The Story of the World

The Story of the World

세계 역사 이야기

영어 리딩 훈련

고대 1

Why do we read about history?
우리는 왜 역사를 읽어야 하는가?

이 책은 까마득히 먼 옛날이야기로 시작된다. 인류가 농사를 짓고 가축을 기르기 시작하기 전, 도시를 건설하기 전, 왕을 뽑거나 지도자를 선출하기 이전의 시절부터 이야기가 시작된다. 첫 번째 장에 나오는 남자들과 여자들은 아직 지중해 해안을 여기저기 떠돌아다니던 유랑민들이다.《The Story of the World》는 이 유랑민들이 어떻게 서서히 여러 민족으로 성장하게 되는지, 이들 민족에게 무슨 일이 일어났는지 이야기해준다.

여러분이 이 책에서 만날 이집트인들, 아카디아인들, 수메르인들, 그리고 여러 다른 민족들은 아주 먼 과거에 흥망을 겪은 사람들이다. 이들은 여러분이 사는 곳에서 아주 멀리 떨어져 살았다. 또한 그들은 여러분이 쓰는 언어와는 전혀 다른 언어를 사용했다. 그 언어들 중 상당수는 이제 더 이상 존재하지도 않으며 그 언어들을 사용한 사람들도 수천, 수만 년 전에 세상을 떠났다.

그럼 왜 우리는 굳이 이 사람들에 대한 이야기를 읽어야 할까? 두 가지 중요한 이유가 있다. 첫 번째 이유는 간단하다. 그동안 사람들이 그다지 많이 변하지 않았기 때문이다! 만 년 전에 살았던 사람들도 오늘날의 남자와 여자들이 원하는 것과 똑같은 것들을 갖고 싶어 했다. 그들 역시 먹을 음식, 마실 물과 술, 안락하게 살 수 있는 곳, 사랑하는 사람을 원했던 것이다. 만 년 전에 살았던 남자와 여자들도 힘을 갈구했다. 오늘날과 다를 바가 없다. 그들도 자신의 부모님을 사랑했고, 의견 충돌을 빚기도 했다. 그들도 자기 자식들을 걱정했다. 그들도 사는 동안 뭔가 훌륭하고 의미 있는 일을 하고자 열망했다. 그들도 우리처럼 죽음을 두려워했다. 이 과거의 사람들에 대해 공부할 때, 사실 우리는 '인간'을 공부하고 있는 셈이다. 우린 우리 자신에 대해 공부하고 있는 것이다.

두 번째 이유 역시 단순하다. 과거에 대해 알지 못하면, 현재를 온전히 이해할 수 없다. 여러분이 어디에서 태어났고, 여러분의 부모와 조부모는 누구이며, 그분들이 중요하다고 여기며 여러분에게 가르친 중요한 가치들이 무엇인지 등등, 아주 어린 시절에 겪은 여러분의 경험은 바로 여러분의 일부이다. 여러분의 부모와 조부모에 대해 모른다면, 여러분의 조상이 누구인지 모른다면, 여러분은 자신에 대해 온전히 알 수 없는 것이다. 고대의 민족들은 바로 오늘날에 존재하는 현대의 국가를 구성하고 있는 사람들의 조상들이기 때문에 우리는 그들이 누구인지 알아야만 비로소 우리 자신을 알 수 있는 것이다.

여러분은 모국어로 고대의 역사에 대해 읽을 수도 있다. 그런데 왜 이 책을 영어로 읽어야 할까? 생각해보자. 영어로 쓰인 세계의 역사에 대해 읽을 때, 여러분은 다음 세 가지 측면에서 여러분의 세계를 확장하고 있는 것이다.

첫째, 여러분은 시간을 초월하게 된다. 이 책을 읽으면서 아주 먼 과거 속으로 들어가 그 시대를 경험함으로써 여러분은 시간 여행자가 되는 것이다! 둘째, 여러분은 공간을 초월하게 된다. 여러분이 살고 있는 친숙한 나라의 경계에서 아주 멀리 떨어져 있는 것을 이해하는 사람이 되는 것이다. 셋째, 여러분은 또 다른 한계, 즉 언어의 한계를 뛰어넘게 된다.

언어마다 생각을 표현하는 방식이 다르다. 한국어로 어떤 사고에 대해 읽으면, 그것을 하나의 방식으로 이해하게 된다. 똑같은 생각에 대해 영어로 읽게 되면, 그것을 새로운 방식으로 이해하게 된다. 미국의 작가인 닐 포스트만(Neil Postman)은 이런 말을 했다. 외국어에 대해 잘 알아서 그 외국어로 쓰인 글을 읽을 수 있다면, "자신의 세계관과는 다른, 또 하나의 세계관을 가질 기회를 얻게 된다". 역사를 영어로 읽으면 여러분이 지금 알고 있는 것을 뛰어넘어, 여러분의 세계관을 훨씬 더 넓힐 수 있다!

이 책을 읽다 보면, 아마 여러분이 모르는 단어들, 이해하지 못하는 개념들도 접하게 될 것이다. 그러나 너무 걱정할 것 없다. 걱정하지 말고, 우선 이 책을 빠짐없이 한 번 이상 읽겠다고 마음먹자.

처음 읽을 때에는 그냥 '이야기' 속에 빠져들면 된다. 즐기자! 그런 다음, 다시 한 번 읽으면서 익숙하지 않은 단어들과 개념들을 확실히 이해하도록 노력하자. 그리고 마지막으로, 앞에서부터 다시 읽어보자. 읽으면서 자문해보자. 이 사람들은 왜 이렇게 행동했을까? 그들이 원한 것은 무엇일까? 그들은 어떻게 그것을 얻으려 했는가? 그들을 '이해하기' 위해 최선을 다하기 바란다.

수잔 와이즈 바우어

2014년 12월

차례

*고대 2는 다음 권에서 만날 수 있습니다

이 책의 구성

영어 학습판

세계 역사의 흐름과 원서 읽는 재미를 동시에 잡은 우리 시대 최고의 텍스트입니다.
함께 읽기를 위한 Read-aloud 기법에 따라 이야기체로 서술되어 있어 기초 문법만
알면 누구나 부담 없이 읽을 수 있습니다. 영단어 설명과 역사 속 Q&A, 구문 해설을
첨부하여 보다 정확한 이해를 도왔습니다.

오리지널 오디오 파일

CNN이 '황금의 목소리'로 경탄한 북텔러, Jim Weiss의 오디오북을 MP3 파일에
담았습니다. 영어 텍스트 전체를 한 편의 소설처럼 실감 나게 읽어줍니다. 귀 기울여
듣다 보면 어느새 역사적 사건들이 하나의 줄기로 이어지며 전체적인 그림을 그리게
됩니다.

셀프 스터디북 Tests and Answer Key

영어 학습판의 영어 문장들과 역사적 내용을 제대로 이해했는지 스스로 파악할 수
있는 익힘책입니다. 100퍼센트 영어로 묻고 대답하면서 영어로 생각하는 법을 익힐
수 있습니다. 별도로 판매하고 있으며 자기주도로 학습할 수 있는 힘이 커집니다.

이 책의 활용법

단어 익히기

중요 영단어를 엄선하여 재치 있는 설명과 예문을 달았습니다.

단순 암기가 아닌 이미지 연상 방식을 채택하여 중고등학교 과정의

필수 어휘들을 완전히 자기 것으로 만들 수 있습니다.

문장 이해하기

대부분 중학교 1학년 수준의 쉬운 영어로 서술되어 있지만 간혹 해석이

어려운 문장은 Sentence Review에서 별도 해설하였습니다.

문법과 숙어를 자연스럽게 익힐 수 있으므로 꼼꼼히 읽어둡니다.

영어 원문 읽기

역사임에도 술술 읽을 수 있는 스토리 중심의 텍스트입니다.

100퍼센트 영어로 되어 있지만 한 문장씩 읽어나갈수록 영어 읽는

재미는 물론 역사적 지식과 생각하는 힘이 점점 커집니다.

오디오 파일 듣기

읽기에만 멈추지 말고 듣기를 반복하여

꾸준히 듣다 보면 직청직해 능력이 향상됩니다. 영어임에도 우리말처럼

편안하게 귀에 쏙쏙 들리는 놀라운 일이 벌어집니다.

How Do We Know What Happened?

What Is History?

Do you know where you were born? Were you born at a hospital, or at home? How much did you weigh when you were born? What did you have to eat for your first birthday?

You don't remember being born, do you? And you probably don't remember your first birthday party! So how can you find the answers to these questions?

You can ask your parents. They can tell you about things that happened long ago, before you were old enough to remember. They can tell you stories about when you were a baby.

These stories are your "history." Your history is the story of what happened to you from the moment you were born, all the way up to the present. You can learn this history by listening to your parents. They remember what happened when you were born. And they probably took pictures of you when you were a baby. You can learn even more about your history from these pictures. Did you have hair? Were you fat or thin? Are you smiling or frowning? What are you wearing? Do you remember those clothes?

You have a history—and so do your parents. Where were they born? Were they born at home, or at a hospital? Where did they go to school? What did they like to eat? Who were their best friends? How can you find the answers to these questions? You can ask your parents. And if they don't remember, you can ask *their* parents—your grandparents.

Now let's ask a harder question. Your grandmother was once a little girl. What is *her* history like? How much did she weigh when she was born? Did she cry a lot? When did she cut her first tooth? What was her favorite thing to eat?

You would have to ask *her* mother—your *great*–grandmother. And you could look at baby pictures of your grandmother. But what if you can't talk to your great–grandmother, and what if you don't have any baby pictures of your grandmother? Is there another way you could find out about your grandmother's history?

There might be. Perhaps your grandmother's mother wrote a letter to a friend when she was born. "Dear Elizabeth," she might write. "My baby was born at home on September 13. She weighed seven pounds, and she has a lot of fuzzy black hair. She certainly cries a lot! I hope she'll sleep through the night soon."

Now, suppose you find this letter, years later. Even though you can't talk to your great–grandmother, you can learn the *history* of your grandmother from her letter. You could also learn *history* if your great–grandmother kept a diary or a journal, where she wrote about things that happened to her long ago.

In this book, we're going to learn about the *history* of people who lived a long time ago, in all different countries around the world. We're going to learn about the stories they told, the battles they fought, and the way they lived—even what they ate and drank, and what they wore.

How do we know these things about people who lived many,

many years in the past? After all, we can't ask them.

We learn about the history of long–ago people in two different ways. The first way is through the letters, journals, and other written records that they left behind. Suppose a woman who lived in ancient times wrote a letter to a friend who lived in another village. She might say, "There hasn't been very much rain here recently! All our crops are dying. The wheat is especially bad. If it doesn't rain soon, we'll have to move to another village!"

Hundreds of years later, we find this letter. What can we learn about the history of ancient times from this letter? We can learn that people in ancient times grew wheat for food. They depended on rain to keep the wheat healthy. And if it didn't rain enough, they moved somewhere else.

Other kinds of written records tell us about what kings and armies did in ancient times. When a king won a great victory, he often ordered a monument built. On the monument, he would have the story of his victory engraved in stone letters. Or a king might order someone in his court to write down the story of his reign, so that everyone would know what an important and powerful king he was. Thousands of years later, we can read the stone letters or the stories and learn more about the king.

People who read letters, journals, other documents, and monuments to find out what happened in the past are called *historians*. And the story they write about the past is called *history*.

What Is Archaeology?

We can learn about what people did in the past through

reading the letters and other writings that they left behind. But this is only one way of doing history.

Long, long ago, many people didn't know how to write. They didn't write letters to each other. The kings didn't carve the stories of their great deeds on monuments. How can a historian learn the story of people who didn't know how to write?

Imagine that a whole village full of people lived near a river, long ago. These people don't know how to write. They don't send letters to their friends, or write diaries about their daily life. But as they go about their duties every day, they drop things on the ground. A farmer, out working in his wheat field, loses the iron blade from the knife he's using to cut wheat from the stalks. He can't find it, so he goes to get another knife—leaving the blade on the ground.

Back in the village, his wife drops a clay pot by accident, just outside the back steps of her house. It breaks into pieces. She sighs, and kicks the pieces under the house. Her little boy is playing in the dirt, just beyond the back steps. He has a little clay model of an ox, hitched to a cart. He runs the cart through the dirt and says, "Moo! Moo!" until his mother calls him to come inside. He leaves the cart where it is and runs into the house. His mother has a new toy for him! He's so excited that he forgets all about his ox and cart. Next day, his father goes out into the yard and accidentally kicks dirt over the clay ox and cart. The toy stays in the yard, with dirt covering it.

Now let's imagine that the summer gets drier and drier. The wheat starts to die. The people who live in the village have less and less to eat. They get together and decide that they will pack up their belongings and take a journey to another place, where there is more rain. So they collect their things and start off down the river. They leave behind the things that they don't want any more—cracked jars, dull knives, and stores of wheat kernels that are too hard and dry to use.

The deserted village stands by the river for years. Slowly, the buildings start to fall down. Dust blows overtop of the ruins. One year, the river floods and washes mud over the dust. Grass starts to grow in the mud. Eventually, you can barely see the village any more. Dirt and grass cover the ruins from sight. It just looks like a field by a river.

But one day a man comes along to look at the field. He sees a little bit of wood poking up from the grass. He bends down and starts to brush dirt away from the wood. It is the corner of a building. When he sees this, he thinks to himself, "People used to live here!"

The next day he comes back with special tools—tiny shovels, brushes, and special knives. He starts to dig down into the field. When he finds the remains of houses and tools, he brushes the dirt away from them. He writes down exactly where he found them. And then he examines them carefully. He wants to discover more about the people who used to live in the village.

One day, he finds the iron knife blade that the farmer lost in the field. He thinks to himself, "These people knew how to make iron. They knew how to grow wheat and harvest it for food. And they used iron tools to harvest their grain."

Another day, he finds the clay pot that the farmer's wife broke. Now he knows that the people of the village knew how to make dishes from clay. And when he finds the little ox and cart that the little boy lost in the yard, he knows that the people of the village used cows, harnessed to wagons, to help them in their farm work.

He might even find out that the people left their village because there was no rain. He discovers the remains of the hard, spoiled wheat that the people left behind. When he looks at the wheat, he can tell that it was ruined by lack of rain. So he thinks to himself, "I'll bet that these people left their village during a dry season. They probably went to find a place where it was rainy."

This man is doing history—even though he doesn't have any written letters or other documents. He is discovering the story of the people of the village from the things that they left behind them. This kind of history is called *archaeology*. Historians who dig objects out of the ground and learn from them are called *archaeologists*.

Chapter 1
The Earliest People

1 The First Nomads

🌐 초기 인류는 수렵과 채취로 식량을 구하며 떠돌던 유목민(nomad)들이었다. 사슴, 들소, 물고기 등을 사냥하는 것이 수렵(狩獵)이고, 자연 상태의 곡물이나 과일 등을 취하는 것이 채취(採取)이다. 한 지역에서 더 이상 먹을거리를 구할 수 없으면 다른 지역으로 이동해야 했다. 많은 인류학자와 고고학자가 현생 인류가 아프리카에서 기원해서 진화하며 유랑을 통해 전 세계로 퍼져나갔다고 믿고 있는데, 이런 주장을 '아프리카 기원설'이라고 한다.

Where do you live? Where do you sleep? Do you sleep in the same bed every night, or do you move into a new house every week?

A long time ago—about seven thousand years in the past—families didn't live in houses and shop at grocery stores. Instead, they wandered from place to place, looking for food and sleeping in tents or caves. Ancient families who lived this way were called *nomads*. Nomad means "a person who wanders or roams around."

Nomads gathered their food from the land around them. They ate plants that they picked, roots that they dug out of the ground, and nuts and berries that they gathered from bushes and trees. When they had eaten most of the food in one place, they would move on to another place. Women and children had the job of digging up roots, picking nuts, berries, and plants, and collecting other kinds of food—eggs, wild honey, and even lizards and snakes. Men hunted for meat with spears, bows and arrows. If the nomads camped near a river or lake, the men would fish too. *When the nomads had hunted in one area for a while, all the animals would move away from them. *When that happened, the nomads would pack up and follow the game.

*In warm places, nomads built tents by stretching animal hides over wooden frames. They could take these tents with them when they moved. Nomads who lived in colder, rocky places used caves for shelter. We know that they lived there because they painted pictures of animals on the walls of the caves; we can still see these pictures today.

Tarak is a seven-year-old girl who lives with her family in the days of the nomads. She likes warm weather the best because she can sleep out in the open and look at the stars until she falls asleep.

One warm morning, Tarak gets up when the sun comes up. *She is sleeping outside, so all she has to do is pick up the piece of animal skin she sleeps on and take it to her mother. *She wears the same clothes all the time, so she doesn't have to change out of her pajamas.

*In the middle of the nomads' camp, the fire is still burning from the night before. *Tarak's uncle and some of the other adults have taken turns staying up through the night, watching the fire and keeping it burning. *They heard a wildcat screaming in the night and wanted to keep it away from the camp. Tarak's uncle says that the wildcat has already frightened away the flocks of small deer that the hunters were tracking. There's no meat for breakfast this morning. If the hunters don't shoot any deer today, the whole group of nomads will pick up their tents and skins and begin to walk towards a new place to hunt.

Tarak doesn't like the grain that her mother offers her for breakfast, so she decides to wait and eat when she goes out to gather food. Every morning, Tarak and her brothers go out with their mother to look for plants and berries. But they've been gathering food in the same place for a long time, and they've already picked most of the leaves that are good to eat. They've already scraped all the honey out of the wild bees' nest that her younger brother found in the crack of a rock. And they've taken the eggs from all the nests that they can climb up to.

•She and her younger brother get their game bags—small bags made out of skin—and start out to look for food. "I'm going to find another bees' nest," brags her brother. "Then we can eat honey again."

"I'm the best lizard catcher in the family," Tarak retorts. "I bet I can find a lizard before you can find a bees' nest."

•Sure enough, as they walk out of a patch of woods into the sunshine, Tarak sees a lizard dart away into the crack of a log. She leaps on the log and turns it over. Three lizards try to scurry away from her, but in a moment, she has scooped them up and dumped them into her bag. There isn't very much meat on a lizard, but her mother is a wonderful cook; she can stew the lizards in boiling water until every shred of meat has come off the bones, add herbs and roots, and serve a good filling stew to the whole camp. All the way back to the nomad camp, Tarak can feel the lizards squirming in her bag. It makes her hungry. She can't wait to taste her mother's lizard stew.

2 The First Nomads Become Farmers

이집트의 나일강 하류 지역과 중동의 티그리스강과 유프라테스강 유역의 고 대 농업 지역을 연결하면 초승달 모양이 그려지는데, 이 지역을 Fertile Crescent 라고 부른다. fertile은 '땅이 비옥하다'는 뜻으로 농작물이 잘 자란다는 의미이며 crescent는 '초승달 모양'이라는 의미이다. 물이 풍부하고 토지가 비옥했기 때문에 이 지역에서 인류 최초로 농사가 시작되었다고 추정한다. 나일강 하류에서는 고대 이집트 문명이, 티그리스·유프라테스강 유역에서는 메소포타미아 문명이 발생했다.

One of the best places for nomads to live was in an area called the Fertile Crescent. It was called a *crescent* because it was shaped like a crescent moon—like this:

And it was called *fertile* because two rivers, called the Tigris and the Euphrates, ran through it. Rich grass, wild barley, and wild wheat grew in the damp soil of the river banks.

When nomads wandered through the Fertile Crescent, they saw herds of animals feeding on the grass. They saw grain that they could harvest, and wide rivers where they could fish and get fresh water to drink. Because it was so easy to find food, nomads returned to the Fertile Crescent again and again. Some of these nomads began to live near the two rivers all year long, instead of wandering from place to place in search of food.

Nomads who settled in the Fertile Crescent couldn't just pick leaves, nuts, and berries to eat. Soon, they would run out of wild plants to harvest. Instead, they had to begin to plant grain for themselves. The nomads of the Fertile Crescent were turning into farmers.

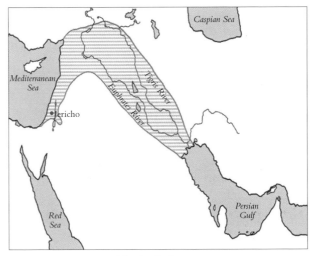

The Fertile Crescent

These new fields of grain needed extra water to flourish. The land near the rivers was damp enough to make growing easy. But it didn't rain very much in the Fertile Crescent, and farther away from the shores, the land was dry for much of the year. So the farmers learned to dig canals from the rivers out into their fields. *That way, even if it did not rain, they could bring water to their crops.

Today, irrigation machines are enormous metal sprinklers, higher than a house and longer than three or four semi trucks. They pump water out of lakes and spray it over entire fields. But long ago, farmers had a simpler machine to get water out of the canals and onto their crops. This machine was called a *shaduf.* Early farmers balanced a pole lengthwise on top of a pillar. They tied a weight to one end of the pole, and attached a leather bucket to the other. *Then the farmers lowered the bucket into the canal, raised the bucket by pushing down on the weight, and then swung the bucket around to pour the water on the crops. The shaduf was one of the first farm machines.

A Farmer with a Shaduf

Farmers had to tend their crops every day for months. So they began to build houses that would stay in one place, instead of living in tents that could be moved every few days. *They used whatever materials were around them. *Farmers who lived near the river built houses out of reeds, or out of bricks that were made from mud and left to dry in the sun.

*Soon, farmers discovered that it was best to build houses close together so that they could help each other to water and tend their fields. These were the first villages. The farmers also learned that they could tame animals such as sheep and goats, feed them grain, and then use them for meat. This was easier than hunting wild animals! Villages were often built around a central pen or field where the tame animals were kept.

Some villages were very successful in growing grain and raising sheep and goats. They even grew rich by trading grain, sheep's wool, and animal skins to others for metals, pottery, wood, and other goods. Because they were afraid that they might be attacked and robbed by bandits, they built stone walls around their villages. These were the first cities.

One of the earliest was the city of Jericho. Jericho had one of the thickest, strongest walls of the ancient world; it was ten feet thick and thirteen feet tall, with a circular tower on one side so that village lookouts could see enemies approaching. The tower was thirty-five feet high—taller than a two-story house!

Not long after the day that Tarak catches enough lizards for her mother's lizard stew, Tarak and her family wander into the Fertile Crescent, searching for food. They find plenty of roots, nuts and berries to eat. Tarak's uncle is excited because he sees large herds of horses and small deer to hunt.

But the most exciting thing Tarak sees is a huge river, flowing by right at her feet. She has never seen so much water in one place in her life. Usually, her family and the other nomads only find small pools of water, or tiny streams trickling through the rocks. They need this water for drinking—so Tarak has never been swimming. As a matter of fact, she has never had a bath in her whole life. Now, she can walk right into the water up to her chin.

At first, Tarak and her brother are afraid to get into the water. They just squat on the shore and splash each other. But slowly they put one foot, and then the other into the water. Tarak wants to show her brother how brave she is, so she wades out almost to her knees. She hears her brother wading in behind her. He splashes her all over, so she turns around and dunks his head under the water. He comes up spluttering and yelling. He's never been under water before.

Tarak and her brother spend the whole morning in the river. When they get out, Tarak notices that her brother smells much better than he used to.

That night at dinner, there is horse meat to eat. Tarak's uncle says, "I met other men a little farther down the riverbank. But they weren't hunting. They were putting seeds into the ground. They told me that if we put seeds into the ground too, grain would grow right here where we are. We could pick it, and we wouldn't have to keep looking for new fields to gather food in. I think we'll stay here for a while and watch what they're doing."

Tarak grins at her brother. She likes living on the bank of the river; she likes eating horse meat instead of lizards; she likes the idea that she won't have to go searching for roots every day. And most of all she likes swimming. 📖

Note to Parent: Nomads roamed through the Fertile Crescent around 7000 BC/BCE. The stone wall at Jericho dates to around 6800 BC/BCE.

The Story of the Words

Chapter 1 The Earliest People

1 The First Nomads

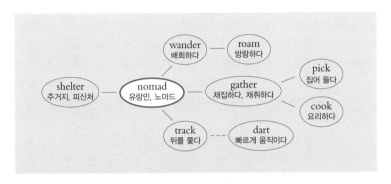

wander ⓥ to walk from place to place without a particular direction

wander는 '여기저기 정처 없이 돌아다니다'라는 뜻이다. 초기 인류는 정해진 목적지 없이 여기저기 먹을 것과 잠잘 곳을 찾아서 걸어 다녔다. 그래서 그들의 '이동'을 표현할 때 wander나 roam이라는 단어를 쓰는 것이다. 새로운 것, 신기한 것에 대해 '궁금하다'라는 뜻의 동사 wonder와 철자를 혼동하지 않도록 주의하자.

Instead, they wandered from place to place, looking for food and sleeping in tents or caves. 대신에 그들은 먹을 것을 찾고 텐트나 동굴 안에서 잠을 자면서 여기저기 정처 없이 돌아다녔다.

nomad ⓝ someone who belongs to a group of people who move from place to place in order to find food and water

원래 '가축을 목초지에 놓아 풀을 뜯게 하다'라는 뜻이다. 한 곳의 풀이 다 없어지면 다른 목초지로 가축을 몰고 이동해야 하기 때문에 '유목(遊牧)하다'의 뜻이고, 그렇게 이동하는 '유목민'을 부르는 말로도 쓰인다. 본문에서는 아직 농사와 목축을 시작하기 전이므로 '유랑민, 노마드'를 뜻하는 말로 이해해야 한다.

Ancient families who lived this way were called *nomads*. 이런 식으로 살았던 고대 가족이 '노마드'라고 불렸다.

Q 인류는 언제부터 유목민으로 살았나요?

A 이 책은 7천 년 전의 이야기로 시작하지만, 유목 생활은 당연히 더 오래 전부터 있었단다. 문자가 없던 시절의 이야기를 어떻게 알 수 있냐고? 고고학자의 발굴이나 우연한 기회에 발견된 역사적 산물 등을 통해 옛사람들의 생활이 밝혀지고 있지. 구석기 시대인의 삶을 들여다볼 수 있는 알타미라 동굴의 발견도 그 하나란다.

1879년 사투올라는 딸 마리아와 스페인의 칸타브리아 지방을 산책 중이었어. 변호사이자 고미술품 수집가, 아마추어 고고학자인 그는 주변 지역을 돌아다니곤 했는데, 마침 동굴을 발견하고는 그 안으로 들어가게 되었지. 그런데 마리아가 "아빠, 천장에 있는 그림을 보세요!"라고 소리치는 거야. 그 순간 2만 5천 년 이상 숨겨져 있던 구석기인의 삶이 우리에게 드러난 거야.

그런데 생각지도 못한 문제가 생겼단다. 1880년 고고학회에서 사투올라가 자신이 발견한 동굴 벽화를 소개하게 되었는데, 보존 상태가 좋은 데다가, 그림 솜씨가 훌륭하다는 이유로 학회에 참석한 사람들은 사투올라를 거짓말쟁이, 심지어는 사기꾼으로 몰았다는구나. 그러나 다행히 그 지역의 다른 곳에서도 동굴 벽화가 차례로 발굴되었고, 과학적 분석으로 알타미라 동굴 벽화가 그려진 시기가 밝혀졌어.

roam ⓥ to walk or travel with no clear direction or purpose

roam도 wander와 마찬가지로 '특정한 목적지 없이 이동하다'라는 의미로, '배회하다, 방랑하다'라는 뜻으로 쓰인다. around가 '주변에, 둘레에'를 뜻하는 부사이므로 to roam around라고 하면 '이곳저곳 주변을 돌아다니다'라는 의미이다.

Nomad means "a person who wanders or roams around." 노마드는 '이곳저곳 정처 없이 돌아다니는 사람'을 뜻한다.

gather ⓥ to search for and find similar things that you need or want

gather는 '모이다'라는 뜻으로 쓰이지만, '모으다'도 된다. My family gathered together에서는 '가족이 함께 모였다'라는 뜻이다. to gather food는 '먹을거리를 모으다'라는 의미로 이때 gather는 '채집하다, 채취하다'이다.
Nomads gathered their food from the land around them. 노마드들은 주변의 땅에서 먹을 것을 채집했다.

shelter ⓝ a place to live, where people can be protected from bad weather or danger

shelter는 '주거지'를 말하는데 아무 곳이나 shelter가 될 수는 없다. 그곳에서 식사를 하고 잠을 자야 하기 때문에 최소한 비바람과 추위 정도는 막을 수 있어야 한다. 그래서 가죽으로 만든 텐트(tent)나 삼면이 막힌 동굴(cave)이 초기 인류의 shelter였다. 위험으로부터 안전한 '피신처, 대피소'의 의미이다.

Nomads who lived in colder, rocky places used caves for shelter. 더 춥고, 바위가 많은 곳에 살던 노마드들은 동굴을 주거지로 사용했다.

track ⓥ to search for a person or animal by following the marks they leave behind

남긴 흔적을 쫓아서 사람이나 동물을 따라가는 행동을 나타내는 동사가 바로 track이므로 The hunters are tracking a deer(사냥꾼들이 사슴을 쫓고 있다)라고 쓸 수 있다. track을 명사형으로 쓰면 '흔적이나 자취가 있어 어디로 갈지 아는 길'을 뜻한다.

Tarak's uncle says that the wildcat has already frightened away the flocks of small deer that the hunters were tracking. 타라크 삼촌은 야생 고양이가 사냥꾼들이 쫓던 작은 사슴 무리 들을 멀리 쫓아버렸다고 말한다.

pick ⓥ to take something with your fingers

동사 pick의 기본적인 의미는 '손가락으로 뭔가를 집거나 잡아채다'이다. 그래서 아이가 콧구멍에 손가락을 넣어 코딱지를 파는 행동을 하면 엄마가 Don't pick your nose!(코 파지 마!)라고 한다. up이 붙은 to pick up은 '집어 올리다'로 to pick up the tent는 '텐트를 걷다'이고, to pick up the phone은 '수화기를 들다[전화 받다]'이다.

If the hunters don't shoot any deer today, the whole group of nomads will pick up their tents and skins and begin to walk towards a new place to hunt. 사냥꾼들이 오늘 사슴을 한 마리도 쏘아 맞히지 못한다면, 노마드 전체가 텐트와 가죽을 챙겨서 새로운 사냥터를 향해 걸어가기 시작할 것이다.

dart ⓥ to move suddenly and quickly in a particular direction

다트(dart) 게임을 해본 적이 있는가? 과녁이 그려진 다트판(dartboard)에 작은 화살을 던져 점수를 내는 게임이다. 이 작은 화살이 바로 dart인데, 던지면 한 방향으로 곧장 날아간다. 그래서 동사 dart는 '일정한 방향으로 휙 움직이다'라는 의미를 지닌다.

Sure enough, as they walk out of a patch of woods into the sunshine, Tarak sees a lizard dart away into the crack of a log. 아니나 다를까, 그들이 작은 숲을 빠져나와 햇살 속으로 걸어갈 때, 타라크는 도마뱀 한 마리가 통나무 틈 속으로 휙 들어가는 것을 본다.

Q 활과 화살을 위해 물물교환이 필요했다면서요?

A 마지막 빙하기가 끝나고 지구의 기온이 따뜻해졌어. 빙하기에 느릿느릿 걸어 다니던 몸집 큰 동물들이 더워진 기후를 못 참고 떠나버린 곳에 동작이 빠른 동물들이 나타났어. 사냥꾼들은 '어떻게 이 녀석들을 잡아 배를 채울 수 있을까' 하고 당황했겠지?

우리는 활과 화살의 발명에 대해 쉽게 이야기하지만, 활이 휘어지는 각도와 화살에 적합한 화살촉을 찾는 일은 말처럼 쉬운 일은 아니었을 거야. 그러니 얼마나 많은 시행착오를 거쳤을까. 화살촉은 돌이 단단하지 않으면 동물의 몸속에 잘 박히지 않아서 흑요석을 써야 제대로 쓸 수 있었어. 그런데 흑요석이 아무 곳에서나 구할 수 있는 돌이 아니었다는 것이 문제였어! 당시 사람들이 어떻게든 흑요석을 구하려면 물물교환을 할 수밖에 없었지. 흑요석이 나오지 않는 지방에서도 화살촉이 발견되었다는 것이 그 증거란다.

---

cook ⓝ someone who prepares and cooks food

Her mother is a wonderful cook(그녀의 어머니는 훌륭한 요리사이다)에서 cook은 명사형으로 '요리사, 요리하는 사람'이다. '요리하다'라는 동사 cook과 형태가 같다. 흔히 teach(가르치다) → teacher(교사), write(쓰다) → writer(작가)처럼 행위 동사에 -er을 붙여 직업을 표현하지만, cook은 예외이다. cooker는 '솥이나 오븐' 등과 같이 요리하는 데 필요한 도구를 뜻한다.

There isn't very much meat on a lizard, but her mother is a wonderful cook. 도마뱀에는 고기가 별로 없지만, 그녀의 어머니는 훌륭한 요리사이다.

2 The First Nomads Become Farmers

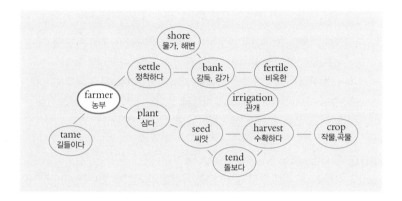

fertile ⓐ able to produce good crops

fertile은 to bear(낳다, 열매 맺다)를 뜻하는 라틴어에서 유래한 말로, '많이 낳다, 열매를 풍성하게 맺다'를 뜻한다. 흔히 농사가 잘되는 땅을 표현할 때 '비옥한, 기름진'을 뜻하는 말로 쓰인다. the Fertile Crescent(비옥한 초승달)는 땅이 비옥해서 인류가 처음 정착해서 농사를 짓기 시작한, 티그리스와 유프라테스 강 사이의 땅과 나일 강의 삼각주를 일컫는다.

And it was called *fertile* because two rivers, called the Tigris and the Euphrates, ran through it. 그리고 그곳이 fertile(비옥한)이라고 불리는 것은, 티그리스와 유프라테스라는 두 개의 강이 그곳을 관통해 흐르기 때문이다.

harvest ⓥ to gather crops from the fields

harvest는 고대 게르만어에서 온 말로, 원래 '가을'을 의미했다. 먼 옛날 사람들은 가을에 들판의 곡식을 거둬들이느라 정신이 없었을 것이다. 가을의 곡식 수확이 겨울 동안의 생존을 결정했기 때문이다. 그래서 harvest는 점차 동사형 '수확[추수]하다'와 명사형인 '수확[추수]'으로 쓰이게 되었고, 16세기 이후부터 autumn과 fall이 harvest를 대신해 '가을'을 뜻하는 말이 되었다.

They saw grain that they could harvest, and wide rivers where they could fish and get fresh water to drink. 그들은 수확을 할 수 있는 곡식과 물고기를 잡고 마실 수 있는 담수를 얻을 수 있는 넓은 강을 보았다.

Q 처음으로 농사를 짓게 된 사람들은 수확 전까지 무엇을 먹고 살았나요?

A 유목민들은 떠돌아다니면서 잡을 수 있는 동물은 무엇이든 먹었어. 동물뿐만 아니라 먹을 수 있는 것이라면 종류를 가리지 않고, 열매와 뿌리, 야생꿀, 심지어는 도마뱀까지 먹어야 했지. 당시에는 생존이 가장 중요한 문제였으니까. 한곳에 정착해서 씨를 뿌리고 조마조마한 마음으로 수확을 기다린 사람들은 하루아침에 '오늘부터 농경 생활이다' 하고 생활 방식을 바꾼 것이 아니라 씨를 뿌리고 농작물의 성장을 지켜보면서 사냥도 하고, 채집도 하고, 물고기도 잡아먹으면서 수확의 날을 기다렸어.

settle ⓥ to begin to live in a new place

settle에는 seat의 의미가 담겨 있다. 즉 자리를 잡고 앉아 있다는 의미로, She settled herself in her seat(그녀는 자기 자리에 앉았다)처럼 쓸 수 있다. 여기저기 돌아다니다가 한곳에 자리를 잡고 산다는 의미의 '정착하다'라는 뜻이다. 그래서 Nomads who settled in the Fertile Crescent는 '비옥한 초승달 지대에 정착한 유랑민들'이라는 뜻이다.

Nomads who settled in the Fertile Crescent couldn't just pick leaves, nuts, berries to eat. 비옥한 초승달 지역에 정착한 유목민들은 단지 잎과 견과와 열매만 채집해서는 먹고 살 수 없었다.

plant ⓥ to put seeds or trees in the ground to grow

plant의 기본적인 의미는 fix, 즉 '한곳에 고정시키다'이다. 어떤 식물의 씨앗이나 묘목 등을 땅에 고정시킨다는 의미에서 동사로 '심다'라는 뜻이 된다. 식물은 이동하지 않고 땅에 고정되어 있기 때문에 plant가 명사형으로 '식물'이라는 뜻이고, '공장, 설비'도 한곳에 고정시켜 사용하는 것이므로 plant로 표현한다.

Instead, they had to begin to plant grain for themselves. 대신에 그들은 자신의 힘으로 곡식을 심기 시작해야 했다.

crop ⓝ a plant grown for food, usually by farmers

쌀, 배추, 사과, 고구마 등의 열매, 줄기, 뿌리를 먹기 위해 키우는 식물이 모두 crop이다. 쉽게 말해 '농작물'이다. 쌀(rice), 보리(barley), 밀(wheat)처럼 농부가 농사짓는 곡물(grain)도 crop에 포함된다. 이 식물들은 먹기 적당한 시기가 되면 수확하므로 crop은 this year's rice crop(올해의 쌀 수확량)처럼 '수확, 수확량'이라는 뜻으로도 쓰인다.

That way, even if it did not rain, they could bring water to their crops. 그런 식으로 비가 오지 않더라도 그들은 농작물에 물을 댈 수 있었다.

irrigation ⓝ the act of bringing water to land in order to grow crops

irrigation은 irrigate의 명사형이다. irrigate는 '안(in)'을 뜻하는 ir-와 '물(water)'을 뜻하는 rigate가 합쳐진 말이다. 즉 '안으로 물을 대다'라는 뜻이다. 농사와 생활을 위해 강이나 호수에서 물을 끌어오는 것이 바로 irrigation이고, 이를 우리말로 '관개(灌漑)'라고 한다. 두 한자 모두 '물을 대다'라는 뜻이다. 인류는 오래전부터 운하(canal), 방아 두레박(shaduf, shadoof) 등의 관개 시설을 이용해왔다.

Today, irrigation machines are enormous metal sprinklers, higher than a house and longer than three or four semi trucks. 오늘날, 관개 기계들은 거대한 금속 살수 장치로, 집보다 더 높고 나무나 작은 트럭 서너 대의 길이를 합쳐 놓은 것보다 더 길다.

tend ⓥ to take care of something or someone

tend의 기본적인 의미는 stretch이다. '어떤 것에 손을 뻗으려고 하는 마음'이 담겨 있는 것이다. tend는 '흔히 ~하다, ~하는 경향이 있다'라는 뜻과 여기에서처럼 '돌보다'로도 쓰인다. to tend crops는 '농작물이 잘 자라도록 돌보다'이다. Farmers had to tend their crops every day for months. 농부들은 여러 달 동안 날마다 자신의 작물을 돌봐야 했다.

tame ⓥ to train an animal to live with people

tame은 사람의 말을 잘 듣도록 동물을 '길들이다'는 뜻으로, The farmers tamed animals such as sheep and goats(농부들은 양과 염소 같은 동물들을 길들였다)처럼 쓸 수 있다. '길들여진'이라는 형용사로도 쓰인다. wild animals(야생 동물들)를 잡아 '길들이면' tame animals가 된다.

The farmers also learned that they could tame animals such as sheep and goats, feed them grain, and then use them for meat. 농부들은 양과 염소 같은 동물들을 길들이고, 그들에게 곡물을 먹이고 나서 고기를 얻기 위해 그 동물들을 이용할 수 있다는 것도 알게 되었다.

shore ⓝ the land along the edge of a river, lake or sea

강, 호수, 바다의 가장자리 땅, 즉 '해안, 해변'을 shore라고 한다. shore 앞에 sea가 붙은 seashore는 바다 가장자리 땅, '바닷가'이다. seaside도 같은 뜻이다. 여름에 해수욕을 즐길 수 있는 모래나 자갈이 덮인 땅을 beach라고 한다.
'강가'와 '호숫가'는 각각 riverside, lakeside로 달리 표현할 수 있다.

They just squat on the shore and splash each other. 그들은 그냥 물가에 쪼그리고
앉아서 서로 물을 끼얹는다.

seed ⓝ a small grain from which a new plant grows

식물의 열매 속에 들어 있는 '씨, 씨앗'이 seed이다. to put seed into the
ground는 '씨를 땅에 심다'라는 의미로, to sow seeds나 to plant seeds와 같
은 뜻이다. 씨가 땅에 떨어져 발아하면 새로운 식물이 자라난다. 이러한 맥락
에서 사업을 위해 모아둔 밑천인 '종자돈'을 seed money라고 한다.

They were putting seeds into the ground. 그들은 땅에 씨앗을 심고 있었다.

bank ⓝ a raised area of land along the side of a river or lake

강의 양쪽 가장자리는 물이 흐르는 수로보다 지대가 높다. 침식과 퇴적 작용 때
문에 오랜 세월 동안 가장자리에 흙이 쌓였기 때문이다. 물론 범람을 막기 위해
사람들이 흙을 쌓기도 했다. 이렇게 강을 따라 솟아 있는 지형인 '강둑'이 바로
bank이다.

She likes living on the bank of the river. 그녀는 강둑에서 사는 것을 좋아한다.

Q 동굴을 하나 더 소개해줄까?

A 한 가지 더 소개하고 싶은 동굴이 있어. 탐험 대장의 이름을 따라 '쇼베
동굴'이라 불리는 곳인데, 1994년 12월 발견되었어. 이 동굴의 발견으로 구
석기 시대 동굴 벽화의 역사를 다시 쓰게 되었다고 할 정도였지. 그만큼
이 동굴에서는 생생하고 다양한 그림이 발견되었어.
쇼베 동굴은 '잊혀진 꿈의 동굴'이라는 제목의 다큐멘터리 3D 영상을 통해
생생하게 만날 수 있어. 구석기 시대 수업에서 반드시 소개하는 다큐멘터
리 목록 중 1번이기도 하지. 알타미라, 라스코, 쇼베 동굴을 직접 보러 갈
기회를 얻기란 쉽지 않은 일이잖아. 정말 간다고 해도 극장에서 3D로 영
상을 보듯 그렇게 리얼하게 제대로 보는 것도 어려울 테니, 오늘은 이 다큐
멘터리를 보면서 구석기 여행을 떠나보는 것은 어떨까.

Chapter 2

Egyptians Lived on the Nile River

1 Two Kingdoms Become One

🌍 약 6,000년 전에 이집트에는 두 개의 왕국이 존재했다. 하나는 나일강 상류 지역에 자리했던 상이집트(Upper Egypt)였고, 다른 하나는 하류의 삼각주를 중심으로 번성했던 하이집트(Lower Egypt)였다. 두 왕국은 각각 남북으로 세력을 확장하면서 끊임없이 경쟁하고 전쟁을 벌였는데, 기원전 3100년경에 상이집트의 나르메르 왕이 하이집트를 멸망시키고 통일 왕국을 세우게 된다. 이때부터 이집트의 역사는 고(古)왕조 시대를 맞게 되며 남북의 경제와 문화가 하나로 합쳐지면서 찬란한 '이집트 문명'을 꽃피우게 된다.

Tarak could go swimming almost any day she wanted to, because the Tigris River was full of water all year round. *But the farmers who lived along the banks of the Nile River had a very different kind of river to deal with. Sometimes the river was very low—so low that you could almost see the bottom. Other times, it was so full that it flooded all over their farmland.

The Nile River is a long river in Africa. At the top, it splits into several different little rivers and runs into the Mediterranean Sea. This area is shaped like an upside-down triangle. The Greek letter for D, *delta*, is shaped like a triangle too. So this part of the river is called the Nile Delta, after the Greek letter of the alphabet.

Every year, the Nile flooded. During rainy seasons, water would fall on the mountains in the south, where the Nile River begins. The water would pour down the mountains, into the river, and run down towards the delta. So much water poured into the Nile at once that it overflowed its banks and spread all over the farmland on either side. The wettest place of all was the Nile Delta—all the little rivers ran over their banks and spread out so that the whole delta was underwater. Would you like to live on the banks of the Nile? Do you think it would be a good place to build a house? What would happen to your house?

If a farmer had a river flood all over his crops today, he'd think it was a disaster. It would wash his crops away. But the farmers who lived along the Nile liked to see the river flood. The river flooded at the same time every year, so they were ready for it. When the water came up out of the river, rich dirt from the bottom of the river came with it. This dirt was called *silt*, and it was full of good vitamins and minerals for plants. The floodwater would spread the silt all along the edge of the river, and then the water would recede—go back into the river until the next year. Then the farmers, who lived a little ways away from the riverbank so that their houses wouldn't flood, would come out and plant their crops in the rich silt. They learned to dig canals leading away from the river, so that floodwater would run into their canals. Then they would block the ends of the canals so that the water couldn't run back into the river. They could use the water in the canals during dry seasons.

The people who lived along the Nile were called *Egyptians*. Early in Egypt's history, there were two Egyptian tribes who lived along the Nile. The Egyptians who lived in the north, in the Nile Delta, were called the "Lower Egyptians." The Egyptians who lived along the straight part of the river, further south, were called the "Upper Egyptians."

When you look at a map, "north" is usually at the top and " south" is usually at the bottom. So it might seem to you that the Nile Delta should be "Upper Egypt." After all, it's on the upper part of your map.

But the ancient Egyptians didn't think about the world in that way. The Nile River flowed from the mountains in the south, down to the delta in the north. So the ancient Egyptians thought

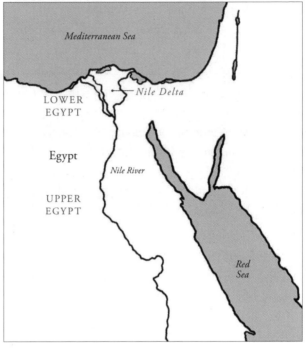

The Nile Delta

about the southern part of their country, Upper Egypt, as "up the river," and the northern part, Lower Egypt, as "down the river." If you turn the map at the top of this page upside down, you'll see the world as the Egyptians did.

The Lower Egyptians were ruled by a king who wore a red crown, and the Upper Egyptians were ruled by a king who wore a white crown. Both kings wanted to rule over *all* of Egypt. So for years, the White Crown King and the Red Crown King fought with each other, and the Upper Egyptians and the Lower Egyptians sailed up and down the Nile and fought with each other too.

Finally, the two kings fought one great battle to settle, once

King Narmer

and for all, who would rule Egypt. The Upper Egyptian king, the White Crown King, was named King Narmer. Around five thousand years ago, King Narmer defeated the Red Crown King and took his crown away. Then he put the red crown overtop of his own white crown and announced that he was the king of all Egypt. From now on, the king of Egypt would wear the Double Crown of Egypt, which had a white spike at the center and a red band around the outside. This showed that he was the ruler of the entire country.

2 Gods of Ancient Egypt

고대 이집트인은 약 700여 명의 인격화된 신들을 믿었다. 대표적인 신들 중에서 '라(Ra)'는 '창조자'라는 뜻으로, 하늘의 지배자인 태양을 상징하는 신이다. '아톤'이나 '아몬'으로 불리기도 했다. 오시리스(Osiris)는 동생인 세트(Set)에게 살해되었는데, 아내인 이시스(Isis)가 그의 몸을 미라로 만들어 부활시켰다. 그래서 오시리스는 저승과 부활의 신으로 여겨졌다. 오시리스의 아내인 이시스(Isis)는 이집트 최고의 여신으로, 풍요와 다산의 상징이었으며 죽은 사람을 보호하는 신으로 숭배되었다. 반면 형을 죽인 세트(Set)는 어둠과 악을 상징하는 신으로 여겨졌다. 오시리스의 아들인 호루스(Horus)는 이승과 태양을 상징하는 신으로, 아버지로부터 전쟁의 비법을 전수받아 세트를 죽이고 이집트를 통일하고 왕이 되었다.

Now that the Egyptians were all part of one country, the king of Egypt became known as the *pharaoh*. He carried a shepherd's crook to show that he was supposed to lead and take care of all the Egyptian people, just like a shepherd takes care of and feeds his sheep. Soon, the Egyptians began to think that the pharaoh was actually a god. They believed that he was able to make the Nile overflow its banks every year so that their crops could grow. The pharaoh got more and more powerful—no one wanted to make a god angry!

The pharaoh wasn't the only god the Egyptians worshipped. Ra was the god of the sun. He was the chief god; other gods were part of his family. Osiris was the god who judged the dead and decided whether they had been good or bad. Isis was Osiris's wife, and the mother of Horus, who was the god of the sky.

Egyptian stories about the gods often tried to explain why the Nile overflowed every year. One Egyptian story, or *myth*, tells about Osiris and his brother, Set. Here's the myth of Osiris as an Egyptian child might have heard it from his mother, long ago.

Once upon a time, the great god Osiris and his wife Isis were ruling over the whole land of Egypt. Osiris went on a trip around the world and left Isis in charge of the kingdom. But while he was gone, Osiris's evil brother Set decided that he wanted to be king. When Osiris came back from his trip, Set invited him to a great feast with all the other gods. "Dear brother," he said, "come to my house so that we can celebrate your safe return!"

Isis was afraid that Set wanted to harm Osiris, but Osiris laughed at her fears. "He's my own brother!" he said. "Why would he want to hurt me?"

So they went together to the feast. After all the gods had eaten until they were full, Set said, "Look what I have found!" He brought out a beautiful coffin, all carved and decorated with gold and pictures. When the gods all admired it, Set said, "I will give this beautiful coffin to whichever god fits into it the best."

The gods didn't know that Set had ordered the coffin made so that it would only fit Osiris. One by one, they lay down in the coffin. But all of the gods were too large or too small—until Osiris got in, and found that the coffin fit him perfectly. Osiris was so pleased that he lay all the way down in the coffin. "Look!" he said. "I've won the coffin!" But as soon as he lay down, Set slammed the coffin closed and threw it into the Nile, where it floated away. "Now I'm the king of the gods, because Osiris has drowned!" Set announced. He took over the throne and began to rule Egypt.

But Isis went on a long journey down the Nile to find the coffin. Finally she discovered it, caught in the reeds beside the Nile's bank. She opened it, but Osiris had drowned. Isis sat down and wept and wept for grief. Even the Nile cried over the death of Osiris, so that the river ran dry and all the Egyptians were desperate for water.

Finally Isis wrapped Osiris's body in linen—so that he became the first mummy. But as soon as she wrapped him in linen, he came back to life again. The whole earth was glad to see Osiris alive again! The Nile filled back up and overflowed its banks, so that all the Egyptians had water to drink, and their crops began to grow again. And that's why the Nile overflows every year—because it remembers that Osiris came back to life. 📖

Note to Parent: The Upper and Lower Kingdoms were united around 3000 BC/BCE. King Narmer is also known as King Menes.

The Story of the Words

Chapter 2 Egyptians Lived on the Nile River

1 Two Kingdoms Become One

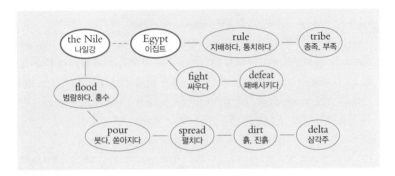

flood ⓥ to cover or fill a place with water

flood는 강이나 호수 등이 범람하여 주변이 '물에 잠기다'라는 뜻이다. The river flooded(강이 범람했다)와 목적어를 취해 The river flooded the fields(강물이 넘쳐 농경지가 잠겼다)처럼 타동사로 쓸 수 있다. flood damage(홍수 피해)처럼 '홍수'라는 뜻의 명사형으로도 쓰인다.

Other times, it was so full that it flooded all over their farmland. 다른 때에는, 물이 너무 가득 차서 그들의 농경지로 범람하기도 했다.

> **Q** 나일 강이 세계에서 가장 긴 강이 아니라면서요?
> **A** 나일 강은 6,000킬로미터가 넘는 강으로 2007년까지는 세상에서 제일 긴 강으로 알려졌단다. 그러나 2008년 라마에서 열린 지리 학회에서 '아마존 강'이 나일 강보다 긴 것으로 발표된 후부터 그 기록은 수정되었어. 하지만 중요한 것은 세상에서 제일 긴 강의 순위가 아니라, 나일 강이 고대 이집트인의 삶에서 어떤 역할을 했는지야. 이집트는 국토의 대부분이 사막이라서 사람들이 살기에 적합한 땅이 별로 없었어. 이집트인들은 주로 나일 강 주변에 모여 살았어. 그들에게 나일 강은 생명의 원천이었지.

delta ⓝ the fourth letter of the Greek alphabet; an area of low land where a river spreads into many smaller rivers near the sea

그리스어 알파벳에서 네 번째 글자인 △를 delta(델타)라고 부른다. 이 글자의 모양이 삼각형(triangle) 모양이기 때문에 강 하류의 삼각주(三角洲)를 영어로 delta라고 한다. 삼각주는 강 하구의 여러 지류로부터 바다로 들어가는 지형을 말하는데, 나일 델타(Nile delta)는 나일 강의 삼각주이다.

The Greek letter for D, *delta* is shaped like a triangle too. D에 해당하는 그리스어의 글자 delta도 삼각형처럼 생겼다.

pour ⓥ to flow continuously and in large amounts

pour는 액체를 위에서 밑으로 '붓다'라는 뜻이다. She poured coffee for me(그녀는 나를 위해 커피를 따라주었다)처럼 음료, 물 등을 컵에 부을 때 쓴다. 또한 It's pouring outside라고 하면 물을 퍼붓듯 '밖에 비가 엄청 온다'라는 의미가 된다. The water would pour down the mountains, into the river는 '빗물이 산을 흘러내려 강으로 들어가곤 했다'라는 뜻으로, '많은 양의 물이 지속적으로 흐른다'라는 의미와 느낌을 전달하기 위해 pour를 쓴 것이다.

The water would pour down the mountains, into the river, and run down towards the delta. 그 물은 산을 흘러내려 강으로 들어가, 삼각주 쪽으로 내려가곤 했다.

dirt ⓝ soil or mud

dirt는 원래 '배설물'이었다. 그래서 형용사 dirty의 뜻도 '더러운'이다. 옷이나 몸에 묻으면 더러워지는 '오물, 때, 얼룩'이 모두 dirt에 해당한다. 흙도 옷에 묻으면 더러워지므로 '흙, 진흙'의 의미이기도 하다. rich dirt from the bottom of the river는 '강바닥의 비옥한[기름진] 흙'으로, 이런 흙이 바로 silt(토사, 유사)이다.

When the water came up out of the river, rich dirt from the bottom of the river came with it. 물이 강에서 넘칠 때, 강바닥에 있던 비옥한 흙이 함께 나왔다.

spread ⓥ to put soft substance over a surface

spread는 '쭉 펴다'라는 뜻이다. Spread your arms!는 '양팔을 옆으로 쭉 펴라'는 것이고, Spread jam on your toast!라고 하면 '빵에 잼을 펴서 발라라'이다. The floodwater would spread the silt all along the edge of the river에서 spread도 잼을 바르듯 '부드러운 물질을 표면에 바르다'라는 뜻으로 쓰였다. 즉 범람한 물이 기름진 흙을 강변을 따라 '펼쳐 놓는다'라는 의미이다.

44

The floodwater would spread the silt all along the edge of the river, and then the water would recede—go back into the river until the next year. 범람한 물은 강의 가장자리를 따라 진흙을 펼쳐 놓는데, 그 뒤에 물이 다시 빠져서 이듬해까지 강으로 되돌아갔다.

tribe ⓝ a large group of people who live in the same area and share a common language and culture

tribe는 같은 지역에 살면서 같은 언어와 문화를 공유하는 사람들, 즉 '종족, 부족'을 일컫는 말이다. tribe는 라틴어 tribus에서 왔다. 고대 로마에는 람네스(Ramnes), 티티에스(Tities), 루케레스(Luceres) 등 성격이 다른 세 종족이 살았는데, 이들을 tribus라고 칭했다.

Early in Egypt's history, there were two Egyptian tribes who lived along the Nile. 이집트 역사의 초기에 나일 강을 따라 살던 두 이집트 종족이 있었다.

rule ⓥ to have the official power to control a country and its people

rule은 원래 straight edge(곧은 자)를 일컫는 말이었다. 어떤 물체나 공간의 길이를 측정하거나 직선을 그리기 위해 사용하는 곧은 막대가 rule이어서 지금도 '자'를 ruler라고 한다. 눈금이 있는 자는 하나의 측정 기준이 되므로 '규칙'을 rule이라고 한다. 규칙을 만들고 그 규칙에 따르게 하는 행위는 권력자만이 할 수 있으므로 rule이 '통치하다, 지배하다', ruler가 '통치자'를 뜻한다.

The Lower Egyptians were ruled by a king who wore a red crown, and the Upper Egyptians were ruled by a king who wore a white crown. 하(下)이집트인은 붉은 왕관을 쓴 왕이 통치했고, 상(上)이집트인은 흰 왕관을 쓴 왕이 통치했다.

Q 이집트에서 수학이 발전한 이유는 무엇인가요?

A 홍수가 끝나고 일상으로 돌아온 이집트인들은 다음 홍수를 대비해 지대가 높은 곳에 집을 지었어. 덕분에 집이 물에 잠기는 것을 피할 수 있었지만, 농토의 경계가 허물어지는 것까지는 막을 수 없었어. 결국 관리자들이 홍수가 끝나고 나서 농토의 경계를 세우는 일에 분쟁이 생길 것을 대비하여 땅의 넓이를 재는 일을 감독했단다. 이렇게 생활의 필요로 발전하게 된 것이 바로 '수학'이야. 농토를 제대로 측량하기 위해 알아낸 수학적 개념들은 피라미드와 신전을 짓는 일에도 큰 도움이 되었지.

fight ⓥ to take part in a war or battle

fight는 '싸우다'이다. 전쟁을 벌이든, 몸싸움을 하든, 선거에서 경쟁하든, 전부 fight로 표현할 수 있다. to fight with each other(서로 싸우다)나, to fight a battle(전투를 벌이다)처럼 쓰인다. fight-fought-fought

So for years, the White Crown King and the Red Crown King fought with each other, and the Upper Egyptians and the Lower Egyptians sailed up and down the Nile and fought with each other too. 그래서 오랫동안 흰 왕관 왕과 붉은 왕관 왕은 서로 싸웠고, 상이집트인과 하이집트인도 배를 타고 나일 강을 오르내리면서 서로 싸웠다.

defeat ⓥ to win against someone in a fight

King Narmer defeated the Red Crown King은 defeat의 의미와 용법을 잘 보여주는 문장이다. 나르메르 왕이 '이긴' 것이다. 'defeat=win against'로 기억하면 된다. defeat를 명사형으로 쓰면 She admitted defeat(그녀는 패배를 인정했다)처럼 '패배(failure to win), 좌절'이 된다.

Around five thousand years ago, King Narmer defeated the Red Crown King and took his crown away. 약 5천 년 전에, 나르메르 왕은 붉은 왕관 왕을 물리치고 그의 왕관을 빼앗았다.

2 Gods of Ancient Egypt

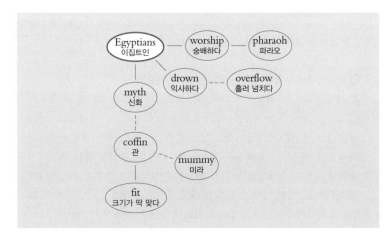

pharaoh ⓝ a king in ancient Egypt

pharaoh는 원래 거대한 집(great house)을 뜻하는 이집트어에서 왔다. 처음에는 '왕궁'을 일컫는 말이었으나 기원전 15세기 이후부터 '왕'을 칭하는 말로 사용되었다. 지금은 최초의 통일 왕국을 건설한 나르메르 왕부터 기원전 30년 로마 제국에 멸망할 당시의 마지막 파라오인 클레오파트라에 이르기까지 '고대 이집트의 모든 왕'을 가리키는 용어로 쓰인다.

Now that the Egyptians were all part of one country, the king of Egypt became known as the *pharaoh*. 이제 이집트인이 모두 한 나라의 구성원이 되자, 이집트의 왕은 '파라오'로 알려지게 되었다.

worship ⓥ to feel or show respect and love for a god

원래 '존경과 제물을 바칠 만한 가치가 있는 지위'가 worship이었다. 그러다가 점차 신에게 '존경과 복종을 표하다'라는 의미로 발전되어 지금은 '숭배하다, 예배하다'라는 동사와 '숭배, 예배'라는 뜻의 명사로도 쓰인다.

The pharaoh wasn't the only god the Egyptians worshipped. 파라오는 이집트인이 숭배하는 유일신은 아니었다.

myth ⓝ an ancient story about gods, heroes and magic

myth는 우리말로 '신화(神話)'인데, '신에 관한 이야기'라는 뜻이다. 원래의 뜻이 '사람의 입에서 나온 소리'이기 때문에 '근거 없는 믿음'이라는 의미도 있다. 신, 영웅, 마법 등, 인간의 상식과 능력을 뛰어넘는 이야기라는 점이 myth의 특징이다.

One Egyptian story, or *myth*, tells about Osiris and his brother, Set. 한 이집트의 이야기 혹은 신화는 오시리스와 그의 형제인 세트에 대해 이야기하고 있다.

coffin ⓝ a long box in which a dead person is buried

coffin은 원래 '나무로 만든 바구니, 상자'를 통칭하는 말이었다. 그래서 옛날에는 물건이나 돈을 담는 '나무 궤짝'이나 나무로 만든 '배(boat)'도 coffin이라고 했으나, 지금은 시신을 보관하는 '관'의 의미로만 쓰인다.

He brought out a beautiful coffin, all carved and decorated with gold and pictures. 그는 아름다운 관 하나를 가져왔는데, 그 관은 온통 금과 그림으로 조각되고 장식되어 있었다.

fit ⓥ to be the right size for something or someone

fit은 작지도 크기도 않고 '크기가 딱 맞다'라는 의미이다. 옷의 크기를 말할 때 This shirt fits me very well(이 셔츠는 나한테 아주 잘 맞는다)처럼 옷을 주어로, 사람을 목적어로 쓴다.

I will give this beautiful coffin to whichever god fits into it the best. 나는 이 아름다운 관을 누구든지 가장 잘 맞는 신에게 주겠습니다.

drown ⓥ to die under water because you cannot breathe

drown은 '물에 빠져 죽다, 익사하다'라는 뜻이다. Osiris has drowned!처럼 자동사와, Set drowned Osiris(세트는 오시리스를 물에 빠뜨려 죽였다)처럼 타동 사로도 쓰인다. 그냥 물에 빠지는 것은 to fall into water라는 표현을 쓴다. A drowning man will catch at a straw(물에 빠진 사람은 지푸라기라도 잡는다)라는 유명한 속담이 있다.

Now I'm the king of the gods, because Osiris has drowned! 오시리스가 물에 빠져 죽었으므로, 이제는 내가 신들의 왕이다!

mummy ⓝ a dead body that has been preserved by wrapping it in cloth, especially in ancient Egypt

mummy는 밀랍(wax)을 뜻하는 페르시아어에서 유래했다. 밀랍을 부어 썩지 않고 오래 보관하는 방식이 페르시아에서 유럽으로 전해졌기 때문에 '방부 처리'를 뜻하는 말로 쓰였다. 흔히 이집트에서 발굴된 '미라'를 의미했는데, '미라 (mirra)'라는 말은 같은 의미의 포르투갈어에서 왔다.

Finally Isis wrapped Osiris's body in linen—so that he became the first mummy. 마지막으로 이시스는 오시리스의 몸을 린넨으로 둘러쌌다. 그래서 오시리스는 최초의 미라가 되었다.

overflow ⓥ of a river or lake being so full that the water flows over its edges

물이 '흐르다'라는 의미의 동사 flow 앞에 '~넘어, ~을 넘는'을 뜻하는 over가 붙은 말이다. The Nile overflowed its banks(나일 강이 둑을 넘쳐흘렀다)처럼 타동 사나 The Nile overflows every year(나일 강은 해마다 범람한다)처럼 자동사로 쓰인다.

The Nile filled back up and overflowed its banks, so that all the Egyptians had water to drink, and their crops began to grow again. 나일 강이 다시 가득 범람해서 모든 이집트인이 마실 물을 갖게 되었고, 작물도 다시 자라기 시작했다.

Q 이집트의 진짜 이름은 따로 있었다면서요?

A 맞아. 우리가 무심코 쓰는 지명이나 국가명 중에서는 고대 그리스인이나 로마인이 붙인 이름이 많아. 이집트라는 지명도 그리스어에서 온 거야. 그렇다면 이집트 사람들은 자신들의 나라를 뭐라고 불렀을까? '케메트'가 정답인데, 그것은 검은색이라는 뜻이야. "이상하네요, 나라 이름이 검은색이라니" 라는 반응이 들리는 듯하지만 생각해봐. 국토 전체의 대부분이 사막인 나라에서 붉은색과 검은색의 의미를 말이야! 붉은색이 생명이 자라지 못하는 색이라면 검은색은 생명을 키우는 색을 의미했어. 홍수 후 물이 빠지고 남은 검은 흙이야말로 이집트인들에게는 일 년 농사의 성공을 보장하는, 생명의 색이었지.

Chapter 3
The First Writing

1 Hieroglyphs and Cuneiform

🌐 인간에게는 사실과 경험을 남기고 기록하고자 하는 본능이 있다. 그래서 알파 벳이나 한글 같은 문자가 사용되기 이전의 고대인도 그림이나 원시적인 형태의 문자를 사용해 기록을 남겼다. 대표적인 고대 문자가 상형(象形) 문자와 설형(楔形) 문자이다. 상형 문자는 사물의 모양象形을 본떠 만든 문자로, 이집트의 고대 유물에서 많이 발견된다. 설형 문자는 문자의 모양이 '쐐기'를 닮았다고 해서 붙여진 이름으로, '쐐기 문자'라고도 한다. 쐐기는 창이나 화살촉처럼 V자 모양으로 뾰족한 것을 말한다. 기원전 3000년경부터 수메르인은 점토판에 설형 문자를 새겨 기록을 남겼다.

The Egyptians were among the earliest people to use writing. Why do you think it's important to be able to write things down?

Suppose I write a message for you on a piece of paper and put it on the table. Then I leave the room. If you look at the paper, you'll know what I wanted to say to you—even though I'm nowhere around. That's one reason writing is important. Once the Egyptians learned to write things down, they could send messages from one part of the kingdom to another.

What if you found my message a year after I wrote it? You would still be able to "hear" my words—even though I had written them down long before. That's the second reason that writing is so important. The Egyptians could write down the important events that happened during their lifetimes, and leave them for their grandchildren and great-grandchildren to read.

The Egyptians used pictures to write with. We call these pictures *hieroglyphs*. *The pictures stood for certain words. The Egyptians used to carve these hieroglyphs into stone tablets.

The stone tablets lasted for a very long time—but they were heavy to carry, and carving the pictures into stone took weeks of work.

Another country near Egypt had a better idea. They carved their pictures into tablets of wet clay. This country was called Sumer.

Sumer was in the Fertile Crescent, between the Tigris and Euphrates rivers. This place between the rivers is called "Mesopotamia." The word *Mesopotamia* means "between two rivers." Do you know what the word *hippopotamus* means? *Hippo* means "horse," and *potamus* means "river." A hippopotamus is a "river-horse"! In Mesopotamia, we can see the word *potamus* again, only this time it has a different ending. *Potamia* means "rivers," and *meso* means "between."

The Sumerian picture-writing was called *cuneiform*. Because the Sumerians lived between two rivers, they had plenty of damp clay. Instead of carving their cuneiform onto stone, they would mold this clay into square tablets. Then, while the clay was still wet, they would use a sharp knife or stick to make the cuneiform marks. After the message was carved into the clay, the Sumerians could either wipe it out and write another message (if the message was something unimportant, like a grocery list), or else bake the clay until it was hard. Then the message would last for a very long time.

Writing in clay is easier than carving stone. But even clay

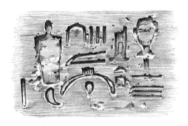

Egyptian Hieroglyphs

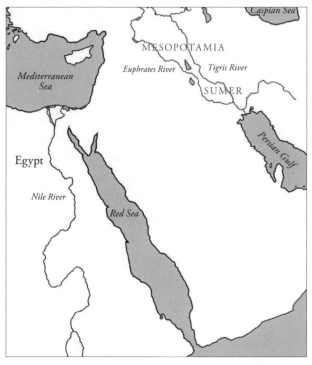

Mesopotamia and Egypt

tablets can be heavy. And clay tablets are thick; if you want to store a whole lot of them, you need a lot of space—whole buildings full of rooms for even a small library.

After several hundred years, the Egyptians came up with an idea that was even better than clay. They learned how to make paper and ink.

Egyptian paper was made from reeds that grew along the banks of the Nile. The Egyptians learned how to soften and mash them into a pulp. They would then spread the pulp out to dry in thin sheets. These sheets became reed-paper, which the Egyptians called *papyrus*. It was much easier to write on paper than on clay or stone. Paper was also easier to carry around; you could fold it up and put it into your pocket, or roll it up into a scroll. *And paper took up less room. When they started using paper, the Egyptians thought they had found the best way to keep records.

But paper has a problem. When paper gets wet, the ink on it dissolves and the paper falls apart. And paper also starts to fall apart over time. The older paper gets, the more likely it is to crack up and turn into dust. We know a lot about Egyptian history from the times that Egyptians wrote on stone, because those stone writings have lasted for centuries—from Egyptian days until now. We know a lot about Sumerian history too, because clay tablets last for a long time if they've been baked hard. But we don't know a great deal about what happened in Egypt after the Egyptians started writing on paper, because in the thousands of years that have gone by, the paper writings of the Egyptians have crumbled and disappeared. 📖

———

Note to Parent: The Sumerians and Egyptians used cuneiform from about 3200 BC/BCE, with Sumerian writing developing slightly earlier.

The Story of the Words

Chapter 3 The First Writing

1 Hieroglyphs and Cuneiform

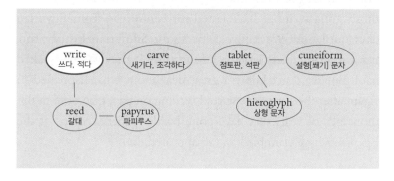

write ⓥ to make letters or words on a surface of something

'글자를 적다, 글을 쓰다'라는 뜻의 write는 원래 scratch(긁다, 할퀴다)를 뜻하는 고대 영어 writan에서 온 말이다. 끝이 뾰족한 돌이나 뼈로 나무껍질을 긁어 기록한 원시적인 형태의 글쓰기에서 유래했다. Write down this phone number(이 전화번호를 적어)처럼 to write down은 뭔가를 '적다, 쓰다'이다.

Why do you think it's important to be able to write things down? 여러분은 왜 뭔가를 기록할 수 있는 것이 중요하다고 생각하는가?

hieroglyph ⓝ a picture or symbol used to represent a word, especially in the ancient Egyptian writing system

hieroglyph는 희랍어에서 유래한 말로, hiero는 '성스러운(sacred)'을 의미하고, glyph는 '새겨진(carved)'을 뜻한다. 유럽인이 석판이나 점토판에 새겨진 '상형 문자'를 처음 발견했을 때 대단히 '신비롭고 신성한' 듯 보였다고 하여 붙여진 명칭이다. 단순화된 그림이나 기호로 기록된 고대 이집트의 '상형 문자'를 hieroglyph라고 한다.

We call these pictures *hieroglyphs*. 우리는 이 그림들을 '상형 문자'라고 부른다.

Q 수메르인이 만든 글자를 왜 설형(쐐기)문자라고 하나요?

A 수메르인은 이집트인과 더불어 최초로 문자를 만들었다는 영광을 누린 사람들이야. 그런데 수메르인들은 왜 문자를 필요로 했을까? 도시 국가가 만들어지면 씨족이나 부족 단위로 농사를 짓고 살던 시대와는 달라져서 의사소통을 제대로 하기 위해 문자가 필요해졌어.

처음에는 사물의 모양을 본떠 그림처럼 문자를 그렸겠지만, 그림만으로는 표현하기 어려운 것이 많았겠지? 소, 양, 집, 해 이렇게 구체적으로 모양을 떠올릴 수 있는 것은 누구나 알아보기 쉬웠지만 적대감, 용기, 의리처럼 추상적인 의미를 표현하는 것은 상당히 어려웠어. 시간이 지나 두 가지 글자를 합해 새로운 뜻을 만들고, 추상적인 의미도 합의해서 표현했지. 수메르인들은 문자를 만든 다음에 그 지역에서 흔히 볼 수 있는 점토판에 글씨를 새겼는데, 그 곡선을 그리는 것은 쉽지 않았다고 해. 그렇다고 포기할 수는 없는 법! 곡선이 어려우면 직선으로라도 표현하려고 했더니 쐐기 모양의 문자가 된 거야.

tablet ⓝ a flat piece of stone, or clay with writing cut into it

tablet은 납작하고 평평해야 한다. flat, board를 뜻하는 라틴어 tabula에서 유래했기 때문이다. 철자로 유추할 수 있겠지만, tablet은 table(식탁)과 친척 관계로 중세 프랑스어에서는 '작은 식탁'을 tablet이라고 했다. 본문에서는 '글이나 그림이 새겨진 평평한 석판이나 점토판'을 뜻한다.

The stone tablets lasted for a very long time—but they were heavy to carry, and carving the pictures into stone took weeks of work. 석판은 대단히 오랫동안 보존되었으나, 석판은 들고 다니기에 무거웠으며 돌에 그림을 새기는 것은 여러 주가 걸리는 작업이었다.

carve ⓥ to cut a pattern or letter on the surface of something

carve는 '조각하다'이다. '조각하다'는 '나무나 돌 등을 깎아서 원하는 모양으로 만드는(to cut wood or stone into shapes)' 것과 본문에서처럼 '물체의 표면에 그림이나 글을 새기는' 것을 의미한다. They carved pictures into stone(그들은 돌에 그림을 새겼다)처럼 주로 carve into를 써서 표현한다.

They carved their pictures into tablets of wet clay. 그들은 젖은 점토판에 그림을 새겼다.

cuneiform ⓝ letters used in the ancient Mesopotamia that look like wedges

cuneiform은 '쐐기(wedge)'를 뜻하는 라틴어에 '형태'를 뜻하는 form이 합쳐진 말로, '설형 문자, 쐐기 문자'이다. '쐐기처럼 생긴 것'이라는 뜻인데, 고대 메소포타미아의 점토판에 새겨진 '설형 문자'가 쐐기 모양과 비슷하다고 해서 붙여진 명칭이다.

The Sumerian picture—writing was called *cuneiform*. 수메르의 그림 글자는 '쐐기 문자'라고 불렸다.

reed ⓝ a tall thin plant that grows in or near water

강가나 호숫가에서 흔히 볼 수 있는 '갈대'가 reed이다. 이집트의 파피루스(papyrus)도 갈대로 만든 것이다. 갈대는 줄기가 가늘고 길어서 바람이 조금만 불어도 잘 흔들려서 마음이 흔들리는 인간을 갈대에 비유하곤 한다. 철학자 파스칼(Pascal)도 Man is a thinking reed(인간은 생각하는 갈대다)라는 말을 했다.

Egyptian paper was made from reeds that grew along the banks of the Nile. 이집트 종이는 나일 강의 강둑을 따라 자라는 갈대로 만들었다.

papyrus ⓝ a type of paper made from reeds in ancient Egypt

papyrus는 이집트 강변에서 많이 자라는 '갈대(reed)'를 지칭하는 희랍어에서 유래했다. 고대 이집트인들이 이 식물로 만들어서 사용했던 종이인 '파피루스'도 같은 이름으로 부른다. '종이'를 뜻하는 영단어 paper도 papyrus에서 온 말이다. 기원전 3세기 이전에 발명된 것으로 추정되는 중국의 종이는 4세기쯤에 유럽으로 전파되었는데, 성질과 용도가 파피루스와 비슷했기 때문에 같은 단어로 표현된 것이다.

These sheets became reed—paper, which the Egyptians called *papyrus*. 이 시트들은 갈대 종이가 되었고, 이것을 이집트인들은 '파피루스'라고 불렀다.

> **Q** 수메르에 최초의 영광이 돌아간 것이 많다면서요?
>
> **A** 《문명은 수메르에서 시작되었다》라는 제목의 책이 있단다. 최초의 도시 국가가 생긴 지역이 수메르이다 보니 아무래도 필요한 것을 스스로의 힘으로 만들 수밖에 없는 환경이었어. 필요가 발명을 낳는 법이니까 수메르에서 최초로 만들어진 것들은 많아.
>
> 앞에서 말한 문자를 시작으로, 바퀴도 수메르인이 처음으로 만든 거야. 인

류 최초의 서사시 《길가메시》도 수메르인들이 만든 이야기였지. 수메르 신화는 바빌로니아와 이집트를 거쳐 그리스 신화에도 영향을 주었단다. 수학도 빼놓을 수 없지. 60진법과 제곱의 개념도 여기에서 생겼으니 한 시간을 60분으로 계산하는 것도 수메르인이 만든 것을 이어 쓰고 있는 것이란다. 또한 그들은 달의 모양이 변하는 것을 관찰하여 태음력을 만들기도 했어. 그러니 '문명은 수메르에서 시작되었다'는 책 제목이 그저 허풍이 아니라는 것이 이해되지?

Chapter 4
The Old Kingdom of Egypt

1 Making Mummies

고대 이집트 신화에는 동생 세트(Set)에게 살해당한 오시리스(Osiris)의 시신을 아내인 이시스(Isis)가 미라로 만들어 부활시켰는데, 이것이 최초의 '미라(mummy)' 라는 내용이 나온다. 고대 이집트인은 사후 세계를 믿었기 때문에 파라오가 죽으면 방부 처리를 해서 미라로 만든 후에 그 시신을 돌무덤 속에 안장했다. 사후 세계에서도 현세와 똑같이 살 것이라는 믿음에서 육체를 보존하고자 했던 것이다. 그런데 미라 풍습은 남아메리카의 아즈텍과 잉카 문명, 중국을 비롯한 아시아 지역에서도 발견되었다.

After King Narmer united Upper and Lower Egypt into one country, Egypt grew to be rich and powerful. We call this time in Egyptian history the "Old Kingdom of Egypt." The Old Kingdom lasted for almost a thousand years—until about the year 2100.

Before we go on, let's look at that date a little more closely. Usually people write this date with a "BC" or "BCE" after it. "BC" means "Before Christ," and "BCE" means "Before the Common Era."

About fifteen hundred years ago, historians began to use the birth of Jesus as a way to count years. In this system, Jesus was born in "Year 1." Dates before Year 1 count down from highest to lowest (for example, 99, 98, 97 … and so on), and end at Year 1. The "Common Era" begins with Jesus' birth. The years after Jesus' birth are called "AD" or "CE." "AD" stands for Anno Domini, or "The Year of Our Lord" in Latin. "CE" means "Common Era." In the Common Era, dates are counted forward (for example, 2006, 2007, 2008, 2009 … and so on). The timeline on the next page shows the BC/BCE years getting smaller as they approach Year 1, and the AD/CE years getting larger as they move away from it.

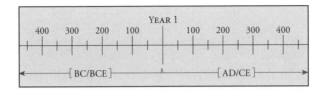

During the Old Kingdom of Egypt, the Egyptians began to make mummies for the first time. Mummies were the bodies of dead people, treated with spices and salts and wrapped in linen so that they wouldn't decay. The Egyptians believed that dead people went on to another life in the afterworld. But they also believed that the dead could only enter the afterworld if their bodies were preserved. This was called *embalming*.

Embalming was a very complicated process. Only *priests*—men who were in charge of worshipping the gods—were allowed to make mummies. And it took more than two months to make a mummy!

Let's imagine that we're back in the Old Kingdom of Egypt, at the time of the pharaoh Cheops. Cheops has been pharaoh for years. He has made Egypt's army strong, and he's kept Egypt safe from enemies. But in the middle of the night, word comes from the palace that Cheops is dead.

Instantly the priests start to make preparations. They collect all the things they'll need to make Cheops's body into a mummy—salt, spices, oil, and linen. Cheops is carried from the palace to the temple, where the priests are waiting for him.

The priests take the body to a holy place inside the temple. They wash it with wine and spices. Then they take all of Cheops's organs—his liver, his stomach, his lungs, and his intestines—out of his body. They cover the organs with special spices to preserve them.

Cheops's heart gets special treatment. The chief priest takes the heart out, washes it, wraps it in linen strips, and puts it back into Cheops's chest. The Egyptians believe that Cheops will need his heart in the afterlife. They think that when Cheops reaches the afterworld, the god Osiris will weigh his heart on a special scale. If his heart is good, it will be light and Cheops will spend the rest of the afterlife in happiness. *But if his heart is full of sin, it will be heavy—and a monster will eat it!

After they finish with the heart, the priests cover the pharaoh's body with salt and more spices and leave it covered for forty days. During this time, Egyptians mourn the death of their king.

When forty days have passed, the priests come back and uncover the body and the organs. They wash the organs and the body again and cover them with oil and more spices. They put the liver, the stomach, the lungs, and the intestines into four special jars called *canopic jars*. Each jar has the head of a god on top of it. These gods are supposed to protect Cheops's organs.

Then the priests wrap Cheops's body in strips of linen. They put special pieces of jewelry between the linen strips. The jewelry is supposed to protect Cheops on his journey to the afterworld— just like magic. Then they make a gold mask that looks just like Cheops, and put it onto the mummy's face, so that the gods will recognize the mummy when Cheops arrives in the afterlife. Finally, the chief priest holds a special ceremony. He touches the mummy's mouth with a special tool. He thinks that this will allow Cheops's mummy to hear, see, and talk in the afterworld.

Finally the mummy is finished. But before Cheops is buried, he has to be put into three coffins. The first coffin is gold and has Cheops's face on the outside. This gold coffin is put into a wood coffin to protect it. Then Cheops's wooden coffin is carried through the streets in a huge funeral procession, all the way to his tomb—a pyramid!

Inside the pyramid is a special burial chamber. The chamber has a big stone coffin in it, called a *sarcophagus*. The wooden coffin is placed inside the sarcophagus. The stone lid of the sarcophagus is so heavy that four men have to push it into place. Now Cheops's mummy is safe inside its coffin. His spirit can begin the journey to the underworld.

Before the Egyptians leave the burial chamber, they make sure that Cheops has everything he'll need to be comfortable in the next life. They fill the chamber with furniture, jewelry, clothes, and food for him to use. They leave toys and games for Cheops to play with, and scrolls for him to read. They even bury a fullsized boat beside the pyramid, so that Cheops can sail through the afterworld. Finally, they leave the burial chamber and seal up the door. Cheops's body will lie undisturbed for years—until grave robbers discover that his tomb is full of treasure.

2 Egyptian Pyramids

마스타바는 고대 이집트의 무덤 양식으로 밑면이 윗면보다 넓고 윗면이 평평한 형태이며 벽돌과 돌로 지어졌다. 마스타바는 피라미드가 만들어지기 전부터 이집트의 왕과 귀족들의 무덤으로 지어졌다. 피라미드는 사각뿔 모양의 거대 석조물로, 파라오(pharaoh)의 무덤으로 지어졌다. 쿠푸(케오프스) 왕 이후 피라미드는 왕만이 묻힐 수 있는 무덤이었고, 마스타바는 귀족의 무덤으로 이후 약 1,000년 동안 존재한 양식이었다.

All of the kings and important people buried in Egypt had gold and jewels in their graves. And everyone in Egypt knew that the graves were full of treasure. What do you think happened?

At first, the Egyptians of the Old Kingdom dug underground

rooms in the desert to bury their mummies. But thieves knew that the mummies had jewelry and treasures buried along with them. Grave robbers often broke into these underground rooms and stole all the treasure. So the Egyptians started to build stone tombs out of huge stone blocks with a hole, or shaft, cut into the middle. *The mummy and all its clothes, furniture, and jewelry were lowered down the shaft into a treasure room. Then the shaft was filled with stones to keep anyone else from climbing in. These tombs were called *mastaba tombs*.

But even mastaba tombs weren't good enough for pharaohs. The pharaohs were buried in the biggest tombs of all—*pyramids*. Pyramids were giant fortresses to keep the pharaohs and their treasures safe. And pyramids were important for another reason. They pointed upwards to the sky. The Egyptians believed that the pharaoh was a god, and that he would rise up and join the other gods after his death. *They thought that the dead pharaoh would climb up to heaven, using the sides of the pyramids like steps.

Cheops spent over twenty years building his pyramid before he died. He knew that he would be buried in this pyramid when he died, and he wanted his pyramid to be the biggest of all. His pyramid still stands in the desert near Giza (which today is called Cairo, Egypt). *It is called the Great Pyramid, because it is the largest of all the 35 pyramids that the Egyptians built for their pharaohs.

The Great Pyramid was built around 2550 BC/BCE. It was the highest building in the world for four thousand years. It was built with over two million blocks of stone—and each block weighs almost three tons. *That's as heavy as an elephant! And the Egyptians didn't have any cranes, bulldozers, or earthmovers. Instead, they cut the stone blocks out by hand, with copper and stone tools. *Then they built *ramps* out of rocks and earth up the sides of the pyramids, and dragged the stone blocks up the ramps with ropes. Hundreds of men pulled together to move the largest stones. Thousands of Egyptians worked on the Great Pyramid, year after year. Finally, the pyramid was finished. Then the Egyptians pulled the ramps down and covered it with sheets of white limestone. Archaeologists think that the pointed stone at the very top of the Great Pyramid even had a golden cap on it. The white stone and golden top are gone now, but when the Great Pyramid was first built, it shone in the sun.

Inside the Great Pyramid was a burial chamber, just for Cheops. But there were also empty chambers and unfinished rooms, and passages that led off into dead ends. Cheops hoped that any thief who broke into the pyramid would get lost in the maze of rooms before he could find the treasure. And after the pyramid was finished, workmen sealed off the door to the outside. They slid huge plugs of stone down the passage to block the way into the

Pyramids of Egypt

pyramid—and then went out through a small escape passage that had been dug down into the ground and came up in the desert outside.

The Great Pyramid even has its own watchdog. Near the Great Pyramid, the Egyptians built a mysterious monument shaped like a *sphinx*—an imaginary animal with a man's head and a lion's body. We now call this giant limestone animal the Great Sphinx. *The Great Sphinx is as tall as eleven men, standing on each other's shoulders. And it is almost as long as a football field. The Sphinx was made out of limestone, which is a kind of stone that is easily chipped and broken. *Desert sand keeps burying it and wearing it away. Its nose is broken. But even though it is almost five thousand years old, you can still see that the Sphinx has the face of a man. Many people think that the Sphinx was built to protect the pyramids.

But thieves found Cheops's burial chamber anyway. They got past the Sphinx and through the maze of passages inside the Great Pyramid and stole Cheops's treasure—and his mummy. *By the time archaeologists made their way into the pyramid, Cheops and his gold had disappeared forever. 📖

Note to Parent: Cheops is also known as Khufu.

The Story of the Words

Chapter 4 The Old Kingdom of Egypt

1 Making Mummies

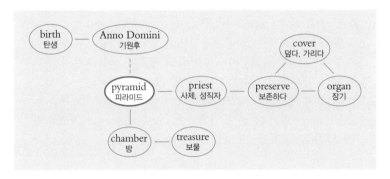

birth ⓝ the occasion of a baby being born

birth는 '아기 태어남, 탄생'을 의미한다. 생일은 birthday이고, '예수 탄생'이 Jesus' birth이다. 어머니의 입장에서는 아기를 낳는 것, 즉 '출산'이므로 She gave birth to a boy yesterday는 '그녀는 어제 사내아이를 출산했다'라는 의미가 된다.

The "Common Era" begins with Jesus' birth. '공통의 시대(CE)'는 예수의 탄생으로 시작된다.

Anno Domini ⓝ after the year of Jesus' birth

라틴어로 Anno는 '해(year)'이고, Domini는 '주님의(of Lord)'를 뜻한다. 그래서 Anno Domini는 '주님[예수]이 태어난 해'를 의미하는데, AD로 줄여서 '기원후'라는 뜻으로 쓴다.

"AD" stands for Anno Domini, or "The Year of Our Lord" in Latin. 'AD'는 라틴어로 Anno Domini, 즉 '주님의 해'를 의미한다.

preserve ⓥ to keep something from being damaged or changed

preserve는 '미리, 먼저'를 뜻하는 접두사 pre-와 '지키다, 간직하다(keep)'를 뜻하는 동사 serve가 합쳐진 말이다. 미리 지키고 간직하니까 변형되지 않도록 '보존하다, 보호하다'라는 의미다. 명사형은 preservation이다.

But they also believed that the dead could only enter the afterworld if their bodies were preserved. 그러나 그들은 또한 육체가 보존되어야만 죽은 자들이 사후 세계로 들어갈 수 있다고 믿었다.

Q 나르메르가 고왕국 최초의 파라오가 아니었다고요?
A 상이집트와 하이집트를 통일한 나르메르(네메스)가 세운 왕조를 이집트 역사에서는 초기 왕조라고 부른단다. 이집트 전체 역사 중에서 30왕조까지 이어졌는데, 3왕조부터가 고왕국으로 불리지. 사실 초기 왕조에 대해서는 그다지 알려진 것이 없었어. 그렇다면 어떻게 우리는 나르메르 이야기를 알게 되었을까? 1899년 히에라콘폴리스 신전에서 발굴된 부장품 중에 나르메르 왕의 석판이 발견된 거야. 기원전 3000년경의 것으로 추정되는데 이집트 초기 왕조를 알 수 있는 귀한 유물이야.

priest ⓝ someone whose job is to perform religious ceremonies and duties

priest는 종교 의식, 예배를 주관하는 '성직자, 사제'를 말한다. 원래의 의미는 the oldest(가장 나이가 많은 사람)이다. 옛날에는 '나이가 가장 많은 사람'만이 종교 의식을 행할 권한을 갖고 있었기 때문에 '성직자'의 뜻이 되었다.

Only priests—men who were in charge of worshipping the gods—were allowed to make mummies. 오직 사제들, 즉 신들을 숭배할 권한과 책임을 가진 사람들만이 미라를 만들도록 허용되었다.

organ ⓝ a part of the body that does a special job

organ은 tool(도구), instrument(기구)를 뜻하는 희랍어에서 온 것이다. 음악을 연주할 수 있는 악기 '오르간'도 하나의 '기구'이기 때문에 organ이라고 한다. 사람 몸 안의 장기(臟器)들도 마치 하나의 도구처럼 각기 고유의 역할을 하므로 심장, 폐, 위, 간, 신장 등도 organ이라고 한다.

Then they take all of Cheops's organs—his liver, his stomach, his lungs, and his intestines—out of his body. 그다음에 그들은 케오프스의 몸에서 간, 위, 폐와 내장의 장기를 모두 꺼낸다.

cover ⓥ to put something over something else

cover는 어떤 것 위에 다른 것을 놓아 '덮다, 가리다'라는 뜻이다. cover A with B(B로 A를 덮다), A is covered with B(A는 B로 덮여 있다)의 형태로 쓸 수 있다. 덮은 것을 걷어내는 것은 uncover이고, cover앞에 re가 붙은 recover는 '상처 난 곳이 다시 아물다'라는 의미에서 '회복하다'이다.

After they finish with the heart, the priests cover the pharaoh's body with salt and more spices and leave it covered for forty days. 심장의 처리가 끝난 후에 사제들은 소금과 더 많은 향료들로 파라오의 몸을 덮은 다음 40일 동안 그대로 덮어둔다.

Q 임호테프가 세계 최초의 건축가라면서요?

A 이 책에서는 '기자'의 피라미드를 중점으로 소개하고 있어. 기자에는 멘카우레, 케오프스(쿠푸), 카프레 파라오의 대피라미드가 있는데, 모두 4왕조에 속했어. 그런데 고왕국을 연 3왕조의 조세르가 사실은 피라미드에 처음 묻힌 파라오였어.

특이한 것은 조세르의 피라미드를 만든 '임호테프'는 목수이자 조각가이며 건축가로서 수많은 재능의 소유자였지. 그는 처음부터 건축을 하지는 않고, 돌항아리를 만들던 장인이었는데 조세르에게 능력을 인정받아 궁중 건축가로 발탁되었어. 그가 처음에 만든 피라미드는 마스타바(사각형 무덤)였으나 사카라의 조세르의 무덤은 계단식으로 변형한 거야. 파라오의 영혼이 계단을 올라가 하늘로 갈 수 있도록 설계한 것이란다.

chamber ⓝ a room used for a special purpose

chamber는 원래 room(방, 공간)이었는데 점차 특별한 용도의 방을 나타내어 '막힌, 공개되지 않는 방, 공간'을 의미하게 되었다. 전에는 '침실(bedroom)'을 chamber라고도 했다. 지금도 공개되지 않은 방의 용도인 의원회의실(council chamber), 가스실(gas chamber), 무덤방(burial chamber) 등으로 쓰인다.

Inside the pyramid is a special burial chamber. 피라미드 안에는 특별한 무덤방이 있다.

treasure ⓝ a group of valuable things such as gold, jewels and money

treasure는 원래 '저장해 두는 것, 모으는 것'을 의미했다. 대개 식량, 돈, 귀금속 같은 귀중한 것을 모아 두기 때문에 treasure는 '보물'을 뜻하는 말로 쓰인다. 물질로서의 '보물'을 뜻할 때는 항상 단수형이고, '대단히 귀중한 것'을 비유적으로 표현할 때는 복수형으로 쓸 수 있다.

Cheops's body will lie undisturbed for years—until grave robbers discover that his tomb is full of treasure. 케오프스의 시신은 오랫동안 아무 방해도 받지 않고 누워 있게 될 것이다. 도굴꾼들이 그의 무덤에 보물이 가득하다는 사실을 알게 될 때까지는 말이다.

2 Egyptian Pyramids

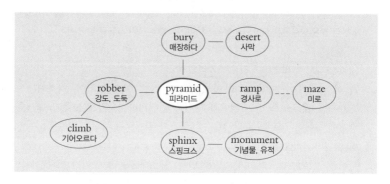

bury ⓥ to put a dead body into the ground

bury는 땅에 뭔가를 묻는 행동을 표현하는 동사로, '중요한 것을 땅에 묻어 감추다'라는 의미로 쓰인다. 시신도 땅에 묻으므로 '매장하다'라는 뜻이다. 명사형 burial에는 '매장, 장례'라는 뜻만 있다.

At first, the Egyptians of the Old Kingdom dug underground rooms in the desert to bury their mummies. 처음에, 고왕국의 이집트인들은 사막에 지하 방을 미라를 매장하기 위해 팠다.

robber ⓝ someone who steals something

rob은 '강제로 빼앗다'라는 뜻의 동사이다. steal(훔치다)과 같은 의미로 쓰이기도 하지만, 엄밀히 말하면 '완력이나 협박으로 빼앗다(to take something from by force or threat)'가 rob이다. 즉 강도짓을 하는 것이다. rob에 어미를 붙일 때는 b를 하나 더 써서 '강도짓을 하는 사람'을 robber라고 한다. robber는 thief(도둑)와 같은 의미로 쓰인다.

Grave robbers often broke into these underground rooms and stole all the treasure. 무덤 도둑들은 종종 이 지하 방을 뚫고 들어가 보물을 몽땅 훔쳤다.

climb ⓥ to move up, down or across something using your hands and feet

climb은 원래 의미가 '힘들게 기어가다'이다. 위, 아래, 옆으로 힘들게 기어가면 전부 climb을 쓸 수 있다. 경사가 가파르면 오르기 힘들기 때문에 '오르다'가 대표적인 의미이다. mountain hiking(등산)은 남녀노소 누구나 할 수 있지만, mountain climbing(등반)은 훈련받은 산악인만 할 수 있다.

Then the shaft was filled with stones to keep anyone else from climbing in. 그런 다음 다른 누구도 들어가지 못하도록 수직 통로에 돌을 가득 채워 넣었다.

ramp ⓝ a slope connecting two levels of a building

계단은 높이가 다른 두 곳을 이동하기 위해 만든 것이다. 또한 걸음이 불편한 사람들의 보행이나 바퀴 달린 휠체어나 카트의 이동을 위해 계단 대신 경사로(slope)를 만들기도 한다. 이런 인공적인 경사로가 바로 ramp이다. 고대 이집트인들은 피라미드를 지으면서 크고 무거운 돌을 가능한 쉽게 위로 옮기기 위해 층마다 ramp를 설치했다.

Then they built ramps out of rocks and earth up the sides of the pyramids, and dragged the stone blocks up the ramps with ropes. 그런 다음 그들은 바위와 흙으로 피라미드의 측면 위에 경사로를 만들었고, 밧줄을 이용해 경사로 위로 돌덩어리들을 끌어 올렸다.

> **Q** 파라오 혼자서 이 넓은 땅을 통치했나요?
>
> **A** 고왕국 시대의 이집트는 중앙 집권 체제였어. 중앙 집권 체제란 수도에서 파라오가 절대 권력을 갖고 통치한다는 의미야. 그래서 이집트의 정치 구조를 피라미드식이라고 한단다. 파라오의 무덤인 피라미드 형태에서 밑변이 넓고 위로 올라갈수록 좁아지는 것처럼, 권력의 꼭대기에는 파라오 한 사람, 그 아래로는 파라오의 명령을 대행하는 신관과 관리가 있고 마지막에는 일반 백성이 있었어. 아무리 파라오가 신과 동급인 대리인이라고 해도 혼자서 이 넓은 땅을 다스릴 수는 없었으니 그의 통치를 돕는 재상이 있었지. 재상이 왕의 오른팔 노릇을 하면서 행정부를 이끌었고, 각 부서에는 우두머리인 장관이 있었어.

maze ⓝ a specially designed path which is difficult to find your way through

이집트 피라미드에서 무덤의 주인이 아닌 유골이 다수 발견되었는데, 그들은 도굴꾼들(grave robbers)이었다. 복잡한 무덤의 구조, '미로' 때문에 나가는 길을 찾지 못하고 헤매다가 굶어 죽은 것이다. 영어 maze에도 confusing(혼동하게 만드는)의 의미가 담겨 있는데, 바로 미로(迷路)가 '헷갈리게 하는 길'이라는 뜻이다.

Cheops hoped that any thief who broke into the pyramid would get lost in the maze of rooms before he could find the treasure. 케오프스는 피라미드에 침입한 어떤 도둑도 보물을 찾기 전에 방들의 미로 안에서 길을 잃게 되기를 원했다.

monument ⑩ a very old building or place that is important historically
monument는 '역사적으로 중요한 유적, 기념물'로 remind(다시 생각나게 하다)를 뜻하는 라틴어에서 유래했다. 그래서 monument를 보면 그때 그 시대의 사건이나 인물을 다시 떠올리게 된다. 요즘 만들어지는 '기념물'도 이러한 역할을 하기 때문에 monument라고 한다.
Near the Great Pyramid, the Egyptians built a mysterious monument shaped like a *sphinx*—an imaginary animal with a man's head and a lion's body. 대피라미드 근처에 이집트인들은 스핑크스처럼 생긴 신비로운 기념물을 지었는데, 그것은 인간의 머리에 사자의 몸을 한 상상의 동물이었다.

sphinx ⑩ an ancient Egyptian image of a lion with a human head
sphinx는 '단단히 묶다, 꼼짝 못하게 움켜쥐다(hold fast)'를 뜻하는 희랍어에서 온 것이다. 그리스 신화 중에 스핑크스라는 괴물이 쳐다보는 상대는 몸을 움직일 수 없게 된다는 내용이 나오는데, 거기에서 유래한 이름이다. 이집트의 스핑크스는 머리는 사람, 몸은 사자의 형상을 하고 있다. 이집트인들에게 sphinx는 '호루스[태양신]의 형상'이었으며 신과 같은 힘을 지닌 파라오를 상징했다.
We now call this giant limestone animal the Great Sphinx. 지금 우리는 이 거대한 석회석 동물을 대스핑크스라고 부른다.

desert ⑩ a large area of dry land with few rain and plants
기후학의 개념에서 보면, desert는 '비가 거의 오지 않는 지역'을 의미한다. 비가 오지 않는 땅은 건조하고, 식물이 거의 자라지 않으며 모래나 돌로 이루어져 있다. 그래서 desert라고 하면 모래로 덮인 지역, 즉 '사막(砂漠)'을 말한다.
Desert sand keeps burying it and wearing it away. 사막의 모래가 그것을 계속 덮으며 마모시킨다.

Chapter 5
The First Sumerian Dictator

1 Sargon and the Akkadians

🌐 사람들이 많이 모여 도시가 만들어지면 예외 없이 지배층과 피지배층이 형성된다. 권력의 개념이 생기고, 사회의 질서를 유지하기 위한 규칙과 법, 도시를 보호하기 위한 군대도 만들어진다. 도시 자체가 하나의 국가처럼 기능을 하는 것이다. 이런 형태의 국가가 바로 도시 국가(city-state)이다. 전쟁과 정복을 통해 통합되어 왕국이나 제국이 형성되기 전 단계에서 도시 국가가 세계 전역에서 존재했다.

Do you remember how the Egyptians used to be divided into two countries—Upper Egypt and Lower Egypt? They spent all their time and energy fighting each other. But once King Narmer conquered Lower Egypt and made the Egyptians into one country, the Egyptians could spend their time on farming and on building instead of on war. *Egypt grew richer and stronger, once all the quarrelling Egyptians were united into one.

The same thing happened over in Mesopotamia, between the Tigris and Euphrates rivers. People called the Sumerians lived in Mesopotamia. You've learned a little about the Sumerians; they wrote picture writing, called cuneiform, on clay tablets. The area where the Sumerians lived was called Sumer. But Sumer wasn't really one country. It was filled with villages of farmers. The villages grew larger and larger until they became cities. Each city built thick walls and high towers to protect itself. Each city had its own king and its own army. And the cities fought with each other all the time! *We call them *city-states* because each city was like a separate country. The cities put all their energy into protecting themselves from their neighbors.

But one Sumerian wanted to make all the quarrelling cities into one country—just like King Narmer made Egypt into one country. This man was named Sargon.

There are many stories about Sargon. One of the oldest stories says that he had no parents—he just floated down the Euphrates River in a basket when he was a baby. The basket got stuck in the reeds at the edge of the river near a city–state called Kish. One of the servants of the king of Kish happened to be down at the river, getting water in a jug. He heard a strange sound. Where was that sound coming from? The servant saw a basket. He bent down to look inside and saw a crying baby—the baby Sargon.

The servant took the basket back to the palace of the king of Kish. The king gave him permission to keep the baby and raise it. So Sargon grew up inside the palace. He became strong, handsome, and popular with the other courtiers. He even became the cup–bearer to the king; at every meal, he would bring the king his wine in a golden cup. The king's cup–bearer was one of his most trusted servants, because it would have been very easy to poison the king's wine. But the king of Kish trusted Sargon.

He shouldn't have. Sargon made friends with the most powerful people at the palace—including the commanders of the army. He became so popular that he convinced the army to follow him instead of the king. And he even persuaded the army to kill the king, and make him, Sargon, the ruler instead. This happened around 2334 BC/BCE.

But that wasn't enough for Sargon. He didn't just want to be king of one city—he wanted to be king of the whole land of Mesopotamia. So he started to attack the cities all around him. He fought over fifty wars to conquer Mesopotamia. Eventually, Sargon ruled all the country between the Tigris and Euphrates rivers. He built a new capital city called Akkad, and named his new empire Akkadia. Now Sumer was united into one country under one ruler.

But many of the cities Sargon conquered didn't like being

part of the Akkadian empire. They were used to making their own laws and running their own affairs. Sargon knew that to stay in charge, he would have to make the cities all obey *his* laws.

So he used his army to force all the Akkadian cities to follow him. He sent soldiers from the Akkadian army to live in each conquered city. They made sure that the people who lived in the city were following Sargon's laws instead of their own. If the conquered cities didn't obey, the soldiers punished them. This is called a *military dictatorship*. *Military* means "having to do with the army." A *dictatorship* is when people have to obey the government without asking any questions. In a military dictatorship, the army is in charge. Sargon's empire lasted for years—but only because he used the power of his army to keep it together. 📖

Sargon, King of Mesopotamia

The Story of the Words

Chapter 5 The First Sumerian Dictator

1 Sargon and the Akkadians

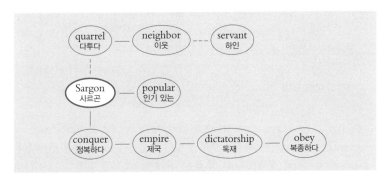

quarrel ⓥ to have an angry argument

quarrel은 complain(불평하다, 따지다)을 뜻하는 라틴어에서 유래했다. 불평을 하고 시비를 가리다 보면 말다툼이 일어나기 마련이다. quarrel은 티격태격 '말 다툼을 하다, 언쟁하다'라는 뜻의 동사인데, 흔히 '싸우다, 다투다'의 의미로 쓰인다.

Egypt grew richer and stronger, once all the quarrelling Egyptians were united into one. 일단 서로 다투던 이집트인들이 모두 하나로 통일되자, 이집트는 점점 더 부유해지고 강해졌다.

neighbor ⓝ a country or city that is next to another one

neighbor는 '가까이'를 뜻하는 neigh와 '사는 사람'을 뜻하는 bor가 합쳐진 단어이다. '자기와 가까이 사는 사람(someone who lives near you)'이니까 '이웃'이다. 이웃처럼 가까운 국가나 도시들도 Korea and its powerful neighbors(한국과 힘센 이웃국가)처럼 neighbor로 표현할 수 있다.

The cities put all their energy into protecting themselves from their neighbors. 그 도시들은 이웃 도시로부터 자신들을 보호하는 데 모든 에너지를 쏟았다.

Q 사르곤과 모세 이야기 중에서 어떤 것이 더 먼저인가요?

A 사르곤 이야기를 읽자마자 익숙한 이야기라고 생각했다면 성당이나 교회를 다니거나 《구약 성서》를 읽은 적이 있다는 증거야. 이미 《로물루스와 레무스》 이야기를 알고 있다면 고개를 갸웃하고 있을지도 모르지. 어떻게 서로 다른 지역의 이야기가 이렇게 비슷할까? 사르곤과 모세 이야기는 시간적인 순서로 당연히 '사르곤' 이야기가 먼저야. 수메르 지역의 키시에 흘러온 어린아이가 모세보다 명백하게 앞선 시대에 태어났으니까.

사르곤도 모세도 부모가 지은 이름은 아니었어. 모세의 부모는 누구인지 알려졌지만, 사르곤은 그저 바구니에 실려 떠내려온 거야. 당시 메소포타미아 지역에서는 물이 갖는 상징성 때문에 물에 떠내려온 아이는 이전의 상태와 상관없이 물로 정화되어 새로운 존재로 태어난다고 생각했어. 어디서 왔는지 모르는 이 아이는 그를 구해준 사람의 양자가 되어 키시에서 성장하게 되었지.

servant ⓝ someone whose job is to do housework for someone else

servant는 동사 serve에 사람을 뜻하는 명사형 접미사 -ant가 붙은 단어이다. serve는 '봉사하다, 섬기다'라는 뜻으로, 원래 '노예(slave)'를 뜻하는 라틴어 servus에서 온 것이다. 고객이나 주인을 섬기고 봉사하는 행동이 serve이고, servant는 '하인(下人), 종'이다.

One of the servants of the king of Kish happened to be down at the river, getting water in a jug. 키시 왕의 하인들 중 한 명이 우연히 강으로 내려와 항아리에 물을 긷고 있었다.

popular ⓐ liked by many people

popular는 라틴어에서 온 popul에 형용사 어미 -ar이 붙어 만들어진 단어이다. popul은 people(사람들)을 뜻해서 population이 '인구'이다. popular는 '사람들이 많이 있는' 상태를 나타낸다. 사람들이 모이는 것은 관심이 많고 좋아하기 때문이다. 그래서 popular가 '인기 있는, 대중적인'이라는 뜻이다. 명사형은 popularity(인기)이다.

He became strong, handsome, and popular with the other courtiers. 그는 힘이 세지고, 잘 생겨졌으며, 다른 신하들로부터 인기를 끌게 되었다.

conquer ⓥ to get control of land or people by fighting

conquer는 '완전히(completely)'를 뜻하는 접두사 con과 '얻다, 취하다(obtain)'

라는 뜻의 quer가 합쳐진 말이다. '쟁취하다'에서 '정복하다'라는 의미로 확장된 것이다. 인류의 역사는 전쟁과 정복의 역사이기 때문에 역사책에 자주 등장하는 동사이다. 명사형 '정복'은 conquest이고, '정복자'는 conqueror이다.

He fought over fifty wars to conquer Mesopotamia. 그는 메소포타미아를 정복하기 위해 50여 차례 전쟁을 치렀다.

empire ⓝ a group of countries ruled by one government

empire는 '명령하다(command), 지배하다(rule)'라는 뜻의 라틴어에서 온 것이다. 다른 국가와 민족을 정복해서 하나의 국가처럼 지배하는 '제국(帝國)'이 empire이다. 아카드(Akkadia)의 사르곤(Sargon)처럼 제국을 건설하고 지배하는 '제왕, 황제'는 emperor라고 한다.

He built a new capital city called Akkad, and named his new empire Akkadia. 그는 아카드라고 불리는 새로운 수도를 건설했고, 자신의 새로운 제국을 아카드라고 명명했다.

obey ⓥ to do what someone or a law tells you to do

obey는 '귀 기울여 듣다'라는 의미를 담고 있다. 즉 '복종하다, 명령에 따르다'의 뜻이다. He always obeys his parents(그는 항상 부모에게 순종한다)처럼 사람에게 복종할 때나 We must obey the law(우리는 법을 따라야 한다)처럼 규칙이나 법을 지킬 때도 쓴다.

Sargon knew that to stay in charge, he would have to make the cities all obey *his* laws. 사르곤은 권력을 유지하기 위해서 도시들이 모두 자신의 법에 복종하도록 만들어야 한다는 것을 알고 있었다.

Q 사르곤이 컵을 나르던 사람이라는 사실이 왜 대단한 것일까요?

A 당시 키시 궁전에서는 왕에게 음식이나 음료를 가져다주는 사람들이 혹시라도 음식에 독이 들어 있는지 확인하기 위해 미리 맛보았단다. 먼저 음식을 먹어보다가 죽으면 억울하지 않았을까? 그래서인지 왕의 음료를 나르는 사람은 누구보다 왕의 신임이 두터운 사람이었다고 해. 그 일을 하면서 왕을 찾아오는 사람들을 선별해 어떤 사람은 왕을 만나게 하고, 다른 사람에겐 그런 기회를 아예 주지 않을 수도 있었어. 그러니까 왕에게 잘 보이고 싶은 사람들은 음료를 나르는 사람과 친해지려고 했겠지? 그렇게 해서 사르곤은 군대의 요직에 있는 사람들과 인연을 맺으며 그들을 설득해 왕을 제거할 수 있었던 것이란다.

dictatorship ⓝ the state of being governed by a ruler who has complete power

dictatorship은 dictator에 접미사 -ship이 붙은 형태이다. 독재자가 절대적인 권력을 갖고 지배하는 형태가 바로 dictatorship이다. 흔히 군사력을 바탕으로 독재 정치를 하기 때문에 military dictatorship(군사 독재)라는 표현을 자주 쓴다. dictate는 '말하다, 명령하다'라는 뜻이고, dictator는 dictate하는 사람(명령하며 군림하는 '독재자')이다.

A *dictatorship* is when people have to obey the government without asking any questions. 독재는 사람들이 어떤 의문도 제기하지 않고 [무조건] 정부에 복종해야 하는 상태를 말한다.

Chapter 6
The Jewish People

1 God Speaks to Abraham

유대인을 뜻하는 jew는 유다(Judah)에서 유래했다. 유대인의 '유대'도 Judah 를 차음한 것이다. 과거에는 유대 민족을 칭했으나 지금은 '유대교(Judaism)'를 믿는 사람'을 통칭하는 말로 쓰인다. 유대인이 중요한 것은 그들이 처음으로 유일신 '야 훼'를 믿었고, 그 유일신 신앙이 세계 전역으로 퍼진 기독교의 뿌리가 되었기 때문 이다. 이 책을 끝까지 공부하면 느끼겠지만, 유일신 신앙은 지금까지 인류의 역사를 이끌고 변화시킨 가장 강력한 주요 원인이었다.

Sargon the Great ruled over many cities in Mesopotamia. One of the cities in Sargon's empire was called Ur. And a very important man lived in the city of Ur. His name was Abram. The book of Genesis, in the Bible, tells us about Abram:

Long ago, Abram lived with his father Terah in the city of Ur. He helped his father to run his business. Terah was a merchant; he bought and sold copper, gold, purple and scarlet cloth, cinnamon, and salt. He grew rich buying and selling in Ur.

Terah should have been happy. Ur was the perfect place for a merchant to live. The city was built right on the banks of the Euphrates River, so that traders could sail right up to the city with their goods. But Terah lived in difficult times. After Sargon's death, his empire had fallen apart. The kings of the cities around Ur were fighting with each other. Tribes of wild people called Gutians were invading the land between the rivers. If Ur was attacked, the city might be burned. Terah could lose all of his riches in the war.

Terah worried and worried. He asked the ancient Mesopotamian gods what he should do. He made extra sacrifices to the moon-god—the special god of the city of Ur. He even went to Ur's largest *ziggurat* and asked the moon-god to protect him from evil. (The ziggurats were special pyramids, built with steps up the sides so that priests could go up to the top and sacrifice to the gods.)

Finally, Terah decided that he would take his family and leave Ur. He took Abram and Abram's wife Sarai with him, and set off to find a better place to live. They traveled along the banks of the Euphrates River, looking for a city to settle in. When they arrived at the city of Haran, up in the north of Mesopotamia, Terah liked what he saw. Haran was a rich city where people came to trade. And the people of Haran also worshipped the moon-god, so Terah felt right at home.

Terah and Abram and Sarai settled into Haran. Terah started to work as a merchant again. Abram took care of the sheep, goats, and cows that Terah bought with all the money he earned. The whole family was doing well.

But Terah was an old man, and after several years in Haran, he died. Then Abram became the head of the family.

One night after Terah's funeral, Abram went out for a walk in the dark. He leaned his arms on the fence surrounding his flocks, and listened to the noise of the sheep and goats. He wondered whether he should keep on farming, or whether he should become a merchant like his father. Maybe he should go back to Ur, where the rest of his relatives were. He thought to himself, "Maybe I will ask the moon god, or one of the other gods, to tell me what to do."

Suddenly he heard a voice say, "Abram!"

He looked around, but he didn't see anyone! "Who are you?" he said. "Are you one of the gods?"

"I am the one God," the voice said, "and there is no other

God except for me!"

"What do you want me to do?" Abram asked.

"Leave Haran," God said, "and go to the land I will show you. I will give it to you and your children. I will make you into a great nation! I will bless your friends and curse your enemies. And everyone on earth will be blessed because of you."

God told Abram to go to Canaan. Abram had never thought about going to Canaan. After all, there were no large trading cities there. There were no rivers. It was far, far away from Mesopotamia—the only civilized place that he knew. Strange, wild tribes lived in Canaan. Why would he go there?

But Abram decided to do what God told him. He took Sarai, all his servants, and all of his sheep, goats, cows, and camels. And all of them left the safe city of Haran and started off into the wilderness.

Finally they arrived in Canaan. When they got there, God appeared to Abram again.

"I will make an agreement with you," God said to Abram. "Obey me and worship me. You will be the father of a whole new nation, and I will give the whole land of Canaan to you and your children and grandchildren. I am going to change your name from Abram to Abraham, because Abraham means 'father of many children.' And I am going to change Sarai's name to Sarah, because Sarah means 'princess.' Sarah will be the mother of a whole nation of people!"

Abraham thought this was very funny, because he was an old man—older than your grandparents. He laughed and laughed at God's promise. "How can Sarah and I have children?" he asked God.

"Nothing is impossible for God!" God said. And the next

year, Sarah had a baby—when she was at least ninety years old! Abraham and Sarah named their son Isaac, which means "laughter," because they had laughed at God.

Isaac had a son named Jacob. And then Jacob had sons—twelve of them. These twelve sons all had families of their own. All of these families lived in Canaan.

Eventually, each one of Jacob's sons had a whole tribe of people named after him. The tribe of Judah was named after Jacob's son Judah. The tribe of Benjamin was named after his youngest son Benjamin. These twelve tribes became known as the nation of Israel, or the Jewish people.

2 Joseph Goes to Egypt

《구약 성서》의 창세기에는 야곱의 아들 요셉이 형제들의 미움을 사서 이집트에 노예로 팔려가고, 이후 기근이 들어 야곱의 가족들이 요셉에게 가서 도움을 받아 이집트에 정착했다고 나와 있다. 그러나 이민족과의 전쟁으로 인해 가나안에 살던 유목민 일부가 이집트로 쫓겨 간 것으로 생각하는 역사가도 많다. 성서에는 야곱과 그의 열두 아들이 이스라엘 민족의 시조가 되어 이집트에서 번성하고, 이후 모세가 핍박을 피해 이스라엘 민족을 이끌고 이집트를 탈출해 다시 가나안 땅으로 돌아갔다고 적혀 있다.

Jacob's twelve sons didn't always get along with each other. They all wanted to be their father's favorite. But Jacob loved his son Joseph the best. The book of Genesis, in the Bible, tells us about Joseph and his brothers.

One day, Joseph was out in the fields with his brothers, watching his father's sheep. Suddenly he heard his father Jacob calling, "Joseph! Joseph!"

"Watch my sheep for me!" Joseph told his brothers. He ran quickly to his father's tent. "Yes, Father?" he asked.

"Joseph," Jacob said, "you are very special to me. So I've made you a beautiful coat to wear." He held out a beautiful coat—as colorful as a field full of flowers and as soft as a cloud, trimmed with a border of purple. Joseph could hardly believe his eyes. He was used to plain clothes, made from the skin of goats and the wool of his father's sheep. He took the coat and slipped it on.

"Thank you, Father!" he said. "I'll always wear it—even while I'm tending the sheep!" And he ran back to his flock of sheep. "Look, Judah!" he shouted. "Look, Benjamin! Look, all of you! Father made me a special coat!"

His brothers stared at the coat. "Why didn't I get one?" Judah asked. "I'm older than you are! Why did Father make a coat for you, and not for any of the rest of us?" All the brothers grumbled and complained about Joseph's coat.

But Joseph wore the coat day and night. He boasted about his coat. He bragged about how much his father loved him. Finally, the other eleven brothers could stand it no more.

One morning, they were all out in a field a long way away from Jacob's tent when they heard Joseph coming. "Here comes our father's favorite!" they complained. "Let's get rid of him so that we never have to hear him brag about his colored coat again!" And when Joseph came, they grabbed him, took his coat away, and threw him into a pit in the ground. When they saw some desert traders coming along, they pulled Joseph out of the pit and sold him to the traders as a slave. Then they smeared some goat blood on Joseph's coat and took it back to their father.

"Look," they said. "We found this out in the desert. A lion must have killed Joseph!"

Jacob wept and wept, because he thought that Joseph was dead. But the desert traders took Joseph down to Egypt and sold him to the pharaoh of Egypt as a slave.

•Down in Egypt, Joseph lived in the house of Potiphar, the captain of the pharaoh's guards. He missed his father. He cried at nights because his brothers had been so cruel to him. But he worked hard in Potiphar's house. Soon, Potiphar took notice of him. •He trusted Joseph more and more and gave him more and more responsibility. Soon, Joseph was running Potiphar's whole household!

But Potiphar's wife decided that Joseph had too much power in her husband's house. She told lies about Joseph to Potiphar. Potiphar believed his wife—and he had Joseph thrown in jail.

"What will happen to me?" Joseph thought. "Will I never be free? First my brothers sell me as a slave, and then I end up in the pharaoh's jail! What will I do?"

One morning, one of the other prisoners looked troubled. "What is the matter?" Joseph asked.

"I had a strange dream," the man said. "I dreamed that a vine grew up out of the ground, right in front of me. The vine grew branches, the branches grew grapes, and the grapes got ripe—right there in front of my eyes! Then I squeezed the grapes into a cup, and gave the cup to Pharaoh."

"I know what your dream means!" Joseph exclaimed. "It means that Pharaoh is going to take you out of jail and forgive your crimes!"

"How do you know?" the dreamer asked.

"Only God knows what dreams mean," Joseph said, "and

he showed me the answer to your dream."

Sure enough, three days later soldiers appeared at the jail's door and took the prisoner away. "You've been pardoned," they said. "You can return to Pharaoh's palace and work for him again."

As the dreamer was walking away, Joseph called after him, "Remember me! Tell Pharaoh that I am innocent, so that I can get out of jail!"

But the dreamer forgot all about Joseph, and Joseph stayed in prison for months and months and months.

One night, the pharaoh himself had a terrifying dream. When he woke up, he said, "Who can tell me what my dream means?"

Then the dreamer remembered Joseph. "Great Pharaoh," he said, "the Israelite in your prison knows what dreams mean. His god tells him!"

"Get him at once!" the Pharaoh said.

So Joseph was brought from prison, right to the pharaoh's throne room. Pharaoh said to him, "I had a terrible dream. I dreamed that I was standing by the river Nile, and that seven big, fat cows walked up out of the water and started to graze on the riverbank. Then, seven ugly, thin cows came up from the water—and swallowed the fat cows right up! What does it mean? Can you tell me?"

"My god gives me the wisdom to understand dreams," Joseph replied. "He tells me that the seven fat cows stand for seven good years, when the Nile will overflow, the crops will grow, and the Egyptians will have plenty to eat. But the seven thin cows stand for seven years of famine. The Nile won't flood, and your crops will die. Pharaoh, you should choose a wise man and put him in charge of gathering grain during the seven good years. •Store the grain, so that the Egyptians will have something to eat during the years of famine."

"A wise man?" the Pharaoh said. "No one is wiser than you, Joseph. I will put you in charge of gathering the grain. You will be second in command to me."

So Pharaoh took the ring off his finger and put it on Joseph's finger. And he gave Joseph white linen robes and a gold chain to wear around his neck. He gave Joseph a chariot to ride in, and men to run in front of him and shout "Make way!"

Joseph went all around Egypt, collecting grain from the farmers and storing it. Sure enough, for seven years the Nile overflowed and crops were good. But then famine came. The Nile was low, and the ground became dry and cracked. The sun beat down on the fields, and the crops died. The Egyptians began to get hungry.

Then Joseph started to hand out the grain that he had saved, a little bit for each family. In the lands around Egypt,

The Pharaoh of Egypt

people were hungry because of the famine. But in Egypt, everyone had food to eat!

Up in Canaan, Jacob and his family were starving. There was no water; their sheep and goats were dying and their crops had failed. Finally Jacob said to his sons, "I hear that they have grain in Egypt. Go and get us some!"

Joseph's brothers walked for days and days and days through the hot sand to reach Egypt. When they got to Pharaoh's palace, they were tired and thirsty and sweaty. They waited in a long, long line of hungry people before they could go into the room where Joseph sat, giving out grain. When they got there, they didn't recognize Joseph at all. He had been in Egypt for years and years. He had grown up. And he was dressed like an Egyptian.

But Joseph recognized his brothers. They had sold him as a slave—and now they were here, asking him for food.

For weeks, Joseph didn't tell his brothers who he was. But finally, he could no longer bear to keep his secret. He invited them for a big dinner. And when dinner was over, he sent all his servants away.

"I am Joseph!" he said to his brothers. "Is my father still alive?"

The brothers could hardly believe their eyes. And they were terrified. "Now we are in his power!" they whispered to each other. "He will kill us!"

But Joseph said, "I forgive the evil thing you did to me! God sent me ahead of you so that you could come and get food from me during this famine. Go back to Canaan and get all your flocks and your families and your tents. Come and live in Egypt, where there is plenty of food!"

So Joseph's father and brothers and all their families—the Israelites—came down to Egypt and lived there, on the banks of the Nile. *The Israelite nation grew larger and larger. They kept on worshipping their one god, even though the Egyptians believed in many different gods. *And as long as Joseph lived, Pharaoh was kind to the Israelites and let them have a part of Egypt for their very own. 📖

The Story of the Words

Chapter 6 The Jewish People

1 God Speaks to Abraham

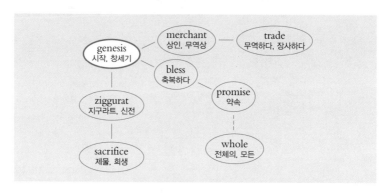

genesis ⓝ the beginning or origin of something

genesis는 '기원(origin), 시작(beginning)'을 뜻한다. 세상의 기원, 시작을 기록한 기독교 성경(the Bible)의 《창세기》를 영어로 the Book of Genesis라고 한다. 첫 부분에 하느님이 세상을 창조한 이야기가 나오기 때문에 붙여진 이름이다. 창세기에는 천지 창조, 아담과 이브, 죄, 노아의 방주의 이야기와 아브라함, 야곱, 요셉의 생애 등의 이스라엘 민족의 뿌리에 관한 이야기가 있다.

The book of Genesis, in the Bible, tells us about Abram. 성경 속 《창세기》는 아브라함에 관해 우리에게 이야기한다.

merchant ⓝ someone who makes money by trading goods

merchant는 물건을 사고팔아서 이윤을 내는 상인을 말한다. 일반적으로 '상인, 장사꾼'으로 해석하지만, 원래는 대량으로 물건을 사들였다가 이윤을 남기고 대량으로 파는 도매상, 무역상을 merchant라고 한다.

Terah was a merchant; he bought and sold copper, gold, purple and scarlet cloth, cinnamon, and salt. 테라는 상인이었다. 그는 구리와 금, 자주색과 진홍색의 천, 계피와 소금을 사고팔았다.

sacrifice ⓝ an object or animal that is offered to a god

sacrifice는 holy(신성한, 성스러운)를 뜻하는 sacri와 make(만들다)의 fice가 합쳐진 것이다. 종교 의식을 '신성한 것으로 만들어주는 것'이 바로 sacrifice, '제물(祭物)'이다. sacrifice는 '희생(犧牲)'이라는 뜻으로도 쓰는데, 이 역시 원래 '신에게 바치는 산짐승'을 의미한다. sacrifice는 '제물을 바치다, 희생하다'라는 뜻의 동사로도 쓰인다.

He made extra sacrifices to the moon—god—the special god of the city of Ur. 그는 우르 시의 특별한 신인 '달의 신'에게 더 많은 제물을 바쳤다.

ziggurat ⓝ a temple tower like a pyramid in ancient Mesopotamia

ziggurat는 '높은 곳'이라는 뜻으로 고대 메소포타미아 지역에 많이 남아 있는 거대 건축물을 지칭하는 말이다. 이것은 신에게 제물을 바치거나 종교 의식을 행하던 '신전(神殿)'으로 사용되었다. 기원전 5세기 그리스의 역사가 헤로도토스(Herodotos)의 기록에 따르면 바빌론의 지구라트는 벽돌을 쌓아 8층으로 지어졌으며 성직자들은 외부의 계단을 통해 꼭대기로 올라가 의식을 치렀다고 한다. 이라크의 우르(Ur)에 대형 지구라트가 남아 있다.

He even went to Ur's largest ziggurat and asked the moon—god to protect him from evil. 그는 심지어 우르에서 가장 큰 지구라트에 가서 달의 신에게 악으로부터 자신을 지켜달라고 빌었다.

trade ⓥ to buy and sell goods

trade는 tread(걷다)를 뜻하는 고대 영어 trod에서 온 것이다. 옛날에 교역을 하는 사람들은 좋은 물건을 사고팔기 위해 우리의 보부상들처럼 여기저기 '걸어서' 돌아다녔다. 그래서 trade가 '거래하다, 물건을 사고팔다'라는 뜻이 되었다. 화폐가 없던 시절에는 물물교환이 곧 장사이고 무역이었기 때문에 trade는 '맞바꾸다, 교환하다'라는 뜻으로도 쓰인다.

Haran was a rich city where people came to trade. 하란은 사람들이 장사하기 위해 오는 부유한 도시였다.

bless ⓥ (of God) to help and protect someone

bless는 blood(피)를 뜻하는 고대 영어에서 유래했다. '축복'을 주고받는 bless가 '피'에서 기원했다는 사실에 당혹스러울 수도 있겠지만, 여기서 '피'는 신에게 제물로 바치는 가축의 '피'다. 그래서 bless는 제물을 바치며 '축복을 빌다'라는 뜻이나 그 피를 보고 신이 감동하여 '축복을 내리다'라는 뜻으로도 쓰인다.

They blessed rain(그들은 (신이) 비를 내려주시기를 빌었다)이나 God bless you!(신의 축복이 있기를!)'처럼 쓸 수 있다.

I will bless your friends and curse your enemies. 내가 네 친구들을 축복할 것이고, 네 적들에게는 저주를 내릴 것이다.

Q 아브라함은 어떻게 종교의 조상이 되었나요?

A 아브라함이 가나안을 향해 떠날 때 아브라함과 사라도 아이를 낳기에는 너무 나이가 많았어. 하란을 떠나 가나안에 도착하자마자 일행은 제단을 쌓고 야훼에게 예배를 드렸단다. 그러나 당시 가나안에는 기근이 들어 그들은 이집트로 가게 되었어. 이집트에서 사라는 하갈이라는 여종을 통해 아이를 낳도록 남편에게 권해 태어난 아이가 이스마엘이야. 이스마엘은 이삭이 태어나자, 아브라함의 집을 떠나 어머니의 고향에서 자랐어. 이슬람 구전에 따르면 이스마엘이 아라비아 반도를 여행하다가 메카의 카바 신전을 건설했다고 전해져. 그러니 이슬람교도에게도 아브라함이 믿음의 조상인 거지. 아브라함은 이삭을, 이삭이 야곱을, 야곱이 열두 명의 아들을 낳았는데, 이 열두 명의 아들이 갈라져 12지파를 이루었어. 그중에서 유다가 이룬 지파에서 유대교가 생겨난 것이란다.

whole ⓐ completely / ⓐ all of something

whole은 '온전한 하나의 전체'로, 깨지지도 않고 조각나지도 않은 상태이다. whole은 명사형 외에 부사형과 형용사형으로도 쓰이는데, a whole new nation(완전히 새로운 나라)에서 whole은 new를 꾸며주는 부사로 '완전히, 전혀'라는 뜻이다. the whole land of Canaan(가나안 전체 땅)에서 whole은 형용사로 '전체의, 모든'을 뜻한다.

You will be the father of a whole new nation, and I will give the whole land of Canaan to you and your children and grandchildren. 너는 완전히 새로운 나라의 시조가 될 것이며 내가 가나안 땅 전부를 너와 너의 자식들 그리고 손자들에게 줄 것이다.

promise ⓝ something you say that you will certainly do

promise는 '앞으로, 미래로(forth, forwards)'를 뜻하는 접두사 pro-에 '보내다(send)'를 뜻하는 mise가 붙은 말이다. 시간이 지나면 만나게 되므로 당연히 지켜야 하는 것이 promise이어서 '약속하다'라는 뜻이다. God's promise(하느님의 약속)에서 promise는 명사형으로 '약속'이다. to make a promise는 '약속하다'라는 뜻으로 자주 쓰이는 표현이다.

He laughed and laughed at God's promise. 그는 하느님의 약속을 듣고 계속 웃었다.

Q 기독교인이 아닌데도 성경을 읽을 필요가 있을까요?

A 신자라면 당연히 성서를 읽겠지만 신자가 아닌 사람들도 성서를 읽을 필요는 있단다. 왜냐고? 서양 역사는 헬레니즘과 헤브라이즘의 두 기둥으로 이루어졌다고 할 수 있거든. 헬레니즘은 그리스 문명과 페르시아를 중심으로 한 동방 문명의 융합을 말하는 것이란다. 헤브라이즘은 유대교를 비롯한 일신교의 믿음에 근원을 둔 것이야. 앞으로 전개되는 인류 역사에서 이 두 가지 문명에 대한 기본적인 지식이 없으면 이해하기 어려운 이야기가 나오니까 성서를 읽는 것은 신앙의 차원이 아닌 문화적 배경으로 꼭 필요하단다. 헤브라이즘의 이해를 위해서 '성서'를, 헬레니즘의 이해를 위해서는 '그리스 로마신화'를 읽으면 도움이 돼.

2 Joseph Goes to Egypt

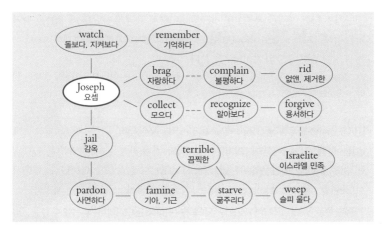

watch ⓥ to take care of someone or something

watch는 '움직이는 것을 보다'라는 뜻이다. 그래서 TV를 시청하는 것을 to see TV나 to look at TV라고 하지 않고 to watch TV라고 하는 것이다. 어떤 사람이나 가축이 움직이는 것을 지켜보는 이유는 잘 있는지 혹은 무엇을 잘하고 있는지 확인하기 위해서이므로 watch가 '돌보다'라는 의미로 쓰인다. Joseph! Will you watch the sheep?이라고 하면 요셉이 목장에 놀러 온 경우가 아니라면 양을 구경하라는 의미가 아니라 돌보라는 것이다.

One day, Joseph was out in the fields with his brothers, watching his father's sheep. 어느 날, 요셉은 형제들과 들판에 나가 아버지의 양들을 돌보고 있었다.

complain ⓥ to say that you are unhappy or angry with something or someone

complain은 강조의 느낌을 주는 접두사 com-과 '한탄하다'라는 뜻의 plain이 합쳐진 것이다. '개탄하다'라는 뜻으로, 생각만 하는 것이 아니라 밖으로 표현하는 것인데, '불평하다, 항의하다'의 의미를 지닌다. to complain about A(A에 대해 불평하다, 항의하다)의 형태로 자주 쓰인다. 명사형은 complaint이다.

All the brothers grumbled and complained about Joseph's coat. 형제들은 모두 요셉의 외투에 대해 투덜거리고 불평했다.

brag ⓥ to talk too proudly about what you have done or what you own

누구나 '자랑스럽게 생각하는(be proud of ~)' 것이 있기 마련이다. He is proud of his son이라고 하면 자신의 아들을 자랑스럽게 여긴다는 의미이다. 자랑도 지나치면 다른 사람을 짜증 나게 하는데, 이렇게 과하게 자랑할 때 쓰는 동사가 brag이다. He bragged about his new coat(그는 자신의 새 외투에 대해 자랑했다)처럼 자랑하는 대상 앞에 about을 쓴다.

He bragged about how much his father loved him. 그는 아버지가 자신을 얼마나 많이 사랑하는지 자랑했다.

rid ⓐ being free from what you hate or do not want

rid는 원래 clear(깨끗하게 정리하다, 청소하다)를 뜻하는 동사로 쓰였다. 쓸데없는 것을 없애면 홀가분해지는데, 형용사 rid는 이런 상태를 의미한다. 형용사로 표현할 때는 거의 'to get rid of ~'의 형태로 써서 '~을 없애다, 제거하다(to throw away or destroy something or someone)'라는 뜻을 지닌다.

Let's get rid of him so that we never have to hear him brag about his colored coat again! 저 녀석이 염색한 외투에 대해 자랑하는 소리를 다시는 들을 필요가 없도록 그를 없애자!

weep ⓥ to cry because you are sad

어떤 식으로 울든 '울다'는 cry로 표현할 수 있는데, weep은 '눈물을 흘리며 슬피 울다'라는 뜻이다. weep은 일상 회화에서는 잘 쓰지 않는 문어체 표현으로,

대개는 그냥 cry를 쓴다. Jacob wept and wept처럼 동사를 and로 연결해 반복해서 쓴 것은 너무 슬퍼서 계속 울었다는 의미를 강조한 것이다.

Jacob wept and wept, because he thought that Joseph was dead. 야곱은 요셉이 죽었다고 생각하여 계속 슬피 울었다.

jail ⓝ a place where people are kept as part of a punishment for their crimes

jail은 cage를 뜻하는 프랑스어에서 온 것이다. cage는 가축을 가두는 데 쓰는 '우리'이다. 옛날에는 죄지은 사람도 '우리'에 가두었다. 그래서 jail이 '감옥, 교도소, 유치장'을 뜻하는 말로 쓰이게 된 것이다. He spent ten years in jail(그는 감옥에서 10년을 보냈다)처럼 명사형으로 쓰거나, He was jailed for robbery(그는 강도죄로 감옥에 투옥되었다)처럼 '감옥에 가두다'라는 의미의 동사형으로도 쓸 수 있다.

Potiphar believed his wife—and he had Joseph thrown in jail. 보디발은 자기 아내의 말을 믿고서, 요셉을 감옥에 가두었다.

pardon ⓥ to allow a person guilty of a crime to go free without being punished

pardon은 '완전히(par) 주다(don)'라는 뜻의 라틴어에서 유래했다. 죄지은 사람은 그 벌로 신체의 자유, 재산권, 시민권 등을 빼앗기게 되는데, pardon하면 그 권리를 '완전히 되돌려주는' 것이다. 그래서 잘못이나 죄에 대해 '용서하다, 사면(赦免)하다'라는 뜻으로 쓰이며 '용서, 사면'을 뜻하는 명사형으로도 쓰인다.

"You've been pardoned," they said. 그들이 말했다. "넌 사면되었다."

remember ⓥ to have something or someone in your mind

remember는 '다시(again), 새로'를 뜻하는 접두사 re-와 '마음에 가득 찬(mindful)'을 뜻하는 member가 합쳐진 것이다. 마음에 담아 두어야 떠올릴 수 있고, 다시 떠올리려면 마음에 있어야 한다. remember에는 이렇게 두 가지 의미가 있다. Remember this number(이 숫자 기억해 둬)나 Do you remember what I said?(내가 한 말 기억나니?)처럼 쓸 수 있다.

As the dreamer was walking away, Joseph called after him, "Remember me! Tell Pharaoh that I am innocent, so that I can get out of jail!" 꿈을 꾼 자가 떠나자 요셉은 그의 뒤에서 소리쳤다. "저를 잊지 마세요! 제가 죄가 없으니 감옥에서 풀려날 수 있게 파라오에게 말해주세요!"

terrible ⓐ making you feel upset or afraid

terrible은 '공포, 무서움'을 뜻하는 terror에 형용사형 접미사 -ble이 붙은 형태로, '공포를 불러일으키는, 무섭게 만드는'의 뜻이다. a terrible dream은 '무서운 꿈'이다. a terrible headache(심한 두통)나 a terrible food(형편없는 음식)처럼 '끔찍한, 심한, 형편없는'의 뜻으로 자주 쓰인다.

I had a terrible dream. 나는 무서운 꿈을 꾸었다.

famine ⓝ a situation in which people have little or no food for a long time

famine은 hunger(굶주림, 배고픔)를 뜻하는 라틴어 fames에서 온 말이다. 먹을 것이 거의 없어서 오랫동안 굶주리는 상황, 즉 '기아, 기근'이 famine이다. 가뭄, 홍수, 냉해 등의 원인과 상관없이 흉년이 들어 먹을 것이 부족하면 famine 상태가 된다.

But the seven thin cows stand for seven years of famine. 그러나 깡마른 일곱 마리의 소는 7년 동안의 기근을 상징한다.

collect ⓥ to bring or gather things together

collect는 '함께, 동시에(together)'를 뜻하는 접두사 col-과 '고르다(choose)'를 뜻하는 lect가 합쳐진 것이다. '골라서 모으다, 수집하다'라는 뜻으로, 흔히 gather(모으다, 합치다)와 동의어로 쓰이지만 느낌은 다르다. collect grain(곡식을 모으다), collect stamps(우표를 수집하다), collect empty bottles(빈 병을 수거하다)처럼 쓸 수 있다.

Joseph went all around Egypt, collecting grain from the farmers and storing it. 요셉은 이집트 전역을 돌아다니며 농부들에게서 곡식을 모아 저장했다.

starve ⓥ to die or suffer because of lack of food

hungry한 상태가 오래 지속되면 아프거나 죽는다. 그 지경이 되도록 굶주릴 때 쓰는 표현이 '굶주리다, 굶어 죽다'라는 뜻의 starve이다. '배고파 죽겠어!'라고 과장해서 흔히 말하는데, 영어로는 I'm starving이라고 말한다.

Up in Canaan, Jacob and his family were starving. 위쪽 가나안에서는 야곱과 그의 가족이 굶주리고 있었다.

recognize ⓥ to know who someone is or what something is because you have met them before

과거에 만나거나 접해 본 적이 있어서 '아, 그 사람이구나!' 또는 '아, 그거구나!'

라고 머리에 떠올리는 것이 recognize이다. 즉 '인식하다, 알아보다'라는 뜻
이다.

When they got there, they didn't recognize Joseph at all. 그들은 그곳에 도착했을 때
요셉을 전혀 알아보지 못했다.

forgive ⓥ to stop blaming or feeling anger toward someone who has done something wrong

'용서하다'라는 뜻의 forgive는 접두사 for와 give(주다)가 합쳐진 것이다. 여기
서 for-는 '많이, 강하게'라는 의미이므로 누군가를 용서하는 것은 그만큼 '많이
주는' 마음, 즉 너그러운 마음이 있어야 가능한 일이다. 용서를 빌 때는 Please
forgive me!(제발 용서해 주세요!)라고 한다.

I forgive the evil thing you did to me! 저는 형들이 제게 한 악한 행동을 용서합니다!

Israelite ⓝ a member of the tribe descended from Jacob

Israelite는 '이스라엘 사람'이다. 야곱을 조상으로 둔 유대인들을 지칭하기도
하고, 기원전 992년부터 721년까지 존속했던 이스라엘 왕국의 백성을 일컫는
말이기도 하다. the Israelites는 '이스라엘 민족'이다. Israel은 '하느님과 (세상
에 맞서) 싸우는 사람'이라는 뜻으로 하느님이 야곱에게 준 새 이름이다. 현재
이스라엘 국민은 Israeli(s)라고 한다.

The Israelite nation grew larger and larger. 이스라엘 국가는 점점 더 커졌다.

> **Q 유일신교의 발상지가 서양이 아니라고요?**
> **A** 당연히 아니라고 대답하면 놀라는 사람들이 있어. 로마 제국 시대에 기
> 독교가 박해의 과정을 거쳐 국교가 되었어. 서로마 제국이 망한 후에도 교
> 회는 살아남아 오히려 서유럽의 중심 조직이 되었지. 그래서 우리 의식 속
> 에는 기독교라고 하면 당연히 서양의 종교라는 인식이 있는 거야. 그러나
> 지도를 보면 가나안 지방은 서아시아에 있단다. 이곳에서 유대교와 기독
> 교가 발생했고, 아라비아 반도에서 이슬람교가 생겼으니 세 종교의 발상
> 지가 모두 서아시아인 셈이지.

Chapter 7
Hammurabi and the Babylonians

1 Hammurabi's Code

바빌로니아의 6대 왕인 함무라비(Hammurabi)는 법치주의를 근간으로 왕권을 강화하기 위해 법전을 만들었다. 최초의 성문법(成文法)으로 인정되는 함무라비 법전의 내용은 바빌로니아의 신(神)인 마르두크(Marduk)의 신전 앞에 세운 돌기둥에 쐐기 문자로 새겨져 있었다. 무역과 세금에 관련된 경제법과 혼인, 노예, 채무 등과 관련된 민법 그리고 절도나 폭행에 관련된 형법 등이 포함되어 있다. 형법 처벌과 관련된 '이에는 이, 눈에는 눈(An eye for an eye, a tooth for a tooth)'은 함무라비 법전을 말할 때 항상 등장하는 문구이다.

You can probably tell that Mesopotamia was not a very peaceful place to live. City-states fought each other. Powerful leaders tried to build empires by conquering other city-states. Sometimes the empires lasted for a long time. Sometimes they collapsed in just a few years—and another powerful leader tried to take over. The people of Mesopotamia lived with war all the time. Sometimes they stayed inside their city walls and hoped that they would be safe. But sometimes they fled. They would travel to another place, hoping to avoid trouble.

Around 1792 BC/BCE, a king named Hammurabi inherited the throne of Babylon from his father. Babylon was a city near Kish (the home of Sargon). At first, Hammurabi only ruled a small area of the land around his own city. But soon he began to conquer some of the smaller cities around him. He convinced the kings of other cities to swear allegiance to him. Soon he ruled over the whole southern part of Mesopotamia. This area was called Babylonia, after the city of Babylon.

Hammurabi didn't want people to obey him just because his army was strong. He wanted his empire to be governed by just laws. He believed that the chief god of Babylon, Marduk, made

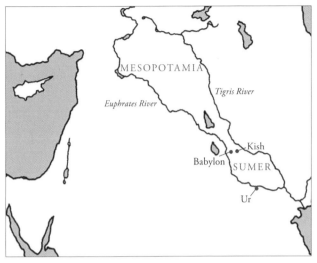

Babylonia

him king so that he could treat people fairly. In one of his letters, Hammurabi calls himself "the reverent god-fearing prince." He says that his job as king is "to make justice appear in the land, to destroy the evil and the wicked so that the strong might not oppress the weak."

Hammurabi wanted people to follow his laws because they were right, not just because soldiers were making them obey. He also wanted his whole empire to follow the same laws and rules. So Hammurabi wrote down all of the laws that he thought were fair. He had them carved in stone, on a monument that showed him getting the laws from the sun-god. These laws are called the Code of Hammurabi. They are the first set of written laws that we know of. They were unusual because everyone had to follow them—rich people, poor people, soldiers, farmers, merchants, and even kings.

Here are some of the laws in the Code of Hammurabi. Do you think these are fair? Why or why not?

- If someone cuts down a tree on someone else's land, he will pay for it.
- If someone is careless when watering his fields, and he floods someone else's field by accident, he will pay for the grain he has ruined.
- If a man wants to throw his son out of the house, he has to go before a judge and say, "I don't want my son to live in my house any more." The judge will find out the reasons. If the reasons are not good, the man can't throw his son out.
- If the son has done some great evil to his father, his father must forgive him the first time. But if he has done something evil twice, his father can throw him out.
- If a thief steals a cow, a sheep, a donkey, a pig, or a goat, he will pay ten times what it is worth. *If he doesn't have any money to pay with, he will be put to death.
- *An eye for an eye, and a tooth for a tooth. If a man puts out the eye of another man, put his own eye out. If he knocks out another man's tooth, knock out his own tooth. If he breaks another man's bone, break his own bone.
- If a doctor operates on a patient and the patient dies, the doctor's hand will be cut off.
- If a builder builds a house, and that house collapses and kills the owner, the builder will be put to death.
- *If a robber is caught breaking a hole into a house so that he can get in and steal, he will be put to death in front of the hole.

Hammurabi was a very religious man. *He believed that the gods themselves had given him the Code of Hammurabi. So he rebuilt many of the temples and ziggurats that had been destroyed in fights between city-states. He encouraged his people to sacrifice to the gods, and to learn more about them.

At that time, people in Babylon believed that they could find out what the gods were doing by watching the movements of the planets and stars. So they spent a lot of time studying the sky. They knew where all the constellations were. They knew the difference between stars and planets.

*From watching the sky, the Babylonians were able to figure out that the earth goes all the way around the sun. They called the time that it took the earth to go all the way around the sun one time "one year." Then they divided this year into twelve months. They were the first people to divide a year into twelve months, just like we do today.

The Babylonians were also the first to divide a day into twenty-four hours, and to divide an hour into sixty minutes. *So whenever you look at a calendar to see what day of the month it is, or look at a clock to see what time it is, you're using methods that we inherited from the Babylonians. 📖

Hammurabi, King of Babylonia

The Story of the Words

Chapter 7 Hammurabi and the Babylonians

1 Hammurabi's Code

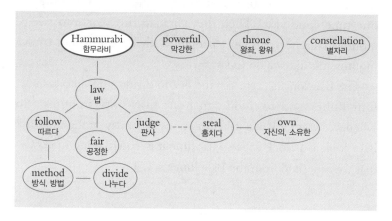

powerful ⓐ having a lot of power and very strong

powerful은 power에 형용사형 접미사 -ful이 붙은 형태인데, power는 ability(능력)을 뜻하는 라틴어에서 유래했고, -ful은 '가득 찬(full), 성질이 강한 (strong)'의 의미이다. 즉 powerful은 '권력과 영향력이 막강한, 힘이 센, 효과가 강력한'으로 a powerful leader는 '영향력이 막강한 지도자, 권력이 막강한 지배자'이다.

Powerful leaders tried to build empires by conquering other city—states. 힘이 센 지도자들은 다른 도시 국가들을 정복함으로써 제국을 건설하고자 했다.

throne ⓝ a special chair that a king or queen sits on

throne은 elevated seat(높은 자리)를 뜻하는 희랍어에서 왔다. 사극을 보면 왕이 앉는 의자는 항상 신하의 자리보다 높은 곳에 있는데, 바로 throne이 그 '왕좌, 옥좌'이다. 왕만이 그 자리에 앉을 권한이 있기 때문에 '왕의 지위와 권력'을 의미하기도 한다.

Around 1792 BC/BCE, a king named Hammurabi inherited the throne of Babylon from his father. 기원전 1792년경에 함무라비라는 왕이 아버지로부터 바빌론의 왕좌를 물려받았다.

law ⓝ a rule that people in a country or area must obey

'법, 법칙'인 law는 '정해진 것, 고정된 것'을 뜻하는 고대 영어 lagu에서 유래했다. law는 정해지고, 고정된 것이므로 아무나 바꿀 수 없으며 모두가 그 정해진 바에 따라 행동해야 한다. 그러려면 law는 누구에게나 공정하게 적용되어야 하는데, just laws가 '공정한 법'이다.

He wanted his empire to be governed by just laws. 그는 자신의 제국이 공정한 법에 의해 통치되기를 원했다.

Q 함무라비 법전이 세계 최초가 아니라고요?

A 함무라비 법전은 오랫동안 세계 최초의 법으로 알려졌어. 그런데 이를 뒤집는 발견이 있었지. 아카드 제국의 몰락 후 수메르 지역에 우르 3왕조가 들어섰지. 우르 남무가 이 지역을 통일한 뒤에 다양한 노력을 했어. 사르곤처럼 우르 남무도 도량형(자, 저울 등) 통일, 경제 질서 회복, 가난한 시민 보호, 서기 양성 학교 설립 등 다양한 정책을 펼쳤어. 우리가 수메르 문명이라고 손꼽는 많은 것이 바로 우르 남무 시절에 만들어졌는데, 법전도 마찬가지였어.

그렇다면 이 책에서는 왜 '우르 남무 법전' 대신에 함무라비 법전을 소개하는 것일까? 우리는 세계 최초에 상당한 의미를 부여하지만, 더 중요한 것은 완성도와 사회에 끼친 영향력이 아닐까? 정확히 말하자면 이제까지 발견된 법전 중에서 오래된 순서로 보면 함무라비 법전은 네 번째(우루 남무, 리시트 이슈타르, 에슈눈나, 함무라비 순)에 해당하지만, 완전한 형태로 남아 있는 것은 함무라비 법전뿐이란다.

follow ⓥ to obey an order or to do what someone tells you to do

follow의 기본적인 의미는 '~의 뒤를 따라가다[오다](to go or come someone or something)'이다. 법, 규칙, 명령에 '따르다'라고 할 때에도 follow를 쓴다. to follow the law는 '법에 따르다, 법을 지키다'라는 뜻이다.

Hammurabi wanted people to follow his laws because they were right, not just because soldiers were making them obey. 함무라비는 군인들이 복종하게 만들기 때문만이 아니라, 법이 옳기 때문에 사람들이 자신의 법을 따르기를 원했다.

fair ⓐ reasonable, acceptable, right and equal for everyone

fair는 '기분 좋은, 만족스러운(pleasing)', 즉 마음에 흡족하다는 뜻이다. a fair price라고 하면 거래가 가능할 만큼 '만족스러운' 가격이라는 뜻이다. 법이나 규칙도 '공정한, 공평한, 온당한' 것이어야 따를 수 있고 a fair law라고 할 수 있다.

So Hammurabi wrote down all of the laws that he thought were fair. 그래서 함무라비는 자신이 공정하다고 생각하는 법을 모두 적었다.

judge ⓝ a person who makes decisions in a law court

'심판하다, 판단하다, 평가하다'라는 뜻의 동사형으로 쓰인다. 재판을 할 때 법정에서 '법과 죄를 심판할 수 있는 사람'은 재판관과 판사뿐이므로 judge는 명사형으로는 '재판관, 판사'이다.

If a man wants to throw his son out of the house, he has to go before a judge and say, "I don't want my son to live in my house any more." 어떤 사람이 자신의 아들을 집에서 내쫓고 싶으면, 그 사람은 판사 앞에 가서 "저는 더는 아들이 제 집에서 사는 것을 원하지 않습니다"라고 말해야 한다.

> **Q 함무라비 법전의 기본 정신은 무엇인가요?**
>
> **A** 함무라비 법전의 내용을 읽어본 적이 없다고 해도 '눈에는 눈, 이에는 이'라는 표현은 들어봤을 거야. 어쩐지 너무 가혹한 법이 아닐까 하는 생각이 들 수도 있지만, 사실 법의 1조항에서 강조하는 것은 '약자의 보호와 정의의 회복'이란다. 실제로 함무라비도 법전은 강자가 약자를 괴롭히지 않으며 일가친척이 없는 여자아이와 과부에게도 정의를 적용하기 위해 만들어졌다고 강조하고 있단다.
>
> '눈에는 눈, 이에는 이'라면 신분에 상관없이 공평하게 적용되는 법이라고 생각하기 쉬우나 그렇지 않았어. 그렇다면 무엇이 정의롭다는 거지? 하고 속단하기 쉽겠지만, 법으로 처벌의 범위를 정한 덕분에 더 심한 복수를 막을 수 있었다는 점이 중요해. 일반 백성이나 노예가 상류층에게 피해를 당했을 경우에 최소한의 법적 보상은 가능하게 한 것이지. 즉 신분이 낮은 사람들에게도 법적 보호 기능이 생겼다는 것이란다. 그런 점에서 함무라비 법전은 신분 제도에 상관없이 적용되는 단계까지는 이르지 못했으나 정의 회복을 위해서는 상당한 의미가 있었던 거야.

steal ⓥ to take something that belongs to someone else without asking for it

다른 사람의 물건을 허락 없이 취하는 행동은 모두 steal로 표현할 수 있지만, 대개는 '몰래' 훔치는 행동을 의미한다. 레이더에 잡히지 않고 '몰래' 기동할 수 있는 전투기를 '스텔스기'라고 하는데, 이때 stealth(몰래 하는 행동)도 steal에서 파생된 것이다. '도둑질하는 사람'을 뜻하는 stealer는 잘 쓰지 않고, 대개는 thief로 표현한다.

If a thief steals a cow, a sheep, a donkey, a pig, or a goat, he will pay ten times what it is worth. 도둑이 소, 양, 당나귀, 돼지나 염소를 훔치면 그 가축의 값어치의 10배를 물어줘야 한다.

own ⓐ belonging to a particular person

own은 '소유하다(possess), 갖고 있다(have)'라는 뜻이다. own을 형용사로 쓰면 '자신의, 자기가 직접 한'의 의미로 항상 '소유격+own+소유한(행동한) 대상'의 형태로 써서 his own eye는 다른 사람의 눈이 아닌 바로 '그 사람의' 눈이고, my own idea는 다른 사람의 생각을 빌린 것이 아니라 바로 '내 머리에서 나온' 생각이라는 뜻이다.

If a man puts out the eye of another man, put his own eye out. 어떤 사람이 다른 사람의 눈을 뺀다면 자신의 눈도 빼야 한다.

constellation ⓝ a group of stars forming a particular pattern in the sky

constellation에서 con-은 together(함께, 모여)를 뜻하는 접두사이고, stella는 star(별)를 뜻하는 라틴어에서 온 것이다. 별들이 특정한 위치에 모여 있는 것, 즉 '별자리'가 바로 constellation이다. 바빌로니아 사람들은 기원전 3000년경에 이미 태양계 행성과 별자리에 대해 알고 있었는데, 그 행성과 별자리마다 신(神)이 있다고 믿었다.

They knew where all the constellations were. 그들은 모든 별자리들이 어디에 있는지 알고 있었다.

divide ⓥ to separate things or people into pieces or parts

divide는 라틴어 divido에서 온 말로, di-는 apart(떨어져)를 뜻하고, vide는 separate(가르다, 분리하다)를 뜻한다. 즉, '나누다, 나뉘다, 가르다'라는 뜻이다. divide A into B처럼 뒤에 into를 붙이면 'A를 나누어 B로 만들다'라는 의미이다.

Then they divided this year into twelve months. 그러고는 그들은 이 1년을 12개월로 나누었다.

method ⓝ a way of doing something

method는 라틴어 methodos에서 온 것이다. met(h) 또는 meta는 after, beyond 의미로 어떤 것을 연구한 후에 나온 결과[발전, 개발]를, hodos는 way(길, 방식)를 뜻한다. 노력 끝에 새로 만든 길, 연구의 결과로 얻게 된 방법이 바로 method이다.

So whenever you look at a calendar to see what day of the month it is, or look at a clock to see what time it is, you're using methods that we inherited from the Babylonians. 따라서 여러분이 날짜가 며칠인지 알기 위해 달력을 보거나 시간이 몇 시인지 알기 위해 시계를 볼 때마다, 여러분은 바빌로니아인에게서 물려받은 방식을 사용하고 있는 것이다.

Q 바빌로니아에도 법관이 있었나요?

A 맞아. 법의 내용 중 아들이 속을 썩여서 고민하던 아버지가 판사에게 가서 하소연하는 장면 기억나니? 판사가 있다는 것은 사법 기관이 존재했다는 증거야. 법의 내용을 살펴보면 당시의 다양한 제도가 눈에 들어온단다. 도둑이 다른 사람의 양이나 당나귀를 훔치다 걸리면 10배로 갚아야 하고, 돈을 내지 못하면 사형 당한다는 구절을 보면 화폐가 있었다는 것을 알 수 있지.

Chapter 8
The Assyrians

1 Shamshi-Adad, King of the Whole World

메소포타미아의 북부 티그리스 강 유역에 세워진 최초의 통일 제국을 아시리아(Assyria) 제국이라고 한다. '아시리아'라는 명칭은 그 지역의 고대인들이 믿은 수호신의 이름이자 제국의 수도 이름이기도 한 '아수르(Assur)'에서 유래했다. 기원전 18세기에 샴시아다드(Shamshi-Adad)는 주변의 도시 국가들을 정복하고 제국을 건설하지만, 그의 사후에 두 아들들의 불화로 인해 국력이 쇠해 남쪽의 바빌로니아 제국에 의해 멸망하고 만다. 아시리아인들은 이후 두 차례 더 메소포타미아 지역에서 제국을 건설했기 때문에 역사에서는 이 첫 번째 제국을 '고(古)아시리아 제국'이라고 구분해서 부른다.

Hammurabi was the most powerful king in southern Mesopotamia. But up to the north, another king was building another empire. His name was Shamshi-Adad, and he didn't want to be a fair ruler who made good laws. He just wanted to rule the whole world.

Shamshi-Adad lived in a city called Assur. Babylon was in the south of Mesopotamia, next to the Euphrates River. But Assur was in the north part of Mesopotamia, beside the Tigris River.

When Shamshi-Adad became king of Assur, he decided that Assur should be the center of a new empire. He started out by building a huge temple to the god he worshipped, The God of Winds and Storms. The temple was made out of cedar logs, covered with silver and gold. Shamshi-Adad even rubbed the foundation with oil, honey, and butter to make his god happy. He wanted The God of Winds and Storms to be on his side and to give him more power, so that he could win battles more easily.

On the day that the temple was finished, Shamshi-Adad announced, "The God of Winds and Storms loves the city of Assur more than any other city in the world! And he wants me to be the king of the whole world." The people of Assur all shouted, "Shamshi-Adad will be king of the whole world!"

*Then Shamshi-Adad gathered his army together and set off to conquer the cities of Mesopotamia. His two sons went with him to fight beside him. Every time Shamshi-Adad conquered a new city, he made his sons the new rulers of that city. Soon the Assyrian army had conquered all the cities nearby!

Shamshi-Adad wanted the people of Mesopotamia to be afraid of him. He was a dictator—he didn't allow any of the people in his new kingdom to ask questions about his laws and his commands. He just wanted them to obey him immediately.

How did he get them to obey? He killed anyone who wouldn't do exactly what he said! When he conquered a city, he chopped off the heads of all the leaders and put them up on stakes around the city. He burned buildings and told his soldiers to destroy everything they could find.

No wonder everyone in Mesopotamia was afraid of the Assyrians! Soon, Shamshi-Adad didn't even have to fight battles to conquer cities. As soon as he got near a city's walls, the leaders would come out and surrender. They would offer to pay him money and to call him their king, if he would just let them live. *Shamshi-Adad would agree to spare their lives—but only if they would do exactly what he said and obey every single one of his decrees.

Now Shamshi-Adad's empire spread all over the northern part of Mesopotamia. He named his empire Assyria, after the city of Assur. And he called himself the King of the Whole World.

But this wasn't exactly true. Remember Babylon, down in the south of Mesopotamia? Babylon had an empire too. Shamshi-Adad never tried to conquer Babylon, or to take Babylon's cities away. He knew that Babylon was too strong for him.

When Shamshi-Adad died, he left one of his sons the job of ruling over the whole Assyrian Empire. He left the other son in charge of one of the biggest cities in Assyria, the city of Mari. He hoped that the two young men would work together to keep his empire strong.

*But the brothers bickered with each other. They wrote each other nasty letters. They complained about each other. They didn't keep Assyria united and strong.

Soon, Hammurabi decided that he wanted to make Assyria part of the Babylonian Empire. He marched up into northern Mesopotamia with his army. He destroyed the city of Mari, and he took over the city of Assur. Now the Assyrians had to pay tribute to Hammurabi, and call Hammurabi "King of the Whole World."

*But Hammurabi wasn't as cruel as Shamshi-Adad had been. He let some of the Assyrian leaders stay in charge of their cities, as long as they followed his Code of Laws. And he didn't chop off the heads of leaders, or burn their houses. The Assyrians agreed to obey Hammurabi—but all the time, they were thinking, "One day we will be free again—and we will try to conquer the world one more time."

2 The Story of Gilgamesh

메소포타미아 지역의 고대 왕국인 바빌로니아와 아시리아에서 전해져 내려온 《길가메시(Gilgamesh)》 이야기는 세계에서 가장 오래된 '서사시(敍事詩)'로 알려져 있다. 서사시에서 서(敍)는 '길게 펼쳐서 쓰다'라는 뜻이고, 사(事)는 '중요한 사건이나 일'을 뜻한다. 대개는 민족의 형성과 관련된 신화나 전설, 영웅의 모험담 등을 이야기 형식으로 길게 쓴 시(詩)를 서사시라고 한다. 영어로는 epic이라고 하는데, epic은 '말(word), 노래(song)'라는 뜻의 그리스어 epikos에서 유래했다. 말과 노

Both the Babylonians and the Assyrians told stories about a great, mythical king named Gilgamesh. The story of Gilgamesh is one of the oldest fairy tales in the world!

Once upon a time, a king named Gilgamesh ruled the city of Uruk. Gilgamesh was half-god, and half-man. He was the strongest man on earth. He could lift huge stones with one hand and leap over high walls without even trying hard. He was young and healthy, and he had all the money and power any man could ever want.

But Gilgamesh was as cruel as he was strong. He made the people of Uruk serve him day and night. He took their money and their food. He took their children to be his slaves. He never thought of others—only of himself.

The people of Uruk were desperate to get rid of this wicked king. So they called out to the sky-god, Anu. "Help us!" they cried. "Our king is evil, and we cannot fight him, because he has the strength of a god!"

A-nu looked down from the sky and was very unhappy. "Look at this king, Gilgamesh!" he said. "He has all the strength and power in the world—and yet he is cruel to the weak and helpless! This is not right. I will send an enemy to teach him a lesson."

So Anu created a monster called Enkidu—a monster who was half man and half animal, with the strength of a dozen lions. "Go and fight Gilgamesh," he told Enkidu, and sent the beast-man down into the wild wastelands around the city of Uruk.

Meanwhile, Gilgamesh had a nightmare! ˙He dreamed that a huge axe appeared at his door—an axe so big and sharp that he couldn't even lift it. When he woke up, he asked his mother what the dream meant. "A man is coming who can destroy you!" his mother told him. "You will have to make friends with him—or die!"

Enkidu came closer and closer to the city of Uruk. ˙But in the forest outside the city's walls, he met the son of a trapper, out checking his father's traps. When the boy saw the naked wildman, he was frightened. But he felt sorry for Enkidu, because the beast-man had no clothes or food, and could not even speak. So he took Enkidu home with him and introduced him to his friends, shepherds who tended their flocks outside the city walls. Enkidu lived with the trapper's son and the shepherds for a long time. They taught him how to talk, how to eat, and how to wear clothes.

One day, Enkidu and his friends went into Uruk, to the wedding of a great man who was giving a feast for the whole city. But during the wedding feast, Gilgamesh decided that he wanted the bride. He marched into the hall, grabbed the beautiful girl, and started to drag her away.

Enkidu was furious. He leaped up in front of the door. "You may be the king," he shouted, "but you'll have to kill me before you take this woman away from her bridegroom!"

No one had ever told Gilgamesh what to do! He leaped at Enkidu and tried to wrestle him to the ground. They fought all up and down the wedding hall until the food was smashed underfoot and both of them were bleeding. Gilgamesh had never before met anyone so strong. Finally he won the match—he pinned Enkidu down and sat on him. But he was so tired from fighting that he could barely move. ˙He gasped out, "Let us be friends from now on!"

From then on, Enkidu and Gilgamesh were friends. Gilgamesh became kinder to the people in his city, and he and Enkidu had many adventures together.

One day, the bull of the gods escaped from the sky and came down to earth. •It came charging through Gilgamesh's kingdom, killing hundreds of people. •It was so powerful that whenever it breathed, huge holes and chasms opened up in the earth. The people called to Gilgamesh and Enkidu for help. Enkidu killed the bull and delivered the whole country.

But the gods were angry with Enkidu for killing their bull. They sent terrible illness upon him. He suffered in pain for twelve days, and then died.

•Gilgamesh mourned his friend's death. He ordered the whole world to weep over Enkidu. He stopped taking baths; he even stopped eating. He could not bear the thought that death had taken Enkidu away. Finally, he decided that he would have to find the secret of eternal life and conquer

Slaying the Bull of Heaven

death itself.

He decided to go see Utnapishtim—the only immortal man on the whole earth. He traveled for a year and a day, and finally reached Utnapishtim's home.

"What is the secret of eternal life?" he asked Utnapishtim.

"If you can stay awake for six days and seven nights," Utnapishtim told him, "you too can become immortal."

Gilgamesh agreed—and instantly fell asleep. He woke up seven days later. "Give me another chance!" he begged.

"Well," Utnapishtim said, "there is one more chance for you. If you can swim all the way down to the bottom of the ocean, you will find a magical plant that lives on the sea's bottom. Pick it and eat it, and you will become young again."

Gilgamesh leaped up, tied a stone to his feet, and jumped into the ocean. He sank all the way down to the bottom. There he found the magic plant. He picked it, swam back up to the top of the ocean, and began the long journey home. "When I get home," he thought, "I will eat the plant, and then I will live forever."

But one night, while Gilgamesh slept, a snake slithered up to him and found the plant. It smelled good—so the snake ate it, and immediately became young again. That is why snakes shed their skins. When they begin to get old, they just climb out of their wrinkled, old skins and become young again.

But Gilgamesh woke up to find his magic plant gone. He went home to Uruk, weeping and mourning. And like all men, he became old and died.

But his story was told to all the children of Uruk, and has been told to all their children, and to their children's children, until this very day. 📖

Note to Parent: The Gilgamesh Epic was composed between 3000–1200 BC/BCE.

The Story of the Words

Chapter 8 The Assyrians

1 Shamshi-Adad, King of the Whole World

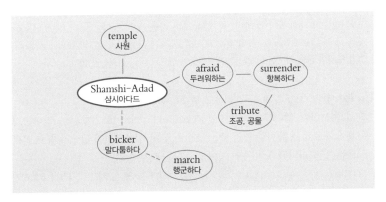

temple ⓝ a building for worship in some religions

고대 로마의 예언자들은 하늘과 땅에 일정한 구역을 정해놓고서 그곳을 보며 신의 계시를 읽곤 했는데, 그 구역을 라틴어로 templum이라고 불렀다. '단절 시킨 구역(a place cut off), 신성한 구역(a sacred place)'이라는 의미이다. 그곳에서만 신의 계시를 받을 수 있고, 신에게 제물을 바치고 종교 의식을 행할 수 있었다. 그래서 temple이 불교, 힌두교 등의 '신전, 사원, 사찰'이 된 것이다. 기독교 '교회'는 temple이라고 하지 않고, 항상 church라고 한다.

He started out by building a huge temple to the god he worshipped, The God of Winds and Storms. 그는 자신이 숭배하는 신인 '바람과 폭풍우의 신'을 위해 거대한 사원을 짓기 시작했다.

afraid ⓐ frightened of someone or something

afraid는 어떤 사람이나 사물, 사건이 자신에게 해를 끼칠까 봐 걱정하고 두려워하는 상태를 말한다. 흔히 'be afraid of ~'의 형태로 쓰는데, They were afraid of Shamshi-Adad는 '그 사람들은 샴시아다드를 무서워했다'는 뜻이다.

I am afraid I cannot help you(도와주지 못해 유감이다)처럼 예의를 갖춰 '거절'할 때도 쓴다.

Shamshi—Adad wanted the people of Mesopotamia to be afraid of him. 샴시아다드는 메소포타미아의 사람들이 자신을 두려워하기를 원했다.

surrender Ⓥ to stop fighting and say to the enemy that you are defeated

surrender는 프랑스어에서 유래하여 over를 뜻하는 접두사 sur-와 give (up)를 뜻하는 render가 합쳐진 형태이다. '넘겨(over)주다(give)'라는 뜻도 있고, '압도되어(over) 포기하다(give up)'로도 이해할 수 있다. 그래서 전투나 경쟁에서 다툼을 멈추고 패배를 인정하다, 즉 '항복하다'라는 뜻이 된다.

As soon as he got near a city's walls, the leaders would come out and surrender. 그가 도시의 성벽 가까이 오자마자, 지도자들이 밖으로 나와 항복하곤 했다.

bicker Ⓥ to argue about things that are not important

흔히 '논쟁하다, 말다툼하다'라고 할 때 argue나 quarrel로 표현한다. 말다툼의 주제가 사소하고 유치한 것일 때는 bicker를 써서 사사건건 말꼬리 잡고 입씨름하는 것을 의미한다. 비슷한 의미로 squabble도 있다.

But the brothers bickered with each other. 그러나 형제들은 서로 사사건건 유치하게 싸움을 벌였다.

march Ⓥ to walk along in formation

march는 원래 '땅에 발자국이 남을 만큼 힘차게 걷다'라는 의미이다. 여러 사람이 함께 걸으면 발소리도 크고 지나간 자국도 선명하게 남으므로 march는 여러 사람이 줄지어 걸어가다, 즉 '행진하다, 행군하다'이다. He marched up into northern Mesopotamia with his army에서 'marched up into ~'는 '위[북쪽]로(up) 행군해(marched) 들어갔다(into)'라는 의미이다.

He marched up into northern Mesopotamia with his army. 그는 군대를 이끌고 북부 메소포타미아를 향해 행군해 들어갔다.

tribute Ⓝ a payment of goods or money by one ruler or country to another more powerful one

역사에서 tribute는 주로 '조공(朝貢), 공물(貢物)'의 뜻이다. 힘이 약한 나라는 힘이 센 나라에 정기적으로 귀한 물건을 바치며 충성과 복종을 표했고, tribute를 받는 나라는 그 대가로 속국의 안전을 보장했다. 그런데 tribute는 원래 '부족

(tribe)끼리 나누는 것'을 일컫는 말로, 친선(親善)을 위해 부족 간에 선물을 주고 받는 것이었다.

Now the Assyrians had to pay tribute to Hammurabi, and call Hammurabi "King of the Whole World." 이제 아시리아인들은 함무라비에게 조공을 바치고, 함무라비를 '온 세상의 왕'이라고 불러야 했다.

2 The Story of Gilgamesh

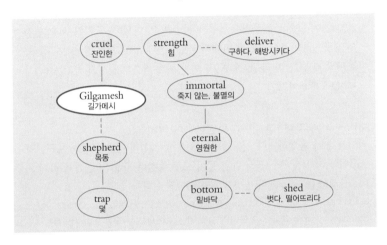

cruel ⓐ causing pain or suffering to others on purpose

cruel은 '잔인한, 잔혹한'을 뜻하는 형용사이다. cruel은 원래 '날 것의(raw), 자연 상태 그대로'라는 뜻을 갖고 있는 crude와 어원이 같다. 그래서 정제되지 않은 석유인 '원유(原油)'를 crude oil이라고 한다. 사람이 감정을 억누르지 못하고 사회적 인식이 부족하면, 동물의[자연 상태의] 성질을 드러내기 마련이다. 분노를 '있는 그대로(crude)' 표출하기 때문에 cruel해지는 것이다.

But Gilgamesh was as cruel as he was strong. 그러나 길가메시는 힘이 센 만큼 잔인했다.

strength ⓝ power and ability

strength는 strong(강한)의 명사형으로 '힘과 능력'을 뜻한다. 물리적인 힘뿐만 아니라 정신적인 힘도 strength이다. 흔히 of를 붙여 the strength of a god(신의 힘과 능력)이나 the strength of a dozen lions(사자 열두 마리의 힘)처럼 쓴다.

뒤에 -en을 붙이면 '강해지다, 보강하다'라는 뜻의 동사 strengthen이 된다.

Our king is evil, and we cannot fight him, because he has the strength of a god!
우리 왕은 사악합니다. 그런데 저희는 그와 맞서 싸울 수 없습니다. 왜냐하면 그는 신의 힘을 갖고 있기 때문입니다!

> **Q** 《일리아스》와 《오디세이》가 세계 최초의 서사시가 아니라고요?
>
> **A** 서양에서는 아주 오랫동안 최초의 서사시는 《일리아스》와 《오디세이》라고 여겨졌지. 그런데 최초라는 명예가 빼앗기는 날이 왔으니 1852년 아시리아 수도였던 니네베(니느웨라고도 함) 발굴 중 호르무즈 라삼이 점토판 2만 4천여 점을 발견한거야. 《일리아스》와 《오디세이》가 기원전 800년경의 작품이라면 호르무즈가 니네베의 도서관에서 발견한 《길가메시》는 그보다 2,000년 전의 작품이었어. 당연히 세계 최초의 서사시 자리는 《길가메시》에게 돌아갔어.

trap ⓝ a piece of equipment for catching animals

먹이를 놓아 유인하거나 지나다니는 길목에 설치해 짐승을 잡는 도구, '덫'이 trap이다. 올무, 포획 도구, 함정 등이 모두 속한다. trap은 '꼼짝 못하게 가두다', trapper는 '덫을 놓아 짐승을 잡는 사냥꾼'이다.

But in the forest outside the city's walls, he met the son of a trapper, out checking his father's traps. 그러나 그 도시의 성벽 밖 숲속에서 그는 덫을 놓아 사냥하는 사람의 아들을 만났는데, 그 아들은 밖에 나와 아버지가 설치한 덫을 확인하고 있었다.

shepherd ⓝ someone who takes care of sheep

shepherd에서 shep는 '양(sheep)'이고, herd는 말 그대로 herd(짐승의 무리, 떼)이다. herd는 herder(목동)의 의미로, 목초지에서 '양을 떼로 몰고 다니는 목동'이다. 다른 동물을 기르는 목동에는 쓰지 않고 오로지 '양치기'에게만 쓴다. '소떼를 몰고 다니는 사람'은 cowboy라고 한다.

So he took Enkidu home with him and introduced him to his friends, shepherds who tended their flocks outside the city walls. 그래서 그는 엔키두를 자신의 집으로 데려와, 성벽 밖에서 양떼를 돌보는 양치기 친구들에게 소개했다.

deliver ⓥ to free someone from a bad situation

deliver에서 de는 away(떨어진, 벗어난)를 뜻하는 접두사이고, liver는 set free(풀어주다, 자유롭게 하다)를 의미한다. 그래서 to deliver the nation(나라를 구하다)처럼 '~을 위험 등에서 구하다, 해방시키다'라는 의미로 쓸 수 있다. deliver는 A의 손에서 '벗어나' B에게 전달된다는 의미에서, '전달하다, 배달하다'라는 의미로 주로 쓰인다.

Enkidu killed the bull and delivered the whole country. 엔키두는 황소를 죽이고 온 나라를 해방시켰다.

eternal ⓐ continuing for ever and having no end

eternal은 '시간(time, age)'을 뜻하는 라틴어에서 유래했다. 시간은 끝이 없으므로 '영원한, 끝없는'을 뜻한다. eternal life는 생명이 영원히 지속되는 '영생(永生)'이다.

Finally, he decided that he would have to find the secret of eternal life and conquer death itself. 마침내 그는 영생의 비밀을 찾아서 죽음 자체를 정복해야겠다고 결심했다.

immortal ⓐ living or existing for ever

'죽음(death)'을 뜻하는 mortal 앞에 '부정(not)'의 의미를 갖는 접두사 im-이 붙어 '죽지 않는, 영원히 사는, 불멸의'라는 뜻이다. mortal는 '죽을 수밖에 없는, 치명적인'을 뜻하는 형용사이다.

He decided to go see Utnapishtim—the only immortal man on the whole earth. 그는 세상을 통틀어 죽지 않는 단 한 사람인 우트나피쉬팀을 찾아가기로 마음먹었다.

bottom ⓝ the ground under a sea, river or pond

bottom은 '지면, 땅(ground, earth)'을 뜻하는 고대 영어 botm에서 온 것이다. 세상의 모든 것은 땅으로 내려오게 되어 있다. 땅을 파도 땅이므로 bottom은 '맨 아래, 바닥'을 뜻한다. the bottom of the ocean처럼 바다, 강, 호수 등을 말할 때는 '물 밑의 땅, 해저(海底)'를 의미한다.

If you can swim all the way down to the bottom of the ocean, you will find a magical plant that lives on the sea's bottom. 네가 바다의 밑바닥까지 헤엄쳐서 내려갈 수 있다면 해저에서 사는 마법의 식물을 발견하게 될 것이다.

shed ⓥ to allow something to fall off, usually as part of a natural process

shed는 '떨어져 나가다(separate out)'라는 뜻의 고대 영어에서 유래했다. 자신의 의지로 떨어지는 것이 아니라, 자연의 법칙에 따라 '저절로 떨어지다'라는 의미이다. 나무의 잎이나 열매도 시간이 지나면 밑으로 떨어지고, 슬프면 눈물이 떨어지며 뱀의 허물도 자연히 몸에서 떨어져 나간다. Snakes shed their skins(뱀은 허물을 벗는다)나 Trees shed their leaves in fall(나무는 가을에 잎이 떨어진다)처럼 쓸 수 있다.

That is why snakes shed their skins. 그것이 바로 뱀이 허물을 벗는 이유이다.

Q 《길가메시》에도 홍수 이야기가 나온다고요?

A 홍수라면 단연 노아의 방주 이야기를 떠올리겠지만 사실 창세기에 나오는 홍수 신화보다 훨씬 오래 전의 이야기가 《길가메시》에 등장한단다. 조지 스미스가 이 점토판을 해석하자 유대교인들은 '창세기 전에 홍수 이야기가 있었다니'라고 혼란에 빠졌다고 해. 그러나 생각해보면 당연한 이야기가 아닐까? 유대교가 성립되기 전에 이미 메소포타미아 문명이 형성되었으니까 아무리 신의 말씀을 기록한 것이라 해도 그들이 살았던 시대와 지역의 영향을 받지 않는다는 것은 불가능한 일이잖아.

수메르 신화에 나오는 홍수 이야기는 다양한 판본이 있어. 그중 수메르 판본에서는 신들이 홍수를 일으켜 생명체를 멸망시키기로 합의했다고 나오는데, 신들로부터 미리 귀띔을 받은 지우스드라(영원한 생명이라는 뜻)가 배에 다른 생물을 태우고 홍수를 피할 수 있었던 거야. 나중에 그는 신들에게 딜문의 땅을 받고, '영원한 생명'을 보장받았어.

Chapter 9
The First Cities of India

1 The River-Road

🌐 인더스 강은 히말라야에서 발원하여 인도의 북서부와 파키스탄의 중심부를 통과해 아라비아 해로 흘러드는 총 길이 약 2,900킬로미터의 강이다. 지금으로 부터 약 4,000년 전에 인더스 강의 중하류 지역에는 도시가 형성되어 문명(文明, civilization)이 태동했는데, 모헨조다로(Mohenjo-Daro)와 하라파(Harappa)에 고 대 인더스 문명의 수준을 엿볼 수 있는 유적이 남아 있다. 인더스 문명, 이집트 문 명, 메소포타미아 문명, 중국의 황하 문명을 '세계 4대 문명'이라고 한다.

The Egyptians lived on the Nile River. The Assyrians and the Babylonians lived on the Tigris and Euphrates rivers, in Mesopotamia. Why do you think that ancient people wanted to live near rivers?

People who lived near rivers had plenty of water to drink and to use on their crops. But there's another reason why ancient cities were built near rivers. Imagine that you live in ancient Mesopotamia, down near Ur. Let's pretend that you're a merchant, like Terah was in our story about Abram. You've got a wonderful crop of wheat this year, and you've just heard that the wheat in Assyria all got washed away in a flood. The people in Assyria will pay twice as much for wheat as the people in Ur—because there's wheat all over Ur, but almost none in Assyria. So you decide that you'll travel north to Assyria with your wheat and sell it there. You can make a lot of money that way.

How will you get from Ur to Assyria? Remember, you don't have a car or truck. If you're going to go all the way to Assyria, you'll have to use a cart pulled by cows. You can't walk, because the wheat is too heavy to carry. And your cart has wheels made out of wood, because rubber hasn't been invented yet.

How long do you think the wheels last? Will you have to stop

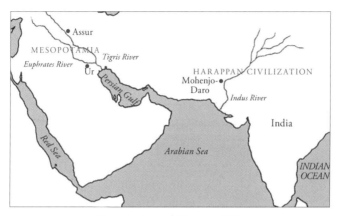

Mesopotamian and Harappan Cities

and fix them, between Ur and Assur? How fast do cows walk?
How long do you think it will take you to walk at the pace
of a cow all the way to Assyria? Let's think about the ground
in Mesopotamia for a minute. In this area, the ground is either
sandy or rocky. Remember—there are no bulldozers and paving
machines to make nice smooth roads. So, part of the way to
Assyria, you'll have to walk on sand.

What's difficult about walking on sand? Think about being
at the beach. Do your feet sink into the sand? What if you were
pulling a very heavy cart with wooden wheels? Would the
wheels sink into the sand? Let's also think about rocky ground.
How will your cart go on rocky ground? Going to Assur with
carts and cows doesn't sound like a very easy trip!

Can you think of another way to get from Ur to Assur? Think
about this: You could put all your wheat on a boat. Then you
could sail from Ur on the Euphrates River down to the Persian
Gulf. And then you could sail back up the Tigris River. By sailing
in your boat, you could get there in less time—and with a lot less
work.

*Cities grew up on rivers because it was easy to ship food, metals, wood, and other goods up and down the water. It was much easier to go by water than to drag heavy loads over land! The cities in Mesopotamia used the Tigris and the Euphrates rivers to trade with each other.

But they didn't just trade with each other. They also traded with countries to the east. And one of the countries they traded with was India. The people of India also used a river as a road. Their river was called the Indus, and the land around the Indus River was called the Indus Valley. The people of India settled in this valley because they could drink the river's water, fish in it, and use it to water their fields. They also sailed up and down the Indus River, trading with each other.

Eventually, the people of India sailed out into the Arabian Sea. The Arabian Sea was the largest body of water they had ever seen! *They must have thought that they were in a sea that had no shores and would never end. But they were brave; they kept exploring. Soon they learned that they could sail up to the cities of Mesopotamia and trade with them.

*If the people of India had tried to go across the land to Mesopotamia, they would have had to cross a mountain range. But by boat, the trip wasn't difficult at all. So the people of India—like the Mesopotamians—built large cities near the Indus River, and made money by trading with other cities. Today we call their civilization the Harappan civilization. It was strongest between 2000 and 1750 BC/BCE.

2 The Mystery of Mohenjo-Daro

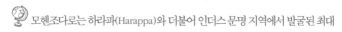 모헨조다로는 하라파(Harappa)와 더불어 인더스 문명 지역에서 발굴된 최대

도시 유적이다. 모헨조다로는 기원전 2500년경에 건설된 계획 도시로, 성채와 광장, 바둑판 형태의 주거지와 넓은 도로, 공동 우물, 대형 목욕탕 등을 갖추고 있었다. 여러 차례 붕괴와 재건을 거듭하며 약 1,000년 동안 존속된 것으로 추정한다. 1922년 영국의 고고학자 존 마샬(John Marshall)이 발굴할 당시에 많은 유골이 나왔는데, '모헨조다로'라는 말 자체가 '죽은 자들의 언덕'이라는 뜻이다. 기원전 1750년경에 멸망한 것으로 보이며 정확한 멸망 원인은 아직 밝혀지지 않았다.

The people who lived in the Indus Valley built cities, just like the people in Mesopotamia. But there weren't any empires in the Indus Valley. No great warrior—like Sargon or Hammurabi or Shamshi–Adad—tried to unite all the Indus Valley cities (the Harappan cities) into one kingdom. The people of the Harappan cities stayed independent.

A farmer living in the Indus Valley had a different life from a farmer in Egypt or in Mesopotamia. He grew grain, but he also grew fruit, like melons, and cotton. And he used water buffalo and elephants to work his fields! A farmer in Babylonia would have been amazed to see an Indus Valley farmer, walking along beside his elephant as he harvested his cotton and melons.

The cities in the Indus Valley were built around huge circular mounds called *citadels.* *Each citadel had a stronghold on it— a place to go in case enemies attacked. All around the citadel, people built their houses out of mud bricks that had been baked hard in ovens. The houses were very comfortable. They had courtyards, wells, and even toilets and drains. People living in the houses could haul water up out of their wells, rather than going all the way to the river for water. Large public baths, like big swimming pools, meant that everyone could stay clean and cool.

And the drains took waste out of the houses, down into deep gutters that ran along the streets. The citadel cities were some of the biggest in the world. Mohenjo-Daro had over forty thousand people living in it.

But something happened to the cities of the Indus Valley. Around 1750 BC/BCE, people began to leave their homes. Eventually, the cities were almost entirely deserted. The buildings, drains, wells, and citadels crumbled. Slowly, sand and dirt covered over the cities. For hundreds of years, no one knew that the citadel cities were even there.

Finally, archaeologists started to dig in the ground around the Indus River. They found the remains of the great citadel cities. They found ruined walls and citadels.

But they couldn't find any clues about why people stopped living there. They found some writing that the Indus Valley people left—but we can't read the writing, so we don't know what it says. In Mohenjo-Daro, archaeologists found skeletons lying in the street, as though people died right there in the road

An Ancient Statue from the Indus Valley

and weren't even buried.

What happened to the citadel cities? We'll probably never know for sure. But the people of India still tell ancient stories, passed down over thousands of years. These stories come from long ago, from the time when the citadel cities were still flourishing. Maybe these stories are clues. One is called "The Hunter and the Quail."

Once, a flock of quail lived on the banks of a river. They had plenty to eat and drink, but they were afraid of the hunter who came every evening to catch them. He would creep up to the edge of the flock with his net and then leap out of the bushes. When the quail scattered, he would catch the nearest bird in his net, carry it back to his house—and eat it for dinner!

One day the oldest of the quail said, "It is easy for the hunter to catch just one of us. But what if he threw his net over all of us? We would be strong enough to escape!"

So the next evening, when the hunter leaped out the bushes, the quail all stayed in one flock. The hunter flung his net over the quail, but they rose up from the ground together, pulled the net out of his hands, and flew away, still side by side. All together, the quail were too strong for the hunter.

The quail were very pleased! Now they didn't have to be afraid. Night after night, they stayed together, pulled the hunter's net out of his hands, and flew away.

But soon the quail began to push and jostle at each other, as they crowded together in their safe, strong group. "You're stepping on my claw!" cried one. "You're rumpling my feathers!" cried another. "You're squeezing me until I can't breathe!" complained a third. Finally they scattered—and the hunter, who had been waiting in the bushes, leaped out and netted them, one by one. As he headed back to his house, he said, "Together, they are free. But apart, they are supper!"

What does this story mean? Perhaps it means that the citadel cities, staying independent and separate from each other, were defeated by invaders. Maybe that's what happened to Mohenjo-Daro. Maybe, if they had united together into one kingdom, the citadel cities would have survived. But we will never know for sure.

The Story of the Words

Chapter 9 The First Cities of India

1 The River-Road

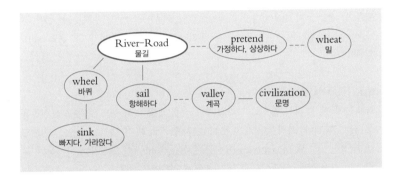

pretend Ⓥ to imagine

'닭 잡아먹고 오리발 내민다'라는 속담이 있다. 아닌 척 거짓으로 꾸미는 행동인데, pretend가 이런 의미를 담고 있다. pretend는 접두사 pre-(앞으로)와 tend(내밀다)가 합쳐진 것으로, 진짜는 뒤에 감추고 가짜를 '앞으로 내미는' 것이다. 그래서 '~인 척하다, 가장하다'라는 뜻이다. Let's pretend that you're a merchant(여러분이 상인이라고 상상해보자)처럼 사실이 아니지만 그렇게 생각해보자는 의미에서 '상상하다, 가정하다'라는 뜻으로도 쓰인다.

Let's pretend that you're a merchant, like Terah was in our story about Abram. 아브람에 관한 우리의 이야기에 나오는 테라처럼, 여러분이 상인이라고 가정해보자.

wheat Ⓝ a kind of grain that is made into flour for bread, noodle and other foods

강수량이 많은 일부 아시아 지역을 제외하고, 세계 전역에서 가장 중요한 곡물은 wheat(밀)이다. 우리의 쌀(rice)처럼 밀은 그 자체로 세상을 움직이는 동력이자 생명의 근원이다. 곡물인 '밀'도 wheat, 밀이 열리는 식물도 wheat라고 한다.

You've got a wonderful crop of wheat this year, and you've just heard that the wheat in Assyria all got washed away in a flood. 여러분은 올해에 밀 풍년을 맞았는데, 방금 전에는 아시리아에서 홍수로 밀이 전부 물에 쓸려갔다는 소식을 들었다.

wheel ⓝ one of the round things under a vehicle that turns around and makes it move

wheel에는 circle(원)의 의미가 담겨 있다. 둥근 것을 이동과 운반에 활용한 '바퀴'의 발명은 역사의 혁명이었다. 자동차나 수레 등의 밑에 달린 바퀴도 wheel이고, 자동차의 핸들이나 배의 키를 작동하는 타륜(舵輪)도 wheel이라고 한다. 모두 둥글고 돌기 때문이다.

How long do you think the wheels last? 여러분은 그 바퀴가 얼마나 오래 버틸 거라고 생각하는가?

sink ⓥ to move below the surface of water or soft ground

sink는 물에 빠져서 밑으로 가라앉거나 진흙에 발이 빠지는 것 등을 표현하는 동사로, '빠지다, 가라앉다'라는 뜻이다. 하수구로 '빠져' 나가는 부엌 싱크대도 sink이다. to sink into the sand는 '모래 속으로(into) 빠진다'라는 의미이다.

Do your feet sink into the sand? 발이 모래 속으로 빠지는가?

valley ⓝ an area of low land between hills or mountains

산과 산 사이, 언덕과 언덕 사이에 꼭대기에서부터 밑으로 길게 움푹 들어간 지형이 있는데, 이런 곳을 valley라고 한다. 우리말로는 '골짜기' 또는 '물이 흐르는 골'이라는 뜻의 '계곡(溪谷)'이라고 한다. 영어권 나라에 '베일(Vale)'이라는 지명이 많은데, 모두 처음부터 골짜기에 삶의 터전을 잡았다는 특징이 있다. valley와 vale은 어원과 의미가 같다. 모두 '계곡'이다.

The people of India settled in this valley because they could drink the river's water, fish in it, and use it to water their fields. 인도 사람들은 이 계곡에 정착했는데, 그 강의 물을 마시고, 그 강에서 물고기를 잡고, 경작지에 물을 대는 데 강을 이용할 수 있기 때문이었다.

sail ⓥ to travel on water in a boat or ship

sail은 배에 다는 넓은 천, 즉 '돛'이다. to set sail(돛을 달다)이라고 하면 '항해를 시작한다'는 의미가 된다. 오랫동안 항해용 배에는 돛을 달아 거의 바람의 힘으로 움직였다. 동사형 sail이 '항해하다'라는 뜻으로 쓰이게 되었고, sailor가 '뱃 사람, 선원'이다.

They also sailed up and down the Indus River, trading with each other. 그들은 또한 인더스 강을 오르내리며 서로 무역했다.

civilization ⓝ a society that is well organized and developed, usually with laws, government and education

civilization은 '문명(文明)'이다. 간단히 정의하기 쉽지 않은 개념이지만, 어원으로 보거나 역사적으로 볼 때 '도시(city)'의 형성과 문명 발생은 불가분의 관계에 있다. civilization에서 civil은 '도시, 도시 사람'이라는 의미가 있어서, 동사형 civilize도 '세련되다, 문명화되다'라는 뜻이다. 사람이 많이 모여 도시가 형성되면 생산과 소비 규모가 커지고, 제도와 규칙이 만들어지고, 지배와 피지배의 개념도 생겨난다. 또한 공통적인 생활 양식과 사고방식을 지닌 문화도 생겨난다. 이러한 역사적인 발전 단계를 '문명'이라고 한다.

Today we call their civilization the Harappan civilization. 오늘날 우리는 그들의 문명을 '하라파 문명'이라고 부른다.

> **Q** 인더스 문명과 하라파 문명은 같은 것인가요?
>
> **A** 같은 명칭이야. 그런데 왜 다르게 표현할까? 인더스 강 주변 계곡에서 태어난 문명이라는 의미로 '인더스 문명'이야. 그런데 오래전에 소멸했던 이 문명의 터를 찾아낸 것은 세월이 많이 흘러서였어. 1856년 이 지역에서 철도 공사를 하던 중, 영국인 브룬튼(Brunton) 형제가 우연히 발견한 옛 유적의 흔적을 발견하고 보고하자, 1920년부터 고고학자들이 본격적으로 발굴을 시작했어. 인더스 강을 따라가면서 여러 유적지가 발견되었는데, 상류부터 발굴하기 시작하여 하라파 유적지가 먼저 발견된 거지. 그래서 하라파의 이름을 따서 '하라파 문명'으로도 불리는 거야. 상류의 하라파와 하류의 모헨조다로 사이에 600킬로미터 정도의 거리가 있었는데, 그 사이에 70여 개의 크고 작은 도시가 발견되었어.

2 The Mystery of Mohenjo-Daro

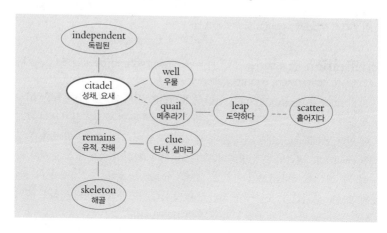

independent ⓐ free and not controlled by others

dependent는 '의지하다'라는 뜻의 동사 depend의 형용사형이다. depend에서 de-는 down(밑으로, 아래에)이고, pend는 hang(매달리다)이라는 뜻이다. 아기가 엄마를 잡고 매달리듯, 등산가가 밧줄에 몸을 의지하듯 '매달리는' 것이 depend이다. 즉 '의존[의지]하다'라는 뜻이다. dependent 앞에 붙은 in-은 not을 의미해서 independent는 '매달리지 않는, 의존하지 않는, 독립된'이다. 명사형은 independence(독립, 자립)이다.

The people of the Harappan cities stayed independent. 하라파 도시의 사람들은 독립된 상태로 남아 있었다.

citadel ⓝ a castle built on a high place for the defense of a city

citadel도 civilization과 마찬가지로 city(도시)를 뜻하는 라틴어에서 유래했다. 옛날에 도시는 대개 주변 지형보다 높은 곳에 위치해 있었다. 홍수도 피할 수 있고, 적이 침입했을 때 높은 곳에 있는 것이 방어에 유리했기 때문이다. 도시 중심부는 가장 높은 곳에 있고, 둘레에 돌로 성을 쌓아 최후의 보루로 활용하는 곳을 citadel(성채, 요새)라고 한다.

The cities in the Indus Valley were built around huge circular mounds called *citadels*. 인더스 계곡에 있는 도시들은 '성채[요새]'라고 불리는 거대한 원형의 언덕 주위에 건설되었다.

well ⓝ a deep hole dug in the ground where people get water

well은 원래 '물이 샘솟는 모습'을 표현한 것이다. 땅을 파다가 물이 솟아 나오면 그곳이 well(우물)이다. 우물을 뜻하는 well과 '잘, 좋은'의 의미로 쓰이는 well은 형태는 같지만 어원은 다르다.

People living in the houses could haul water up out of their wells, rather than going all the way to the river for water. 그 집에 사는 사람들은 물을 얻기 위해 강까지 가지 않고, 자신의 우물에서 물을 길어 올릴 수 있었다.

remains ⓝ parts of something that are left

remains는 동사 remain에 -s가 붙어 만들어진 명사형이다. remain에서 re-는 back(뒤에)을, main은 stay(머물다)를 뜻한다. 뒤에 머무는 것이므로 '남다, 계속 ~의 상태로 있다'라는 뜻이다. 명사형 remains는 어떤 과정이 끝난 후에나 시간이 흐른 뒤에도 남아 있는 것을 의미한다. the remains of the citadel cities (요새 도시들의 유적)처럼 '유적, 잔해'의 의미로 역사책에서 자주 볼 수 있다.

They found the remains of the great citadel cities. 그들은 거대한 요새 도시들의 유적을 발견했다.

skeleton ⓝ all the bones in a person or animal

시체가 부패 과정을 겪은 후에 '남는 것(remains)'이 바로 skeleton이다. dry up(완전히 마르다)를 뜻하는 희랍어에서 유래했다. 몸에서 수분이 다 빠져 나가고 남은 뼈, '해골(骸骨)'이 skeleton이다. 사람이나 동물 모두에게 쓸 수 있다. 모헨조다로(Mohenjo-Daro) 유적에서 사람의 skeleton이 많이 발견되었는데, '모헨조다로'라는 말 자체가 '죽은 자들의 언덕'이라는 뜻이다.

In Mohenjo—Daro, archaeologists found skeletons lying in the street, as though people died right there in the road and weren't even buried. 모헨조다로에서 고고학자들은 거리에 누워 있는 해골을 발견했는데, 마치 사람들이 바로 도로 위에서 죽어 매장조차 되지 않은 듯 보였다.

clue ⓝ something that helps you find the answer to a difficult problem

clue는 문제 해결의 열쇠가 되는 '단서, 실마리'라는 뜻이다. 실이 엉키면 우선 실의 끄트머리인 '실마리'를 찾아야 풀 수 있는데, clue의 원래 의미도 '실뭉당이(a ball of thread)'다. 나중에 형태가 달라졌지만, 원래 clew(실꾸리)와 의미가 같다. 그리스 신화에서 미로를 벗어날 수 있는 수단으로 실꾸리(아리아드네의 실)가 나온 데에서 유래해 clue가 '단서, 실마리'의 의미가 된 것이다.

Maybe these stories are clues. 어쩌면 이 이야기들이 단서가 될 수 있을 것이다.

quail ⓝ a small fat bird with a short tail that people hunt and eat

quail은 몸길이가 20센티미터 정도인 꿩과의 새인 '메추라기'이다. 옛날부터 주변에서 흔히 볼 수 있는 새였기 때문에 사냥감으로 많이 잡혔고, 대개는 '생각이 짧거나 시야가 좁은' 동물로 우화(寓話)에 자주 등장한다.

Once, a flock of quail lived on the banks of a river. 옛날에 메추라기 떼가 강둑에 살고 있었다.

leap ⓥ to jump suddenly from one place to another

토끼 한 마리가 굶주린 호랑이 눈에 들어와서, 호랑이는 살금살금 다가가다가 갑자기 훌쩍 뛰어오른다. 이렇게 힘차게 높이, 멀리 도약하는 것이 leap이다. to leap out of the bushes는 갑자기 덤불에서 나오며(out of) 뛰어오른다는 의미이다. leap은 명사형(도약, 비약)으로도 쓰인다.

He would creep up to the edge of the flock with his net and then leap out of the bushes. 그 사냥꾼은 그물을 들고서 (메추라기) 떼의 가장자리 쪽으로 기어간 다음에 덤불에서 나와 훌쩍 뛰어오르곤 했다.

scatter ⓥ to move away in different directions

높은 곳에서 바닥에 물을 쏟으면 물방울이 사방으로 튄다. 총소리가 나면 새들이 사방으로 흩어져 날아간다(The sound of gunfire makes the birds scatter). 이렇게 '사방으로 흩어지다'라는 뜻을 표현하는 동사가 scatter이다. She scattered the seeds on the ground(그녀는 씨앗을 땅 위에 흩뿌렸다)처럼 '~을 흩뿌리다, 흩어지게 하다(to make things spread)'라는 뜻으로 쓰인다.

Finally they scattered—and the hunter, who had been waiting in the bushes, leaped out and netted them, one by one. 마침내 메추라기들은 흩어졌고, 덤불 속에서 기다리고 있던 사냥꾼은 뛰어나와 한 마리씩 그물로 잡았다.

Q 인더스 문명은 왜 갑자기 끝나버렸나요?

A 번성하던 인더스 문명은 갑자기 끝나버렸어. 이에 대해 학자들은 서로 다른 견해를 내놓고 있단다. 한동안은 중앙아시아에서 온 유목민인 아리아인들이 정복했다는 설이 우세하여 실제로 그렇게 쓰인 책도 많았어. 그런데 유적지에서 나온 두개골에 전쟁으로 인한 상처가 보이지 않는다는 점과 아리아인의 편잡 지역 이주를 기원전 1500년경으로 보는 견해를 감

안하면 인더스 문명이 갑자기 끝난 시기와 약 200여 년 차이가 나. 벌목을 많이 하면 홍수가 나는 경우에 감당하기 어려웠을 것이라는 추측도 있어. 벽돌을 굽기 위해 나무 연료가 필요한데, 모헨조다로 유적지만 해도 3만 정도의 인구가 살았으니 그들에게 필요한 벽돌을 굽자면 상당한 나무가 필요했을 거야. 마지막으로 강수량이 줄어 사람이 살기 어렵게 되자 그 마을을 모두 떠났다는 설도 있어.

Chapter 10
The Far East: Ancient China

1 Lei Zu and the Silkworm

Huang Di는 중국의 신화에 등장하는 지배자인 '황제(黃帝)'이다. emperor
를 뜻하는 황제(皇帝)와는 글자 표기가 다르다. 황(黃)은 땅(土)을 상징하는 것으로,
황제(黃帝)란 땅을 다스린 지배자를 뜻한다. 영어로도 Huang Di를 the Yellow
Emperor라고 부른다. 황제는 기원전 2500년을 전후해 황허 강(Yellow River)과
양쯔 강(Yangtze River) 유역을 기반으로 나라를 세우고 중국을 통치한 것으로 전
해지는 전설 속 인물이다. 농기구와 무기, 농경법과 직조 기술 등을 사람들에게 가
르쳐 중국 문명의 시조가 되었다고 전해지며, 중국인들은 중국의 역대 왕조와 한
(漢)족은 모두 그의 자손이라고 믿고 있다.

The people who lived in Mesopotamia, between the Tigris
and the Euphrates rivers, thought they lived at the very center of
the world. They called India the East, because they had to sail east
to reach it. They thought of India as a strange and distant place.

But there was a country that seemed even stranger and was more
distant than India: China. To the Assyrians and the Babylonians,
China was the "Far East." It was all the way on the edge of the
world!

The people of China and the people of the Fertile Crescent
didn't know very much about each other. But even though they
lived far away, the Chinese people chose to live near a river, just
like the Egyptians and Babylonians and Assyrians did. Ancient
people needed rivers to survive.

The people of China first lived between two rivers called the
Yellow River and the Yangtze River. The area between the rivers
was called the Yellow River Valley. The earliest people of China
settled between these rivers, in the Yellow River Valley, and grew
crops—especially rice, because it grows well in wet ground.

At first, the Chinese lived in separate villages, just like the

Huang Di united the villages of the Yellow River Valley

people of Mesopotamia. But eventually a great leader united the different villages of the Yellow River Valley into one kingdom. The leader who united the Chinese villages was named Huang Di. He lived so long ago that we really don't know very much about him—but there are plenty of stories about his rule. Legends say that Huang Di first discovered medicine, and taught the Chinese people how to cure illnesses. His wife, the empress Lei Zu, discovered that silkworms make their cocoons out of silk threads.

One day the empress Lei Zu sat in her garden beneath the mulberry trees. Outside the palace walls, she could hear the noises of trading caravans, the sound of camel-hooves on stone, and the cries of street-merchants selling candy, jewelry, and tea. But Lei Zu's walled garden was quiet and peaceful.

The breeze moved the leaves of the mulberry tree above her.

"Min Lai!" she called to her maid. "Bring my lunch out here. I will eat in the garden today!"

Soon Min Lai brought out the empress's favorite meal—turtle meat with garlic and ginger, candied fruit, rice, and a pot of steaming, fragrant tea. Lei Zu breathed in the rich smell of tea as she poured it into her cup. She lifted the cup to her mouth. Something splashed into it, right in front of her nose.

She looked down into her cup. There, floating in the hot water, was something small and round and white. She glanced up into the branches of the mulberry tree. Hundreds of little white cocoons were dangling just over her head—the cocoons of the silkworm. Inside the cocoons, the silkworms were changing into moths. Soon they would chew through the cocoons and fly away.

"Look, Min Lai," she said. "A silkworm cocoon fell right into my tea!"

"Let me get you a fresh cup, Empress Lei Zu," the maid offered.

"Wait," Lei Zu said. She carefully lifted the cocoon out of her cup. It seemed to be made from a thin, bright thread, wrapped a hundred thousand times around the silkworm within. The hot water had begun to unravel it. Lei Zu pulled gently at the end of the thread and drew it out, longer and longer and longer. She rose from her seat and walked through the garden, trailing the thread behind her. It was so long that she circled the garden with it a dozen times. The thread was so light that it floated on the wind, and it shone in the sun like melting silver.

"If only I could weave this into cloth!" Lei Zu marveled. "What a robe I could make for my husband, the emperor!"

"But it is too thin to weave!" Min Lai said.

"Pick me another cocoon, Min Lai," the Empress said. "We will unravel another thread."

All afternoon, the Empress and her maid unraveled the fine, shining threads from the silkworm cocoons. They twisted the threads together until they were as thick as a thread of cotton. And then the Empress called her dressmaker. "Can you weave a cloth from these threads?" she asked.

"I have never seen threads like these!" the dressmaker exclaimed. "They are as fine as hairs, but as soft as the petal of a flower." She took the threads away and wove them into a cloth that shone like water in the sunshine, and from that cloth Lei Zu made a robe for her husband, the emperor. When he saw it, he gasped with wonder.

"From now on," he said, "we will call this *silk*. The secret of making this wonderful cloth must never leave the palace. *Only the royal family can know this treasure was yielded by the silkworm cocoons!"

So from then on, Lei Zu and her court made the wonderful cloth called silk. They fed the silkworms on trays of mulberry leaves, waited until the worms wove their cocoons, and then carefully unraveled the cocoons for their precious threads of silk. Soon China became famous for its silk—the cloth that no one else in the world knew how to make.

2 The Pictograms of Ancient China

그림 문자는 사물의 형상을 그림으로 단순하게 표현한 글자를 말한다. 영어 pictogram은 painting(그림)을 뜻하는 picto와 writing(글, 글자)을 뜻하는 gram 이 합쳐진 것이다. 말 그대로 '그림 글자'이다. pictograph도 pictogram과 같은 의미이다. 문자 발생 시기로 볼 때 그림 문자는 상형 문자(hieroglyph) 이전 단계의 문자 형태로, 세계 전역에서 다양한 형태의 그림 문자들이 적힌 유물을 볼 수 있다. 중국의 한자(漢字)도 그림 문자에서 발전한 것이다.

We don't know much for certain about Huang Di, or about the rulers who followed him—because they didn't leave any written records about their empires. *Almost everything that we know about these very ancient Chinese rulers has been passed down in stories and legends, from person to person over thousands of years. We don't know what parts of the stories are true, and what parts were added to make them more interesting and more exciting.

We do know that the Chinese went on living in the Yellow River Valley, and that they grew rice, raised silkworms, and tried to defend themselves against invaders. And we know that a new leader came to power, hundreds of years after Huang Di. His name was T'ang, and his family was called the Shang family.

T'ang became king around 1766 BC/BCE. His family would rule the Yellow River Valley for the next five hundred years. In China, this was called a *dynasty*—one family keeping control of a country for many, many years, passing the crown along from father to son, from brother to brother, or from uncle to nephew.

We know much more about the Shang dynasty than we do about the rulers who came before it.

*During the rule of the Shang family, the Chinese began to use bronze. They made weapons, wheels, and farming tools out of bronze. *These tools and weapons made of bronze didn't rot away like wooden tools. Thousands of years later, archaeologists discovered the bronze tools and weapons, buried beneath the ruins of Shang buildings. *The bronze weapons tell us that the

Chinese who lived during the rule of the Shang dynasty knew how to fight with bows and arrows. They used chariots when they attacked their enemies, and they wore shields and armor to protect themselves. The farming tools tell us that they grew wheat and mulberries, as well as rice, and that they used plows pulled by horses to farm their fields.

But that's not all the Shang dynasty left us. During the rule of the Shang, the Chinese began to use writing for the very first time. And we can still read this writing, because it was often engraved on bones and on bronze plaques that have lasted for thousands of years.

At first, this early Chinese writing was made up of pictures. These special pictures are called *pictograms*. Picto means "picture" and *gram* means "writing." Pictograms are words that look like pictures. For example, here's a pictogram for "sun":

It's a picture of the sun, with the sun's rays shining out at both sides. The pictogram for "water" looks like this:

Can you see the waves in the water?

Here's a Shang dynasty pictogram that means "house":

Here is a Shang pictogram that means "bow and arrow":

And here's a more complicated pictogram that means "soldier":

This soldier is carrying a *halberd*, a weapon that has an axe on one side and a dagger on the other.

The Chinese people used these pictograms to write simple messages. The pictograms look almost exactly like the words they represent.

3 Farming in Ancient China

중국과 인도의 고대 유적에서 발굴된 탄화미(炭化米: 불에 타거나 지층에서 자연 탄화되어 남은 볍씨)와 원시 농기구의 형태로 볼 때 벼농사는 약 4,000~5,000년 전 신석기 시대에 시작되었을 것으로 추정한다. 물론 그전에도 야생의 벼를 채집해서 식량으로 먹었을 것이다. 모판에 볍씨를 파종하고 난 후에 어린 벼를 논에 옮겨 심는 '모내기' 농사법은 중국에서 춘추전국 시대에 시작되었다.

Most people who lived in ancient China were farmers. They raised animals like pigs, chickens, and cows. They grew grain, just like people in Egypt and in Mesopotamia. But the people of China grew a kind of grain that the Egyptians and Mesopotamians couldn't grow—rice.

Rice will only grow where the ground is very wet for most of the year. The ground in Egypt and Mesopotamia was too dry for rice. But near the Yellow River in China, whole fields stayed wet for months and months. Rice could grow there.

Chin was seven years old. He lived in ancient China with his father, a rice farmer, his mother, his grandfather, and his little sister.

One spring morning, Chin woke up before sunrise. The room where he slept with the rest of his family was still dark. But Chin was too excited to go back to sleep. This morning, he would go with his father to work in the rice fields for the very first time! He hoped that it wouldn't rain. But he couldn't see out past the stiff paper that covered the windows.

Chin got up and tiptoed out of the room, past where his parents, his grandfather, and his little sister lay sleeping on their pallets on the floor. He opened the door as quietly as he could. From his front steps, he could hear the roar of the Yellow River. The river was fuller than usual because of the spring rains, and it was so noisy that the people in Chin's little village could hear it a mile away.

Chin looked up. The sky was just beginning to turn a beautiful clear pink. A spring breeze was blowing. It was going to be a beautiful day! He could hear the pigs rooting and grunting behind the house, and the chickens scratching around the edges of their pen. Chin fed the three pigs and the four chickens every morning. He decided that he would feed them right away, before his father got up. Then all his chores would be finished.

After he fed the animals, Chin washed his hands, combed his hair, and dressed. He picked up his sleeping mat and put it outside to air. Then he knelt down beside his father's pallet and whispered, "Father? Are you awake? Are you well this morning? Can I bring you water or food?" Chin did this every morning; it was his duty, as the oldest son, to make sure that his father had everything that he needed.

Chin's father opened his eyes and laughed. "Are you ready to go to work already?" he said.

"Can we go right now?" Chin asked eagerly.

"Wait until I've had my rice and tea!" Chin's father said, getting up.

Chin waited impatiently by the door. His mother was grinding rice into flour; she would make the flour into little sweet cakes for dinner. Chin's baby sister played on the floor with her favorite rag doll. Finally, Chin's father finished his breakfast. He led Chin down the hill towards the river, where the rice fields stood.

Weeks ago, the Yellow River had flooded out over the rice fields. It spread water all over the flat land, deeper than Chin was tall. Then the water began to flow away back into the river, leaving soft, fertile mud from the river's bottom all over the ground. But water still stood ankle-deep all over the rice fields.

"Do you see these tiny rice plants, here in this special bed?" Chin's father asked. "Today I'll be moving them out into the field so that they can grow larger. Your job will be to pull weeds out of the field while I plant."

Chin rolled up the legs of his pants and waded out into the water. The water was ice-cold. At first his feet from the cold. Then they started to go numb. He had to put his hands down into the water to pull weeds. His fingers were stiff with cold. But he kept working. He could see his father, planting rice seedlings up ahead of him. His father never stopped working! Chin was determined to work as hard as his father. The sun rose up higher and higher, and Chin's back and head grew warm in the sunshine. But his fingers and feet ached with cold.

Finally his father called him back to dry land. "You've worked like a man this morning!" he said. "Let's go back to the house for our midday meal."

Chin followed his father back up to the house. His back hurt from bending over. His feet were wet and chilly. His hands were covered with cold mud. But he was proud of the work he had done.

Back at the house, his mother had fixed him a special treat— meat to go along with his rice. And his father poured him a cup of hot steaming tea to warm him. Chin huddled beside the clay stove, listening to his grandfather tell about the great floods of long ago. "When I was a boy," his grandfather said, "the spring rains came down and down and down, day after day, until the Yellow River rose up and overflowed its banks. But it didn't just flood our fields. Great rushing floods swirled down on our village and swept our houses away. We were left homeless!"

Chin shivered. He hoped that the Yellow River would never flood his home!

Note to Parent: According to legend, Huang Di ruled around 2690 BC/BCE. Lei Zu is also known as Xiling Ji. The Shang dynasty ruled 1766–1122 BC/BCE.

1 Lei Zu and the Silkworm

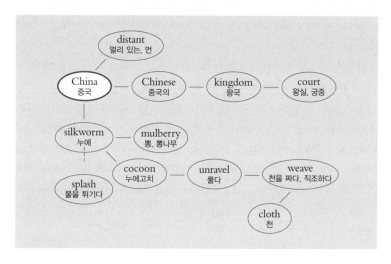

distant ⓐ far away

distant는 away(떨어져)를 뜻하는 접두사 dis-와 stand(서 있다)를 뜻하는 라틴 어 stant가 합쳐진 것이다. 떨어져 서 있다는 의미로, '멀리 있는, 먼'이라는 뜻 의 형용사이다. a distant place(멀리 있는 곳)나 China is more distant than India from Mesopotamia(메소포타미아에서 중국은 인도보다 더 멀다)처럼 쓸 수 있다. 명사형 distance는 '거리, 먼 곳'이다.

They thought of India as a strange and distant place. 그들은 인도를 낯설고 먼 곳으 로 생각했다.

Chinese ⓐ of China; relating to China

Chinese는 형용사 '중국의'이다. Chinese people은 중국 사람들, Chinese food는 중국 음식이다. Chinese는 '중국인, 중국어'를 뜻하기도 한다. China는 최초로 중국 대륙을 통일한 '진(秦; Chin)'에서 유래했다. 자주 듣고 보게 되는 나라와 국민을 일컫는 영어 명칭은 알아 두는 것이 좋다.

But even though they lived far away, the Chinese people chose to live near a river, just like the Egyptians and Babylonians and Assyrians did. 그러나 비록 멀리 떨어져 살았지만, 중국인들도 이집트인들과 바빌로니아인들, 아시리아인들이 그랬던 것처럼 강 근처에서 살기로 선택했다.

kingdom ⓝ a country ruled by a king or queen

도시가 생기면서 그 도시 사회와 사람들을 지배하는 king(왕)도 생겨났다. king 뒤에 붙은 -dom은 domain(영역)을 뜻한다. 그래서 kingdom은 '왕이 다스리는 영역', 즉 '왕국'이다. 한자의 왕(王)은 복근이 멋진 사람이 아니라, '하늘, 땅, 사람' 셋(三)을 꿰뚫어(l) 다스리는 사람이다. 여왕(queen)이 다스리는 '여왕국'을 뜻하는 queendom이라는 단어도 있지만, 일반적으로 쓰지는 않는다.

But eventually a great leader united the different villages of the Yellow River into one kingdom. 그러나 결국 한 위대한 지도자가 황허 강의 다른 마을들을 하나의 왕국으로 통합했다.

Q 물을 잘 다스리는 것이 지도자의 능력이라고요?

A 황허 강이 범람하면 주변의 가옥이 물에 잠기고, 사람들의 목숨까지 빼앗아갔지. 처음에는 둑을 쌓아 해결하려고 했지만 쉽지 않았어. 실제로 이 일을 맡았으나 제대로 해내지 못해 처형당한 담당자도 있었다고 해. 둑으로 어렵다면 다른 방법을 쓰는 수밖에 없어서 새로운 담당자 '우'가 강바닥의 흙을 파내고, 물길을 여러 곳으로 내는 작업을 해보기로 했지. 그러나 문제는 노동력이 엄청나게 필요해서 각 지역의 대립하는 씨족들을 모아서 협력해야 한다는 점이었어. 설득 작업을 거쳐 그들에게 일하는 방법을 지시하기까지 십 년이나 걸렸어. 드디어 물길을 내는 데 성공하여 능력을 인정받은 '우'가 중국 최초의 나라(하나라) 시조가 되었다는 것은 사마천의 《사기》에도 기록되어 있단다.

silkworm ⓝ a worm that produces silk thread

silkworm은 명주 실을 만드는 벌레, '누에'이다. 실크는 '비단, 명주(明紬)'라고도 한다. silk는 명주 실을 뜻하는 중국어 '쉬絲'의 발음에서 유래했는데, 우리말의 '실'과도 관련이 있는 것으로 추정한다. worm은 지렁이, 송충이, 배추 벌레처럼 '꿈틀거리며 기어다니는 벌레'를 통칭한다.

His wife, the empress Lei Zu, discovered that silkworms make their cocoons out of silk threads. 그의 아내인 황후 누조는 누에가 비단 실로 자신의 고치를 만든다는 사실을 발견했다.

mulberry ⓝ a dark purple fruit that can be eaten

본 적이 있는지 모르겠지만 뽕나무에 열리는 열매인 '오디, 뽕'이 mulberry이고, '뽕나무'가 mulberry tree이다. mulberry에서 berry는 작은 나무 열매이고, mul은 black, dark를 뜻한다. 먹을 수 있을 만큼 익으면 색깔이 검어지기 때문에 붙여진 이름이다.

One day the empress Lei Zu sat in her garden beneath the mulberry trees. 어느 날, 황후누조가 정원의 뽕나무 아래에 앉아 있었다.

splash ⓥ to fall into a liquid, making a noise

Something splashed into the tea cup은 찻잔에 뭔가 '풍당' 소리를 내며 떨어졌다는 의미이다. 액체의 표면에 어떤 힘이 가해지면 소리가 나면서 방울이 튄다. 이런 모습을 표현한 동사가 splash이다. '풍당[철썩, 첨벙] 소리를 내며 물이 튀다'라는 뜻으로 물이 튀는 소리를 표현한 것이다.

Something splashed into it, right in front of her nose. 바로 그녀의 코앞에서, 뭔가가 풍당 물을 튀기며 그 속으로 들어갔다.

cocoon ⓝ a silk cover that young moth makes to protect themselves while growing

누에가 만드는 둥근 보호막인 '고치'가 cocoon이다. '알껍데기(eggshell)'를 뜻하는 프랑스어 cocon에서 온 단어로, 누에고치의 생김새가 알 모양 같아서 붙여진 것이다. silkworm은 질기고 튼튼한 cocoon 속에 들어 있어서 cocoon은 '보호막'의 의미로도 자주 쓰인다.

Inside the cocoons, the silkworms were changing into moths. 누에고치 안에서 누에가 나방으로 변하고 있었다.

unravel ⓥ to separate or undo things that are twisted or tangled

ravel은 '꼬다(twist), 엉키다(tangle)'이다. '부정, 반대'를 뜻하는 un-이 붙어 '꼬이지 않게, 엉키지 않게 하다'라는 뜻이 되었다. 원래 꼬여 있는 것이나 엉켜 있는 것을 원래대로 '푸는' 행동을 나타낸다.

The hot water had begun to unravel it. 뜨거운 물이 고치실을 풀기 시작했다.

weave ⓥ to make threads into cloth, by moving one thread over and under another

초기 인류는 직조(織造) 방법을 알지 못해서 동물 가죽을 입고 살았다. 그럼 누구한테 옷 짜는 법을 배우게 되었을까? 혹시 '거미(spider)'는 아닐까? weave는 원래 '거미줄(web), 거미줄을 치다'를 의미했다. 거미줄 치듯 '실(thread)'을 엮어서 천(cloth)을 만들다'라는 뜻이다. weave-wove-woven

"If only I could weave this into cloth!" Lei Zu marveled. 누조가 감탄하며 말했다. "이것으로 천을 짤 수만 있다면!"

cloth ⓝ woven material made from wool, silk or cotton

cloth와 clothes는 단순히 단 . 복수의 관계가 아니기 때문에 잘 구분해서 발음해야 한다. cloth는 실을 엮어서 만든 '천, 옷감'이다. cloth를 '여러 개' 붙여 꿰매서 원하는 모양으로 만들어야 '옷', clothes가 된다. cloth를 '재료'의 의미로 쓸 때는 She wove cloth out of thread(그녀는 실로 천을 짰다)처럼 셀 수 없는 명사로 쓴다.

"Can you weave a cloth from these threads?" she asked. 그녀가 물었다. "이 실로 천을 짤 수 있겠느냐?"

court ⓝ a king or queen, their family, their advisers and servants

왕과 그의 가족, 신하, 하인을 통칭하는 단어가 court이다. 즉 왕궁에서 살거나 일하는 사람들을 뜻하는데, 우리말로는 '궁중(宮中)'으로 해석한다. 궁중은 '장소'를 뜻하기도 하는데, court도 원래 '폐쇄된 곳(an enclosed place)'을 뜻하는 라틴어 cors에서 유래했다. court는 아무나 못 들어가는 곳이었다.

So from then on, Lei Zu and her court made the wonderful cloth called silk. 그때부터 계속 누조와 그녀의 궁중 하인들은 비단이라고 불리는 멋진 천을 만들었다.

2 The Pictograms of Ancient China

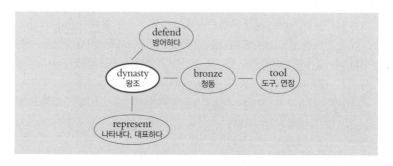

defend
방어하다

dynasty
왕조

bronze
청동

tool
도구, 연장

represent
나타내다, 대표하다

defend ⓥ to protect someone or something from an attack

defend는 '반대로(opposite), 떨어져(away from, off)'를 뜻하는 접두사 de-와 '치다, 공격하다(strike)'를 뜻하는 fend가 합쳐진 단어이다. 공격에 맞받아치든, 공격에서 벗어나려고 하든, 모두 스스로를 '방어하다'라는 의미이다. 명사형은 defense(방어)이다.

We do know that the Chinese went on living in the Yellow River Valley, and that they grew rice, raised silkworms, and tried to defend themselves against invaders. 우리는 중국인들이 계속 황허 계곡에 살았고, 쌀을 재배하고 누에를 길렀으며 침략자들에 맞서 스스로를 방어하려고 했다는 사실을 알고 있다.

dynasty ⓝ a family whose members have ruled a country for many years

dynasty는 '지배(rule), 권력(power)'을 뜻하는 희랍어에서 온 것이다. 한 가문이 대대로 권력을 쥐고 통치할 때 그 '가문'이나 '통치 기간'을 dynasty라고 하는데, 우리말로는 '왕조(王朝)'라고 한다. 대개 나라가 망하면 왕조도 바뀌기 때문에, 역사의 단계를 구분하는 데 Shang dynasty(상 왕조)나 Chosun dynasty(조선 왕조)처럼 dynasty가 자주 나온다.

In China, this was called a *dynasty*—one family keeping control of a country for many, many years, passing the crown along from father to son, from brother to brother, or from uncle to nephew. 중국에서는 이것을 왕조라고 불렀다. 왕조란 한 나라를 아주 오랫동안 통치하며 왕권을 아버지에서 아들로, 형제에서 형제로, 삼촌에서 조카로 전해주는 한 가문을 뜻한다.

bronze ⓝ a hard metal, made by mixing copper and tin

bronze는 17세기경부터 사용된, '놋쇠(brass)'를 뜻하는 페르시아어에서 유래한 것으로 추정한다. bronze는 '동(銅)'을 말하는데, 구리(copper)와 주석(tin)을 섞어서 만든 금속이다. 제작 방식에 따라 색이 달라질 수 있기 때문에, '황동(黃銅), 청동(靑銅), 백동(白銅)' 등을 bronze라고 부른다. 석기 시대 이후 인류가 청동을 사용한 '청동기 시대'를 Bronze Age라고 한다.

During the rule of the Shang family, the Chinese began to use bronze. 상 왕조 통치 동안 중국인들은 청동을 사용하기 시작했다.

tool ⓝ something that helps you to do tasks

tool은 '준비하다(prepare)'라는 뜻의 고대 영어에서 온 것이다. 어떤 일을 하기 전에 준비해야 하는 것이 tool, '도구'이다. 어떤 일에 이용할 수만 있으면 망치나 삽과 같은 연장도 tool이고, 무기도 일종의 tool이며 심지어 사람도 tool의 범주에 속한다.

They made weapons, wheels, and farming tools out of bronze. 그들은 청동으로 무기, 바퀴, 농기구를 만들었다.

> **Q** 상나라(은나라)의 존재가 '갑골 문자' 때문에 알려졌나요?
>
> **A** 하나라의 마지막 왕 '걸'을 무너뜨리고 새로운 왕조를 세운 사람이 '탕'이야. 그는 상족 출신이어서 이 나라를 '상나라'라고 부른단다. 사실 상나라도 오랫동안 전설 속의 왕조로 여겨졌어. 그러나 1899년 말라리아의 특효약으로 알려진 용골 표면의 글자에 주목한 학자들 덕분에 상나라의 존재가 드러나게 되었단다. 당시 한약방에서는 그들이 가져오는 용골이 어느 지역의 것인지 비밀로 하고 있었어. 아무래도 상업적인 이윤을 위해서 알리고 싶지는 않았던 모양이야. 학자들의 탐문으로 용골은 상나라의 도읍지인 허난성 안양현 샤오툰촌의 농민들이 파낸 것으로 밝혀졌어. 1928년 이후 15차례의 발굴로 '갑골 문자'가 새겨진 골편 10만여 점, 당시 사용되었던 청동기, 궁전 터, 거대한 지하분묘(무덤)가 발견되었단다. 상나라의 마지막 수도가 은허라서 이 나라를 은나라라고도 부르지.

represent ⓥ to be a sign or mark that means something

represent는 '강조'의 의미를 담고 있는 접두사 re-와 '나타내다, 내보이다'를 뜻하는 present가 합쳐진 것이다. 즉 '확실하게 내보이다, 정확하게 나타내다'라는 뜻이다. 예를 들어 십자가 모양을 보면, 기독교나 적십자를 나타낸다는 것을 알 수 있다.

The pictograms look almost exactly like the words they represent. 그림 문자들은 그것이 나타내는 글자와 거의 똑같이 생겼다.

3 Farming in Ancient China

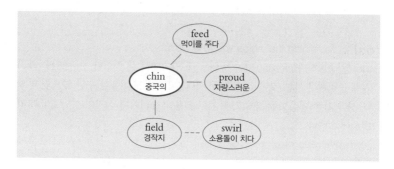

field ⓝ a piece of ground used for a particular purpose

흔히 field라고 하면 그냥 넓고 탁 트인 땅이나 들판을 떠올리지만, field의 정확한 뜻은 '특정한 목적을 위해 사용하는 넓은 땅' 또는 '특정한 용도에 맞는 모습을 취하고 있는 넓은 땅'이다. 그래서 풀이 많이 난 들판은 grass field, 벼가 자라는 '논'은 rice field, 축구장은 soccer field라고 한다. 농촌 지역을 말하면서 fields라고 하면 '농경과 목축 등을 위해 사용하는 넓은 땅'을 의미한다.

But near the Yellow River in China, whole fields stayed wet for months and months. 그러나 중국의 황허 강 근방에서는 모든 경작지가 여러 달 동안 축축한 상태로 있었다.

feed ⓥ to give food to a person or an animal

food와 feed 모두 같은 고대 영어의 단어에서 유래했다. food는 '먹을 것, 먹이, 식량'이고, feed는 food를 '먹이다'라는 뜻이다. 대개 혼자서는 먹을 것을 찾아 먹을 수 없는 가축이나 애완동물, 어린아이에게 쓴다. feed는 '먹이, 모이'를 뜻하는 명사형으로도 자주 쓰인다. '동물 사료'는 animal feed, '닭 모이'가 chicken feed이다.

Chin fed the three pigs and the four chickens every morning. 친은 매일 아침 세 마리의 돼지와 네 마리의 닭에게 먹이를 주었다.

proud ⓐ feeling very pleased about your actions or people around you because you think they are very good

자신이 한 행동, 가족이나 친구 등에 대해 '자랑스러워하는' 마음을 표현하는 형용사이다. 흔히 'be proud of ~'의 형태로 쓴다. '자부심, 자랑스러움'을 뜻하는 명사형 pride도 proud와 어원이 같다. 모두 '가치(value)'라는 뜻을 담고 있다.
But he was proud of the work he had done. 그는 자신이 한 일에 대해 자랑스러워했다.

swirl ⓥ to move quickly in a twisting, circular pattern

swirl에서 s는 '강조(세게)'의 의미이고, wirl은 '빙글 돌다'를 뜻하는 whirl의 다른 형태이다. 그래서 swirl은 '몸을 꼬듯, 빙빙 돌 듯 세차게 움직이다, 소용돌이치다'라는 뜻이다. '빙글 돌리다'라는 타동사로도 쓰인다.
Great rushing floods swirled down on our village and swept our houses away. 거대하게 밀려드는 홍수가 소용돌이치듯 우리 마을을 덮쳐 우리 집을 휩쓸었다.

The Story of the World

Chapter 11
Ancient Africa

1 Ancient Peoples of West Africa

🌐 아프리카는 대서양과 인도양, 지중해로 둘러싸인, 세계에서 두 번째로 큰 대륙이다. Africa라는 말은 고대 로마인들이 북아프리카의 카르타고 사람들을 Afri라고 부른 데에서 유래했다. 동북쪽에는 이집트 문명의 토대가 된 나일 강이 흐르고, 서북쪽에는 세계 최대의 사막인 사하라(Sahara Desert)가 있으며 남쪽으로는 밀림과 초원 지대가 펼쳐져 있다. 오스트랄로피테쿠스를 비롯해 많은 고생(古生) 인류의 화석이 발견되면서 현생 인류가 아프리카에서 진화되어 전 세계로 퍼져 나갔다는 아프리카 기원설(起源說)이 등장했다.

When you first started to learn about ancient times, you read about the nomads who settled in the Fertile Crescent, between the Tigris and the Euphrates rivers. If you were to put your finger on a map right between those two rivers and then move your finger *right*, you would cross over the land of the Sumerians and of the Babylonians and the Assyrians. You would cross the top part of India, where Mohenjo-Daro used to be. If you kept on going right, you would end up in China, where Chin and his family grew their crops beside the Yellow River.

If you put your finger on the Fertile Crescent and then moved it *left*, you would come to Egypt and the Nile River, where the pharaohs lived. ˙We know a great deal about the history of Egypt, because the Egyptians left thousands and thousands of *artifacts* (treasures and everyday objects) behind them. Archaeologists dug up the artifacts and used them to learn more about ancient Egypt. And the Egyptians also left us writing on stone tablets. Historians read these tablets and wrote down the history of the ancient Egyptian empire.

But if you keep moving your finger on down the Nile River, you will see that Egypt is only one small part of a whole huge

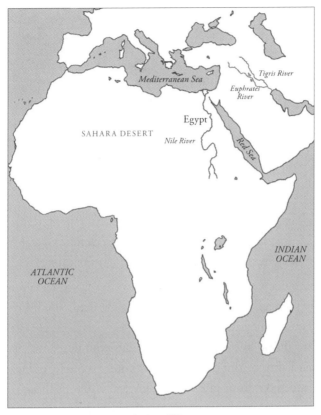

Ancient Africa

continent (a large piece of land with many countries on it). This continent is called Africa.

The people of Africa did not leave written records or thousands of artifacts behind them. So we don't know as much about ancient Africa as we do about ancient Egypt. But we do know that people have lived in Africa from the very earliest times.

If you were to move your finger left from the Nile River, you would come to a huge, sandy desert—the Sahara Desert. Today, the Sahara Desert is as hot and dry as an oven. The ground is cracked and parched. Sand drifts over the iron-hard ground and piles up in huge drifts called dunes. The only water lies in *oases*—

little patches of land where water collects and a few scrubby palm trees can grow. Tiny villages sometimes settle in these oases. The people raise desert animals that don't need much water—sheep, camels, and goats. They eat the dates that grow on the palm trees. Sometimes, one tree is owned by several families who share it!

Life in the Sahara Desert is difficult and dangerous. But long ago, this part of Africa wasn't a desert. It was a green, fertile place full of water and trees. Rivers and streams used to run where rocky, dried valleys now lie. Grassy meadows once grew where shifting sands now blow. Herds of gazelles and antelopes roamed through the green plains. Fish, crocodiles, and hippopotami swam in the rivers. Wild cows and sheep lived in the forests. The people of the Sahara were farmers, just like those who lived in the Fertile Crescent. They hunted wild animals and raised their own plants and animals for food.

How do we know this? Archaeologists who dug down through the hard dirt of the Sahara Desert found ancient pollen from trees and seeds from grasses and flowers. None of these trees or flowers grow in the Sahara today—they left their seeds long, long ago. The archaeologists also found bones of animals that used to live in the Sahara, back when there was enough water for them. In one place, the people who lived in a Saharan village had eaten a feast of turtle. There were hundreds of shells that had been cracked open for their meat. In another place, the villagers had eaten an entire giraffe—except for its head.

The ancient people of Africa also left paintings behind them. They drew pictures of their way of life on the stone walls of caves. In these paintings, we see men growing crops and taking care of herds of animals. We see women in beautiful clothes, riding tame cows. These pictures tell us about the way the Sahara used to be.

But then something happened in the Sahara. The rains got scarcer and scarcer. Trees began to wither and die. The grass died too, and the ground dried up until it was nothing more than dust and sand. The rivers stopped flowing and the streams disappeared. The animals went further and further south, down to the parts of Africa where there was still water and food. And the people of the Sahara went south too. They traveled for weeks and weeks. They settled around the lakes and rivers in central Africa and began a new life. And above them, the Sahara turned into desert.

From now on, Africa would be divided by the huge dangerous desert. Up along the coast of the Mediterranean Sea, people from Mesopotamia and Egypt would settle down and live in the northern part of Africa. And down below the Sahara Desert, the people of Africa would live for centuries in peace, cut off from the rest of the ancient world by the massive sands between them.

2 Anansi and Turtle

아난시 이야기는 아주 오래전부터 서아프리카의 아샨티(Ashanti) 부족이 대대로 전해온 구전 문학이다. '아난시'라는 말 자체가 '거미'라는 뜻이 있는데, 이야기 속에서 주인공 아난시는 거미나 인간의 모습으로 등장한다. 대부분의 이야기는 지혜와 교훈을 주는 내용으로 우화 형식을 띠고 있다. 아난시 이야기는 서아프리카 전역으로 퍼졌고, 흑인 노예들의 이동으로 인해 카리브해 연안과 중앙아메리카 지역에도 전래되었다.

The ancient people of Africa didn't leave mummies or clay tablets behind them. But they did leave stories, passed down from person to person.

Anansi the Spider is a favorite character of African storytellers.

Anansi is a tricky spider who often gets his way. But sometimes he is outwitted. Here is a story about Anansi and his friend Turtle. It comes from the Yoruba people of Nigeria, a West African country that is just south of the Sahara Desert. In this story, Anansi is hungry, and he's looking forward to eating a good supper of yams! Yams are a little bit like potatoes, only rough on the outside like a coconut. The people of Africa have grown them in the ground for thousands of years.

Anansi the Spider was hungry! He had dug some of the fattest yams ever out of his garden, and had baked them carefully in his clay oven. Now they were ready to come out. The yams smelled wonderful, and he couldn't wait to dig in.

But just as he was sitting down to his meal, along wandered Turtle. Now, Anansi and Turtle were friends. But when Anansi looked at his yams and then looked at Turtle, he thought, "There are just enough yams for me! If Turtle eats half of them, I'll still be hungry!"

"Oh, Anansi!" Turtle said. "How wonderful those yams smell! It has taken me all day to crawl over to your house for a visit, and I haven't eaten my lunch or my supper. Please, share your yams with me."

Now, in Africa it is the custom to share your meal with any visitor who asks. So Anansi couldn't say no. He said grumpily, "I would be happy to share my yams with you, Turtle. Have a seat. Help yourself."

Turtle sat down and reached for the fattest yam. But just as he was about to touch it, Anansi shouted, "Stop! Are you going to eat with those filthy flippers? Really, Turtle, don't you think you should wash off first?"

Now, Turtle had been crawling all day. He was dirty and

sandy and hadn't come across any water. But he looked at his flippers. They certainly were dirty.

"Where should I wash?" he said.

"Go wash in the river," Anansi said. "It's only half a mile away."

Poor Turtle! He got up and crawled off to the river to wash his flippers. By the time he came back, the yams were half gone. Anansi said with his mouth full, "Sorry, Turtle, you were so long that I had to start eating. But go ahead and have some yams."

Turtle reached for the yams. But his flippers had gotten dirty again from his journey back up from the river. "Turtle!" Anansi yelled. "Didn't I say that you should wash yourself off? Don't come to the table dirty!"

Turtle crawled wearily off to wash himself again. When he climbed slowly back up from the river, he was very careful to stay on the grass. But when he got to the table and reached out his clean flipper for a yam, the last crumbs were gone.

Turtle looked sadly at the empty platter.

"Well," he said, after a little while, "thank you for inviting me to supper, Anansi. The next time you come by my house, be sure to share my dinner with me."

And he got down and crawled away, still hungry.

Anansi the Spider and Turtle

A few days later, Anansi was going by Turtle's house on the riverbank. "Turtle told me that he would share his food with me," he thought. "I'll stop and eat with him." So he bounced up and knocked on Turtle's door. "Turtle, Turtle!" he cried. "I'm ready for supper!"

Turtle opened the door and blinked at Anansi. "Supper is all ready," he said. "Come along with me. It's right down here." And with that he led Anansi to the river's edge. "I've set the table right down there at the bottom of the water," he said. "Dive on down and eat." And with that he slipped into the water, swam down to the river's bottom, and started to eat.

Anansi ran back and forth on the bank. First he tried jumping into the water. But he was so light that he floated on the top. He tried to swim down. He tried to make himself sink. But nothing worked. Down below, he could see Turtle polishing off all the food.

Finally Anansi stuffed the pockets of his tiny jacket full of pebbles and jumped back into the water. He sank like a stone right down to the bottom, where Turtle was eating his way through a whole platter full of delicious food.

Turtle pushed the platter over. "Here," he said. "Have some. But first, Anansi, take off your jacket. It's so rude to wear a coat at the table."

Anansi took off his jacket. And as soon as it was off his shoulders, he popped right back up to the surface of the water. When he stuck his head underwater, he could just see Turtle finishing off the very last morsel of food.

"Thank you for supper, Turtle," he said gloomily. And he swam back to the river bank, wet and hungry.

•Moral: If you try to be too smart, you might find that someone else outsmarts you instead.

3 Anansi and the Make-Believe Food

'아난시 이야기'처럼 동물이 등장하는 이야기를 우화(寓話)라고 하는데, 영어로 는 fable이다. 우화의 특징 중 하나는 항상 교훈적인 내용이 담긴다는 점인데, 이때 '교훈'을 moral이라고 한다. moral은 '도덕, 도덕을 배우게 되는 교훈'을 뜻한다.

Another story about Anansi tells us about a time when food was very scarce and the rivers and streams were drying up. It may even come from the days when the people of Africa were leaving the Sahara for greener places. Here is the story:

There had been no rain for many, many days. The crops had all withered away. The animals were starving. Anansi and his whole village were hungry too. And day after day, the sun shone down and the blue sky stayed empty of clouds.

Finally, Anansi said, "If someone doesn't go find some food, we will all die of hunger! I am going to walk until I find a village where there is food, and bring some back for all of us.

So Anansi started out. He walked and he walked and he walked until the sun went down. He walked all night. When the sky began to get light the next morning, he saw smoke from the chimneys of a village, far in the distance.

He walked until he reached the village. And then he stood with his mouth open. The village was full of—cassava! Cassava are vegetable roots that look like large potatoes. Anansi loved roasted cassava almost as much as he loved yams. And in this village, there were no people, just cassava—walking around in the streets, sweeping the steps of their huts, and sitting under the palm trees, talking to each other. When the cassava saw him, they all jumped up.

"A visitor! A visitor!" they said. "Would you like to eat us roasted, boiled, or fried?"

"I—I don't care," Anansi stammered.

"Roasted!" all the cassava cried. They jumped into the fire one by one until they were nicely roasted, and then lined up for Anansi to eat them. He was just getting ready to take a bite out of the first one when he saw another spire of smoke, far away.

"What is that?" he asked.

"Oh, that's just the plantain village," the cassava said. "Aren't you going to eat us?"

Now, a plantain is like a banana. And Anansi liked fried plantain even more than he liked roasted cassava. So even though the cassava begged him to stay and eat them, Anansi jumped up and ran towards the plantain village.

It took him hours to get there, and by the time he arrived he was hot and thirsty and even hungrier. But all the plantains ran out to meet him. The little baby plantains danced around his feet, and the big plantains jumped up and down for joy. "How would you like to eat us?" they asked. "Roasted, boiled, or fried?"

"Any way you want!" Anansi cried.

"Fried!" the plantains shouted. So they jumped into a big pot of oil, one by one, and lined up to be eaten. But just as Anansi was getting ready to sink his teeth into the first one, he saw another spire of smoke, far off in the distance.

"What's that?" he asked.

"Oh, that's just the rice village," the plantains said. "Aren't you going to eat us?"

Now, if there was one thing that Anansi liked even more than a roasted plantain, it was a big bowl of boiled rice. So even though the plantains begged him to stay and eat them, Anansi got up and began to walk towards the rice village.

By the time he reached it, the sun was setting. He was so hungry that he grabbed the first little pieces of rice who ran out to meet him and started to eat them raw. But the other rice grains squeaked, "No, no! We will cook ourselves! How would you like to eat us—roasted, boiled, or fried?"

"Any way you like!" Anansi moaned. "Just feed me!"

"Boiled!" the rice shouted. So the rice grains threw themselves into a big pot of boiling water and climbed out into a big bowl. Just as Anansi was getting ready to plunge his hand into the bowl, he saw one more spire of smoke.

"What's that?" he asked.

"We don't know!" the rice grains shrilled at him. "Just eat us!" But Anansi thought, "Each village has been better than the one before! If I can get to that village, I'll get to eat something even better than rice!" So he left the bowl of rice and ran towards the strange village.

It was night-time when he got there. He ran eagerly into the center of the town—and stopped. It was his own village, and there was no food anywhere to be seen. Anansi fainted. When he woke up, the people of his village were all gathered around him. "Here," they said. "We boiled a fish bone and made you some fish-bone-and-water soup. It's all we have. Where have you been?"

Anansi told them all about the cassava village, the plantain village, and the rice village. But no one could ever find those villages again.

What do you think the moral of this story is? Maybe it is "Don't be greedy—eat whatever you're given." 📖

Note to Parent: The climate changed in the Sahara around 3500 BC/BCE. We know little about the cultures that flourished in southern Africa before medieval times; the second volume of The Story of the World deals much more extensively with African history.

The Story of the Words

Chapter 11 Ancient Africa

1 Ancient Peoples of West Africa

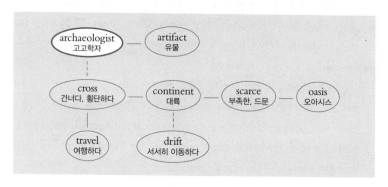

cross Ⓥ to go over from one side of something to the other

가로줄 위에 세로줄을 긋는 것이나 세로줄 위에 가로줄을 긋는 것, 이렇게 십자가(cross) 형태의 움직임을 표현하는 동사이다. '강을 건너다'는 to cross the river이고, '도로를 건너다'는 to cross the road이다. 즉 cross는 '가로지르다, 건너다, 횡단하다'라는 뜻이다.

If you were to put your finger on a map right between those two rivers and then move your finger *right*, you would cross over the land of the Sumerians and of the Babylonians and the Assyrians. 지도 위에서 손가락을 바로 그 두 강 사이에 대고서 오른쪽으로 움직이면 수메르인과 바빌로니아인, 아시리아인이 살던 땅 위를 가로지르게 된다.

artifact Ⓝ an object that was made in the past and is historically important

artifact는 artefact로 표기하기도 한다. artifact는 라틴어에서 와서 arti는 '예술기법을 사용해(by using art)'라는 뜻이고, fact는 '만들어진 것(something made)'을 뜻한다. 즉 '예술적[기술적]으로 만들어진 것'이 artifact이다. 과거에 만들어진 다양한 예술 작품, 농업기구나 무기류, 생활용품 등의 역사적으로 가치 있는 것들을 통칭하는 용어이다.

We know a great deal about the history of Egypt, because the Egyptians left thousands and thousands of *artifacts* (treasures and everyday objects) behind them. 우리는 이집트의 역사에 대해 상당히 많은 것을 알고 있다. 이집트인들이 대단히 많은 유물(보물과 일상용품)을 남겨 놓았기 때문이다.

archaeologist ⓝ someone who studies very old things made by people who lived a long time ago

archaeology는 '고고학(考古學)'이고, archaeologist는 '고고학자'이다. archeo 는 '고대의(ancient), 먼 옛날의'라는 뜻이고, -logy는 '학문(science, study)'을 뜻한다. 즉 archaeology는 고고학(考古學)이라는 말로 '옛것을 고찰하는 학문'이라는 뜻이다.

Archaeologists dug up the artifacts and used them to learn more about ancient Egypt. 고고학자들은 유물을 발굴했고, 그것을 활용해 고대 이집트에 대해 더 많은 것을 알아냈다.

continent ⓝ a large mass of land that has many countries

continent는 분명 대단히 넓은 땅이다. 가도 가도 '계속 나오는 땅(continuous land)'을 뜻하는 라틴어 continens에서 온 단어이기 때문이다. 그래서 우리말로도 '넓은 땅'이라는 뜻의 '대륙(大陸)'이다. 지리학적으로 아시아, 유럽, 아프리카, 북아메리카, 남아메리카, 오스트레일리아, 남극의 7개 대륙으로 나뉜다.

But if you keep moving your finger on down the Nile River, you will see that Egypt is only one small part of a whole huge continent (a large piece of land with many countries on it). 그런데 나일 강 밑으로 손가락을 계속 움직이면, 이집트는 단지 하나의 거대한 대륙(많은 나라들이 있는 큰 땅덩어리)의 작은 일부분이라는 사실을 알게 될 것이다.

drift ⓥ to move slowly through the air or on the water / ⓝ a large pile of sand or snow formed by the wind

drift는 원래 바람에 휩쓸려 쌓인 눈 더미를 일컫는 단어이어서 명사형으로 '바람에 휩쓸려 쌓인 더미'를 뜻한다. 바람을 타고 천천히 움직이는 모습을 표현하는 동사형으로는 '서서히 이동하다, (물, 공기 위로) 떠가다'라는 뜻이다. 예문에서 첫 번째 drift는 동사형이고, 두 번째 drift는 명사형이다.

Sand drifts over the iron-hard ground and piles up in huge drifts called dunes. 모래는 바람을 타고 단단한 땅 위를 서서히 이동해 거대한 모래더미로 쌓이는데, 이것을 '사구(砂丘)'라고 한다.

oasis ⓝ a place in the desert with water and trees

oases는 oasis의 복수형이다. 사막에서 물이 있고 식물이 자라는 지역을 오아시스라고 한다. 물이 없으면 살 수 없기 때문에 사막 지형에서는 사람들이 오아시스에 모여 살 수밖에 없으므로, oasis는 '사는 곳(a place to live)'을 뜻하는 이집트어에서 온 말이다.

The only water lies in oases—little patches of land where water collects and a few scrubby palm trees can grow. 물은 오아시스에만 있다. 오아시스는 물이 고여 있고, 몇 그루의 키 작은 야자나무들이 자랄 수 있는 좁은 땅을 말한다.

scarce ⓐ not enough; not very much of

scarce는 수, 양, 크기 등이 적거나 작다는 의미를 담은 '부족한, 드문'의 뜻으로 쓰인다. scarcer는 scarce의 비교급으로 '더 부족한, 더 드문'을 뜻한다.

The rains got scarcer and scarcer. 내리는 비의 양이 점점 더 줄어들었다.

travel ⓥ to go or move from one place to another, usually far away

travel을 보면 재미와 여흥을 위해 떠나는 '여행'을 떠올리는데, 그것은 travel이 갖고 있는 의미의 일부이다. '집 떠나면 고생이다'라는 말이 있듯이 오히려 travel은 '고생스러운 여행'이라는 의미로 더 자주 쓰이는데, 원래 travail(고생, 고역)에서 파생된 단어이다. travel의 기본적인 의미는 '먼 거리를 이동하다'이다.

They traveled for weeks and weeks. 그들은 몇 주동안, 또 몇 주동안 이동했다.

> **Q 우리 모두의 고향이 아프리카라고요?**
>
> **A** 이런 말을 들으면 설마! 하면서 고개를 젓는 사람이 많을 거야. 그러나 사실이란다. 아프리카는 세상에서 가장 오래된 대륙이고, 현생 인류가 태어난 곳이기도 해. '호모 사피엔스'라는 말 들어봤니? 사피엔스는 슬기롭다는 뜻으로, 호모 사피엔스는 '지혜로운 사람'이야. 바로 그들이 출현한 곳이 약 20만 년 전의 동아프리카야.
>
> 그곳에서 고고학자들이 최초의 여성 화석을 발견하여 '이브'라는 이름을 붙였어. 그 이름이 붙여진 여성이 우리 모두의 조상이라는 사실이 놀랍지 않니? 10만 년 전에 동아프리카를 떠난 소그룹의 호모 사피엔스가 시나이 반도를 넘어 지금의 중동 지역으로 진출했고, 그곳에서 점점 다른 지역으로 퍼져나간 거야. 이들이 4만 년 전 유럽 대륙에 도착했고, 1만 5천 년 전에는 아직 육지로 연결되어 있던 지금의 베링 해협을 건너 아시아로, 북아

2 Anansi and Turtle

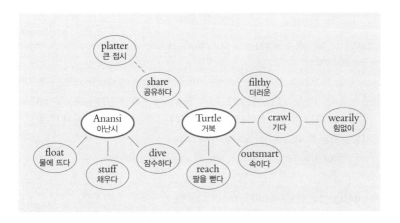

share ⓥ to divide something between two or more people
어떤 것을 여럿이 함께 사용하고, 소유하고, 나누는 것을 표현하는 동사로, '공
유하다, 함께 쓰다'이다. 물건을 share하면 그 물건은 나중에도 그대로 있지만,
음식을 share하면 '나누어(divide) 먹다'라는 의미이다.
Please, share your yams with me. 네 얌을 나와 나누어 먹자.

reach ⓥ to stretch out your hand to touch or hold something
reach는 일정 거리를 이동해 '어떤 곳에 도착하다(to arrive somewhere)'라는 뜻
이지만, 더 기본적인 의미는 무언가 손으로 잡거나 만지기 위해 '팔을 뻗다'이
다. 그래서 권투 중계에서 선수의 팔 길이를 말할 때 '리치(reach)가 길다, 짧다'
라고 하거나, The boy was too small to reach the book on the shelf(그 소년
은 너무 작아서 서가의 책에 손이 닿지 않았다)처럼 쓸 수 있다.
Turtle sat down and reached for the fattest yam. 거북은 자리에 앉아 가장 통통한 얌
을 잡기 위해 팔을 뻗었다.

filthy ⓐ very dirty

filthy는 '더러운 오물'을 뜻하는 filth에 -y가 붙은 형용사형이다. filth는 원래 '썩은 것, 부패'를 뜻하는 고대 영어에서 유래한 것이다. 세상에 부패한 것만큼 '더러운' 것이 없다.

Are you going to eat with those filthy flippers? 너 그 더러운 손[지느러미발]으로 먹으려는 거니?

crawl ⓥ to move along on your hands and knees with your body close to the ground

crawl은 '엎드려서 기다'라는 뜻이다. Turtle had been crawling all day는 '거북은 종일 기어왔다'라는 뜻이다. 거북 입장에서는 그냥 걷는(walk) 것인데, 느리게 걷기 때문에 기는 것처럼 보이는 것이다. 걸음이 느린 것 중에서 벌레들의 이동을 표현할 때도 흔히 crawl을 쓴다.

Now, Turtle had been crawling all day. 자, 거북은 종일 기어왔다.

wearily ⓐ in a tired way

wear(동사) → weary(형용사) → wearily(부사)처럼 형태가 변한다. 동사형 wear는 '옷을 입다'라는 뜻이다. 옷을 계속 입다 보면 낡고 해어진다. 그래서 wear에는 '낡다, 닳다, 해어지다'라는 뜻도 있다. 몸과 정신에 대해 말할 때는 '지친, 피곤한, 싫증 난'의 뜻으로 쓰인다.

Turtle crawled wearily off to wash himself again. 거북은 다시 몸을 씻기 위해 힘없이 기어서 출발했다.

dive ⓥ to jump into water with your head and arms going in first

물속으로 상체부터 들어가게 뛰어드는 행동이 dive이다. '다이빙(diving) 선수'의 동작을 떠올리면 쉽게 이해된다. 그런데 '물속에서 헤엄치는(to swim under water)' 동작, 즉 '잠수하다'도 dive이다. 그래서 '다이빙 선수'뿐만 아니라 '잠수부'도 diver라고 부른다.

Dive on down and eat. 밑으로 잠수해서 먹어.

float ⓥ to stay on the surface of a liquid

액체 속으로 가라앉지(sink) 않고 표면에 뜨는 것이 float이다. '뜨다, 띄우다, 떠가다'라는 뜻으로 쓴다. 왜 물에 뜰까? 잠수를 못하는 거미(Anansi)의 경우를 보면 너무 가벼우면 물속으로 가라앉지 않고 뜬다는 것을 알 수 있다.

But he was so light that he floated on the top. 그러나 그는 너무 가벼워서 물 위에 떴다.

stuff ⓥ to fill space with something

속이 빈 공간에 뭔가를 채워 넣는 것이 바로 stuff이다. 그런데 채울 때 욱여 넣거나 꽉 채우는 느낌이 있어야 stuff를 쓸 수 있다. a pillow stuffed with feathers(깃털이 가득 채워진 베개)처럼 쓸 수 있는데, 동물을 박제할 때도 빈 가죽 속에 뭔가를 가득 채워 넣기 때문에 stuffed tiger(박제된 호랑이)라고 표현한다.

Finally Anansi stuffed the pockets of his tiny jacket full of pebbles and jumped back into the water. 마침내 아난시는 작은 재킷의 주머니에 조약돌을 가득 채우고서 다시 물속으로 뛰어들었다.

platter ⓝ a large plate used for serving food

음식이 담긴 그릇(dish, bowl)을 나르는 '쟁반'이나 음식을 담는 '큰 접시'를 뜻한다. platter에서 plat은 원래 '평평한(flat)'을 뜻하는 희랍어에서 유래하여 그 자체로 a large dish(큰 접시)라는 뜻이었다. '둥근 접시'를 일컫는 plate와도 어원이 같다.

He sank like a stone right down to the bottom, where Turtle was eating his way through a whole platter full of delicious food. 아난시는 마치 돌멩이처럼 곧장 바닥으로 가라앉았는데, 강바닥에서는 거북이 커다란 접시에 가득 담긴 맛있는 음식을 마음껏 먹고 있었다.

outsmart ⓥ to gain an advantage over someone using tricks or cleverness

outsmart에서 out은 '능가하는(better than, more than)'이고, smart는 '영리한, 똑똑한'을 뜻한다. 즉 '남보다 더 영리하고 똑똑하다'라는 의미이다. smart는 형용사형이지만, outsmart는 동사형으로만 써서 '속임수나 머리를 써서 다른 사람에게서 이익을 취하다'라는 뜻이다.

If you try to be too smart, you might find that someone else outsmarts you instead. 너무 똑똑하게 굴려고 하면, 도리어 다른 사람이 당신을 속이는 일이 생길 수도 있다.

3 Anansi and the Make-Believe food

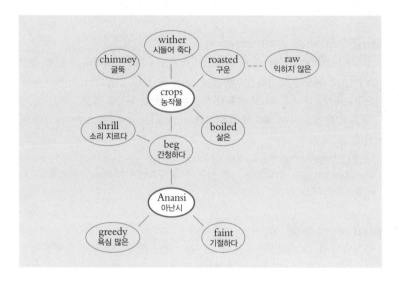

wither ⓥ to become drier and smaller, and then to die
wither는 식물이 '시들고 말라서 죽다'라는 뜻이다. wither는 weather가 변형
되어 생겼는데, weather에는 '날씨(햇빛, 바람 등) 때문에 형태나 성질이 변하다'
라는 뜻이 있다. 나물이나 과일을 햇빛과 바람에 말리면 형체가 쪼그라든다.
이 의미를 차용하여 단어의 형태를 weather에서 wither로 바꾸어 쓴 것이다.
The crops had all withered away. 농작물이 모두 시들어 죽어서 없어졌다.

chimney ⓝ a pipe that allows smoke to go up and out of a building
《아기 돼지 삼형제》에서 늑대가 뜨거운 최후를 맞는 곳이 바로 chimney
다. chimney는 원래 '불을 때는 곳, 아궁이'를 뜻했는데, 아궁이나 화로는
fireplace, furnace로 대체되었고, 연기를 뿜아내는 '굴뚝'만 chimney로 남은
것이다.
When the sky began to get light the next morning, he saw smoke from the
chimneys of a village, far in the distance. 다음날 아침, 하늘이 다시 밝아오기 시작할
때, 그는 아주 멀리 어떤 마을의 굴뚝에서 연기가 나는 것을 보게 되었다.

roasted ⓐ cooked over a fire or in an oven
음식을 직접 불에 굽거나 오븐의 뜨거운 온도로 굽는 조리법을 roast라고 한다.

고기를 굽거나 요리할 때 주로 사용하는 방법인데, 형용사 roasted를 써서 구운 닭고기나 닭구이는 roasted chicken, 갈비구이는 roasted ribs라고 한다. roast 는 '볶다'는 뜻으로도 쓸 수 있어서 '볶은 커피콩'을 roasted coffee beans라고 한다. 물이나 기름을 사용하지 않고, 불과 열로만 요리한 음식에 모두 roasted 를 붙일 수 있다.

Anansi loved roasted cassava almost as much as he loved yams. 아난시는 얌을 좋 아하는 만큼 구운 카사바도 무척 좋아했다.

beg ⓥ to ask someone very strongly for something

뭔가를 요청할 때는 I asked her to stay with me(난 그녀에게 곁에 있어 달라고 부탁했다)처럼 ask로 표현하면 되지만, 간절히 원할 때는 I begged her to stay with me처럼 beg를 써야 느낌이 처절해진다. 옛날에는 beg해서 얻을 것이 주 로 음식과 돈이어서 '구걸하다'라는 뜻으로 쓰였고, beggar가 '거지'이다. 상 대에게 무언가를 구걸하듯 청해야 한다면 Please stay with me. I'm begging you처럼 말하면 된다.

So even though the cassava begged him to stay and eat them, Anansi jumped up and ran towards the plantain village. 그래서 카사바가 가지 말고 자신들을 먹어달라고 간청했지만, 아난시는 자리를 박차고 일어나 플랜테인 마을을 향해 뛰어갔다.

boiled ⓐ cooked in very hot water

boil은 '거품(bubble), 거품이 나다'를 뜻하는 라틴어에서 유래한 것이다. 물을 가열해 100 °C가 넘으면 '보글보글' 거품을 내며 끓기 때문에, boil은 '끓이다, 끓다'라는 뜻이다. 물을 붓고 요리할 때도 boil을 써서 찌개, 국 등을 끓이면 to boil soup이라고 한다. '삶다, 데치다'는 것도 boil이다. 쌀밥은 boiled rice, 삶 은 달걀은 boiled egg, 데친 시금치는 boiled spinach라고 한다.

Now, if there was one thing that Anansi liked even more than a roasted plantain, it was a big bowl of boiled rice. 자, 아난시가 구운 플랜테인보다 훨씬 더 좋아하는 것 하 나가 있다면, 그것은 커다란 공기에 담긴 쌀밥이었다.

raw ⓐ not cooked

raw는 '날것의, 익히지 않은'을 뜻하는 형용사로, 요리되지 않은 상태의 음식을 말한다. raw meat는 '날고기'이고, 일본어에서 유래한 sashimi(생선회)도 sliced raw fish(저민 날생선)로 쓸 수 있다. 또 Oyster can be eaten raw(굴은 날것 상태 로 먹어도 된다)처럼 쓸 수 있다.

He was so hungry that he grabbed the first little pieces of rice who ran out to meet him and started to eat them raw. 그는 배가 너무 고픈 나머지, 그를 맞으러 앞서서 뛰어나온 쌀을 붙잡아 생으로 먹기 시작했다.

shrill ⓥ to complain loudly

소리가 듣기 싫게 '크거나(loud)' 톤이 '높을(high-pitched)' 때 shrill을 쓴다. a shrill voice(날카로운 목소리)처럼 형용사나, She shrilled at me(그녀는 내게 소리를 질렀다)처럼 동사로도 쓸 수 있다. 대개 심하게 아프거나, 짜증 날 때, 놀랄 때 '새된' 목소리가 나오는데, shrill에는 이런 감정이 실려 있다.

"We don't know!" the rice grains shrilled at him. "우린 몰라요!" 쌀들이 그에게 소리를 질렀다.

faint ⓥ to suddenly become unconscious for a short time

faint의 어원은 무척 흥미롭다. '실신하다, 기절하다'라는 뜻의 동사형 faint는 원래 '가장하다(pretend), 속이다(deceive), 비겁하다(be cowardly)'라는 뜻의 고대 프랑스어에서 유래했다. 이 의미는 같은 어원에서 온 feint에 그대로 남아 있다. 축구에서 '페인트(feint) 동작'은 상대 선수를 '속이는' 동작이다. 아마도 어떤 책임을 회피할 목적으로 기절한 척하기 때문에 faint가 쓰인 듯하다.

Anansi fainted. 아난시는 기절했다.

greedy ⓐ wanting too much of something

너무 많은 것을 원하는 사람은 '욕심이 과한' 사람이다. 이런 사람에게는 Don't be greedy!라고 충고해야 한다. 이처럼 greedy는 '욕심 많은, 탐욕스러운'을 뜻하는 형용사이다. '과욕, 탐욕'을 뜻하는 명사형은 greed이다. 탐욕의 대상을 표현하고자 할 때는, 'greedy for ~'를 쓴다. She is greedy for money라고 하면 '그녀는 돈 욕심이 많다'라는 의미이다.

Maybe it is "Don't be greedy—eat whatever you're given." 아마도 교훈은 '너무 욕심 내지 말고, 무엇이 됐든 주어진 것을 먹어라'일 것이다.

Chapter 12
The Middle Kingdom
of Egypt

1 Egypt Invades Nubia

이집트의 중(中)왕국 시대는 기원전 2040년경부터 1750년경까지 제11 왕조 와 제12 왕조를 거치는 시대를 말한다. 고왕국 시대가 끝나며 이집트는 다시 분열 되었는데, 상(上)이집트의 제11 왕조의 네 번째 왕인 멘투호셉 2세가 다시 이집트를 통일함으로써 이집트 중왕국 시대가 열리게 된다. 이후 재상 출신으로 파라오가 된 아메네메트 1세가 제12 왕조를 열고 중왕국 시대의 번영을 이끌게 되지만, 기원전 17세기에 세력을 키운 힉소스인들에게 이집트가 점령당하면서 고왕국 시대는 막 을 내린다.

Do you remember reading about the Old Kingdom of Egypt? The Egyptians of the Old Kingdom built pyramids and temples. They traded with the Babylonians and the Assyrians. They worshipped their gods, made mummies, and buried treasure along with them. Egypt had good pharaohs and a strong army. Life in Egypt was good.

But these peaceful times didn't last. The pharaohs of Egypt became weaker and weaker. They lost control of their armies. They even lost control of their own courts and temples. Priests and palace officials fought over who would be in charge. Egypt's power started to vanish. For a little while, it seemed that Egypt might fall apart, just like the kingdom of Sargon did.

But then, around 1991 BC/BCE, a new ruler came to the throne of Egypt. His name was Amenemhet. Amenemhet wasn't a pharaoh—he just worked for the government. But he was determined to make Egypt strong again. He seized the throne and became the new pharaoh of Egypt. This was the beginning of a new time in Egypt's history—the Middle Kingdom of Egypt. During the Middle Kingdom, Egypt became a powerful country once more.

Amenemhet decided that his first job was to make Egypt bigger. He planned to conquer the countries that surrounded Egypt. And his first target was the kingdom of Nubia.

Nubia was south of Egypt, in Africa. Unlike the people of ancient West Africa, the Nubians didn't go down into the central part of Africa. After all, they had the Nile River for water, and the rich mud of the Nile overflow for their crops. So the Nubian people stayed in their own country.

The Nubians traveled up the Nile River to sell many beautiful things to the Egyptians. They sold ivory, animal furs, ostrich feathers, and gems. And they brought gold up into Egypt. Amenemhet knew that the Nubians dug gold out of the hills and ground of their kingdom. He thought that if he could become the ruler of Nubia, he would have plenty of treasure to make him rich.

So Amenemhet set off to conquer Nubia. He fought dozens of battles against the Nubians, but finally he won. The Egyptians renamed Nubia "Kush." They painted pictures of their new Afric an subjects on the walls of their tombs. The pictures show Nubians carrying gold, ebony, incense, furs, and monkeys as presents to the Egyptians.

For the next seven hundred years, the Nubians were ruled by the Egyptians. Slowly, they began to think of themselves as Egyptians. They learned the Egyptian language and followed the Egyptian religion, and obeyed the Egyptian pharaoh. The Egyptians began to respect them. And they gained power of their own in Egypt. One Nubian woman even became the queen of Egypt, when she married the pharaoh Amenhotep III! Her name was Queen Tiye. And Queen Tiye wasn't the only Nubian who moved into the palaces of Egypt. Eventually, the Nubians who lived in Kush founded their own dynasty—and became pharaohs

Queen Tiye

of Egypt themselves.

So the Egyptians were also Africans. And the people of Africa brought their own stories, traditions, and skills into the Egyptian empire. When we read about the greatness of the Egyptians, we are also reading about the greatness of Africa.

2 The Hyksos Invade Egypt

힉소스(Hyksos)는 기원전 1640년경에서 1548년경까지 약 100년 동안 이집트를 점령해 통치한 유목 민족이다. 힉소스 민족은 중동의 셈족을 중심으로 한 여러 유목민의 연합체로 추정되지만 정확한 기록은 없다. 이들은 발달된 청동기와 철기 무기, 기마술 등을 기반으로 나일강 델타 지역과 중부 이집트까지 점령했다. 힉소스인들은 이집트 상왕국의 아흐모세 왕에 의해 이집트에서 쫓겨났지만, 그들의 선진적인 전쟁 기술과 철기 문화는 이후 이집트의 발전에 큰 영향을 미쳤다.

Back up in northern Africa, Amenemhet's sons and grandsons were still ruling the Middle Kingdom of Egypt. They were strong pharaohs who kept all of Egypt united. They didn't allow conquered people, like the Nubians, to rebel. They made money by selling iron and gold to other countries. Egypt was rich and prosperous again.

Amenemhet's family was a powerful dynasty. Do you remember what a dynasty is? It's when one family rules a country for many years. But after the dynasty of Amenemhet, other families ruled Egypt. The kings in these families were not good pharaohs! They couldn't keep control over all of Egypt's land. Once again, the priests and government workers started to quarrel with each other about who had the most power. There was no army that could fight off invaders. No one was really in charge.

But this was a bad time for Egypt to become weak. Fierce enemies were getting ready to attack the pharaoh and take away his throne.

These enemies were from Canaan. Do you remember reading about Canaan? In your story about Abraham, Abraham heard the voice of God, telling him to go to Canaan. And do you remember what he thought? He thought, "Why would I go to a wilderness filled with strange, wild tribes?"

Well, one of the strange wild tribes that lived in Canaan was called the Hyksos. They were warlike nomads who moved from place to place, looking for new land to conquer and new wealth to steal. They had been wandering around Canaan for years. A few at a time, the Hyksos had moved down into Egypt and settled. Now a huge number of Hyksos lived in the Nile Delta. There were so many Hyksos that they had an entire city all their own.

Now they were ready to rule their new home. They picked up weapons and charged down to attack the pharaoh and his army.

Egypt's weak army wasn't ready for such a vicious attack.

And the Hyksos had weapons that the Egyptians had never used before. They used new bows that could shoot arrows much farther than the Egyptian bows. They used war chariots pulled by horses. The Egyptian army didn't know how to fight off these invaders with their strange new weapons. So the Hyksos defeated the Egyptian soldiers and captured the largest cities of Egypt. They even took over the pharaoh's palace. From now on, the Hyksos were the rulers of Egypt. This was the end of the Middle Kingdom of Egypt.

The Egyptians hated their Hyksos kings. They called them the "shepherd kings." *They thought that the Hyksos were rude, unclean, and uncivilized. But the Hyksos stayed in Egypt for over a hundred years.

Finally, a group of Egyptian princes got together and organized a rebellion. They armed themselves with strong bows, like the Hyksos bows. They got themselves war-chariots pulled by horses, just like the Hyksos war-chariots. They made bronze sickle-shaped swords, just like the Hyksos swords. And they drove the Hyksos out of Egypt—using fighting methods that they had learned from the Hyksos themselves. The leader of the rebellious Egyptian princes, Ahmose, became the new pharaoh of Egypt.

Under Ahmose and his descendents, Egypt became stronger than ever. Egypt got back the land it had lost to the Hyksos. And the Egyptian pharaohs used their new bows, chariots, and swords to conquer even more territory. Egypt became one of the most powerful kingdoms in the whole world. This time in Egyptian history is called the New Kingdom of Egypt. 📖

Note to Parent: The rule of Amenemhet is approximately 1980–1926 BC/BCE (the first portion of his reign was probably a co-regency with his father). The Middle Kingdom of Egypt dates from 2040 to approximately 1720 BC/BCE. The Hyksos were expelled by Ahmose in approximately 1567 BC/BCE.

The Story of the Words

Chapter 12 The Middle Kingdom of Egypt

1 Egypt Invades Nubia

peaceful ⓐ not fighting; quiet and calm

peace는 '평화'를 뜻하는 라틴어 pax에서 온 것이다. 팍스 아메리카나(Pax Americana)라는 표현은 20세기에 미국 중심으로 세계 질서가 유지되는 '평화' 상태를 의미한다. peaceful에서 -ful은 '성질이 강한, 가득한(full)'을 뜻해서, '평화로운, 평화적인'을 뜻하는 형용사로 쓰인다.

But these peaceful times didn't last. 그러나 이 평화로운 시절도 계속 이어지지는 못했다.

vanish ⓥ to disappear suddenly in a way that cannot be explained easily

vanish는 to die away를 뜻하는 라틴어에서 유래했다. 죽어서(die) 없어지는 (away) 것이므로 '소멸하다, 없어지다'라는 뜻이다. 대개는 소멸의 이유를 알 수 없을 때 vanish를 쓴다.

Egypt's power started to vanish. 이집트의 힘은 소멸되기 시작했다.

seize ⓥ to take hold of something quickly and firmly

seize는 재빨리 힘을 주어 뭔가를 잡는 동작을 표현한다. She suddenly seized my hand(그녀는 갑자기 내 손을 움켜잡았다)처럼 빨리 강하게 잡는 행동이다. 또한 He seized the throne(그는 왕위를 차지했다)처럼 자기 것이 아닌 재산, 권력, 기회 등을 '신속하게 잡거나 빼앗아 차지하다'라고 할 때도 쓴다.

He seized the throne and became the new pharaoh of Egypt. 그는 왕좌를 차지하고서 이집트의 새로운 파라오가 되었다.

Q 파라오는 왜 신관에게 권력을 빼앗겼나요?

A 상이집트와 하이집트를 하나로 통일하여 파라오 칭호를 처음 쓴 인물이 메네스(나르메르)야. 첫 파라오 이후로 이집트에서는 30왕조에 걸친 파라오가 있었단다. 4왕조에서는 기자의 대피라미드를 만든 세 명의 파라오 '쿠푸, 카프레, 멘카우레'가 등장했어. 이렇게 거대한 피라미드를 만들기 위해서는 엄청난 노동력을 동원해야 했는데, 그것이 그리 쉽지 않은 일이었다는 것은 피라미드의 규모가 멘카우레에 와서 확 줄어드는 것을 보면 알 수 있단다. 결국 고왕국은 5, 6왕조에 와서는 힘이 줄어들게 되었지.

파라오는 '신의 현현'이라고 하는데 왜 이런 현상이 벌어졌을까? 이집트에서 파라오는 최고 사제였으나 모든 신전에 동시에 존재할 수는 없어서 파라오를 대리하는 사제가 있었지. 이집트 사람들이 신에게 바치는 최고의 농산물이나 수공예품을 관리하는 사람들이 바로 사제였어. 사제가 각 신전에서 자신의 힘을 키우게 되면서, 세월이 흘러 최고 권위자인 파라오와 힘의 관계가 역전되는 상황이 벌어지게 된 거야.

target ⓝ an object, person or place chosen as the aim of an attack

target은 '공격 대상, 표적, 성취해야 할 목표'라는 뜻인데, 원래는 '모양이 둥근 방패'를 나타냈다. '둥근 방패'가 보이면 그 뒤에는 반드시 적군이 있는 것이므로 target이 '공격해야 할 목표'가 되는 것이다. 양궁이나 사격 경기에서 쓰는 '둥근' 모양의 과녁도 target이라고 한다.

And his first target was the kingdom of Nubia. 그리고 그의 첫 번째 공격 목표는 누비아 왕국이었다.

subject ⓝ someone who was born in a country that has a king or queen

subject는 under(아래에, 밑으로)를 뜻하는 접두사 sub-와 throw(던지다)를 뜻하는 ject가 합쳐진 말이다. 다양하게 해석될 수 있는 어원인데, 신(神)의 손이나 권력에 의해 '밑으로 던져진 사람들'로 이해할 수 있다. 그래서 명사형으로 '지배를 받는 사람들', 즉 '백성, 신민(臣民)'의 의미로 쓸 수 있다.

They painted pictures of their new African subjects on the walls of their tombs. 그들은 새로운 아프리카 백성들의 그림을 자신들의 무덤 벽에 그렸다.

found ⓥ to start an organization such as a company, school or nation
우선 동사 found를 find(발견하다)의 과거형과 혼동해서는 안 된다. 형태만 같다. found는 '바닥, 기초'를 뜻하는 라틴어에서 유래한 것이다. 건물을 지을 때 항상 바닥부터 짓기 시작하고, 학문도 기초부터 배워야 하므로 found는 어떤 조직, 기관, 국가 등을 '처음 만들다(설립하다), 건립하다, 건국하다'라는 의미로 쓰인다. '우리 학교는 10년 전에 개교했다'는 Our school was founded 10 years ago처럼 쓸 수 있다. found-founded-founded
Eventually, the Nubians who lived in Kush founded their own dynasty—and became pharaohs of Egypt themselves. 결국 쿠시에 살던 누비아인들은 자신들의 왕조를 세우고서 스스로 이집트의 파라오가 되었다.

greatness ⓝ the impressive quality of something
great은 겉모습이 '대단히 크다(very big)'라는 형용사로 쓰이지만, 내적인 성질과 성격을 표현할 때는 '위대한, 훌륭한'의 의미이다. great에 명사형 접미사 -ness가 붙은 greatness는 '위대함, 훌륭함'을 뜻한다.
When we read about the greatness of the Egyptians, we are also reading about the greatness of Africa. 우리가 이집트인의 위대함에 대해 읽을 때 우리는 아프리카의 위대함에 대해서도 읽고 있는 셈이다.

2 The Hyksos Invade Egypt

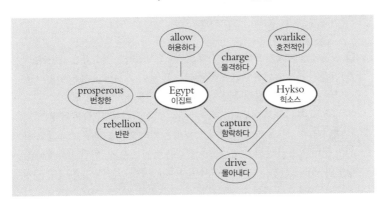

allow ⓥ to give someone permission to do or have something

'허락[허용]하다, 용납하다'라는 뜻으로 자주 쓰는 동사이다. Smoking is not allowed here라고 하면 '흡연이 허용되지 않는다'라는 의미이다. 허락하는 행위와 사람을 넣어 'allow A to ~(A가 ~하는 것을 허용하다)'라고 표현할 수 있다.

They didn't allow conquered people, like the Nubians, to rebel. 그들은 누비아인들처럼 정복당한 사람들이 반란을 일으키는 것을 용납하지 않았다.

prosperous ⓐ well-off and successful

prosperous는 '번영[번성, 번창]하다'를 뜻하는 동사 prosper의 형용사형인 '번창하는'이다. prosper는 '계속, 앞으로(onwards)'를 뜻하는 접두사 pro-와 '희망(hope)'을 뜻하는 sper가 합쳐진 것이다. '희망만이 계속되다'라는 의미이므로 '계속 발전[성장, 성공]하다'가 된다. prosper의 명사형은 prosperity이다.

Egypt was rich and prosperous again. 이집트는 다시 부유하고 번창했다.

warlike ⓐ liking war

전치사 like는 '~와 비슷한, ~ 같은'의 뜻으로 쓰이는데, 명사 뒤에 붙어서 새로운 단어가 된다. child(아이) + like(같은) = childlike(아이 같은)처럼 거의 모든 명사 뒤에 like를 붙여 '~같은, ~와 비슷한'을 뜻하는 형용사로 만들 수 있다. 그런데 The Hyksos were warlike nomads에서 warlike는 명사 war(전쟁)에 '좋아하다'라는 뜻의 like가 붙은 것이다. '힉소스는 전쟁을 좋아하는[호전적인] 유목민들이었다'라는 의미이다. a warlike stance(전쟁도 불사하겠다는 자세)처럼 warlike가 '전쟁을 의미하는 듯한, 전쟁을 일으킬 것 같은'의 의미로도 쓰인다.

They were warlike nomads who moved from place to place, looking for new land to conquer and new wealth to steal. 그들은 호전적인 유목민들로, 정복할 새로운 땅과 약탈할 새로운 재산을 찾으며 이곳저곳 이동했다.

> **Q** 중앙 집권 체제가 무너지고, 지방 호족이 대두했다는 것이 무슨 뜻인가요?
> **A** 지방 관리들은 파라오의 힘이 약해진 틈을 타 자신의 세력을 넓히며 그 지역의 왕처럼 행동하게 되었어. 중앙의 통제를 받지 않게 된 이들을 그 지역의 '호족'이라고 한단다. 호족이 관리보다 강하냐고? 물론이야. 관리는 파라오의 명령을 따라야 했지만, 호족은 파라오의 눈치를 보지 않고 자신의 군대를 동원해 다른 호족들과 전쟁을 하기도 했지. 이런 상황에서 고왕국의 파라오들은 자신이 죽어서 묻힐 피라미드 만드는 것은 꿈도 꾸지 못했지. 파라오의 권위가 약해진 틈에 귀족과 부자들은 영생을 얻고 싶다

는 마음에 미라를 만들며 장례 의식을 거행하게 되었으니 달라진 사회 풍토를 엿볼수 있지.

charge ⓥ to rush towards someone or something in order to attack them
charge는 원래 '바퀴 달린 탈것(wheeled vehicle)'을 일컫는다. '전차(戰車), 마차'를 뜻하는 chariot도 charge와 어원이 같다. '전차나 마차를 타고 전속력으로 달리다'에서 '돌진하다, 맹렬히 공격하다'라는 의미로 발전했다.
They picked up weapons and charged down to attack the pharaoh and his army.
그들은 무기를 집어 들고서 남쪽으로 맹렬히 진격해 파라오와 그의 군대를 공격했다.

capture ⓥ to get control of a place that once belonged to an enemy
capture에서 어근 capt-는 '잡다, 쥐다, 취하다(hold, seize, take)'의 의미가 있다. 노력하거나 의도적으로 손에 쥐는 행동을 표현하는 동사가 capture이다. 즉 '함락하다, 점령하다, 사로잡다'라는 뜻이다. 명사형도 capture인데, 화면 캡처(screen capture)는 순간의 화면을 정지시켜 취하는 것이다.
So the Hyksos defeated the Egyptian soldiers and captured the largest cities of Egypt. 그래서 힉소스인들은 이집트 병사들을 물리치고 이집트의 대도시들을 함락시켰다.

rebellion ⓝ the act of fighting against a leader or government
'반란, 반항'을 뜻하는 rebellion은 동사 rebel의 명사형이다. rebel에서 re는 '다시(again), 새로(anew)'를, bel은 '전쟁(war)'을 의미한다. 즉 전쟁을 다시 하는 것이 바로 rebel이다. 고대에는 전쟁에서 패하면 속민이 되거나 노예가 되어야 했다. 그 속박에 벗어나려면 '다시 전쟁을 해서' 이기는 수밖에 없으므로 rebel은 '반란을 일으키다, 반항하다'라는 뜻이 되었다.
Finally, a group of Egyptian princes got together and organized a rebellion. 마침내, 이집트의 왕자들이 함께 모여서 반란을 준비했다.

drive ⓥ to force someone to leave a place
drive는 뒤에서 힘을 가해 사람이나 동물을 원하는 방향으로 가도록 만드는 행동을 의미한다. 힘을 가해서 자동차를 원하는 방향으로 가게 하니까 '운전하다'도 to drive a car이다. drive-drove-driven
And they drove the Hyksos out of Egypt—using fighting methods that they had learned from the Hyksos themselves. 그리고 그들은 바로 힉소스인들에게서 배운 전투 방법을 사용해서 힉소스인들을 이집트에서 쫓아냈다.

Q 이집트는 왜 힉소스에게 쉽게 패했나요?

A 사방이 확 트여 적의 공격에 쉽게 노출되는 메소포타미아 지방과는 달리 이집트는 천연의 국경 지대가 있었어. 나일 강 유역 양편에는 사막이 있었고, 남쪽에는 폭포가 많아서 자연히 국경 역할을 해준 거야. 그것이 장점이자 단점이 되기도 했단다. 아무래도 군사 기술을 개발하는 일에 소홀하게 된 거야.

보병 위주의 이집트 군대는 힉소스가 쳐들어오기 전에는 말의 존재도 몰랐다고 해. 힉소스는 이집트어로 외국의 족장들이라는 뜻인데, 이런 별명이 붙여질 정도로 유목민들이 나일 강 삼각주 주변 무역로를 따라 모여들었어. 기원전 1640년경, 힉소스인은 말이 끄는 전차를 이끌고, 성능이 좋은 화살을 날리며 이집트를 대규모 기습 공격했지.

Chapter 13
The New Kingdom of Egypt

1 The General and the Woman Pharaoh

🌐 이집트 신(新)왕국 시대는 이집트에서 힉소스인들을 몰아내고 제18 왕조를 세운 아흐모세 1세부터 기원전 1070년경까지 약 500년 동안 이어진 시기를 말한다. 18왕조의 파라오들은 남쪽의 누비아 지역을 장악했고, 동쪽으로는 히타이트인들을 공격해 가나안 지역까지 영토를 넓혔다. 이후에도 지속적인 정복 전쟁과 점령지 수탈을 통해 국력이 융성했고, 이집트 왕국의 역사에서 가장 영토가 넓었기 때문에 이 시기를 '이집트의 제국 시대'라고도 한다.

After the Egyptians learned how to fight from the Hyksos, the New Kingdom of Egypt got more and more powerful. This is sometimes called the "Golden Age of Egypt," because Egypt was richer than ever before. Pharaoh after pharaoh came to the throne, ruled well, and kept the New Kingdom of Egypt strong.

We could never learn about all of these pharaohs! But we are going to read about two of the most interesting pharaohs: Thutmose I and his daughter, Hatshepsut.

Thutmose I: The General

Before he became pharaoh, Thutmose I was a general in the Egyptian army. *Leading the army into wars was what he did best. And he liked to fight!

Thutmose helped the Egyptian princes drive the Hyksos out of Egypt. When the leader of the Egyptian princes became king, Thutmose was his right-hand man. Then Thutmose married his daughter! And when the king died, Thutmose became the new pharaoh of Egypt. His rule began around 1524 BC/BCE.

Thutmose decided that his job as pharaoh was to make Egypt's empire even bigger by conquering other countries. *Thutmose's first battles were against the Nubians, who were trying to break away from Egypt. He went down and conquered the Nubian chiefs and reminded them that they were still part of Egypt.

But that wasn't enough for Thutmose. *Next, he took his army and followed the Hyksos all the way up to Canaan. He defeated the tribes living in the south part of Canaan and made the land part of Egypt. Thutmose was very pleased with himself. *The Hyksos had come down and taken over Egypt. *Now he had gone up and taken over the land of the Hyksos.

*The victory made him so happy that he wanted to keep on fighting. He turned his army east, and he started to march. He conquered land all the way to the Euphrates River. But he didn't cross the river—because Babylon was ruling between the Tigris and the Euphrates. Thutmose knew better than to start a fight with Babylon.

Thutmose I

*By the time Thutmose died, Egypt was twice as big as it had been!

Hatshepsut: The Woman Who Pretended To Be a Man

Hatshepsut was a princess of Egypt—the daughter of a pharaoh. Her father Thutmose was one of Egypt's greatest pharaohs. Thutmose had three children, but his favorite child was his daughter, Hatshepsut.

Hatshepsut loved to listen to her father's stories of battles and conquest. She wanted to grow up to be pharaoh too. But back in ancient times, most people thought that women were too weak to rule countries. In ancient Egypt, women were allowed to get married and have children. If they didn't want to get married, they could work at the temple, serving the gods. Or they could become dancers. But those were the only jobs women could have.

So when the pharaoh Thutmose died, Hatshepsut's brother became the next pharaoh. Hatshepsut didn't think this was fair. Her brother was sick most of the time, and he didn't pay much attention to his job of ruling Egypt. "I would be a better pharaoh than my brother!" she told herself. "But he is a man, and I am a woman. Will I ever get the chance to show what a good ruler I can be?"

Hatshepsut's brother got sicker and sicker, and one day he died. He had only been pharaoh for four years. Before he died, he told Hatshepsut that he wanted his son to be the next pharaoh. But his son was just a baby.

So Hatshepsut said to the Egyptians, "I will help my brother's son rule Egypt until he is old enough to be pharaoh on his own."

The Egyptian people agreed, and Hatshepsut was finally able

to rule Egypt. She wasn't the real pharaoh; everyone knew that her nephew would soon be old enough to rule.

But when that day came, Hatshepsut announced that she would not give up the throne. "My father always meant me to be the Crown Prince," she told her people. "He wanted me to become pharaoh, rather than my brother."

"You can't do that!" the people in the palace said. "Only men can be pharaohs!"

Hatshepsut answered, "But the god Amon—Ra told me that I would rule Egypt. He said, 'Welcome, my sweet daughter, my favorite, the ruler of Upper and Lower Egypt. Hatshepsut, you are the Pharaoh!' So the gods themselves want me to rule Egypt!"

"But no woman has ever been pharaoh!" the people complained.

"Then pretend I am a man," Hatshepsut said. And she started to wear men's clothing. Whenever she sat on the throne, she even put on a false beard.

Hatshepsut was so determined to be pharaoh that the Egyptians finally agreed to have her as their ruler. For over twenty years, Hatshepsut ruled Egypt—a queen pretending to be a king. She didn't fight any wars, but she did lead expeditions into Africa. There, she bought gold, incense, monkeys, elephants, and other things that the Egyptian people loved. She built more monuments than any other Egyptian queen. She ruled over the Egyptians until her death.

2 Amenhotep and King Tut

🌐 이집트 신(新)왕국 시대 역대 파라오들의 무덤이 있는 나일 강 서쪽 계곡(룩소르 소재)을 '왕들의 계곡(The Valley of the Kings)'이라고 부른다. 기원전 약 1500년대 초부터 1,000년경까지 약 500년 동안에 투트모세 1세부터 람세스 11세까지 역대 파라오들이 모두 이곳에 묻혔는데, 피라미드를 짓지 않고 절벽에 무덤을 만든 것은 도굴을 막기 위해서였다. 그러나 이곳에서도 도굴되지 않은 것은 투탄카멘의 무덤 뿐이었다. 1922년 영국의 하워드 카터(Howard Carter)는 투탄카멘의 무덤에서 시신을 비롯해 많은 보물과 유물을 발굴했다.

Thutmose I and Hatshepsut were powerful rulers. But we remember two other pharaohs of Egypt for different reasons. The pharaoh Amenhotep tried to change the way that the Egyptians worshipped their gods. And we remember the pharaoh Tutankhamen because of the way he was buried.

Amenhotep: Many Gods or One God?

Amenhotep's father was pharaoh, so when he died Amenhotep inherited his throne. He became pharaoh around 1350 BC/BCE. He was the fourth pharaoh named Amenhotep, so he was known as Amenhotep IV.

At first, Amenhotep acted like any other pharaoh. He made laws. He sent the army out to stop rebellions. He married a princess from Nubia and had a daughter. He worshipped all of Egypt's many gods. As a matter of fact, he was named after one of Egypt's most important gods—Amun, a god of the sun who was sometimes called "The King of the Gods." *Amenhotep sacrificed to Amun, gave money to his priests, and held big celebrations to honor this powerful god.

But then something happened to Amenhotep. He decided that Amun didn't exist. As a matter of fact, he decided that none of Egypt's gods were real.

The Egyptian people were horrified. After all, they worshipped dozens of gods. They were *polytheists*. *Polytheism* means "the worship of many gods." The Egyptians thought that the gods controlled every part of life. The gods made the Nile flood; they made rain fall; they made women have babies; they provided food; they decided whether you would live or die. How could this pharaoh suddenly stop worshipping the gods?

Amenhotep didn't pay any attention to what his people thought. His mind was made up. Instead of many gods, he believed, there was only one god. He called this god Aten. The old gods of Egypt had looked like human beings, but Aten didn't look like a man. He had to be drawn by a symbol.

Amenhotep did his best to drive all worship of the old gods—polytheism—out of Egypt. He closed temples and made priests stop performing rituals. He told people not to sacrifice to the old gods. He even changed his name, so that he wouldn't be named after Amun, the King of the Gods, any more. Now, instead of Amenhotep, he wanted to be called Akhenaten. This name means "worshipper of Aten."

Amenhotep was the first Egyptian *monotheist*. *Monotheism* means "worship of only one god." He spent much of his reign worshipping Aten. He built a whole new city with a huge, new temple in it for Aten. He wrote *poetry* to his god. One of his poems says:

Earth brightens when you dawn in lightland,
When you shine as Aten of daytime …
The entire land sets out to work,

All beasts browse on their herbs;
Trees, herbs are sprouting,
Birds fly from their nests ...
Ships fare north, fare south as well,
Roads lie open when you rise;
The fish in the river dart before you,
Your rays are in the midst of the sea.

As long as Amenhotep lived, he kept the Egyptians from worshipping all their gods. But as soon as Amenhotep died, the Egyptians rebelled! They closed the temple to Aten. They reopened all their other temples. They went back to worshipping all the old gods of Egypt. And they erased Amenhotep's name from all the monuments he had built. They took him out of all their records. They moved out of his new city and let it crumble away into ruins. They were so angry at Amenhotep for trying to make them worship just one god that they tried to forget he had ever been pharaoh. Monotheism in Egypt had failed. Polytheism—the worship of many gods—had won, after all.

The Boy Buried With Treasure: King Tut

Tut became king of Egypt when he was only seven. He grew up in the house of Amenhotep, the pharaoh who changed his name to Akhenaten. There, Tut was originally named Tutankhaten, a name honoring the god Aten. But when he became king, Tut changed his name to Tutankhamen, a name honoring Amun, the old "King of the Gods"! King Tut helped to wipe out the worship of Aten. He encouraged the people to start worshipping the old gods again. He helped to erase Akhenaten's name from all Egyptian records.

But King Tut did not have much time to rule. He died when he was eighteen.

Tut wasn't buried in a pyramid. You see, robbers knew that the pyramids of Egypt were full of treasure. They broke into the pyramids and robbed them of all their gold and jewels. Sometimes they even dumped the mummies of pharaohs out onto the floor and stole the golden coffins. So the Egyptians began to hide their tombs in the hills and mountains. They carved caves into the cliffs, put their pharaohs and treasures inside, and then blocked up the doors with stone to hide them. Their favorite place to bury pharaohs was a long, rocky valley catacombed with caves and passageways. This valley, now called the Valley of the Kings, has sixty tombs in it. And the tombs are well hidden. Robbers never found King Tut's tomb. As a matter of fact, no one knew it was there for thousands and thousands of years.

Over three thousand years later, a man named Howard Carter was working in the Valley of the Kings. He had spent years looking for the tombs of the pharaohs. He found Hatshepsut's tomb. He was convinced that another royal grave was hidden in the Valley of the Kings. But he was simply unable to find it.

One day, Howard Carter was moving a stack of stones when he found something unexpected—a step! He ran for help. His men, digging all through the day, uncovered more steps, leading down to a door in the stone. On the door, Carter found a name in hieroglyphs: TUTANKHAMEN.

Carefully, Carter cut a hole in the door. He held up a light to the door. At first, all he could see was darkness. He moved his light from side to side. Suddenly, a beautiful golden gleam sprang out from the blackness. The room was full of gold.

Carter's friends were pressing in behind him. "What do you

see?" one of them asked. "Can you see anything?"

"Yes!" Howard Carter said. "Wonderful things!"

*The workmen slowly pried the door open. In front of them was a room filled with treasures. King Tut's throne, golden statues of the young king, game boards inlaid with ivory and jewelry, rings, necklaces, jars, jewel-encrusted chests, figures of the gods and goddesses—all of these were crowded into King Tut's tomb.

Howard Carter and his friends kept on exploring. They found a whole series of rooms, linked together by hallways. Each room held more treasures. Finally, they came to the last locked door. Carter opened it carefully. Inside, he found the body of the young king, Tutankhamen himself.

At first, all Carter saw was a huge golden box. Then he realized that the box opened at the top. Inside this golden box, he found a heavy stone chest. Inside the stone chest, he found a golden statue of the king, lying on its back.

As soon as he touched the statue, he knew that it was actually a wooden coffin, carved to look like the king and then coated with gold. He pried the coffin open, expecting to see Tut's body. Instead, he found another wooden coffin, covered with gold. And when he opened this coffin, he found yet another coffin—this one solid gold, through and through.

Carefully, he opened this final coffin. *There was Tutankhamen's mummified body, wrapped in linen and soaked with spices. It was so well preserved that Howard Carter could even see the dead king's face.

Soon, people began to say that there was a curse on Tut's tomb. The man who helped Howard Carter open Tut's tomb, Lord Carnarvon, died only seven weeks after the burial chamber was first opened. Was this a result of the inscription found on the statue of Anubis, the god of death, inside Tut's treasure? *The inscription reads, "It is I who hinder the sand from choking the secret chamber. I am for the protection of the deceased." Five months after Lord Carnarvon's death, his younger brother also died unexpectedly. And that's not all—Howard Carter's pet canary was swallowed by a cobra on the very day that the tomb was first opened! A cobra was also carved on Tut's mask—so that it would spit fire at all enemies of the king.

There were 26 people present when the tomb was opened. Within ten years, six had died. But the others lived into old age. So you decide: was there a curse in Tut's tomb? 📖

Note to Parent: Thutmose I was pharaoh of the 18th dynasty and ruled 1524–1518 BC/ BCE. Hatshepsut was also a pharaoh of the 18th dynasty and ruled 1498–1483 BC/BCE. There are several pharaohs named Amenhotep; this is Amenhotep IV (1350–1334 BC/ BCE), who married Nefertiti and changed his name to Akhenaten. Titankhamen was born around 1343 BC/BCE and died around 1325, when he was probably 18. Carter found his tomb in AD/CE 1922.

The Story of the Words

Chapter 13 The New Kingdom of Egypt

1 The General and the Woman Pharaoh

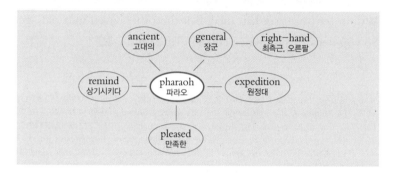

general ⑩ a very important officer in the army

general은 '종족(race), 종류(kind)'를 뜻하는 라틴어 genus에서 온 것이다. 로마 제국의 군대는 여러 종족(race)의 군사들로 구성되었고, 직책도 보병, 기병, 궁병 등으로 다양했다. 각각의 종족과 직책으로 구성된 군대를 통솔한다는 의미에서 general은 '대장, 장군'의 뜻으로 쓰이게 되었다. 지금은 주로 별(star)을 단 장군 계급에게 general을 붙인다.

Before he became pharaoh, Thutmose I was a general in the Egyptian army. 파라오가 되기 전에 투트모세 1세는 이집트 군대의 장군이었다.

right-hand ⓐ being on the very important position for someone

Thutmose was his right-hand man을 '투트모세는 그의 오른손잡이인 부하였다'라고 이해하면 곤란하다. 문장 속의 right-hand man은 오른손과 같이 '중요한, 믿음직한' 사람이라는 뜻이다. '오른손잡이'는 right-handed로 표현한다. 왼손잡이는 억울하겠지만, 동서양을 막론하고 예로부터 '오른쪽'이 왼쪽보다는 중요하게 취급되었다. 기독교 성경에도 Jesus(예수)가 God(하느님)의 오른쪽에 있다는 표현이 자주 나온다.

When the leader of the Egyptian princes became king, Thutmose was his right-hand man. 이집트 왕자들의 지도자가 왕이 되었을 때 투트모세는 그의 오른팔과 같은 중요한 부하였다.

remind ⓥ to make someone remember something

remind는 '마음, 생각, 관심'을 뜻하는 mind 앞에 again(다시)을 뜻하는 접두사 re-가 붙은 형태이다. 다시 마음에 떠올리게 하는 것이므로 '생각나도록 알려주다, 상기시키다'라는 뜻이다.

He went down and conquered the Nubian chiefs and reminded them that they were still part of Egypt. 그는 내려가 누비아의 족장들을 정복하고서 그들이 여전히 이집트의 일부라는 사실을 상기시켰다.

pleased ⓐ happy or satisfied

동사형으로 누군가를 '기쁘게 하다, 만족을 주다'라는 뜻이다. She always pleases her parents(그녀는 부모님을 항상 기쁘게 한다)처럼 표현할 수 있는데, 부모가 주어 자리에 오면 Her parents are always pleased with her처럼 수동형의 형용사 pleased로 쓴다.

Thutmose was very pleased with himself. 투트모세는 스스로에게 만족했다.

ancient ⓐ a very long time ago; very old

ancient는 before(이전에)를 뜻하는 라틴어에서 온 말이다. 원래는 '지나간 과거 시점'을 뜻하는 말로 쓰였지만, 지금은 역사 단계에서 '고대(古代)'에 해당하는 것 앞에 ancient를 붙인다. '고대 역사'는 ancient history, '고대 문명'은 ancient civilizati on, '고대 이집트'는 ancient Egypt이다.

But back in ancient times, most people thought that women were too weak to rule countries. 그러나 고대에는 대부분의 사람들이 여자는 너무 약해서 나라를 다스릴 수 없다고 생각했다.

expedition ⓝ a long difficult trip, especially to a dangerous place

expedition에서 ex-는 '밖으로(out)'를 뜻하는 접두사이고, pedi-는 '발(foot)'을 나타낸다. 즉 '밖으로 걸어나가다'라는 뜻이다. 옛날에는 내가 살고 있는 곳의 '밖'은 낯설고 신기하고 때론 위험한 곳이었다. 그런 곳으로 걸어나가는 것이므로 명사형 expedition은 '탐험, 원정' 혹은 '탐험대, 원정대'를 뜻한다.

She didn't fight any wars, but she did lead expeditions into Africa. 그녀는 전쟁을 하지는 않았지만, 아프리카 원정대를 이끌기도 했다.

2 Amenhotep and King Tut

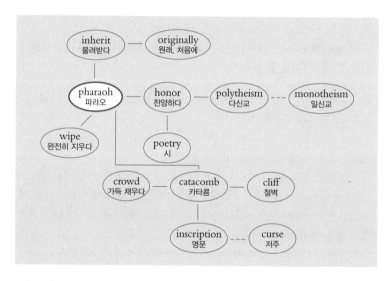

inherit ⓥ to receive something from someone when he or she dies

inherit에서 in-은 en-의 변형으로 '실행, 사용'이라는 의미가 있다. herit는 '상속받을 권리'를 의미하는데, heir(상속인)와 어원이 같다. 상속받을 권리를 실행하는 것이므로 inherit는 '상속받다, 물려받다'라는 뜻이다. 명사형은 inheritance 이다.

Amenhotep's father was pharaoh, so when he died Amenhotep inherited his throne. 아멘호테프의 아버지는 파라오였기 때문에, 그가 죽었을 때 아멘호테프가 그의 왕좌를 물려받았다.

honor ⓥ to respect much

저명인사를 만났을 때 흔히 It's my great honor to meet you라는 말을 하는데, '당신을 뵙게 되어 큰 영광입니다'라는 의미이다. 명사형 honor는 '영광, 영예' 이다. honor를 동사형으로 쓰면 영광으로 여길 만큼 '대단히 존경하다'라는 뜻 이다. 그토록 존경하기 때문에 '찬양하다, 받들어 모시다, (신을) 예배하다'라는 의미로 쓰인다.

Amenhotep sacrificed to Amun, gave money to his priests, and held big celebrations to honor this powerful god. 아멘호테프는 아문 신에게 제물을 바쳤고, 사제들에게 돈을 주었으며이 강력한 신을 기리기 위해 성대한 축제를 열기도 했다.

polytheism ⓝ the belief that there are more than one god

polytheism에서 poly-는 '여럿, 많은(many)'을 뜻하고, theism의 어원은 '신 (god)'을 뜻하는 희랍어 theos이다. 여러 신을 믿는 '다신교(多神敎), 다신론'이 polytheism이고, '다신론자'는 polytheist이다.

Polytheism means "the worship of many gods." 다신교는 '여러 신을 섬기는 것'을 뜻한다.

monotheism ⓝ the belief that there is only one god

'오직 한 명의 신'을 믿는 종교관을 monotheism이라고 하는데, mono-가 '하나 (one)'를 의미한다. 세상에 '신'은 자신이 믿는 신 하나밖에 없고, 다른 신은 다 가짜라고 여기는 '일신교(一神敎), 유일신 사상'이다.

Monotheism means "worship of only one god." 일신교는 '단 하나의 신만 섬기는 것' 을 의미한다.

Q 아멘호테프 4세가 갑자기 일신교를 믿게 된 이유가 있었나요?
A 신왕국의 시작인 18왕조 하반기에 들어서면서 아문신을 모시는 테베 의 성직자들의 권력이 지나치게 커졌단다. 신전에 속한 농경지는 세금을 면제받았는데, 그들이 거두어들이는 농산물의 양이 어마어마했지. 신전에

속한 인부와 가축의 수도 늘어났고, 성직자들은 자신의 권력을 이용해 정부의 중요한 관직을 차지한 후에 그 자리를 상속하기도 했어.

성직자들이 국가의 권위를 위협하는 지경에 왔다고 판단한 파라오 아멘호테프 4세는 아문신 숭배를 금지했어. 아문신 숭배를 금지하면 신전을 폐쇄할 수 있는 명분이 생겼지. 물론 사제들은 크게 반발했지만, 파라오는 이를 무시했어. 다신교였던 이집트에서 파라오가 신은 태양을 상징하는 아텐밖에 없다고 선언한 거야. 이집트 최초의 유일신 선언이었지만, 아멘호테프 사후에 다시 다신교로 돌아갔으니 최초이자 마지막이었던 셈이지.

poetry ⓝ poems in general, or the art of writing them

'시(詩)'를 뜻하는 poem은 '만들다(make), 창조하다(create)'를 뜻하는 희랍어에서 유래한 것이다. 행(行)만 바꾼다고 전부 시(詩)가 되는 것이 아니라 비유와 상징을 담은 언어로 운율을 맞춰 '창의적으로(creative)' 써야 시라고 할 수 있다. 한 편의 시는 a poem이고, 복수형은 poems이다. 반면에 poetry는 여러 편의 시를 통칭하거나 문학 장르로서의 '시'를 뜻한다. '시집(詩集)'은 a poetry book이라고 한다.

He wrote *poetry* to his god. 그는 자신의 신에게 시를 썼다.

originally ⓐ in the beginning

origin은 rise(떠오르다, 일어나다)라는 뜻의 라틴어에서 유래했다. 해가 '떠오르는' 동쪽 땅인 orient(오리엔트)와 어원이 같다. 해가 떠서 하루가 시작되고, 식물의 싹이 '올라와서' 성장이 시작되는 시점을 나타낸다. 그래서 origin은 '기원, 시작, 태생', original은 '원래의, 처음의, 독창적인', originally는 '처음에는, 원래'라는 뜻으로 쓰인다.

There, Tut was originally named Tutankhaten, a name honoring the god Aten. 그곳에 있을 때, 투트는 원래 아텐 신을 기리는 이름인 투트앙크아텐으로 불렸다.

wipe ⓥ to remove or destroy someone or something

wipe는 원래 '빠르게 움직이는(moving quickly)' 동작과 관련이 있다. 앞뒤로, 좌우로 반복적으로 빨리 움직이는 동작으로, '걸레질'하는 모습을 떠올리면 된다. 그래서 wipe는 물기나 눈물 등을 '닦다, 지우다'이다. 뒤에 out이 붙으면 '철저하게, 완전히 지우다'라는 뜻이 된다.

King Tut helped to wipe out the worship of Aten. 투트 왕은 아텐 신 숭배를 완전히 없애는 일을 도왔다.

cliff ⓥ an area of high, steep rock at the side of a mountain

'절벽'을 뜻하는 cliff는 cleave와 같은 어원에서 유래했을 것으로 추정한다. 침식과 풍화 작용에 의해 '쪼개지고 갈라져서(cleave)' 생기는 것이 바로 cliff다. 산과 해안의 '절벽, 낭떠러지'를 뜻한다.

They carved caves into the cliffs, put their pharaohs and treasures inside, and then blocked up the doors with stone to hide them. 그들은 절벽에 동굴을 파서 파라오와 보물들을 동굴 안에 넣은 다음에 그것을 감추기 위해 입구를 바위로 막아 놓았다.

catacomb ⓝ a tomb with many passages and rooms, below ground where dead people are buried in the walls

catacomb은 '2세기경부터 만들어진 로마 시대의 기독교인 매장지'를 부르는 명칭이었다. 당연히 라틴어에서 유래했는데, cata는 '밑(down)'을, comb는 '속이 빈 공간, 구멍(hollow)'을 뜻한다. 즉 초기 기독교의 지하 묘지이다.

Their favorite place to bury pharaohs was a long, rocky valley catacombed with caves and passageways. 그들이 선호했던 파라오 매장지는 카타콤처럼 동굴과 통로를 파낸, 길고 바위가 많은 계곡이었다.

crowd ⓥ to fill a place with things or people

crowd는 '누르다(press), 밀다(push)'라는 뜻의 고대 영어에서 유래한 것이다. 공간에 뭔가를 꾹꾹 '눌러서' 채우거나, '밀어서' 넣는 동작을 표현한다. 그래서 crowd는 동사형으로는 '가득 메우다, 채우다'라는 뜻이고, 명사형은 '많은 무리, 군중'이다. 발 디딜 틈 없이 콩나물시루처럼 승객이 들어찬 '만원 버스'가 a crowded bus이다.

All of these were crowded into King Tut's tomb. 이 모든 것들이 투트의 무덤 속에 가득 채워져 있었다.

curse ⓝ a word or wish that, with the help of gods or some magical power, something bad will happen to someone

심한 욕을 하거나 악담을 퍼붓는 것을 curse라고 하지만, curse의 원래 의미는 '저주, 저주하다'이다. 어떤 사람에게서 심한 피해를 입으면 그 사람을 저주하기도 하는데, 본문에서 자신의 힘으로는 불가능하므로 신의 힘을 빌어 보복하겠다고 말하고 있다.

Soon, people began to say that there was a curse on Tut's tomb. 곧 사람들은 투트의 무덤에 저주가 있다고 말하기 시작했다.

inscription ⓝ a piece of writing carved on a stone

inscription의 동사형 inscribe는 '속으로(into)'를 뜻하는 접두사 in-과 '쓰다 (write)'를 뜻하는 scribe가 합쳐진 것이다. 그냥 쓰는 것이 아니라 돌이나 나무 등에 '새겨서 쓰는' 것이다. 명사형 inscription은 돌이나 나무, 금속 등에 '새겨 진 글, 명문(銘文)'을 뜻한다.

Was this a result of the inscription found on the statue of Anubis, the god of death, inside Tut's treasure? 이것이 투트의 보물 속에 있던 죽음의 신 아누비스 조각상 에서 발견된 명문 때문에 벌어진 일일까?

Q 파라오의 저주는 사실이었나요?

A '이집트하면 생각나는 것은?'이라고 물으면 대부분 피라미드와 스핑크 스 그리고 투탕카멘을 꼽더라. 그 정도로 유명한 투탕카멘은 18세의 나이 로 세상을 떠났으니 제대로 정치를 한 지도자는 아니었어. 그의 유명세는 무덤 발굴로 인한 거야. 유일하게 제대로 보존된 무덤에서 상상을 초월하 는 다양한 부장품이 나와서, 우리가 말로만 듣던 이집트의 문화와 만날 수 있게 된 거야.

무덤 발굴의 지휘자는 영국 출신 고고학자 '하워드 카터'였는데, 그가 이 끄는 발굴팀이 무덤을 열었을 때 파라오의 관에는 '사자의 안녕을 방해하 는 자에게 저주 있으라'와 '파라오의 이름을 알리는 자에게 복이 있으라'라 는 말도 적혀 있었대. 이렇게 모순된 내용을 함께 적어놓은 의도는 뭘까? 투탕카멘은 오히려 카터의 발굴로 이집트에서 가장 유명한 파라오가 되어 지금도 사람들의 입에 오르내리고 있으니, '파라오의 이름을 알리는 자에 게 복이 있으라'라는 말에 해당된 경우가 아닐까? 파라오의 저주라는 말은 무덤 발굴에 관련된 사람들이 차례로 죽자 언론인들이 퍼트린 거였어. 그 러나 정작 발굴의 주인공인 하워드 카터는 무사했단다.

Chapter 14
The Israelites Leave Egypt

1 The Baby Moses

🌏 모세는 《구약 성서》에서 가장 중요한 유대 민족의 지도자로 그려지고 있다. 이 집트에서 태어난 모세는 강에 버려졌다가 파라오의 딸에 의해 구해져 왕궁에서 자라는데, 성장기에 자신이 이집트인이 아니라 유대인임을 깨닫는다. 어느 날 유대인을 괴롭히는 이집트 병사를 죽이고 미디안 광야로 피신하는데, 오랜 세월 후에 호셉 산에서 하느님의 명령을 받아 유대 민족을 구원하는 지도자로 거듭나게 된다.

Do you remember reading about Abraham? When Abraham lived in Ur, he was a polytheist—he believed in the moon god and many other gods. But after Abraham heard a voice telling him to go to Canaan, he became a monotheist. He believed there was only one god, and that the voice that spoke to him was the voice of that one god.

Abraham had a son named Isaac, and Isaac had a son named Jacob. Jacob didn't have just one son. He had twelve! Each one of those sons had a big family too. All together, Jacob's sons and their families made up a whole new nation. This nation was called "Israel." The Israelites—the people of Israel—were unusual in the ancient world, because they were monotheists. They only worshipped one god, and they tried to obey his commands.

Because God had told them to live in Canaan, the Israelites tried to stay there, even though it was a dry and rocky place. But then a famine came. It stopped raining. Plants wouldn't grow. Animals died. The Israelites had no food for their flocks, or for themselves. They were afraid that they would die, too.

Do you remember the story of Joseph? Joseph's brothers sold him to be a slave in Egypt. But Joseph became a very important man in Egypt. And he had plenty of grain and water. So he invited the Israelites down into Egypt. They packed up their tents, their animals, their families, and all their belongings and traveled down to Egypt. They started to keep their flocks and grow their crops on the banks of the Nile.

At first the Egyptians didn't mind having the Israelites in their country. But then they saw the Israelite nation growing larger and larger. Soon, the Egyptians started saying to each other, "'What if these people decide to attack us? They might even take our kingdom away!" After all, that was exactly what the Hyksos had done, years before.

So the Egyptians made the Israelites into slaves. They forced the Israelites to make the mud bricks that they used to build their houses and temples. The Israelites were not allowed to carry any kind of weapons. They had to work hard for no pay.

But the Israelite nation kept growing bigger and bigger, and the Egyptians were still afraid. The book of Exodus, in the Bible, tells us the story of what happened next.

The pharaoh of Egypt sat on his throne, a frown on his face. "What will I do about all those Israelites in my country?" he thought to himself. "There are more and more of them all the time! Soon they will take over Egypt. If only they didn't have so many children."

And then he had an idea—a terrible, cruel idea. He called his soldiers to him. "Men," he said, "go out into the land of Egypt, to every Israelite home. Find out when the Israelite mothers are about to have their babies. Then kill every baby boy as soon as it is born!"

When the Israelites heard about this dreadful command, they wept and mourned. "God, save us!" they cried out. "Send us someone to deliver us from this wicked pharaoh of Egypt!"

An Israelite woman who lived near the banks of the Nile

was just getting ready to have her baby when she heard the order. "Quickly!" she said to her daughter Miriam. "Help me hide! I don't want the soldiers to see me!"

So Miriam helped her mother hide in a back room of their house. When the baby was born, it was a boy—a fine, strong boy with a very loud cry.

"Quiet!" the mother whispered to her baby. "Don't cry so loud, or the soldiers will hear you!"

For three months, the mother and baby hid from the soldiers of the pharaoh. But the baby got older and louder. He started to giggle and coo. The mother knew she could not hide him forever.

So she wove a basket out of reeds and coated the outside with tar so that it would float. She wrapped the baby in a warm, soft blanket, put him into the basket, and pushed it out onto the Nile River. And she sent her daughter Miriam to stand by the riverbank and watch to see what would happen next.

The baby floated down the river. He smiled at the sunshine and at the bird that landed on the edge of the basket to see what was inside. Finally, the gentle rocking of the basket lulled him to sleep. The basket drifted closer and closer to the side of the Nile, until it caught in the weeds at the water's edge.

Now, the daughter of the pharaoh liked to walk down to the Nile at the hottest part of the day, so that she could swim. She came to the edge of the water and saw the basket.

"What's in that basket?" she demanded. "Get it for me!"

One of her maids ran to fetch the basket. When the daughter of the pharaoh looked inside, she saw the baby boy. He opened his eyes and smiled at her. "Oh!" she cried out! "Such a beautiful baby! I'll keep him and raise him as my own!"

When Miriam heard this, she ran forward. "Lady," she said, "would you like me to find you a nurse to take care of the baby?"

"Yes," the daughter of the pharaoh said. "*Bring me this woman and she can take care of my baby for me."

*So Miriam hurried home and got her mother. And so the baby and his mother were together again. She took care of him until he was old enough to live in the pharaoh's palace alone. The daughter of the pharaoh named him Moses.

2 The Exodus From Egypt

출애굽기(出埃及記)는 기독교《구약 성서》를 구성하는 책의 하나다. 출(出)은 '탈출'을 뜻하고 애굽(埃及)은 '이집트'를 부르는 중국어 음을 차용한 것이다. 쉽게 바꾸면 '이집트 탈출기'이다. 출애굽기에는 이스라엘 민족의 이집트 생활과 노예로 전락하는 과정, 모세를 따라 이집트를 탈출하는 과정 등이 기술되어 있다. 영어로는 The Book of Exodus라고 하는데, exodus는 '대규모로 동시에 탈출하거나 이동하는 것'을 의미한다.

Moses grew up in the palace of the pharaoh. But when he got older, he discovered that he wasn't an Egyptian. He was an Israelite. *And he saw that his people were being beaten and mistreated.

So he went to see the pharaoh. "I am an Israelite," he said, "and I worship the one God of the Israelites. God says: Let the Israelites go!"

But the pharaoh didn't want to lose all his slaves. So he refused to let the people of Israel go. When Moses saw that the pharaoh would not free the slaves, he told the pharaoh that God would send ten plagues on Egypt. Each one of these plagues showed that the God of the Israelites was more powerful than all the gods of the Egyptians. The Egyptians thought that Horus was the god of the Nile, and protected all the life in the river—but the God of Moses turned the river to blood and killed all the fish. Frogs were sacred to the Egyptians, because they belonged to Isis, the wife of Osiris— but God sent so many frogs that the Egyptians found frogs in their beds, their clothes, their bathtubs, and even in their food. The Egyptians thought that Ra was the god of the sun, and was stronger than any other god—but the God of Moses covered up the sun and made darkness last all day long.

Finally the pharaoh told Moses that the Israelites could leave Egypt. They packed up all their belongings and left that very night. But then the pharaoh changed his mind and sent his army after them.

The Israelites were running as fast as they could go. But when they looked behind them, they saw dust rising up from the hooves of the Egyptian army. "Faster!" they cried. "Faster! Or the Egyptians will take us back to Egypt, and we will be slaves again!"

Then they looked up. Ahead of them they saw the shore of a sea—the Red Sea. Water lay in front of them, as far as they could see. And the Egyptians were behind them. They couldn't go forward, and they couldn't go backward.

"We are trapped!" they said. "Moses, have you led us out of Egypt only to kill us here on the shores of the Red Sea?"

Then Moses raised his staff. God parted the waters so that the Israelites could walk through. Huge walls of water rose up on either side of them. They could see fish, swimming in the

Moses

walls. But the ground beneath them was dry.

They walked all the way through the Red Sea, to the other side. But behind them the Egyptians were still coming. The Egyptians drove their war chariots down into the sea as well.

Then Moses lifted his staff again. The water flooded back over the Egyptians and drowned them all! The Israelites were finally free.

This part of Israel's history is now called the Exodus. The story of the Exodus shows monotheism winning out over polytheism, because the one god of Israel was able to conquer the many gods of Egypt. The Israelites walked from Egypt all the way back up to Canaan, where Abraham had once lived. They lived in Canaan for many years and became a powerful kingdom in their own right.

The story tells us something else, too. Egypt, which had been powerful for a long time, was once again growing weak. The New Kingdom of Egypt had come close to ruling the world. But now, even a band of slaves without weapons could escape from the clutches of the Egyptian army. Egypt was losing its strength once again.

The Story of the Words

Chapter 14 The Israelites Leave Egypt

1 The Baby Moses

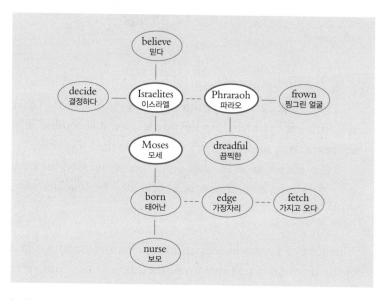

believe ⓥ to think that something is true

believe와 trust는 모두 '믿다'이지만 정확한 의미와 용법이 다르다. I trust you 라고 하면 너를 신뢰하고 의지한다는 것이고, I believe you는 너의 말이나 행동이 옳다고 믿는다는 의미이다. believe는 옳고 그름, 사실 여부와 상관없이 어떤 것이 '사실이고 옳다고 생각하다'라는 뜻이다. He believed in the moon god(그는 달의 신을 믿었다)처럼 'believe in ~'은 '존재를 믿다'라는 뜻인데, 주로 종교적 믿음, 신념 등을 표현할 때 쓴다. 명사형은 belief이다.

When Abraham lived in Ur, he was a polytheist—he believed in the moon god and many other gods. 우르에서 살 때 아브라함은 다신교도로서 달의 신과 다른 여러 신을 믿었다.

decide ⓥ to choose what to do

decide에서 de-는 off(단절, 분리), cide는 cut(자르다)을 뜻한다. 즉 잘라서 끊는 다는 '결단(決斷)'의 의미이다. 즉 decide는 '결정하다, 결심하다'이고, 명사형은 decision이다.

What if these people decide to attack us? 만약에 이 사람들이 우리를 공격하기로 마음먹으면 어쩌지?

frown ⓝ a look on your face when you move your eyebrows together, showing you are angry or unhappy

frown은 '찡그린 표정'이다. He looked at me with a frown(그는 인상을 찌푸리고 나를 쳐다보았다)처럼 쓸 수 있고, He frowned while thinking about the problem(그는 그 문제에 대해 생각하며 얼굴을 찡그렸다)처럼 '얼굴을 찡그리다, 인상을 쓰다'라는 동사형으로도 쓸 수 있다.

The pharaoh of Egypt sat on his throne, a frown on his face. 이집트의 파라오는 인상을 쓰고서 왕좌에 앉아 있었다.

> **Q** 모세에 관하여 볼 만한 작품이 있나요?
>
> **A** 모세에 관한 기록은 너무 많아서 다 읽거나 보기 어려울 정도야. 어린 아이를 위한 애니메이션이나 동화, 어른을 위한 소설, 영화, 다큐멘터리에 이르기까지. 그중에서도 BBC에서 만든 다큐멘터리 '모세'를 보면 당시를 이해하는 데 큰 도움이 될 거야. 모세는 다양한 조각과 그림으로도 형상화 되었어. 가장 인상적인 작품을 소개하자면 조각가 슬뤼테르의 모세의 우물, 미켈란젤로의 모세, 화가 렘브란트의 십계가 있어.

dreadful ⓐ causing great fear; terrible

dread는 명사형으로 앞으로 닥칠 일에 대한 '두려움', 동사형으로는 앞으로 닥칠 일을 '두려워하다'라는 뜻이다. dread에 '가득한(full)'을 뜻하는 형용사형 접미사 -ful이 붙었으니, dreadful은 '끔찍한, 무시무시한'이라는 의미이다.

When the Israelites heard about this dreadful command, they wept and mourned. 이 끔찍한 명령에 대해 들었을 때 이스라엘인들은 울면서 슬퍼했다.

born ⓐ coming out of your mother's body

born을 형용사로 취급하는 이유는 동사 bear의 완료형이 borne이기 때문인데 (bear-bore-borne), 사실상 borne과 born이 같다. 동사 bear는 여성이 아기를 낳다(to give a birth to a baby)라는 뜻으로 I want to bear a son(전 아들을 낳고 싶어요)처럼 쓸 수 있다. 아기의 입장에서는 스스로 낳는 것이 아니라, 엄마 몸에서 태어나는 것이므로 I was born in 2000(저는 2000년에 태어났어요)처럼 수동태 be born의 형태로 쓴다.

When the baby was born, it was a boy—a fine, strong boy with a very loud cry. 아기가 태어났는데, 사내아이였다. 그것도 울음소리가 아주 우렁찬, 잘생기고 건강한 사내아이였다.

edge ⓝ the outside end of something

edge는 '끝'을 의미한다. 중심에서 가장 멀리 있는 곳이고, 새로운 것과 만나는 경계선이다. 그래서 the edge of the basket은 '바구니의 가장자리'이고, the water's edge는 물과 땅이 만나는 지점, 즉 '물의 가장자리, 물가'를 뜻한다.

He smiled at the sunshine and at the bird that landed on the edge of the basket to see what was inside. 그 아기는 햇빛을 보고 미소 지었고, 바구니 안에 무엇이 있는지 보려고 바구니 가장자리에 내려앉은 새를 보고도 미소를 지었다.

fetch ⓥ to go and get something and bring it back with you

fetch의 fet은 '발(foot), 걸음(step)'의 의미를 담고 있다. '걸어가다[오다]'라는 뜻에서 '걸어가서 뭔가[누군가]를 가지고[데리고] 오다'로 발전한 단어가 fetch이다. 간단히 말해서 '가지고[데리고] 오다'라는 뜻으로 이해할 수 있다.

One of her maids ran to fetch the basket. 공주의 하녀 중 하나가 달려가 그 바구니를 가지고 왔다.

nurse ⓝ a woman whose job is to look after a young child

nurse가 '음식을 먹이다'라는 뜻의 라틴어에서 유래했기 때문에 원래 의미는 '젖을 먹이는 여자'였을 것이다. nourish(영양을 공급하다), nutrition(영양)과 어원이 같다. 그래서 엄마 대신 젖을 먹이며 보살피는 '보모'가 nurse이고, 환자도 아기와 마찬가지로 보살핌이 필요하기 때문에 '간호사'도 nurse이다.

"Lady," she said, "would you like me to find you a nurse to take care of the baby?" 그녀가 말했다. "아씨, 제가 그 아기를 돌봐줄 보모를 찾아드려도 되겠습니까?"

2 The Exodus From Egypt

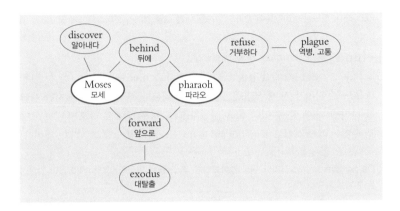

discover ⓥ to learn about something for the first time; to find something that was hidden

dis-는 '제거하다(remove)'이고, cover는 '~을 덮다, 덮개'라는 의미이다. 즉 덮개를 제거하면 그 안의 내용물이 보이므로 '발견하다, 알아내다'라는 뜻이다.

But when he got older, he discovered that he wasn't an Egyptian. 그러나 나이를 먹으면서 그는 자신이 이집트 사람이 아니라는 사실을 알게 되었다.

refuse ⓥ to say that you will not do or accept something

refuse에서 접두사 re-는 back(뒤로, 반대)을, fuse는 pour(쏟다, 붓다)를 뜻한다. 누군가 내 컵에 물을 부어 '마셔!'라고 했는데, 그 물을 상대 물잔에 부으며 '너나 마셔!'라고 말하는 상황을 떠올릴 수 있다. refuse는 '거절하다'라는 뜻으로, 이렇게 어떤 제안이나 부탁 등을 거부할 때 쓰는 동사이다.

So he refused to let the people of Israel go. 그래서 그는 이스라엘 사람들이 가도록 놓아주기를 거부했다.

plague ⓝ a thing causing serious trouble

plague는 strike(때리다), wound(다치게 하다)를 뜻하는 라틴어에서 유래했다. 가벼운 타격이나 부상이 아니라, 강력한 타격과 심각한 부상을 의미한다. plague는 '심하게 괴롭히다'라는 뜻으로 쓰이고, 그렇게 심한 피해를 주는 것이나 느닷없이 퍼져 많은 인명을 앗아가는 '전염병, 역병'도 plague이다. 전염병도 인류 역사에 큰 영향을 미쳤으므로 이 책에서도 앞으로 plague라는 단어를 여러 번 만나게 될 것이다.

When Moses saw that the pharaoh would not free the slaves, he told the pharaoh that God would send ten plagues on Egypt. 모세는 파라오가 노예들을 풀어주지 않으려고 하자, 하느님이 이집트에 10가지 고통을 내려 보낼 것이라고 파라오에게 말했다.

behind (prep) at the back of something

behind는 be는 '존재[있다]'를 의미하는 것이고, hind는 '뒤(back)'를 뜻한다. behind는 위치가 '뒤에' 있음을 표현하는 전치사나 부사로, 공간과 시간 개념을 나타낼 때 에 쓸 수 있다. Stay behind!라고 하면 '앞으로 나오지 말고 그냥 뒤에 있어'라는 것이고, I am behind in my work는 '일이 밀려 있다'는 것이다. But when they looked behind them, they saw dust rising up from the hooves of the Egyptian army. 그러나 뒤를 돌아보았을 때, 그들은 이집트 군대의 말발굽이 일으키는 먼지를 보았다.

forward (ad) in the direction that is in front of you

앞에 어떤 단어가 ward를 이끄는가에 따라 방향이 달라지는데, ward 앞에 '앞'을 뜻하는 for가 붙으면 '앞으로'가 되고, '뒤'를 뜻하는 back이 붙으면 '뒤로'가 된다. forward는 '앞으로'이고, backward는 '뒤로'라는 뜻이다. They couldn't go forward, and they couldn't go backward. 그들은 앞으로도 갈 수 없었고, 뒤로도 갈 수 없었다.

exodus (n) a situation in which many people leave a place at the same time

exodus는 희랍어에서 유래한 말로, '밖으로, 벗어난(out of)'을 뜻하는 ex-와 '길(road, way)'을 뜻하는 odus가 합쳐진 것이다. 길을 통해 어딘가로 빠져나간다는 의미이다. 전쟁이나 자연재해가 일어나면 사람들이 대규모로 피난을 가는데, 이런 '대탈출, 대이동'의 상황을 exodus라고 한다. 대문자로 쓰는 Exodus는 기독교 《구약 성서》에 나오는 '모세와 이스라엘 민족의 이집트 탈출'을 뜻한다. This part of Israel's history is now called the Exodus. 이스라엘 역사의 이 대목을 지금은 '엑서더스'라고 부른다.

Chapter 15
The Phoenicians

Black Sea

Carthage

Mediterranean Sea

Tyre

Canaan

Egypt

Nile River   Red Sea

PHONECIA
PHONECIAN SETTLEMENTS

1 Phoenician Traders

🌐 페니키아 문명은 가나안 북부, 현재의 레바논과 시리아의 지중해 연안에서 번성했던 해양 도시 문명을 말한다. 페니키아(Phoenicia)라는 단어는 보라색(purple)과 관련이 깊다. 페니키아인들이 발전된 염료 기술을 사용해 보라색 옷을 즐겨 입었기 때문에, 그리스인들이 페니키아인들을 '보라색, 뿔고둥'을 뜻하는 'phoinix'라고 불렀다. 페니키아인들은 가나안 북부에 풍부한 나무인 백향목(柏香木)으로 항해에 적합한 튼튼한 선박을 만들어 지중해 무역을 독점했고, 아프리카 북부에 식민 도시들을 건설하기도 했다. 염료와 유리 제조 기술이 발달했으며 고유의 문자를 사용했는데, 이 페니키아의 문자는 그리스로 전파되어 알파벳의 기원이 되었다.

When the Israelites walked from Egypt back up to Canaan, they weren't moving into an empty country. There were already people living in Canaan. The people who lived up in the north of Canaan were called Phoenicians, and they were the greatest sailors in the ancient world.

The northern part of Canaan wasn't a very good place to grow wheat, because it was rocky and sandy and dry. It wasn't a good place to raise animals, because there wasn't enough grass or water to make them fat and healthy. And it was hard to get into or out of—it was surrounded by steep craggy hills.

So the Phoenicians pushed their boats out onto the water and sailed around the Mediterranean Sea. They became traders. They cut down the tall cedar trees that grew in their homeland and floated the logs to other countries. They built beautiful furniture and sold it for a high price. They sold salt and dried fish and embroidered cloth. And they sailed around the coast of the Mediterranean and found the best places to dig up tin and other metals.

The Phoenicians were famous for making glass. Ancient glass-

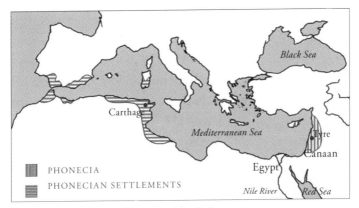

Phoenicia and Its Settlements

making was a long, complicated process. First, the Phoenicians made a special chemical called *lye* by pouring water over the ashes from a wood fire and collecting the liquid that oozed out. They mixed this lye with pure sand and melted the sand—lye mixture over a hot, hot fire. To get the fire hot enough to melt sand, slaves probably had to fan the fire with special pumps called *bellows* for hours and hours.

Once they had melted the sand and lye together, the Phoenicians would pour the mixture into special molds. When the sand—lye mixture cooled, it was hard, shiny glass. Sometimes the Phoenicians colored the glass by putting red, blue, and yellow dyes into it, or wound colored threads around the molds so that the finished glass had a pattern of threads all through it. Sometimes the glass even had gold and jewels in it.

Other ancient peoples made glass too. But the Phoenicians were the first glassmakers to invent *glass blowing*. Have you ever blown bubbles in your milk through a straw? That's exactly what the Phoenicians did with their hot liquid glass. Instead of pouring the glass into a mold, a Phoenician glassmaker would dip a hollow pipe made out of thin metal into the sticky melted glass. Some of the glass would cling to the end of the pipe in a glob. Then the glassmaker would blow very gently through the pipe. The glass at the other end would puff out into a big round bubble. As long as the glass was still soft, the glassmaker could stretch it out so that bubble was long and thin, or twist it into different shapes. Finally, the glassmaker would cool the glass and break it carefully off the pipe. Blown glass was the most beautiful and expensive kind of ancient glass. All around the Mediterranean Sea, people were happy to pay the Phoenicians for this blown glass.

The Phoenicians were also known for making a beautiful purple dye out of snails. They collected snails, called *murex*, from the sea and boiled them with salt water and lemon juice for ten days. The boiling snails smelled awful. As a matter of fact, Phoenician cities like Tyre were famous for their stench—caused by the dye-factories that were boiling snails. "You stink like a man from Tyre" was a favorite insult in ancient times!

When the dye was finished, the Phoenicians dipped wool into it. The dye turned the wool a dark, beautiful purple. It took so many snails to make purple dye that the cloth made from purple wool was expensive. Sometimes it cost a whole year's pay to buy a purple cloak. So *purple* was often called "the color of kings" because only kings could afford to wear it.

2 The Founding of Carthage

처음 정착한 가나안 북부 지역은 환경이 척박했기 때문에 페니키아인들은 일찍부터 지중해의 다른 지역에 눈을 돌렸다. 발달된 조선술을 기반으로 지중해에서 활발하게 해상 무역을 벌이던 페니키아인들은 아프리카 북부의 여러 지역에 식민

지를 건설하는데, 그중에서 대표적인 곳 중 하나가 '카르타고' 였다. 기원전 9세기 초
에 건설된 카르타고 식민지는 크게 번성하여 남부 유럽의 세력과 힘을 겨루었고, 기
원전 3~2세기경에는 로마 제국과 '포에니 전쟁'을 벌이게 된다.

The Phoenicians sailed all around the Mediterranean Sea. And they started *colonies*—little settlements of Phoenician people—in many of the places where they landed. One of the most famous cities was Tyre, over in Canaan. Another was Carthage, all the way over in North Africa.

Carthage was first settled around 814 BC/BCE. At first, Carthage was just a tiny village. But soon it grew to be a huge, busy city where merchants from all different countries came to trade their goods.

We don't know the names of the first Phoenicians who settled in Carthage. But later, a great writer named Virgil told this famous story about the beginnings of the city of Carthage:

Dido was a Phoenician princess, the sister of the king of Tyre. She should have been happy. She was married to a very rich man, and she lived in a palace. But Dido's brother, the king, was jealous of her and of her husband's wealth. He wanted all that money for himself!

So the king had Dido's husband arrested and put to death. Dido was terrified. Would she be next? She gathered together all of her friends and left Tyre in the middle of the night. They pushed away from the shore in a boat and sailed away, never to return.

Dido and her friends traveled and traveled. Finally, they spotted land. "Let's go ashore here, and build a new city!" Dido urged her friends. They agreed, but when they reached the place where Dido wanted to settle, they found that the land was already settled.

"We should go somewhere else," Dido's friends said. But Dido was determined to build her new city on that very spot. She wanted to live close to the water, so that ships would visit her new city and trade with her. So she said to the owner of the land, "Will you sell me as much land as I can cover with the skin of a bull?"

"Of course!" the owner agreed. He thought that Dido would put her bull hide down over a little patch of ground, just large enough to stand on. But instead, Dido got out a very sharp knife and cut her bull hide into hundreds of long, thin strips. She laid the strips out, end to end, around a huge portion of land.

"There!" she said. "Now keep your promise and sell me this ground."

The owner of the land was forced to agree. So Dido and her friends built a tower on the ground and named their tower "Bull's Hide." They settled around the tower and named their city Carthage. Soon, ships from all over the world came to Carthage to buy and sell their goods. The city bought with a bull's skin became one of the most powerful in the world.

Note to Parent: The Phoenician civilization was at its height between 1200–700 BC/BCE.

The Story of the Words

Chapter 15 The Phoenicians

1 Phoenician Traders

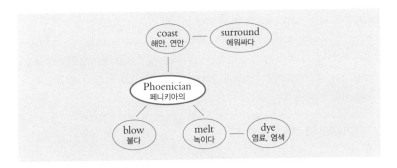

surround ⓥ to be all around something

surround에서 sur-는 over, above(위로, 너머), round는 '둥근 모양(circle)'을 뜻한다. 그래서 surround는 '둘러싸다, 에워싸다'라는 의미인데, 대개 무엇으로 둘러싸여 있기 때문에 be surrounded by ~(~로 둘러싸이다)의 수동태로 많이 쓴다.

And it was hard to get into or out of—it was surrounded by steep craggy hills. 그래서 그곳으로 들어가거나 나오기가 힘들었다. 가파르고 바위투성이인 언덕으로 둘러싸여 있었기 때문이다.

coast ⓝ the land next to the ocean

coast는 '옆구리(side), 갈비(rib)'를 뜻하는 라틴어에서 유래해서 어떤 것의 '옆(next, side)'에 있음을 나타냈다. 배를 타고 항해하다 보면 바다 '옆으로' 육지가 있다. 따라서 바다 옆의 육지, 즉 '해안(海岸)'을 가리키는 말로 coast가 쓰이게 된 것이다. 해안이 '선(line)'으로 이어진 듯한 '해안지대'를 coastline이라고 한다.

And they sailed around the coast of the Mediterranean and found the best places to dig up tin and other metals. 그래서 그들은 지중해 연안을 항해해, 주석을 비롯한 금속을 캐내기에 가장 적합한 곳을 찾았다.

melt ⓥ to change from a solid to a liquid by heating

얼음을 '녹이면' 물이 되고, 설탕을 가열해 녹이면 시럽이 된다. 이처럼 고체를 가열해서 액체로 만드는 것이나 고체 상태의 물질이 액체 상태로 변하는 것을 melt로 표현한다. 즉 '녹이다, 녹다'라는 뜻이다. 여러 민족이 섞여 하나의 국가를 형성한 미국을 melting pot(용광로, 도가니)에 비유하기도 한다.

They mixed this lye with pure sand and melted the sand-lye mixture over a hot, hot fire. 그들은 이 잿물을 순수한 모래와 섞은 다음에 모래와 잿물의 혼합물을 아주 뜨거운 불에 녹였다.

blow ⓥ to send out air through your mouth

blow는 '공기의 흐름'을 표현하는 단어이다. to blow out the candle(바람을 불어 촛불을 끄다)처럼 '입으로 바람을 불다'라는 뜻으로도 쓰이고, It's blowing hard outside(밖에 바람이 심하게 분다)처럼 '자연적으로 바람이 불다'도 된다. blow-blew-blown

Have you ever blown bubbles in your milk through a straw? 빨대로 공기를 불어 우유에 거품을 내본 적이 있는가?

dye ⓝ a liquid or powder that is used to change the color of something

우리가 입고 있는 옷은 거의 다 염색된 것이다. 집안에 벽지, 책 표지, 장난감 등의 물건에 염료가 들어가지 않은 것은 거의 없다. 이렇게 원료에 색을 더하거나 변화시키는 것이 '염색하다'의 dye이다. '머리 염색제'도 hair dye라고 한다.

The Phoenicians were also known for making a beautiful purple dye out of snails. 페니키아인들은 고둥으로 아름다운 보라색 염료를 만드는 것으로도 유명했다.

Q 페니키아가 자주색이라는 뜻이라고요?

A 유치원이나 초등학교 미술 시간에 빨강, 노랑, 파랑의 기본색(primary colors)을 섞어 다양한 색깔을 만들어 본 적이 있을 거야. 빨강(red)과 파랑(blue)을 섞으면 무슨 색이 나올까? 보라[자주]색, purple이야. 그런데 purple이라는 단어 자체는 보라색 염료를 만드는 원료인 특정 '조개(shellfish)'인 뿔고둥(murex)의 희랍어 이름에서 유래한 거란다. 페니키아인들의 염색 기술과 purple이라는 말의 역사가 비슷하다고 추정할 수 있어. purple은 자연에서 얻기 힘든 귀한 색이었기 때문에 왕실을 상징하는 색이기도 했단다. 티레에서 자주색 염료로 만든 자주색 천은 royal purple이라는 말을 낳을 정도였어. 왕만 입을 수 있을 정도로 귀하고 값이 비싸

다는 의미였지. 자주색 천은 상품으로도 가치가 높았단다. 기원전 8세기의 그리스 문헌에 페니키아라는 말이 바로 '자주색'을 의미했다고 나와 있어.

2 The Founding of Carthage

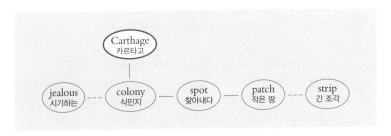

colony ⓝ a country or area that is under the political control of a more powerful country, usually located in a place far away

colony는 '정착지, 농장'을 뜻하는 라틴어에서 유래한 것이다. 페니키아인들이 본국에서 멀리 떨어진 아프리카에서 '농사짓기 좋은 땅'을 찾아 '정착해' 살면, 그곳이 페니키아의 colony(식민지)가 되는 것이다. 제국주의 시대 유럽의 강국들과 아시아, 아메리카와의 관계를 떠올리면 식민지의 의미를 쉽게 이해할 수 있다.

And they started colonies—little settlements of Phoenician people—in many of the places where they landed. 그리고 그들은 상륙한 곳의 많은 지역에서 식민지들(페니키아인들의 작은 정착지)을 만들기 시작했다.

jealous ⓐ feeling unhappy or angry because you want what someone else has

jealous는 zealous와 마찬가지로 명사형 zeal에서 파생된 형용사형이다. zeal은 뭔가를 성취하고 싶어 하는 '열정'이다. 그 열정으로 열심히 노력하는 태도를 나타낸다. 그런데 열정이 과해진 태도를 표현하는 형용사가 jealous(시기하는, 질투하는)로, She was jealous of Snow White's beauty(그녀는 백설 공주의 아름다움을 시기했다)처럼 쓸 수 있다. 명사형은 jealousy(시기, 질투)이다.

But Dido's brother, the king, was jealous of her and her husband's wealth. 그러나 디도의 오빠인 왕은 그녀와 그녀 남편의 부를 시기했다.

spot ⓥ to see or notice someone or something

spot은 '얼룩, 점'이라는 뜻으로, He has a lot of spots on his face(그의 얼굴에는 점이 많다)처럼 표현할 수 있다. 점이나 얼룩은 보기에도 작기 때문에 시간적으로도 찰나의 '한 순간', 공간적으로 한정된 '한 부분, 자리'를 의미한다. to build her new city on that very spot(자신의 새로운 도시를 바로 그 작은 자리에 세우다)처럼 표현할 수 있다. spot을 동사형으로 쓰면 잘 보이지 않은 것을 '찾아내다, 발견하다'라는 뜻이다.

Finally, they spotted land. 마침내 그들은 육지를 발견했다.

patch ⓝ a small area that looks different from the area around it

patch는 원래 piece(조각)를 뜻하는 말에서 유래했다. 옷이 귀하던 시절에는 옷이 낡아 해지거나 구멍이 나면 다른 옷감의 자투리(piece)를 잘라 기워서 입었다. 그런 옷감 자투리가 patch이다. 눈병이 나서 눈을 가리는 '안대'나 몸에 붙이는 의료용 '파스'도 patch이다. a patch of ground는 주위의 땅과는 다른 목적으로 사용하거나 다른 모습을 한 '작은 면적의 땅'을 의미한다.

He thought that Dido would put her bull hide down over a little patch of ground, just large enough to stand on. 그는 디도가 서 있을 만한 크기의 작은 땅 위에 소가죽을 놓을 것이라고 생각했다.

strip ⓝ a long narrow piece of cloth, leather or paper

옛날에 이발소에 가면 면도용 칼을 가는 긴 가죽 끈이 있었는데, 이것을 영어로 strop이나 strap라고 한다. strip과도 어원이 같으므로 천이나 가죽, 종이 등을 가늘고 길게 잘라낸 조각을 strip이라고 한다. 즉 '폭이 좁고 긴 땅'이나 신문의 직사각형 지면에 연재하는 a comic strip(연재 만화)처럼 가늘고 긴 모양을 뜻한다.

But instead, Dido got out a very sharp knife and cut her bull hide into hundreds of long, thin strips. 그러나 대신에 디도는 아주 잘 드는 칼을 꺼내서 소가죽을 수백 개의 길고 가는 조각으로 잘랐다.

Q 페니키아는 언제 지중해를 누비고 다녔나요?

A 히타이트와 이집트가 해적질을 하면서 지중해 지역 사람들을 공포에 떨게 했던 시절, 동부 지중해는 교역 활동이 완전히 끊겼단다. 생명이 우선이니 바다로 배를 띄울 엄두가 나지 않았겠지? 기원전 1000년경에 다시 무역이 시작되었는데, 이 시기의 무역을 주도한 나라가 바로 페니키아야. 페니키아는 아시리아에게 망하기 전까지 무역의 왕자 노릇을 하면서 지중해를 누볐고, 심지어 브리타니아(지금의 영국) 지방에까지 주석을 사러 갔어.

Chapter 16

The Return of Assyria

1 Ashurbanipal's Attack

🌐 소왕국으로 명맥을 유지하던 아시리아는 기원전 10세기 초부터 7세기 초까지 다시 메소포타미아 지역을 장악하며 제국을 건설하는데, 이 시기의 아시리아를 '신 (新)아시리아 제국'이라고 부른다. 이슈르바니팔은 기원전 669년부터 627년까지 재위하며 신아시리아의 후반기를 이끈 왕이다. 선대의 왕들과 마찬가지로 끊임없이 정복 전쟁을 벌여 영토를 확장했으며 니네베에 대규모 도서관을 짓고, 학문을 후원한 것으로 유명하다.

Do you remember reading about Shamshi-Adad, the Assyrian king who wanted to rule the whole world? He led his armies out to conquer the cities all around him, and he built an empire—the Assyrian Empire. But when they fought the Babylonians, the Assyrians lost. They became part of Babylon's empire, and had to obey the king of Babylon. But all the time they were thinking, "One day we will be free, and we will try to conquer the world again!"

Finally, that day came. The Assyrians rebelled against their masters, the Babylonians. They dug canals through the city of Babylon and flooded it with water, washing the city away. And then they started out to rebuild their empire. "We are like an evil rain that washes its enemies away!" they boasted. "We are like a net that tangles the feet of those who fight against us!"

The Assyrians raged up and down the Tigris and Euphrates rivers, taking over every city in their path. They stampeded over to Canaan and scattered the Israelites like dust; the Israelites were never allowed to return back to their own land again. They marched up into Asia Minor and forced the people there to obey them. And one of the greatest Assyrian kings of all, Ashurbanipal, led his soldiers all the way down into Egypt—and took it over!

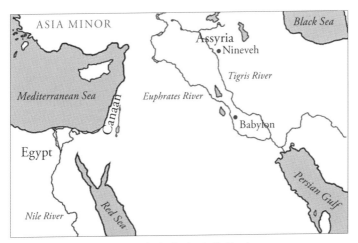

The Spread of Ashurbanipal's Empire

Even the mighty pharaohs of Egypt had to obey Assyria.

Ashurbanipal became king of Assyria around 668 BC/BCE. He terrified his enemies. For fun, he went on lion-hunts, chasing the lions down on horseback and shooting arrows at them. And when he led his soldiers into battle, he fought like an angry lion himself. With Ashurbanipal leading them, the Assyrians were almost impossible to beat.

Why were they so hard to conquer? The Assyrian soldiers fought in pairs. One man would hold a shield made out of baskets, tied together with leather. The other would shoot arrows from behind the shield. These basket shields were very light—but they kept arrows and spear-points out. The Assyrians would put their basket shields side by side and march towards their enemies like a moving wall with arrows spitting out from behind it.

Soon, the only way to escape the invading Assyrians was to hide inside a city with strong brick or stone walls. But Ashurbanipal, the king who was as strong as a lion, knew how to get over city walls. First, he ordered his soldiers to build a ramp out of

Ashurbanipal, the king who was as strong as a lion

dirt. They hauled buckets of earth up to a city's wall, holding their basket–shields over their heads to protect themselves. They dumped the earth into a heap against the wall and went back for more. Slowly, the heap grew larger and larger until it reached all the way up to the top of the wall.

Then Ashurbanipal commanded his men to build a *siege tower*—a wooden tower on wheels. The soldiers pushed the tower up the ramp, towards the city walls. On top of the tower, Assyrian archers fired arrows into the city. A battering ram jutted out of the tower's front. The soldiers pushed it right into the wall, breaking up the brick and stone. Soon, a section of the wall tottered and fell. The Assyrian army poured through the gap, into the city. Another city had fallen to Ashurbanipal and his army.

Ashurbanipal was cruel and ruthless to the cities he conquered. He burned houses, smashed walls, and killed anyone who tried to disobey him. He scattered salt in their fields, poisoning the land so that no crops would grow. He took captured people off to be slaves and never let them go home again. Most cities were too frightened to resist Ashurbanipal for long. They agreed to become part of the Assyrian empire and to pay part of their money to the Assyrian king.

Ashurbanipal became very rich. He ruled the biggest empire that the world had ever seen. But all across Assyria, people hated him. The cities conquered by Ashurbanipal obeyed him because they were afraid, but all the time they hoped that Assyria would soon collapse. "When we finally hear the news of your destruction," one conquered man wrote, "we will clap our hands with joy! And no one will cry over you."

2 The Library of Nineveh

니네베는 신(新)아시리아 제국의 수도로, 현재의 이라크 북부 모술 지역 티그리스 강변 동쪽에 세워졌는데, 기원전 612년에 바빌로니아에게 함락되어 파괴되었다. 19세기 말과 20세기 초에 영국의 고고학자들이 처음 발굴했는데 유적에서 궁전의 벽화와 청동상 등의 많은 유물이 나왔다. 특히 아슈르바니팔 궁전에서 수만 점의 점토판이 발견되었는데, 그 점토판에는 다양한 이야기들이 담겨 있었다. 사실 그 점토판들은 책이었으며 니네베에 거대한 도서관이 존재했다는 사실을 말해준다.

Ashurbanipal, the king of all Assyria, stood on his palace walls looking out over the city of Nineveh. He had spent years making Nineveh beautiful. It was his favorite city, and he was the strongest king in the world! He had built himself a magnificent palace, full of high, cool rooms hung with silk and painted with rich colors: royal blue, scarlet, and yellow as bright as the sun. The fifteen great gates of Nineveh's walls had been decorated with sculptures of bulls and lions and edged with gold. Carved pictures of Ashurbanipal's conquests lined the walls of Nineveh's greatest buildings. *Canals brought water into the city, so that all Nineveh's people could drink; and throughout Nineveh,

Ashurbanipal had planted gardens of strange and beautiful plants, so that his subjects could wander through green grass and admire the trees and flowers from far away.

"But it isn't enough!" Ashurbanipal thought. "I have made this city beautiful, but will it last after I am dead? A hundred years from now, how will anyone know of my greatness?"

"Excuse me, sir." A voice interrupted him. He turned to see one of his chief scribes, holding a clay tablet. The scribe held the tablet out. Ashurbanipal saw that it was covered with writing.

"Have you brought me a new book to read?" he asked. Ashurbanipal's scribes, the men who were in charge of writing down all the events of his reign, knew that he loved to read. They were always on the lookout for new books for him. And in those days, books weren't written on paper. They were carved into clay.

"We've found you a wonderful book!" the chief scribe said. "It's a tale from the court of Hammurabi, the great king who ruled Babylon so long ago. No one has ever read it before! One of your men found it in the ruins of Babylon's old walls, and kept it safe until we could bring it here to you."

Ashurbanipal glanced down at the tablet. This was indeed a find—a story from the days of a famous king of old. Now he could look forward to a good long evening of reading.

That night, as Ashurbanipal sat in his room reading his new tablet by lamplight, he had an idea.

"How many of these tablets are left in the ruins of old cities?" he said to himself. "If they are not rescued, they will crumble away into dust. Then we'll never know these stories from old times. What if I were to collect them all together, and keep them here in my palace? That would be a great project indeed! And then I would become known as the king who collected books—

and people could read my books hundreds of years from now."

Ashurbanipal set his new idea into action at once. *He sent his scribes out into all parts of the vast kingdom of Assyria, ordering them to collect all the tablets they could find and bring them back to Nineveh. He commanded other scribes to go out and ask the people of Assyria to repeat the stories they had heard from their grandfathers and grandmothers. *These stories had been told to children for centuries—but no one had ever written them down. Ashurbanipal's scribes wrote them on clay tablets, so that they could be kept forever.

He ordered the priests of Assyria to write down the words of their prayers. *The court astrologers wrote down the movements of the sun, moon and stars. The court doctors wrote down everything that they knew about illness and medicine. The court historians recorded all of the details of Ashurbanipal's reign, and everything that they knew about the kings who had come before him.

All of those clay tablets were thick and heavy. So Ashurbanipal built more and more rooms to keep them in. Soon he had collected thousands and thousands of clay tablets full of stories, prayers, instructions, history, science, medicine, and law. He had created the first library in the world.

And Ashurbanipal's wish came true. Although many of the tablets were destroyed in Assyria's wars with other countries, some of them still survive today, thousands of years later. They can still be read. And because we have Ashurbanipal's clay tablets, we remember him as the king who collected books—the first librarian ever. 📖

Note to Parent: Assyria's expansion took place between 1300–1200 BC/BCE; it reached its greatest extent under Tiglathpileser III (745–727 BC/BCE). Ashurbanipal, the last great Assyrian king, ruled 668–627 BC/BCE.

The Story of the Words

Chapter 16 The Return of Assyria

1 Ashurbanipal's Attack

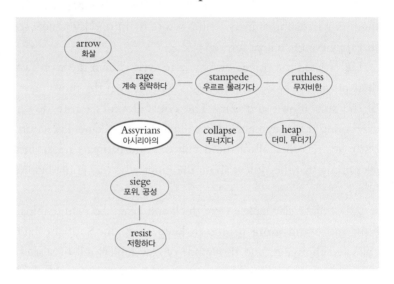

rage ⓥ to continue to invade with a great violence

rage는 머리끝까지 치밀어 오르는 화, 눈이 뒤집힐 정도의 분노를 말한다. 그렇게 화가 나면 가만있지 못하고 여기저기 돌아다니며 감정을 표출하게 되는데, 그런 동작을 표현하는 동사가 rage이다. 즉 '격렬하게 화를 내다'나 '계속 맹렬히 침략하다'이고, 명사로 쓰면 '분노'라는 뜻이다.

The Assyrians raged up and down the Tigris and Euphrates rivers, taking over every city in their path. 아시리아인들은 티그리스 강과 유프라테스 강을 오르내리며 계속 맹렬히 침략했고, 발길이 닿는 모든 도시들을 점령했다.

stampede ⓥ to start to run very fast to somewhere, in a large group

stampede는 에스파냐어에서 온 단어로 '쿵쿵거리며 걷다(stamp), 짓밟다

(crash)'라는 뜻이 있다. '무리지어 한꺼번에 어딘가로 질주하는' 동작이 바로 stampede이다.

They stampeded over to Canaan and scattered the Israelites like dust; the Israelites were never allowed to return back to their own land again. 그들은 가나안으로 우르르 몰려가 이스라엘 사람들을 먼지처럼 흩어지게 했다. 이후 이스라엘 사람들은 다시 자신들의 땅으로 돌아가도록 허락되지 않았다.

arrow ⓝ a weapon like a sharp stick that is shot from a bow

'활'에서 나가는 '살'인 '화살'을 arrow라고 한다. 둥글게 굽어 있는 '활'은 bow라고 한다. 총이 발명되기 전까지 활과 화살(a bow and arrow)은 대표적인 원거리 공격 무기였기 때문에 전쟁의 역사에서 항상 등장했다. 또한 arrow는 '쏘아야' 하기 때문에 He shot arrows at lions(그는 사자들에게 화살을 쏘았다)처럼 동사 shoot과 붙어 다닌다. 화살 모양을 닮은 기호 '화살표(→)'도 arrow라고 한다.

For fun, he went on lion-hunts, chasing the lions down on horseback and shooting arrows at them. 재미삼아 그는 사자 사냥을 했는데, 말을 타고 사자들을 쫓으며 활을 쏘았다.

heap ⓝ a large untidy pile of something

heap은 뭔가 쌓인 '더미, 무더기'를 의미하는데, 대개는 단정하게 차곡차곡이 아니라 대충 쌓은 것을 말한다. rubbish heap(쓰레기 더미)이나 a heap of stones(돌무더기)처럼 아무렇게나 쌓여 있는 것이다.

They dumped the earth into a heap against the wall and went back for more. 그들은 벽에 흙을 부려서 쌓은 다음 더 많은 흙을 나르기 위해 돌아갔다.

siege ⓝ an attack in which an army surrounds a place in order to gain control of it

siege는 sit(앉다), seat(자리)를 뜻하는 라틴어에서 유래하였다. 즉 '자리 잡고 앉는 것'이다. 전투에서 성 안에 있는 적군을 나오게 하거나 항복하게 만들려면 계속 성 주위에 자리를 잡고 '앉아' 있어야 한다. 식량이나 무기가 떨어지면 나와서 싸우거나 항복하거나 선택할 수밖에 없기 때문에 siege는 '포위, 봉쇄'라는 뜻이다. a siege tower는 성을 포위해서 공격할 목적으로 높이 지은 망루[전망대]이다.

Then Ashurbanipal commanded his men to build a siege tower—a wooden tower on wheels. 그런 다음 아슈르바니팔은 부하들에게 바퀴가 달린 목재 망루인 '공성 망루'를 건설하라고 명령했다.

ruthless ⓐ willing to hurt other people for getting what you want

ruthless는 pity, compassion(연민, 동정심)을 뜻하는 ruth와 '부정(~이 없는)'을 뜻하는 형용사형 접미사 -less가 합쳐진 것이다. '연민과 동정심이 없는' 사람은 단호하고 가차 없다. 울고불고 해도, 살려달라고 애원해도 소용없다. 자신만 생각하고 원하는 것을 얻기 위해서든 무슨 일이든 하는, 피도 눈물도 없는 '몰인정함'을 ruthless로 표현한다.

Ashurbanipal was cruel and ruthless to the cities he conquered. 아슈르바니팔은 자신이 정복한 도시에 대해 잔인하고 무자비했다.

resist ⓥ to fight against someone or something

resist는 '반대(against)'를 뜻하는 접두사 re-와 '서다(stand), 막다(stop)'를 뜻하는 sist가 합쳐진 것이다. 즉 '저항하다, 항거하다, 반대하다'라는 뜻이다. 2차 세계대전 당시 독일 나치에 저항해 싸운 프랑스의 민병대 레지스탕스(Résistance)도 '저항'이라는 뜻이다.

Most cities were too frightened to resist Ashurbanipal for long. 대부분의 도시들은 너무 두려워서 오랫동안 아슈르바니팔에게 저항하지 못했다.

collapse ⓥ to fall down suddenly; to suddenly stop existing

라틴어에서 온 collapse는 '함께(together)'를 뜻하는 col-과 '미끄러진(slipped), 넘어진(fallen)'을 뜻하는 lapse가 합쳐진 말이다. 한두 군데가 아니라 전부 한꺼번에 미끄러지고 넘어진 것을 표현한다. 그래서 collapse는 국가 체제의 붕괴, 망국(亡國)을 표현할 때 '쓰러지다, 무너지다, 붕괴되다'라는 뜻으로 쓰인다.

The cities conquered by Ashurbanipal obeyed him because they were afraid, but all the time they hoped that Assyria would soon collapse. 아슈르바니팔에게 정복된 도시들은 두려웠기 때문에 그에게 복종했지만, 그들은 항상 아시리아가 곧 무너지리라 기대했다.

2 The Library of Nineveh

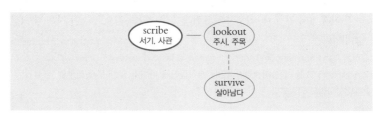

244

scribe ⓝ someone in the past whose job was to make written copies of official documents

라틴어에서 온 scribe에는 write(쓰다, 적다)라는 뜻이 있다. 그래서 describe 가 '서술하다, 묘사하다'이고, script가 '원고, 대본'이다. The scribe held the tablet out(그 서기는 점토판을 내밀었다)에서 scribe는 '쓰는 사람'을 말한다. 항상 왕의 옆에서 왕의 언행을 기록하고 궁정의 일을 기록하는 '서기(書記)'이다. 조선 시대의 '사관(史官)'도 scribe라고 할 수 있다.

He turned to see one of his chief scribes, holding a clay tablet. 그는 점토판을 들고 있는 수석 서기들 중 한 명을 돌아보았다.

lookout ⓝ the state of being watchful or paying attention in order to find something you want

lookout은 말 그대로 '밖(out)을 바라보는(look)' 것이다. 기다리는 사람이 오지 않나, 먹잇감이 지나가지 않나 하고 '내다보는 것'을 말한다. 그래서 lookout은 명사형으로 '망보기, 망보는 곳'을 뜻하는데, 대개 be on the lookout for ~의 형태로 쓴다. 뭔가를 보기 위해(for) '망루 위에 있다(be on the lookout)'라는 의미로, '계속 주시하다, 살피다'라는 뜻이다.

They were always on the lookout for new books for him. 그들은 그를 위해 새로운 책을 찾으려고 항상 주의를 기울였다.

survive ⓥ to continue to exist after a difficult time

survive는 '~을 넘어(beyond)'를 뜻하는 접두사 sur-와 '살다(live)'를 뜻하는 vive가 합쳐진 것이다. survive라고 하면 그냥 쉽게 사는 것이 아니라, 어떤 역경을 버텨내고 생존하는 것이다. survive를 사물에 쓰면 '없어지지 않고 계속 존재하다'라는 의미가 된다. She survived the plane crash(그녀는 비행기 추락에서도 생존했다)처럼 쓸 수 있다. 명사형은 survival(생존, 유물)이다.

Although many of the tablets were destroyed in Assyria's wars with other countries, some of them still survive today, thousands of years later. 비록 그 점토판 중 상당수가 아시리아와 다른 나라 간의 전쟁에서 파괴되었지만, 일부는 수천 년이 지난 지금까지도 남아 있다.

Q 아시리아에서 기억할 왕들은 누구인가요?
A 아시리아의 최초 수도는 아수르였어. 그러나 바빌로니아에게 굴복한 이후 암흑의 세월을 산 아시리아는 여러 번 수도를 옮겼단다. 아시리아 부

흥의 시기를 연 '아슈르나시르팔 2세'는 칼레로 수도를 옮긴 다음에 날개 달린 황소의 몸에 사람 머리를 한 수호상을 세웠어.

그다음 기억할 왕으로는 '사르곤 2세'가 있어. 아카드 제국을 세운 사르곤을 닮아 대제국을 이루겠다는 의지를 표명하느라 이름도 사르곤 2세로 지은 거야. 그는 사르곤 시를 만들고, 거대한 상을 세웠는데, 아시리아의 신마저 배경으로 보일 정도로 큰 상이었다고 해. 자신의 권위를 만방에 알리고 싶었던 거지.

그리고 니네베를 수도로 삼은 왕 산혜립은 《구약 성서》에도 이름이 기록되어 있단다. 아시리아의 최전성기를 만든 왕이지만, 예루살렘 정복에 실패해 그가 이룬 많은 성공에도 불구하고 불운한 왕으로 남았어. 니네베에 왕궁을 새로 만들고, 거대한 부조를 세웠지만 두 아들에게 살해당했으니까.

Chapter 17
Babylon Takes Over Again!

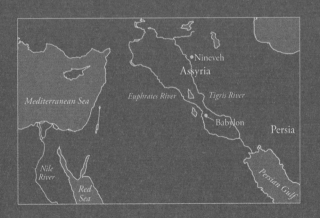

1 Nebuchadnezzar's Madness

🌐 바빌로니아인들은 기원전 625년부터 아시리아 제국을 무너뜨리고 옛 영토인 메소포타미아와 주변 지역을 되찾아 다시 제국을 세웠다. 그런데 성경 속에 묘사된 바빌로니아의 모습은 대단히 부정적이다. 《구약 성서》 창세기에는 바빌로니아인들이 신의 권위에 도전해 '바벨탑'을 세웠고, 그로 인해 인간의 언어가 달라지고 서로 미워하게 되었다는 내용이 등장한다. 또한 다니엘서(the Book of Daniel)에는 '바빌론 유수(Babylonian Captivity)'가 기록되어 있다. 네부카드네자르 2세는 기원전 586년에 예루살렘을 약탈하고 유대교 성전을 파괴한 뒤 많은 이스라엘인들을 포로로 잡아 바빌론으로 끌고 가는데, 이 사건을 '바빌론 유수(幽囚)'라고 한다.

After Ashurbanipal died, the Assyrian empire fell apart. And Assyria's old enemies, the Babylonians, took over Assyria's land. The Babylonians wanted revenge! Assyria had destroyed Babylon, so now the Babylonians destroyed Nineveh, Assyria's most beautiful city. ˙They broke down the walls and gates, ripped the doors off Ashurbanipal's great library, and smashed hundreds of his precious clay tablets! ˙Fortunately, some of the books survived so that we can still read them today.

Then the Babylonians settled down to rule their own empire. ˙The Babylonian Empire wasn't quite as big as the Assyrian Empire, because the Babylonians never took over Egypt. But it was almost as big. And for many years, the Babylonians were the most powerful people in the world.

Babylon, the city flooded by Assyria, was rebuilt. The great Babylonian king Nebuchadnezzar (who became king around 605 BC/BCE) spent much of his reign making Babylon beautiful again. He built huge walls all around the city, to keep it safe from invasion. In one of the walls, he built a great blue gate decorated with yellow and white bulls and dragons, and named it after

Babylon's chief goddess, Ishtar. Underneath this gate, a great parade passed every year in honor of Ishtar. The gate became famous all through Nebuchadnezzar's empire.

Nebuchadnezzar was such a famous ruler that he became known as "Nebuchadnezzar the Great." But he was not a happy man. Clay tablets and scrolls written during his reign talk about "Nebuchadnezzar's madness." These stories say that, for several years, Nebuchadnezzar actually lost his mind!

One story about Nebuchadnezzar's madness is told in the book of Daniel, in the Bible. The story says that Nebuchadnezzar was a little too pleased with himself. He thought he was a god. He even made an enormous golden statue of himself, almost a hundred feet high, and told all of his people to bow down and worship it. Here is the rest of the story:

One day, the great king Nebuchadnezzar was walking on the roof of his palace in Babylon. "Look at this beautiful city I have built!" he said to himself. "I am the most powerful king in the world! No one is greater than I am—not even God."

As soon as he said this, a voice came from heaven. "Nebuchadnezzar!" the voice said. "You have become too proud! You think you are greater than God Himself. Now listen to your doom—you will act like an animal, and eat grass like a cow, until you admit that God is more powerful than you are!"

At once Nebuchadnezzar lost his mind. He ran out into the fields and lived like a wild animal. He walked on his hands and knees, until his knees were as tough as hooves and his fingernails were as long as a bird's claws. He drank from the river, slept under bushes, and woke up in the morning wet with dew. His hair grew long and shaggy, until he looked like a goat. And he ate grass like a cow. His people gathered around at a distance and watched him. "What is wrong with the king?" they whispered. "He has gone mad!"

Finally Nebuchadnezzar looked up at the sky. "I am not a god!" he said. "I am only a man. And God is more powerful than I am."

At once Nebuchadnezzar was sane again. He stood up on his feet. He looked around him and knew that he was the king of Babylon, not an animal. He returned to his palace in Babylon to rule his people once again. But never again did he claim to be a god. Now he knew that he was only a man.

2 The Hanging Gardens of Babylon

'공중정원'은 신(新)바빌로니아 제국의 네부카드네자르(Nebuchadnezzar) 왕이 왕비인 아미티스(Amytis)를 위해 건설한 것으로 알려진 거대한 인공 정원이다. 멀리서 보면 마치 하늘과 땅 사이에 아름다운 산이 떠 있는 듯 보인다고 해서 '공중정원(Hanging Garden)'이라는 이름이 붙여졌다. 거대한 계단식 피라미드를 짓고 각 층마다 온갖 꽃들과 식물들을 심어 놓았으며 유프라테스 강에서 물을 끌어와 정원을 관리했다고 한다. '바빌론의 공중정원'은 고대 세계의 7대 불가사의 중 하나로 꼽힌다.

Nebuchadnezzar, the great king of Babylon, sat on his throne and worried. *He had a great empire—but what if another country attacked him? He wasn't sure that his army could defend Babylon from invaders. And he was very worried about Persia, a country to the east of Babylon. The Persians were expanding their own country. Their army was strong. He had heard frightening stories about Persian soldiers!

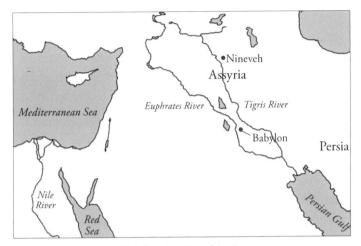

Babylon, Assyria, and Persia

"I know what I'll do," he thought to himself. "I will ask the king of Persia if I can marry his daughter. Then he will be my father-in-law, and he won't want to attack me!"

Nebuchadnezzar had never seen the daughter of the Persian king. But that didn't matter to him. He was willing to marry a stranger to keep Babylon safe. So he sent messages to the king of Persia, offering to marry the princess.

Meanwhile, the king of Persia was sitting on his throne, worrying about Babylon. "What will I do if Babylon attacks me?" he thought. "Their soldiers are such good fighters! I'm not sure that we could defeat them. How can I convince Nebuchadnezzar to leave me alone?"

Just then his servant entered with the message from Nebuchadnezzar. "Sir," he said, "the king of Babylon has sent you a message. He wishes to know if you will give him your daughter in marriage."

The king of Persia was greatly relieved. "Of course I will!"

he said. "Nebuchadnezzar would never attack his own father-in-law!" And he sent for his daughter, the princess Amytis. "My dear," he said, "the king of Babylon wishes to marry you."

"But I've never even met him!" Amytis protested. "And I don't want to leave my home in the mountains to live in Babylon. It's down on flat land, where the air is still and thick."

"If you marry him," the king of Persia said, "Persia will be safe from attack. You will be helping your whole country."

Finally, Amytis agreed. She traveled to Babylon for the great wedding ceremony. As soon as Nebuchadnezzar saw her, he fell in love with her. He built her the most beautiful rooms to live in and filled them with lovely things. He gave her gold jewelry, clothes of silk, pet monkeys from China to play with, beautiful flowers to make her rooms colorful, and servants to do her every wish.

But Amytis wasn't happy. She missed the cliffs and valleys of the Persian mountains. Most of all, she missed the gardens that the Persian people built on the hillsides. "I want to go home!" she said. "I don't want to live in Babylon anymore. It's so flat and dull here!"

"How can I make Amytis happy?" Nebuchadnezzar thought. And then he had an idea. He would build her a garden—a mountain garden, right in the middle of the city of Babylon.

Nebuchadnezzar set to work at once. He ordered his slaves to haul huge slabs of rock in from far away. Out of this rock, he built an enormous hill—an artificial mountain! He covered the rock with dirt and planted it thickly with trees, flowers, and bushes. He had plants brought from Persia, so that Amytis could see familiar flowers again. Nebuchadnezzar's men even built a pump that would pull water up from the Euphrates River to the very top of the garden. Then the water ran down the garden, just like a mountain river. Nebuchadnezzar ordered paths built up and down the mountain. Then he brought Amytis out to see what he had done.

"My dear," he said, "you cannot return to Persia. But I have brought a little bit of Persia to you. Now you can walk in your hillside garden whenever you want."

Amytis's garden became known as the Hanging Gardens of Babylon. People came from all over to admire the mountain Nebuchadnezzar had built in the middle of flat, hot Babylon. And every day, Amytis walked in her garden and pretended that she was back home in Persia.

The Hanging Gardens of Babylon were so beautiful and so huge that they are now called one of the Seven Wonders of the Ancient World. The Seven Wonders are things that ancient people made or built that we still think are incredible, even today! You have already studied about one of the Seven Wonders of the Ancient World—the Great Pyramid of Giza. Today you've learned about the second of the Seven Wonders: The Hanging Gardens of Babylon. 📖

Note to Parent: Nebuchadnezzar reigned from 605–561 BC/BCE.

The Story of the Words

Chapter 17 Babylon Takes Over Again!

1 Nebuchadnezzar's Madness

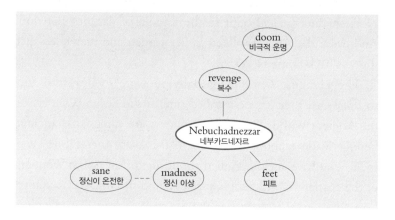

revenge ⓝ something you do in order to punish someone who has done something bad to you

revenge는 '강하게'를 뜻하는 접두사 re-와 avenge(복수하다)의 고어(古語)인 venge가 합쳐진 것이다. revenge는 대개 '복수, 보복, 설욕'을 뜻하는 명사형으로 쓴다. 상대에 대한 보복을 표현할 때는 on을 붙여 revenge on Assyria(아시리아에 대한 보복)처럼 쓰고, 어떤 행위에 대한 보복은 for를 붙여 revenge for the murder(그 살인에 대한 복수)의 형태로 쓴다.

The Babylonians wanted revenge! 바빌로니아인들은 복수를 원했다!

> **Q** 바빌론 유수가 유대교를 촉진시켰다니 정말인가요?
>
> **A** 《구약 성서》의 예레미야서에는 당시의 역사를 생생하게 증언하는 이야기로 가득하단다. 첫 공격에서 왕과 군사는 바빌론으로 끌려 가고, 솔로몬 성전의 보물은 약탈당했지만 도시 자체가 파괴되지는 않았단다. 끌려간 왕도 살아있는 동안은 바빌론에서 호의호식하고 지냈다고 해. 그러나 유

대 왕국이 이집트와 몰래 동맹을 맺고, 바빌로니아에 대항하려던 것이 발각되어 화가 난 네부카드네자르는 예루살렘을 불태우라고 명령했어. 백성들도 바빌론 전역에 포로로 끌려왔지. 이것을 역사에서는 '바빌론 유수'라고 해.

유대인들은 타국에 끌려와 살면서 오히려 '야훼(하느님의 이름)'의 의미가 무엇인지 고민하면서 기록하는 일에 착수했는데, 이것이 《구약 성서》의 기반이 된 거야. 고난 속에서 오히려 유대인 공동체를 유지하려고 그들에게 전승된 이야기를 정리하면서 유대인의 마음을 하나로 묶으려고 노력한 것이지.

madness ⓝ the state of being mad; mental illness

-ness는 '상태(state), 성질(quality)'을 나타내는 명사형 접미사로, 형용사 뒤에 붙어서 특정한 상태나 성질을 표현한다. mad는 '미친, 정신 이상의'라는 뜻의 형용사이다. 명사형 madness는 '미친 상태, 정신이 이상한 상태'를 뜻한다. '정신 이상, 광기, 미친 짓' 등으로 이해하면 된다.

Clay tablets and scrolls written during his reign talk about "Nebuchadnezzar's madness." 그의 통치 시기에 기록된 점토판과 두루마리는 '네부카드네자르의 정신 이상'에 대해 이야기하고 있다.

feet ⓝ plural form of 'foot'(a unit of length)

feet은 foot(발)의 복수형이다. 따라서 '발의 길이'라는 뜻의 foot은 길이를 재는 원시적인 측정 단위로도 쓰였는데, 미국에서는 지금도 미터법을 쓰지 않고 피트법을 쓴다. 1foot은 30.48센티미터이다. 서양 성인 남자의 발 길이가 평균적으로 이쯤 되는 것 같다. 그럼 a hundred feet high는 높이가 몇 미터쯤 될까? 대략 30미터가 넘는다.

He even made an enormous golden statue of himself, almost a hundred feet high, and told all of his people to bow down and worship it. 심지어 그는 약 100피트 높이의 거대한 자신의 황금 동상을 만들었고, 모든 백성에게 그 동상에 절을 하고 숭배하라고 명령했다.

doom ⓝ something very bad that is going to happen

doom은 '심판(judgment)'을 뜻하는 고대 영어에서 온 것이다. 그래서 기독교에서 주장하는 '최후 심판의 날'을 영어로 doomsday라고 한다. 죽음, 파멸 등을 피할 수 없는 비극적인 운명이 doom이다. 운명은 신이 부여하는 것이기 때문에 doom은 동사로 '불행한 운명을 맞게 하다'라는 뜻이다. 따라서 '~할 운명이다'는 We are all doomed to die(우리는 모두 죽을 운명이다)처럼 수동태로 쓴다.

Now listen to your doom—you will act like an animal, and eat grass like a cow, until you admit that God is more powerful than you are! 이제 너의 운명을 들려주마. 하느님이 너보다 더 강하다는 사실을 인정할 때까지, 너는 짐승처럼 행동할 것이며, 소처럼 풀을 먹을 것이다.

sane ⓐ able to think in a normal and reasonable way

sane은 '건강한(healthy)'을 뜻하는 라틴어 sanus에서 온 것이다. 처음에는 육체와 정신의 건강을 모두 뜻하는 말로 쓰였지만, 점차 '정신적으로 건강한'의 의미로만 쓰이게 되었다. sane은 '제정신인, 정신이 온전한, 분별 있는'을 뜻하는 형용사이다. 명사형은 sanity이고, 반대말은 앞에 in-을 붙여 표현한다. 일상 회화에서는 sane보다 insane(제정신이 아닌, 미친)을 훨씬 많이 쓴다. 친구가 황당한 말이나 행동을 하면 Are you insane?(너 미쳤니? 정신 나갔니?)이라고 묻게 된다.

At once Nebuchadnezzar was sane again. 그 즉시 네부카드네자르는 다시 정신이 온전해졌다.

> **Q** 아시리아 제국을 무너뜨리고 새로 세운 왕국은?
> **A** 우선 함무라비 법전으로 유명한 바빌로니아는 새롭게 건설된 바빌로니아와 구분해서 '구바빌로니아'라고 해. 그리고 나보폴라사르 왕이 아시리아 제국을 멸망시키고 건설한 제국이 '신바빌로니아'란다.
> 바빌론의 나보폴라사르 왕이 아시리아의 니네베를 쳐들어가는 것은 혼자의 힘으로는 어려웠어. 그를 도와준 사람이 메디아 왕인 키악사레스였지. 키악사레스는 나보폴라사르를 도와서 아시리아를 공격하는 것이 유리하다고 생각했어. 그들은 굳건한 동맹을 위해 결혼을 추진했는데 그것이 바로 당시 왕자였던 네부카드네자르와 메디아의 공주 아미티스가 맺어지게 된 계기가 되었어.

2 The Hanging Gardens of Babylon

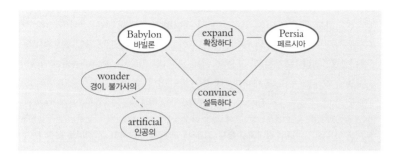

expand ⓥ to make something larger

expand는 '밖으로(out)'를 뜻하는 접두사 ex-와 '퍼지다, 퍼뜨리다(spread)'를 뜻하는 pand가 합쳐진 것이다. 물을 마룻바닥에 쏟으면 물이 한동안 계속 '밖으로(out) 퍼져(spread)' 가는데, 바로 이런 모습을 표현하는 동사가 expand이다. 즉 '확장하다, 확대하다'라는 뜻이다. 명사형은 expansion이다.

The Persians were expanding their own country. 페르시아인들도 자신들의 영토를 넓히고 있었다.

convince ⓥ to persuade someone to do something

다른 사람의 생각을 바꾸도록 설득하고 그것에 대해 확신을 주는 것은 대단히 힘든 일이다. 그래서 '설득하다, 확신을 주다'라는 뜻의 convince에서 접두사 con-은 '강하게'를, vince는 '극복하다(overcome), 정복하다(conquer)'를 뜻한다. 상대의 생각을 힘들게 정복해야 설득이 되고 확신을 줄 수 있는 것이다.

How can I convince Nebuchadnezzar to leave me alone? 어떻게 네부카드네자르가 그냥 내버려두게 설득할 수 있을까?

artificial ⓐ not natural, but made by people

artificial의 art는 '기술'을, ficial은 '만들어진(made)'을 뜻한다. 즉 '사람이 솜씨를 부려 만든' 것이 artificial이다. '자연적인(natural)'과 반대되는 개념으로, '인공의(man-made), 인위적인'을 뜻한다.

Out of this rock, he built an enormous hill—an artificial mountain! 그는 이 바위로 하나의 거대한 언덕, 즉 인공 산을 건설했다!

wonder ⑪ something that makes you feel great admiration

'어, 저게 뭐지?' 입에서 이런 말이 절로 나오면 wonder라는 단어를 쓸 수 있다. 신기하고 놀랍고 멋진 것을 보고서 경탄하며 궁금해 하는 것이 wonder이다. 동사형으로는 '궁금해 하다, 놀라다'이고, 명사형으로는 감탄을 자아내는 '경이로움, 경탄, 불가사의' 라는 의미로 쓰인다. the Seven Wonders of the Ancient World는 '고대 세계의 7대 불가사의'이다.

The Hanging Gardens of Babylon were so beautiful and so huge that they are now called one of the Seven Wonders of the Ancient World. '바빌론의 공중정원'은 너무도 아름답고 너무도 거대해서 현재 '고대 세계의 7대 불가사의' 중 하나로 불린다.

Q 세계 7대 불가사의는 누가 정한 것인가요?

A 세계 7대 불가사의에 이집트의 피라미드, 바빌론의 공중정원이 포함된다고 책에서 소개하고 있는데, 도대체 7가지 유적을 뽑아 불가사의라고 정한 사람은 누구이고, 어떤 근거에서 정한 것일까? 바로 그 주인공은 기원전 200년대에 비잔틴 제국에서 살았던 '필론'이야. 그는 기원전 225년경에 자신이 뽑은 7가지 건축물을 《세계의 7대 경관》라는 제목으로 기록했어. 그 책은 제자들을 가르치기 위한 목적이었다고 하니 건축물의 교육적 가치가 무엇보다 중요했겠지? 필론이 실제로 본 것뿐만 아니라 당시에 존재했던 자료를 읽고 정했다고 보는 것이 맞아. 그가 정한 '세계 7대 불가사의'는 피라미드와 공중정원 이외에도 파로스의 등대, 에페소스의 아르테미스 신전, 로도스 섬의 크로이소스 거상, 마우솔루스의 영묘, 올림피아의 제우스 신상이었어. 그런데 왜 7가지였을까? 숫자 7이 피타고라스가 거론한 우주를 표현하는 완벽한 수이기 때문이었단다.

Chapter 18
Life in Early Crete

1 Bull-Jumpers and Sailors

🌍 기원전 3000년경부터 에게 해의 크레타 섬에는 사람들이 문명을 이루며 살았는데, 이 문명을 크레타 문명이라고 부른다. 그런데 크레타 섬의 유적과 유물에는 이 사람들이 소를 숭배한 토템(totem) 신앙을 갖고 있었음을 짐작케 하는 것이 많다. 특히 크노소스 궁전 유적에서 사람이 황소를 뛰어넘는 곡예 장면이 묘사된 벽화가 발견되었는데, 이를 통해 역사가들은 크레타 사람들이 소를 숭배했을 뿐만 아니라 황소 뛰어넘기 곡예를 즐기며 소에게 사람을 제물로 바쳤을 것으로 추정하고 있다.

We've been learning about people who lived near rivers: the Egyptians, the people of the Indus Valley, the Chinese of the Yellow River Valley, and the Assyrians and Babylonians who lived near the Tigris and Euphrates rivers, in Mesopotamia. But if we look over in the Mediterranean Sea, we'll find something different—people who lived completely surrounded by water. These people built their homes on an island called Crete.

Crete is a long, skinny island in the Mediterranean Sea, a sea that is shaped a little bit like a duck flying. Long, long ago, a tribe called the Minoans settled down on the island of Crete.

The Minoans entertained themselves in an unusual way—by leaping over bulls.

Imagine that you're standing on a hard dirt floor, in the middle of a huge arena. All around you, crowds are shouting your name and cheering. You glance around you and see two other people in the arena with you, a boy and a girl. None of you have any weapons. Your hands are empty, and all you're wearing is a simple loose garment that allows your arms and legs to move freely.

Suddenly a wooden door swings open in the arena wall. A

huge black bull charges out into the arena. The shouts of the crowd get louder and louder. The bull paws the earth and shakes his head back and forth. His horns are sharp and tipped with gold. He swings his head towards you and sees you. *He snorts and charges straight at you.

But you don't run away. You wait until he's only inches away from you—and then you grab his horns and push yourself upwards. You somersault through the air, do a handstand on the bull's back, and land on your feet behind him. The girl who's in the arena with you is there to catch you. The crowd roars! *You turn and see your other teammate vault onto the bull. As he lands on his feet, you grab his arm to help him stay standing. The bull comes to a halt, confused. The three of you bow to the crowd and then turn to do it all over again.

If you were a boy or girl in ancient Crete, you might find yourself part of a bull-jumping team! The Minoans, who lived on the island of Crete, trained athletic children to become bull-jumpers. The children learned the kind of gymnastics that children still learn today—somersaulting, balance exercises, tumbling, and vaulting. But instead of doing their vaulting over a piece of equipment, the students learned how to vault over the backs of small animals such as goats—and then finally were taught how to leap over the backs of bulls.

Bull-jumping festivals were held to honor the Minoan gods, who were thought to take the form of bulls. At the end of every bull-jumping festival, the bulls were sacrificed to the gods.

During festivals, people came from all over Crete to cheer for the bull-jumpers. Bull-jumpers were treated like royalty. They were given the best food and the nicest places to live. They were showered with presents of gold, jewelry, and beautiful clothes. But bull-jumping was a dangerous sport, because bulljumpers were often killed by the bulls they were supposed to leap over. Few bull-jumpers lived past the age of twenty.

The Minoans were known both for bull-jumping and for ship-building. In ancient times, the Mediterranean Sea was full of pirates. No one ruled the sea; it was controlled by bandits who sailed their small boats near the shore. These bandits attacked and robbed anyone who ventured out onto the water. Kings of the ancient world had learned how to build strong armies that fought on land. But none of them knew how to build big ships to carry their soldiers out onto the water. So the pirates roamed free on the Mediterranean Sea.

But the king of the Minoans was different. He knew that the Minoans had to be able to sail safely across the Mediterranean Sea to land, so that they could trade with other countries. *So he ordered his craftsmen to build great ships that he could use to wipe out pirates and patrol the Mediterranean Sea.

The Minoan craftsmen learned how to build the ships. They were the greatest ship-builders of the ancient world. And the king of the Minoans became the first king to have a navy—an army that knew how to fight on the water. This navy drove the pirates out of the Mediterranean Sea and carried Minoan traders to other ancient countries so that they could buy and sell goods. The Minoan navy became the strongest in the world. It was so strong that the greatest palace of Crete didn't even have walls. *No invaders could land on Crete's shores, because the navy kept them away.

2 King Minos and the Minotaur

그리스 신화에는 괴물 미노타우로스에 관한 내용이 나온다. 최고의 신 제우스

262

는 페니키아의 공주인 에우로페를 사랑해 둘 사이에서 미노스가 탄생한다. 미노스
는 크레타의 왕이 되었는데, 바다의 신 포세이돈의 노여움을 산다. 포세이돈은 미노
스의 왕비가 황소를 사랑하게 만들고, 왕비와 소 사이에서 소의 머리에 사람의 몸을
한 괴물 미노타우로스가 태어난다. 미노스 왕은 이 사실을 감추기 위해 왕궁 지하의
미로에 미노타우로스를 가두고, 해마다 아테네에서 소년과 소녀 일곱 명씩을 받아
미노타우로스의 먹이로 희생시킨다.

The Minoans who lived on Crete were named after a legendary
king named Minos. The Minoans told this story about Minos:

Minos was a son of the god Zeus, the chief of all the
gods. But because he was half-human, Minos couldn't live
with the other gods. Instead, he lived on Crete, in a great and
beautiful palace.

*But this shining palace concealed a dark secret. *Below the
foundation of the palace, in a maze so twisty and complicated
that no one could find the way in or out, lived a horrible
monster—the Minotaur. The Minotaur lived in the dark, but
people whispered that he was half man and half bull—and that
he ate human beings.

King Minos didn't want to feed his own people to the
Minotaur, so he ordered the nearby city of Athens to send
him victims for the Minotaur's dinner. *Every year, Athens
had to send seven girls and seven boys to King Minos, or else
(he threatened) he would destroy their city. *Year after year,
the Athenians sent this dreadful tribute to Minos. They put
the names of all the boys and girls of Athens into a bowl, and
picked out fourteen unlucky victims, then put them on a ship
and took them to Crete. And year after year, the seven girls
and seven boys disappeared and were never seen again.

On his eighteenth birthday, Theseus, the son of the king of Athens, decided to walk down to the seaside. The sea was blue, the sky was clear, and the sun shone. ˙But the beach was full of weeping fathers and mothers, and the ship drawn up to the shore had black sails.

"Why does the ship have black sails?" Theseus asked. "Why are you all crying?"

"Because our sons and daughters are going to Crete," one mother answered him. "They'll be eaten by the Minotaur, and we'll never see them again."

Theseus was horrified! "Why didn't I know about this?" he demanded.

"Because you are the prince," another father told him. "Your name is never put into the bowl with the names of all the other young people of Athens! You'll never have to go to Crete and face the Minotaur."

"But that's not right!" Theseus said. "˙Let me go to Crete in the place of one of the young men. I'll face the Minotaur, and try to kill him. If I succeed, we'll put a white sail on this ship instead of the black one, and sail home to Athens. And no one will ever have to be sacrificed as tribute to King Minos again."

Theseus's father, King Aegeus, begged him not to go. But Theseus was determined, and in the end he had his way. He sailed to Crete with the other victims.

˙On the shore of Crete, they were greeted by the cruel King Minos himself, with his beautiful daughter Ariadne walking meekly behind him. "More food for the Minotaur!" King Minos said, with a great laugh. "Tonight, you'll visit the bull-man in the Labyrinth, his maze beneath my palace!"

He sent the fourteen victims to the prisons of Knossos to

wait for nightfall. But Ariadne had fallen in love with Theseus at first sight. Just before dark, she found a torch, a sword, and a ball of wool, and crept secretly out of King Minos's palace, down to Theseus's prison cell. "Theseus!" she whispered. "Do you want to kill the Minotaur?"

"Yes!" Theseus answered. "But how can I? He lives at the center of the Labyrinth, and no one who gets into that maze can ever get out again."

"I've brought you a torch to light your way," Ariadne said, "and a sword to kill the monster. Take this ball of wool and tie it to the doorframe of the Labyrinth. Then drop the ball and let it roll forward. It will lead you to the center of the maze, because the center is the lowest part of the whole Labyrinth. You'll find the Minotaur sleeping there. Kill it, and then follow the string back out to the doorway."

She unlocked the door of the cell and let Theseus out. He did as she told him, making his way through the dark passages of the Labyrinth with his torch throwing strange shadows all

The Minotaur

around him and the ball of wool rolling steadily forward in front of him. Suddenly the ball came to a stop. Theseus held up his torch. He was in the center of a huge underground room. *It stank of some wild animal, and bones littered the floor. In the middle of the room, a monster—half man and half bull—lay asleep on a golden sofa.

Theseus started forward, but the monster woke and leaped from his sofa with a roar. They fought together for hours, until finally Theseus struck the Minotaur dead with his sword. Then he made his way back up to the entrance of the Labyrinth, following the wool string until he saw the door to the outside up ahead of him.

Ariadne had already released his thirteen friends. Together, they slipped away to the harbor, boarded their ship, and set sail for Athens. They sailed into the harbor of Athens just as the sun rose over the city.

*But in their haste, they had forgotten to put a white sail on their ship! The people of Athens came forward to meet them, but although some were rejoicing, others were weeping. "Your Highness," one of them said to Theseus, "your father the king was waiting for you, on top of that far distant cliff. When the sun struck the sails of your ship, and he saw that the sails were black, he thought that you were dead. So he threw himself off the cliff and into the water. You are now the king of Athens."

Theseus was crowned king of Athens, but it was a bitter celebration for him. He built a monument to his father in the harbor of Athens. And he named the water around Athens the Aegean Sea, in memory of his father Aegeus. It is still called the Aegean Sea today.

3 The Mysterious End of the Minoans

🌐 미노스 문명은 기원전 3600년경부터 1450년경까지 에게 해(Aegean Sea) 남쪽 크레타(Crete) 섬에서 꽃피운 유럽 최초의 해양 문명을 말한다. 미노아 문명, 크레타 문명이라고도 하는데, 이 문명을 일군 사람들을 뜻하는 Minoans는 20세기 초에 영국의 고고학자 아서 에반스(Arthur Evans)가 크레타 섬의 유적을 발굴하면서 전설 속 왕인 미노스(Minos)의 이름을 따서 명명한 것이다. 미노스인들은 청동기 문명과 발달된 조선술을 기반으로 에게 해에서 세력을 떨쳤다. 유럽 문명의 '첫번째 고리'로 평가받는 미노스 문명은 화산 폭발로 인해 멸망한 것으로 추정된다.

What happened to the Minoans?

The Minoans of Crete disappeared, mysteriously, more than two thousand years ago. Their civilization came to a sudden end. All the Minoans left Crete. Why did they do this?

Although no one knows for sure, many historians think that the Minoans left when a volcano erupted on a nearby island called Thera. Thera looked like a small island, and people lived on it, grew crops and raised animals in its fields. But Thera was actually the top of an active volcano that poked up from the Mediterranean Sea.

One day, the small island began to shake underfoot. The people of Thera could feel constant small earthquakes. Many left the island at once, taking all their possessions with them! But the earthquakes died away, and the people who were still on Thera decided to stay. They started to rebuild the walls that had fallen down.

But the volcano wasn't finished. *Bits of rock called pumice started to spray out of the volcano's funnel. It covered the whole countryside. Smoke began to come out of the ground.

The rest of the people of Thera decided to leave—and just in time! *The volcano exploded, spraying lava and rock all over the island. *Huge boulders were thrown up from the inside of the volcano and fell like rock bombs on top of the villages of Thera. Suddenly, the volcano collapsed inward. *The sea rushed in to fill the hole, and the whole island of Thera sank beneath the sea! The island of Thera was gone forever.

The island of Crete was still there. *But a tidal wave thrown up by the volcano swept its shores. Huge clouds of ash, dust and smoke floated down the wind to cover it. Ash covered the crops. Food supplies were wiped out. People could hardly breathe, because of all the dust and smoke in the air. Historians think that many of the Minoans left the island of Crete because the volcano ruined the air and land. Others stayed, but they struggled against starvation. Finally they were forced to battle their neighbors for food. Minoan cities were never strong and powerful again. *Ash and dust helped bring the first great civilization of Crete to its end. 📖

Note to Parent: The Minoan civilization reached its peak between 2200–1450 BC/BCE. Since the Minoans are important for elementary students primarily as predecessors of the Greeks, I have included them slightly out of chronological order.

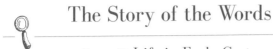

The Story of the Words

Chapter 18 Life in Early Crete

1 Bull-Jumpers and Sailors

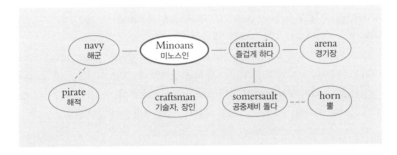

entertain ⓥ to do something to amuse or interest people

entertain은 '서로(inter)'를 뜻하는 enter와 '붙잡다, 껴안다(hold)'라는 뜻의 tain
이 합쳐져 '접대하다, 즐겁게 해주다'라는 뜻이 되었다. 찾아온 손님을 반갑게
환대하는 모습을 연상하면 된다. 음식과 술을 대접하고 여흥을 즐길 수 있게 한
다는 의미이다. 명사형은 entertainment(오락, 여흥, 접대)이다.

The Minoans entertained themselves in an unusual way—by leaping over bulls. 미
노스 사람들은 독특한 방식으로 즐기며 놀았는데, 그것은 황소를 뛰어넘는 것이었다.

arena ⓝ a building with a large central area surrounded by raised seats,
used for sports and entertainment

arena는 '모래'를 뜻하는 라틴어 '하레나(harēna)'에서 온 것이다. 로마 시대에
검투사들이 대결하는 경기장에는 모래가 깔려 있었기 때문에, arena가 '경기
장, 공연장, 무대'를 뜻하는 말이 된 것이다. 비유적으로 자신이 전공하는 분야
나 직업 세계도 '활동하는 무대'라는 의미에서 arena라고 한다.

Imagine that you're standing on a hard dirt floor, in the middle of a huge arena. 여
러분이 거대한 경기장의 한가운데에 있는 딱딱한 흙바닥 위에 서 있다고 상상해보라.

horn ⓝ a hard pointed part that grows from the heads of some animals
소나 사슴의 머리에 나는 '뿔'을 통칭하는 말이 horn이다. 쌍으로 나기 때문에
보통 복수형 horns로 쓴다. 그런데 소, 염소, 산양 등 소과(科)의 동물은 길게 한
줄기로 뿔이 나고, 사슴과의 동물들은 나뭇가지처럼 여러 갈래로 뿔이 자란다.
우리가 약용[녹용]으로 쓰는 수사슴의 뿔은 antler(s)라고 하지만, 전문가가 아
니니까 그냥 '초식 동물의 뿔'은 horn(s)이라고 하면 된다.

His horns are sharp and tipped with gold. 뿔은 뾰족했고, 뿔의 끝은 황금으로 칠해져
있었다.

somersault ⓥ to jump and turn your body in the air so that your feet go
over your head and then touch the ground
somersault에서 somer는 above(위로, 너머로)이고, sault는 jump, leap(도약하
다)을 뜻한다. 위로 뛰어올라 넘는 동작을 말하는데, 그냥 뛰어넘는 것이 아니
라 몸을 한 바퀴 이상 돌려서 넘어야 somersault라고 할 수 있다. 체조 선수들
이 착지하기 전에 꼭 somersault를 하는데, '공중제비 돌다'라고 한다.

You somersault through the air, do a handstand on the bull's back, and land on
your feet behind him. 여러분은 공중제비를 하며 뛰어오르고, 황소 등에 손을 짚고 물구
나무를 선 다음에 황소의 뒤쪽에 착지한다.

pirate ⓝ someone who sails on the ocean attacking and stealing from
other ships
pirate는 '공격하다(attack), 노리다(attempt)'를 뜻하는 희랍어에서 유래한 단어
이다. 평범한 어선이나 상선으로 위장해 다른 배들이 다가오기를 기다렸다가
느닷없이 공격하는 것이 해적들의 수법이다. 고대부터 지중해 연안은 해적이
창궐하는 것으로 유명했다. piracy은 '해적질'인데 지금은 '저작권을 침해하는
행위, 불법복제'를 뜻하는 말로 자주 쓰인다. pirate도 '저작권을 침해하는 사람'
을 뜻한다.

In ancient times, the Mediterranean Sea was full of pirates. 고대에 지중해에는 해적
들이 들끓었다.

craftsman ⓝ a man who makes useful or beautiful things using his hands
craftsman에서 craft는 '기술(skill)'을 뜻한다. 뭔가 실용적이거나 아름다운 물
건을 만들 수 있는 '기술'을 갖고 있는 사람이 바로 craftsman, 즉 '기술자, 장인'
이다. 옛날에 최고의 기술자는 선박을 만드는 사람이어서 craft 자체에 '배(ship,

boat)'라는 뜻이 있다. 미노스의 왕이 craftsmen에게 배(craft)를 만들라고 한 것은 지당한 명령이 아닐 수 없다.

So he ordered his craftsmen to build great ships that he could use to wipe out pirates and patrol the Mediterranean Sea. 그래서 그는 자신의 기술자들에게 해적들을 소탕하고 지중해를 순찰하는 데에 쓸 수 있도록 거대한 배를 만들라고 명령했다.

navy ⓝ a country's military force that fights at sea

navy는 라틴어에서 유래한 말로, '배(ship)' 또는 여러 배들이 모인 '함대(fleet)'를 의미했다. '항해술, 위치 정보 제공 장치'를 가리키는 navigation(내비게이션)의 navi-와 같은 의미이다. navy는 '배, 함대'라는 뜻에서 '해군'을 지칭하는 단어로 발전했다. 지금으로부터 약 4,000년 전, 미노스 왕국이 최초로 해군을 보유했던 것으로 알려져 있다.

And the king of the Minoans became the first king to have a navy—an army that knew how to fight on the water. 그래서 미노아의 왕은 물에서 싸우는 법을 아는 군대인 해군을 소유한 최초의 왕이 되었다.

> **Q** 미노아(크레타) 문명도 20세기에 발굴되었다면서요?
>
> **A** 고대 문명의 대부분은 번영기를 지나 전설 속을 떠다니는 유령 같은 존재였단다. 그러다가 고고학자들의 발굴로 드러나게 된 거야. 기원전 2000년경에서 기원전 1450년경까지 크레타 섬에서 화려하게 꽃피우던 미노아 문명 역시 20세기 초 영국의 고고학자 에번스에 의해 밝혀졌어.
> 크노소스 궁전 터가 발견되면서 그리스 문명 시기에 동부 지중해를 주름잡으며 교역했던 크레타인들의 삶이 드러난 거지. 크레타 섬의 유적 중에서 가장 유명한 것이 크오소스 궁이야. 궁의 1,500개가 넘는 방은 미로라고 불러도 손색이 없을 정도라서 그 궁전이 미궁(라비린토스)이라는 단어의 어원이 되었다는 추측도 있단다.

2 King Minos and the Minotaur

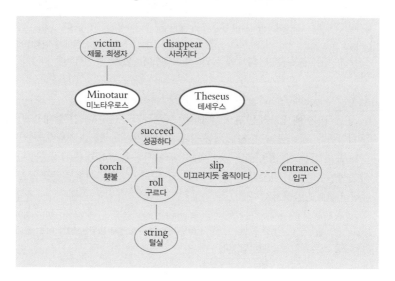

victim ⓝ someone who has been hurt or killed by someone or accidents

victim에서 vict는 '생명(life)'을 뜻한다. 그래서 victim은 '생명을 잃는 사람'인데, 원래 종교 의식에서 제물로 바쳐지는 사람을 일컬었다. 원래의 이 의미는 victims for the Minotaur's dinner(미노타우로스의 식사를 위한 제물들)라는 표현에 고스란히 담겨 있다. 지금은 범죄나 재난의 '피해자, 희생자'를 뜻한다.

King Minos didn't want to feed his own people to the Minotaur, so he ordered the nearby city of Athens to send him victims for the Minotaur's dinner. 미노스 왕은 자신의 백성들을 미노타우로스에게 먹이로 주고 싶지 않아서 근처 도시인 아테네에 미노타우로스의 식사를 위한 제물을 보내라고 명령했다.

disappear ⓥ to go out of sight suddenly

disappear는 '나타나다'라는 뜻의 appear 앞에 '반대, 부정(not)'을 의미하는 접두사 dis-가 붙은 형태이다. appear의 반대말로, '사라지다, 갑자기 없어지다'라는 뜻이다. disappear와 비슷한 말로 vanish가 있다.

And year after year, the seven girls and seven boys disappeared and were never seen again. 해마다 일곱 명의 소녀들과 일곱 명의 소년들이 사라져 다시는 모습을 볼 수 없었다.

succeed ⓥ to do well; to have the result as you want to

succeed는 '근접한(close to, near)'을 뜻하는 suc-과 '가다(go)'를 뜻하는 ceed가 합쳐진 형태이다. 즉 의미상 어느 지점까지 거의 다 간 것이므로 '성공하다'를 의미한다. He succeeded in killing the monster(그는 괴물을 죽이는 데 성공했다) 처럼 succeed in+명사[~ing 구문]의 형태로 쓸 수 있다. 명사형은 success(성공) 이다.

If I succeed, we'll put a white sail on this ship instead of the black one, and sail home to Athens. 내가 성공하면 검은 돛이 아니라 흰 돛을 이 배에 달고서 아테네로 항해해 귀향할 것이다.

Q 지상의 헤파이스토스가 바로 다이달로스라면서요?

A 헤파이스토스는 그리스 신화에 나오는 대장간 신으로 무엇이든 척척 만들어내지. 지상의 헤파이스토스는 바로 '다이달로스'였어. 다이달로스 는 '쪼아서 만드는 자, 명공'이라는 뜻이야.

이 책에 소개된 '미궁'이 다이달로스가 만들었다는 전설이 있단다. 테세우 스가 아리아드네의 도움으로 미노타우로스를 죽이고 미궁을 탈출하자 미 노스 왕은 책임을 물어 다이달로스와 그의 아들 이카루스마저 미궁에 가 두었대.

그러나 다이달로스는 바로 그 미궁을 만든 사람으로서 구조를 잘 알고 있 었지. 그는 깃털을 모아 밀랍을 이용해 날개를 만들고는 미궁을 탈출할 계 획을 세웠어. 떠나기 전에 아들에게, "너무 높이도 너무 낮게도 날지 마 라!"라고 당부했어. 그러나 이카로스는 막상 날기 시작하자 아버지의 당 부를 잊고는 더 높이 더 높이 날다가 태양의 열기에 밀랍이 녹아 추락하고 말았다는 이야기가 있단다.

---

torch ⓝ a long stick that you burn at one end for a light

torch는 어둠을 밝히는 '횃불'이다. '홰[나무막대]'에 '불'이 붙은 것이다. 올림픽 이 열리는 곳까지 여러 사람이 교대로 들고 뛰는 '성화'도 Olympic Torch라고 한다. 영국에서는 '손전등(flashlight)'을 torch라고 한다. 모양이 달라도 어둠을 밝히는 용도가 같기 때문에 횃불과 손전등을 똑같이 torch라고 부를 수 있다.

Just before dark, she found a torch, a sword, and a ball of wool, and crept secretly out of King Minos's palace, down to Theseus's prison cell. 어두워지기 직 전에 그녀는 횃불과 검, 털실뭉치를 찾아서 남몰래 미노스 왕의 궁전을 빠져나와 테세우스 가 있는 감방으로 잠입했다.

roll ⓥ to move by turning over and over

roll은 일정한 방향으로 계속 돌아가는 모습을 표현한 동사이다. 라틴어 어근 rol이나 rot은 turn(돌다)의 의미를 갖고 있다. 그래서 roll은 '구르다, 굴리다, 돌다, 말다'이고, roller는 '돌아가는 것, 바퀴'를 의미한다. 신발에 작은 바퀴들이 달린 탈것 중에 '롤러스케이트(roller-skates)'와 '롤러블레이드(roller-blades)'가 있고, '롤러코스터(roller-coaster)'도 트랙에 롤러가 연결되어 있다.

Then drop the ball and let it roll forward. 그런 다음 털실뭉치를 떨어뜨려 앞으로 굴러 가게 놔두세요.

string ⓝ a long, thin piece of something

가늘고 긴 '줄, 끈'이 string이다. 실, 섬유, 가죽, 철 등 재료와 상관없이 가늘고 길면 모두 string이라고 할 수 있다. 그래서 '양털실'을 wool string, 기타나 첼로처럼 줄을 튕겨서 소리를 내는 '현악기'를 string instruments라고 한다.

Kill it, and then follow the string back out to the doorway. 그 괴물을 죽인 다음에 다시 실을 따라서 출입구로 나오세요.

entrance ⓝ a place where you can go in to a building

entrance는 enter(들어가다)에 '상태, 행위'를 뜻하는 명사형 접미사 -ance가 붙은 형태이다. '들어가는 행동, 들어간 상태'를 의미하므로 '입장, 입학'이나 '입구, 출입문'을 뜻한다. 그래서 the entrance of the Labyrinth를 '라비린토스 입구'라고 한다. labyrinth는 미노타우로스 신화에 나오는 고유 지명에서 유래해 '미로(迷路), 미궁(迷宮)'을 뜻하는 말이 되었다.

Then he made his way back up to the entrance of the Labyrinth, following the wool string until he saw the door to the outside up ahead of him. 그때 그는 다시 라비린토스 입구로 향했는데, 털실을 따라가자 바로 앞에 밖으로 통하는 문이 보였다.

slip ⓥ to move somewhere quickly and quietly

slip의 기본적인 의미는 '미끄러지다(slide)'이다. 미끄러진다는 것은 표면 마찰력[저항]이 작아서 속도가 빠르고 소리도 작다는 의미를 담고 있다. 그래서 slip은 마치 미끄러지듯 '빠르고 조용하게 움직이다'라는 뜻으로도 쓰인다. slip-slipped-slipped

Together, they slipped away to the harbor, boarded their ship, and set sail for Athens. 그들은 다 함께 조용하고 신속하게 항구로 빠져나와 배에 올라 아테네를 향해 항해를 시작했다.

274

3 The Mysterious End of the Minoans

volcano (n) a mountain with a hole at the top from which come burning rock and fire

volcano는 로마 신화에 등장하는 불의 신, 대장장이 신인 불카누스[Vulcan. 그리스 신화의 헤파이스토스(Hephaestos)에 해당] 이름에서 유래한 것이다. 불을 내뿜고 모든 것을 파괴하니 '화산(火山)'에 신의 이름을 붙일 만하다. volcano가 나오면 항상 따라오는 동사가 있는데, 바로 erupt이다. '갑자기 터지다, 폭발하다'라는 뜻이다.

Although no one knows for sure, many historians think that the Minoans left when a volcano erupted on a nearby island called Thera. 확실히 아는 사람은 없지만, 많은 역사학자들이 근처에 있는 테라라는 섬에서 화산이 폭발해서 미노아인들이 떠났다고 생각한다.

earthquake (n) a strong and sudden shaking of the ground

earthquake는 earth(땅)와 quake(떨다, 흔들리다)가 합쳐진 것이다. 땅이 흔들리는 것이 '지진(地震)'이다. earth를 빼고 그냥 quake만 써도 '지진'이 된다. I felt an earthquake last night(지난밤에 지진을 느꼈다)라고 해도 되고, The quake had a magnitude of 8(그 지진은 강도 8이었다)처럼 쓸 수도 있다. 강한 에너지의 분출로 땅이 흔들리는 지진을 '화산 지진(a volcanic earthquake)'이라고 한다.

The people of Thera could feel constant small earthquakes. 테라 섬의 사람들은 지속적이고 미세한 지진을 느낄 수 있었다.

ruin (v) to destroy or spoil something

ruin은 '넘어지다(fall down), 무너지다(collapse)'라는 의미를 갖고 있다. 사람이 넘어지면 몸이 상하고, 건물이 무너지면 못 쓰게 된다. 그래서 ruin은 '망치다, 엉망으로 만들다, 폐허가 되다, 멸망하다'를 뜻한다. '몰락, 붕괴, 파멸, 폐허'를 뜻하는 명사형으로도 쓰인다.

Historians think that many of the Minoans left the island of Crete because the volcano ruined the air and land. 역사가들은 화산으로 인해 공기와 땅이 오염되었기 때문에 많은 미노아인들이 크레타 섬을 떠났다고 생각한다.

Chapter 19

The Early Greeks

1 The Mycenaeans

기원전 2000년을 전후로 발칸반도 북쪽의 아카이아인들이 그리스 본토로 남하해 원주민을 정복하고 미케네, 티린스, 필로스 등의 소왕국을 건설했다. 이들은 지중해 여러 지역의 문화를 흡수하고 군사력과 경제력을 키웠는데, 중심 세력이었던 미케네는 기원전 1450년경 남쪽의 크레타 섬을 정복하면서 에게 문명의 후반기인 미케네 문명을 이룩했다. 그러나 청동기 문명이었던 미케네 문명은 철기로 무장한 북쪽의 도리아인들과 소아시아의 해상 세력에 의해 멸망했다.

Crete was covered with dust and ash. Crops had failed. The Minoans had been a great nation—but now they were just ragged people trying to find enough food to stay alive.

Slowly, the ash and rock began to wash away from the fields and streams. Crops began to grow again. It was too late for the Minoans, though. The volcano had already destroyed their country and their way of life.

Soon, strangers landed on the shores of Crete. They were the Mycenaeans, and they came from the city of Mycenae, in Greece. Greece is the land just north of Crete; it juts out into the Mediterranean Sea like a set of fingers, surrounded by small islands.

The Mycenaeans knew that Crete was now weak. They knew that they could conquer the island easily. And they wanted to own Crete for themselves. So they took over the whole island of Crete and settled there.

Now the Mycenaeans owned both their own city and the island of Crete. They learned how to build ships from the Minoans who were left in Crete. They used these ships to sail to other islands. On each island, the Mycenaeans built a city called a *colony*. All of these cities were controlled by the Mycenaean king and his army. Soon the Mycenaeans had colonies all around the Aegean Sea.

*The Mycenaeans weren't the only people who lived in Greece. Other Greeks lived in the cities of Thebes and Athens. But the Mycenaeans had stronger weapons than the other Greeks. They made spear-tips and sword-blades from bronze. They learned how to use shields to protect themselves during battles. *And they hammered out helmets from bronze, and lined them with fur and cloth to protect their heads from enemy swords.

The Mycenaeans were also the first Greeks to use horses in battle. *Before this, soldiers had always fought on foot. *But the Mycenaeans began to hitch horses to war chariots. They drove these chariots into battle. Enemy soldiers ran when they saw the warhorses and chariots charging straight at them!

With their armor, bronze weapons, and chariots, the Mycenaeans dominated the Aegean Sea and the islands in it. They were the first great Greek civilization.

2 The Greek Dark Ages

미케네 문명이 쇠망하고 이민족인 도리안인들과 '바다 사람들'에 의해 그리스가 점령당한 후, 기원전 1200년경부터 700년경까지 약 500년 동안 그리스에 관한 기록이나 시대상을 알 수 있는 유물이 거의 없기 때문에 이 시기를 '그리스의 암흑시대'라고 부른다. 그러나 이 시기에 그리스에서는 토지의 사유화가 진행되고 폴리스(도시 국가)들이 형성되는 변화가 있었음은 분명하다. 또한 에게 문명과는 다른 그리스의 독자적인 문화가 성장하고 있었다.

The Mycenaean Greeks were great fighters because they had bronze weapons and armor, and chariots that they could drive

Greek Cities

into battle. They ruled the area around the Aegean Sea for several hundred years.

But the Mycenaean Greeks were facing disaster—although they didn't know it yet! All around them, tribes of barbarians were also learning how to use bronze weapons and chariots.

Barbarian wasn't a nice name! *It was an insult. You see, the early Greeks thought of themselves as very civilized people. They lived in nice houses, made of stone or wood. They had their own kitchens and bathrooms. *Greek women stayed home most of the day, supervising the household slaves who did most of the housework and cooking. Some Greek men worked as storekeepers, farmers, or fishermen. Others were craftsmen—they spent their time weaving cloth, creating pottery, or making other things for use in everyday life. Greek children went to school, or had tutors. They lived settled, ordinary lives.

But barbarians didn't have houses of their own or regular

jobs. They couldn't read or write. *And they spent their time wandering around from country to country, attacking the people who lived there and trying to take over.

The Mycenaean Greeks thought that these wandering barbarians were ignorant, smelly, and uncivilized. They knew that Greek weapons and chariots were the strongest around. They figured that they could protect themselves from any barbarian attack.

But they were wrong. The barbarian tribes who lived around the Aegean Sea discovered how to make weapons out of iron. *These iron weapons were even stronger than the bronze weapons of the Greeks. They learned how to use bows and arrows, and how to throw javelins. Now, the barbarians could kill the drivers of Greek chariots from a long distance away—before the Greeks could even get close enough to fight them. Some barbarians even learned how to build warships, so that they could attack the Mycenaean Greeks from the sea. These seafaring barbarians were called the Sea People. (Some of them settled in Canaan, and became known as the Philistines.)

The Greeks tried to fight off the barbarians. They built stronger and stronger walls around their cities. *These walls were so strong and so big that we can still see them today.

*But no matter how many walls the Mycenaean Greeks built, they couldn't keep the barbarians out. The Sea People invaded them from the water. Other barbarians called Dorians came streaming down from the north. Greek cities were burned and destroyed. Greek armies were defeated. The Greeks fled away from these savage tribes. And soon the only people living in Greece were the barbarians.

For hundreds of years, the barbarians lived in Greece. But these tribes were a little bit like a bully who spends so much time fighting that he never gets his homework finished. They put so much energy into battles that they never learned how to read or write. They didn't leave us any written records of their lives. The only thing they left behind them were ruined cities! And so we know very little about Greece during the time that the Sea People and the Dorians lived there. This time in Greece is called the Greek Dark Ages—because the history of the Dorians and the Sea People is completely unknown, or "dark," to us today. 📖

———

Note to Parent: The Mycenaeans settled in Crete around 1450 BC/BCE. The Greek "Dark Ages" stretched from around 1200 to around 700 BC/BCE.

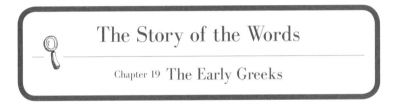

The Story of the Words

Chapter 19 The Early Greeks

1 The Mycenaeans

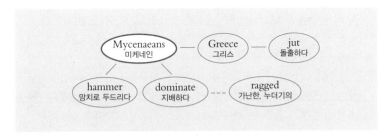

ragged ⓐ wearing old dirty clothes and looking very poor

지금은 모피(毛皮)옷이 비싸고 고급이지만, 먼 옛날에는 가난한 사람들이 입는 옷이었다. 가공하지 않고 그냥 털가죽을 벗겨 몸에 걸친 것이다. ragged는 '털이 붙은'을 뜻하는 말에서 유래해서 '빈궁(貧窮)한' 상태를 의미한다. rag는 '누더기, 넝마'이고, 그런 옷을 입을 만큼 가난한 사람들이 ragged people이다.

The Minoans had been a great nation—but now they were just ragged people trying to find enough food to stay alive. 미노아인들은 위대한 민족이었으나 이제 그들은 생존에 필요한 식량을 구하기 위해 애쓰는 가난한 사람들일 뿐이었다.

Greece ⓝ an ancient country in the Southern Europe

그리스는 유럽 문명의 모태(母胎)이다. 그런데 Greece는 고대 로마인들이 지금의 그리스 지역에 살던 사람들을 부르는 말에서 유래했다. 예로부터 그리스인들은 자신들을 '엘라스[the Hellenes]'라고 불렀고, 지금도 그리스의 정식 국가명은 The Hellenic Republic이다. 헬레니즘(Hellenism)이나 그리스의 중국식 한자 이름 '희랍(希臘)'도 Hellenes에서 유래했다. 지금은 영어로 '그리스'는 Greece이고, '그리스 인, 그리스어'는 Greek이다.

They were the Mycenaeans, and they came from the city of Mycenae, in Greece. 그들은 미케네인들이었는데, 그리스에 있는 도시인 미케네에서 온 사람들이었다.

jut ⓥ to be further forward than other things

jut은 jet(분출, 제트기)과 마찬가지로 '던지다(throw)'를 뜻하는 라틴어에서 유래했다. jut은 밖으로 던져진 듯 볼록 튀어나온 모습을 표현한 동사로, '돌출하다, 튀어나오다'라는 뜻이다. jut-jutted-jutted

Greece is the land just north of Crete; it juts out into the Mediterranean Sea like a set of fingers, surrounded by small islands. 그리스는 크레타 섬의 바로 북쪽에 있는 땅으로, 마치 손가락 모양처럼 지중해 쪽으로 튀어나와 있으며 작은 섬들로 둘러싸여 있다.

> **Q** 미노아 문명은 그리스 문명에 속하지 않나요?
> **A** 화산 폭발 후 미노아인들은 예전의 영화를 되살릴 수 없었단다. 그 틈을 노리고 그리스 본토에서 온 미케네인은 아직 크레타 섬에 남아 있던 미노아인들로부터 배 만드는 기술을 배운 다음, 에게 해 주변에 식민 도시를 건설했어. 그들이 사용한 문자가 크레타 섬 사람들과 다르다는 점은 그들이 서로 다른 종족이라는 증거이기도 해. 이런 점에서 미노아 문명은 미케네 문명에 끼친 영향에도 불구하고 그리스 문명에 포함되는 것은 아니란다. 문자의 해독이 아직 이루어지지 않아서 미노아인들에 대해 많은 부분 미스터리 상태로 남아 있지만, 크노소스 궁전의 프레스코화(회반죽을 벽에 바르고 위에 색을 입힌 그림)를 보면 호전적인 미케네인과는 살아가는 방식이 달랐다는 점을 확연히 알 수 있단다.

hammer ⓥ to hit something with a hammer

'망치' hammer는 '돌(stone, rock)'을 뜻하는 고대 영어에서 유래했다. 석기 시대에 돌은 도구였으므로 hammer는 stone tool의 의미로 쓰였다. 지금도 못을 박을 때 망치가 없으면 돌로 쓸 수 있다. 망치로 할 수 있는 것은 '망치질'이니까 '망치질을 하다, 망치로 두드리다'이다.

And they hammered out helmets from bronze, and lined them with fur and cloth to protect their heads from enemy swords. 그리고 그들은 청동을 망치로 두드려 투구를 만들고, 그 투구에 가죽이나 천으로 안감을 대서 적의 검으로부터 자신들의 머리를 보호했다.

dominate ⓥ to have power and control over someone or something

1951년 할리우드에서 만든 쿼바디스(Quo Vadis)라는 유명한 영화가 있다. 이 영화의 제목은 '쿼바디스 도미네(Quo Vadis, Domine?)'라는 라틴어 성경 구절에서 따온 것이다. 베드로가 십자가를 진 예수에게 묻는 질문인데, '주여, 어디로 가시나이까?'라는 뜻이다. 여기에서 Domine가 바로 dominate의 어원으로 '주인(lord, master)'을 뜻한다. dominate는 주인이 하인을 부리듯 마음껏 권력을 행사하고 통제한다는 의미로, '지배하다, 장악하다, 압도하다'라는 뜻이다.

With their armor, bronze weapons, and chariots, the Mycenaeans dominated the Aegean Sea and the islands in it. 갑옷과 청동 무기, 전차로 무장한 미케네 사람들은 에게 해와 일대의 섬을 지배[장악]했다.

2 The Greek Dark Ages

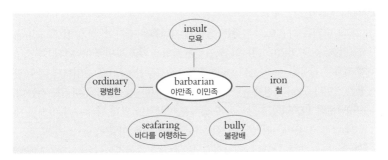

barbarian ⓝ someone from a different tribe or land who is considered to be violent and uncivilized

barbarian의 어원에 대해서는 여러 가지 설이 있는데, 고대 그리스와 로마인들이 '외국인'을 지칭하는 말에서 유래했다는 것이 유력하다. 자신보다 그 '외국인'이 미개하고 난폭하다는 인식을 갖고 있어서 barbarian은 모욕을 담은 표현이었다. 그래서 지금도 barbarian은 '교양 없는 사람'을 일컫고, 형용사형 barbarous는 '야만적인, 잔인한'이라는 뜻이다.

All around them, tribes of barbarians were also learning how to use bronze weapons and chariots. 그들의 주위를 둘러싼 야만족들 역시 청동 무기들과 전차들을 사용하는 법을 배우고 있었다.

insult ⓝ an impolite remark or action that offends someone

insult는 '위에, 위로(on)'를 뜻하는 in-과 '뛰어오르다(jump), 짓밟다(trample)'를 뜻하는 sult가 합쳐져 '함부로 다른 사람의 몸 위로 뛰어오르거나 짓밟는다'는 의미이다. 즉 '모욕하다'라는 뜻이다. 명사형으로는 '모욕적인 언행'이다. 예를 들어 Calling someone a barbarian was an insult(누군가에게 바바리언이라고 부르는 것은 모욕이었다)처럼 쓸 수 있다.

It was an insult. 그 이름은 모욕이었다.

ordinary ⓐ usual; not special or different

원래 ordinary는 orderly(질서 있는)를 의미했다. 세상은 대체로 질서(order)가 잡혀 있고, 그런 상태가 지속되는 것이 바로 평범한 일상이라는 의미에서 '일상의, 평범한, 보통의'라는 뜻이다. 반대로 '기이하고, 비범한' 상태는 extraordinary이다.

They lived settled, ordinary lives. 그들은 안정적이고 평범한 삶을 살았다.

iron ⓝ a hard heavy metal used as a material for construction and manufacturing

iron의 발견과 사용으로 인류는 청동기 시대를 마감하고, 철기 시대(the Iron Age)를 맞을 수 있었다. '철, 쇠'를 일컫는 iron은 가공 방법에 따라 다양한 도구와 원료로 활용할 수 있는데, 요즘 흔히 쓰는 '강철(steel)'은 산업혁명 이후 발명된 것이다. iron은 형용사형으로 쇠처럼 '강인한' 성격을 표현하기도 하는데, 1979년부터 1990년까지 강직하게 영국을 이끌었던 전직 영국 수상 마거릿 대처(Margaret Thatcher)의 별명이 '철의 여인(Iron Lady)'이었다.

The barbarian tribes who lived around the Aegean Sea discovered how to make weapons out of iron. 에게 해 주변에 살던 야만족들은 철로 무기 만드는 법을 찾아냈다.

seafaring ⓐ working or travelling regularly on the sea

seafaring은 sea(바다)와 동사 fare의 진행형 형용사 faring이 합쳐진 말이다. fare는 원래 travel(이동하다, 여행하다)을 의미하여 옛날에는 작별인사로 Fare well!(잘 가세요!)이라고 했다. travel할 때 필요한 '교통 요금'도 fare이고, seafaring barbarians는 말 그대로 육지에 정착해 살지 않고 '바다를 여행하며' 사는 이방인들을 말한다.

These seafaring barbarians were called the Sea People. 바다를 여행하는 이 이방인을 '바다 사람들'이라고 불렀다.

> **Q** 미케네 문명기의 사람들은 어디로 떠났나요?
>
> **A** 바다 민족과 도리아인의 침입으로 미케네 문명은 순식간에 허물어졌어. 그곳에 살던 사람들은 살 길을 찾아 고향을 떠났고, 그중 일부는 이집트의 용병으로 일했다고 해.
> 고향을 떠난 도리아인이 정착한 곳이 펠로폰네소스 반도로, 지도에서 보면 그리스의 남부야. 남부를 피해 아예 바다를 건너 다른 섬이나 아나톨리아(소아시아)로 간 사람들도 있었지. 아나톨리아에 함께 간 사람들끼리 가

족, 씨족, 부족 단위로 살았는데, 왜 그들은 주로 바닷가에 모여 살았을까? 다른 지역으로 이주하여 불안하게 살고 있으니까 어떤 문제가 생기면 언제라도 떠날 준비를 해야 했겠지. 그러나 그들은 다른 지역에서도 그리스 본토에서 살던 방식대로, 그리스인이라는 의식을 지녔다고 해.

bully ⓝ a person who hurts weaker people or make them afraid

bully는 원래 결혼한 여자의 '남자친구(boyfriend), 애인(lover)'을 뜻하는 말이었는데, 지금은 주로 학교에서 '약한 학생들을 괴롭히는 못된 녀석'을 지칭하는 말이 되었다. 동사로 '약한 자를 괴롭히다'라는 뜻으로도 쓰인다.

But these tribes were a little bit like a bully who spends so much time fighting that he never gets his homework finished. 그러나 이 종족들은 싸움질하는 데 너무 많은 시간을 쓴 나머지 자신의 숙제는 마치지 못하는 불량학생과 약간 비슷했다.

Chapter 20
Greece Gets Civilized Again

1 Greece Gets an Alphabet

🌐 기원전 1200년경부터 지중해를 누비며 활발한 교역을 하면서 여러 지역에 식민지를 세웠던 페니키아는 오리엔트 문명을 유럽에 전파하는 역할을 했다. 페니키아인들이 사용하던 간편한 문자가 기원전 9세기경에 그리스로 전파되었는데, 그리스인들은 이 페니키아 문자를 받아들이고 거기에 모음을 더해서 그리스 알파벳 24자를 만들었다. 이후 알파벳은 로마 제국에 전해졌고, 로마를 통해 유럽의 문자로 퍼져나가 각 민족의 언어에 맞게 변형되고 발전되었다.

The Mycenaeans are gone. *Now Greece is full of barbarians—the Dorians from up north, and the Sea People (who are also called the Philistines), who invaded Greece from the Mediterranean Sea. These people can't read or write. *They're not used to living in cities. Greek civilization has ended!

But wait! Something strange is happening. The longer these barbarians live in Greece, the more civilized they become. They're no longer wandering around looking for cities to attack. Instead, they're settling into villages. They're learning how to farm and fish. They're becoming—Greeks!

The Dorians and the Sea People lived in Greece for hundreds of years. They looked less and less like wild warrior tribes, and more and more like civilized merchants, farmers, and storekeepers. They started building houses. Their houses became fancier and fancier, with kitchens, rooms for taking baths, and separate rooms for men and women to entertain their friends. Soon they started building houses close to each other, in villages. Then the villages grew even larger, into cities—each one with its own government and its own army. They learned how to grow olives, grapes, figs, and wheat, and how to make wine from the grapes. *Instead of riding out to kill their neighbors, they learned how to enjoy civilized sports like wrestling, chariot racing, and horseback riding. They loved to dance—at weddings, at funerals, at feasts, and at sports events. As a matter of fact, they soon invented over two hundred dances to use on all occasions.

*The women no longer went out foraging for food, and they certainly didn't spend their time putting up tents, washing and cooking like barbarian women. Instead, they spent their time indoors, away from the sun, so that their skin would remain pale and beautiful. They kept slaves to do all the hard work.

Now these barbarians were known, simply, as Greeks.

We know more about these early Greeks than we know about the barbarians, because the early Greeks soon learned how to read and write. They started to write down stories about their ancestors. They started to write down the myths and fairy tales that they told their children. And we still have some of this writing today.

The early Greeks didn't use the same alphabet that we use. They used their own letters. They probably learned some of these letters from the Phoenicians, who had one of the first alphabets. Here are some Greek letters:

$$\alpha$$

This is called an *alpha*. If you think it looks like an "a," you're right. It sounds like an "a" too. The alphabet that we use today borrowed many of its letters from the ancient Greeks. Here is a *kappa*, a Greek letter that makes the same sound as our "k":

$$\kappa$$

And here is a *tau*, a Greek letter that makes the "t" sound:

τ

And here is a Greek *beta*, a letter that makes the "b" sound:

β

•Our alphabet is named after the Greek letters *alpha* and *beta*. Can you hear the letters *alpha* and *beta* in the word *alphabet*?

Other Greek letters don't look anything like our letters. Here is a Greek letter called a *psi*. It makes the sound "ps"—that's a sound we don't use in English.

ψ

•The *psi* looks a little bit like a trident, a three—pronged weapon carried by the Greek god Poseidon, who lived in the sea. The letter is named after Poseidon too. Can you hear the *psi* sound in Poseidon's name?

Here is one more Greek letter. •It is called a *theta*, and it makes the sound that our letters "th" make when you say them together:

θ

•Even though some of the Greek letters are different from ours, we owe a lot of our alphabet to the Greeks. If you have an A, B, E, H, I, K, M, N, O, P, T, X, Y, or Z in your name, you are using a Greek letter whenever you write your name. How would your name sound if the Greeks had never invented these letters?

2 The Stories of Homer

🌐 호머(Homer)라고도 불리는 호메로스는 그리스의 암흑기 후반인 기원전 9~8 세기 경에 살았던 것으로 추정한다. 호메로스는 구전되던 이야기들을 바탕으로 《일리아드(Iliad)》와 《오디세이(Odyssey)》를 집필했는데, 각각 24권으로 구성된 장편 서사시이다. 《일리아드》는 전설 속의 트로이 전쟁에서 마지막 한 해 동안의 사건을 담고 있으며, 《오디세이》는 영웅 오디세우스가 고향으로 돌아가면서 겪게 되는 모험담을 다루고 있다. 모두 그리스 신화의 내용을 바탕으로 하고 있지만, 《길가메시》 신화를 연상시키는 특징도 있어서 오리엔트 문화의 영향도 받은 것으로 평가 된다.

•When the Greeks began to learn how to read and write, one of them decided to write down the old Greek stories that had been told out loud around Greek fires for years and years. His name was Homer, and he was the first great Greek writer. Tradition tells us that Homer was blind—so he listened to the stories he heard, and then wrote them down using the Greek alphabet.

Homer wrote the story of a famous war—the Greek attack on the city of Troy. This war was called the "Trojan War," and Homer tells about it in his long poem, the *Iliad*. After he finished the *Iliad*, he wrote another story, called the *Odyssey*. The *Odyssey* was about Odysseus, a Greek warrior who fought in the Trojan War. •When Odysseus started to sail back home, he ran into all kinds of trouble! Here is one of the stories from the *Odyssey*:

•Odysseus and his men sailed away from Troy, looking forward to their return home. They praised all the gods of Greece for keeping them alive through the war. And they thanked the gods for their victory.

But they forgot to thank Poseidon, the god of the sea. *Poseidon was furious at being left out. *He sent a strong wind to blow the ships off course, so that Odysseus would have a hard time getting home.

Odysseus and his men got lost, out there on the sea. After many days of sailing, Odysseus and his tired, hungry sailors saw a beautiful island. It was cool and shady, full of wheat and grapevines and wild goats that could be killed for food. So they landed their ships on the beach, got out their bows and arrows, and hunted. When they had killed enough meat, they lit fires, roasted the goats, and feasted. And the next morning, when the dawn lit the sky red, they got up to explore.

Around the other side of the island, Odysseus and his men found a huge cave, carved into a cliff. Laurel trees grew all around it. In front of the cave was a pen, walled with stone and filled with hundreds of sheep and goats.

"Who lives here?" Odysseus asked. "Let's go in and find out." He took with him his twelve strongest men, along with a jug of sweet wine for a present. The rest of his men he sent back to the ships. Odysseus and his twelve companions came up to the cave and peered in—but they could see no one. Carefully, they crept in. There they found pens of lambs and baby goats. *The walls were lined with racks of cheeses, each cheese bigger than a man's head. Beneath them sat the bowls into which the cave's owner milked his goats, each bowl large enough for a man to lie down in.

When they saw this, Odysseus's men were terrified. "A giant lives here!" they said. "Let's take some cheese and some of the lambs, and get back to the ship before he returns!"

But Odysseus refused to run away. "We'll wait here and greet him when he returns!" he said. So the men cut up some cheese and ate it for their dinners, after offering some of it to the gods as a sacrifice. And they waited. Dark fell over the island. *And when it was completely dark, they heard footsteps, each one shaking the ground.

In through the door came the cave's owner. He was a giant, as tall as three men standing on each other's shoulders. He had only one eye, right in the center of his forehead. He was a Cyclops!

*The Cyclops was herding his sheep in front of him. *And he carried over his shoulder three or four trees that he had pulled up for firewood. He flung them onto the floor of the cave with such noise that Odysseus and his men hid themselves in fright. When all the sheep were inside the cave, the Cyclops rolled a huge stone across the cave's entrance—a stone so heavy that twenty men couldn't have shifted it aside. He milked his sheep and goats and got up to light his fire.

When the flames roared up, the Cyclops saw Odysseus and his men, hiding at the far end of the cave. "Well," he roared,

Odysseus and the Cyclops

"what do we have here? Robbers? Have you crept into my cave to take my sheep and my cheese?"

"No," Odysseus said, his voice shaking with fright. "We are merely travelers on our way home. Please, show us some kindness and hospitality—we are hungry and cold!"

"If you are travelers," the Cyclops said, "where is your ship?"

But Odysseus was afraid that the Cyclops might want to find the ship and destroy it. So he lied: "We were shipwrecked on your island," he said, "and our ship is destroyed."

The Cyclops didn't answer. Instead, he snatched up two of Odysseus's men and ate them on the spot. And then he washed down his horrible meal with goat's milk, lay down on the floor, and went to sleep.

"Let's kill him while he sleeps!" Odysseus's men urged him. But Odysseus refused. "If we kill him," he said, "who will let us out of the cave? That stone is too heavy for us to move. We would die in here!"

So Odysseus and his men spent the night huddled at the back of the cave, listening to the Cyclops snore as loud as thunder.

The Cyclops slept all night. When the red dawn came, he woke up, lit his fire, milked the goats, and grabbed two more of Odysseus's men for breakfast. After he ate them and drank some more milk, he pushed the stone away from the entrance to the cave and drove the sheep out. But before Odysseus and his men could dash out of the cave, the Cyclops rolled the stone back again, as easy as putting a lid on a jar.

Odysseus's men were terrified, moaning and crying. But Odysseus paced up and down the cave and thought, hard. Finally he went to the pile of trees that the Cyclops had brought in for firewood. Several of them still lay beside the sheep-pen, where the Cyclops had dropped them. One of the trees there was tall and green.

"Come on," Odysseus said to his men. "Be brave! Do what I say, and we'll escape. Let's cut a long piece off the end of this tree, about as long as a man is tall, and sharpen it. Don't ask why; just do what I say."

The men cut the tree and sharpened it, and then Odysseus burned the sharp point in the coals of the fire until it was hard and black. He hid it underneath a pile of straw. And then he and his men waited, all day long, for the Cyclops to come back.

˙When the monster came back into the cave that evening, he drove his sheep and goats in, and again sealed up the door with the huge stone. Then he grabbed two more of the men and ate them, washing them down with goat's milk. And then Odysseus took his courage in both hands and went forward.

"Cyclops!" he said. "You've eaten so many of my men that you must be thirsty. Milk won't help that thirst! Here, I've got a jug of the best sweet wine you've ever tasted."

He held up the jug of wine that he had brought into the cave, and the Cyclops sniffed at it. It smelled so good that he drank a mouthful, and then another, and then another. Soon the whole jug of wine was gone. And the Cyclops was very sleepy.

"What's your name?" he growled. "Who's giving me this wonderful stuff to drink?"

"My name is Noman," Odysseus said.

"Noman, I'm pleased with your wine," the Cyclops answered. "So I'll eat you last!" ˙And with that he sprawled over and went to sleep, right there on the ground.

Then Odysseus and four of his men dragged out the sharpened log they had hidden in the straw, and drove it right into the Cyclops's single eye.

The Cyclops leaped up and roared with pain. He stumbled all around his cave, grabbing blindly for Odysseus and his men. But they got easily away from him, because he could no longer see them.

Soon, Odysseus and his men heard other footsteps outside the cave. The Cyclops' friends and neighbors had come to find out what all the noise was about. "Why are you making so much noise?" they called to the Cyclops. "You're keeping us from sleeping! Is someone attacking you?"

"Noman!" the Cyclops yelled. "Noman is trying to kill me!"

"No man?" the other monsters answered. "Well, then, go back to sleep!" And they all went away.

The Cyclops, groaning with pain, lay down until morning. ˙Then he got up, feeling his way around with his hands, and rolled the stone away. He started to herd his sheep and goats out of the cave. But he reached down and patted the back of every animal that went past him, so that neither Odysseus nor his men could sneak out with the sheep and goats.

So Odysseus caught three fat sheep for every one of his men, and tied the sheep together in groups of three. ˙He told each one of his men to hold on to the stomach fleece of the sheep in the middle of each group, and to let the sheep carry them out past the Cyclops. The Cyclops put his hands right on the sheep's backs—but he couldn't find the men who were holding on underneath.

When Odysseus and his men had gotten out past the Cyclops, they ran for their ships. The rest of the men saw them coming. Odysseus started to yell, "Pull for the sea! Pull for the sea!" And as soon as they had scrambled aboard, the oarsmen rowed the ships out into the water, safely away from the island of the Cyclops.

Then Odysseus began to shout, "Cyclops! Cyclops! See what happens to you when you eat guests who come to your house? You should have known better than to fall for my tricks!"

The blind Cyclops heard his jeers. In fury, he wrenched a huge boulder off the side of the cliff and threw it towards Odysseus's voice. Waves pushed the ship around, but Odysseus shouted again, "Cyclops, if anyone asks you who put out your eye and spoiled your beauty, tell them that it was Odysseus!"

"Curses on you!" the Cyclops yelled back. "I'm the son of Poseidon, the god of the sea! And I will ask him to send waves and wind that will sink your ship so that you'll never reach home alive!"

Odysseus ignored the Cyclops' threat. He told his men to row for the open water. As soon as they were far away from the island, their sails caught the wind and they headed for home.

But Poseidon heard the Cyclops' request. He sent winds to blow Odysseus off course, and waves to batter his ship into pieces. It took ten long years and many dangerous adventures before Odysseus finally reached his home.

3 The First Olympic Games

고대 올림픽은 기원전 776년부터 서기 393년까지 1,160년 동안 4년마다 한 번 씩 그리스에서 열린 축제이다. 올림포스(Olympus)의 신들에게 제사를 지내는 명목으로 개최되었기 때문에 '올림픽(Olympics)'이라는 명칭이 붙었다. 처음에는 달리기 경주만 했는데, 시간이 지나면서 레슬링, 복싱, 5종 경기, 경마, 전차 경주 등으로 종목이 확대되었다. 시민권이 있는 남성만 선수로 참여할 수 있었고, 여성은 참가할 수 없었다. 고대 올림픽은 그리스가 로마 제국으로 편입된 이후에도 계속되었는데, 서기 394년에 로마 제국의 테오도시우스 황제가 그리스도교를 국교로 정하고 이교 금지령(異教禁止令)을 내리면서 역사에서 사라지게 되었다. 그로부터 약 1,500년이 지난 1896년에 쿠베르탱 남작의 노력으로 올림픽은 부활하게 된다.

The Greeks celebrated courage and strength by telling stories about brave, strong people like Odysseus. They also celebrated courage and strength with a big festival, called the Olympic Games. The bravest and strongest Greeks came to the Olympics to compete for prizes.

The Olympics started when two cities in ancient Greece made peace, after fighting with each other for years and years. To celebrate the peace, they decided to have a festival—a big celebration—in honor of the god Zeus, the chief god of the Greeks. The festival was named after Mount Olympus, the highest mountain in Greece. The Greeks thought that Zeus and the other gods lived on Mount Olympus.

At the festival, the Greeks feasted and made sacrifices to Zeus. And they also ran races. *The winners of the races were given wreaths made out of olive branches to wear on their heads. The olive leaves represented peace.

The Greeks decided that they would get together every four years to have the Olympics, and to run races in honor of Zeus. *As time went on, more and more Greeks from different Greek cities came to the Olympic Games. And the Greeks added more kinds of events to their games. Instead of just running races on foot, they started racing horses as well. They held boxing and wrestling matches. They even invented a competition called the *pentathlon*, where the athletes had to do five different events. *The winner had to throw a discus (a metal Frisbee) and a javelin (a Greek spear) farther than anyone else. He also had to win a long–jump competition, a wrestling match, and a foot race.

But only men were allowed to compete in the Greek Olympics. Girls could watch, but they weren't allowed to race or to do any of the other events. And married women couldn't even watch. They weren't allowed anywhere near the Olympics, on pain of death. That's because the Greeks thought that only men could be truly brave and strong. *They thought that the best way to honor the gods was for men to train their bodies to be as graceful and powerful as possible.

The Olympics were held every four years for almost a thousand years. People came from all over Greece to compete in the Games and to watch the other athletes. They all camped out at the Games and spent their evenings feasting and listening to music. *Poets would recite poems and stories out loud to entertain the crowds. These poems and stories were like movies to the ancient Greeks. Some of the poets probably told the story of the *Odyssey*. Others told the story of the attack on Troy. And others performed new stories and poems that they had written themselves.

The winners of the races and other competitions were treated like heroes. They were given banquets to honor them. And when they went back home, their own cities rewarded them with money and with free food for the rest of their lives.

Today, the Olympic Games are still held every four years. Hundreds of events take place—wrestling, running, and boxing, just like in ancient times, but also gymnastics, ice skating, soccer, basketball, swimming, and much more. Today, women can compete in the Olympics as well as men. Athletes come from all over the world, not just from Greece. But the Games are still called the Olympics, after Mount Olympus. And they still celebrate strength, grace, and courage—just like they did in the times of the ancient Greeks. 📖

Note to Parent: Homer lived around 800 BC/BCE.

The Story of the Words

1 Greece Gets an Alphabet

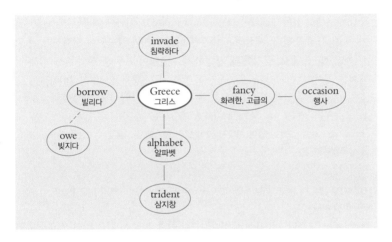

invade ⓥ to attack and enter a country or place with an army

invade는 '안으로(into)'를 뜻하는 접두사 in-과 '가다(go)'를 뜻하는 vade가 합쳐진 것이다. '안으로 들어가다'라는 의미인데, 원래 vade는 그냥 자연스럽게 가는 것이 아니라 '저항을 이겨내며 힘겹게 가는' 것을 의미한다. 그래서 invade는 전쟁에서 다른 나라 땅으로 '침입[침략하다, 쳐들어가다'라는 뜻으로 쓰인다. invade의 명사형은 invasion이다.

Now Greece is full of barbarians–the Dorians from up north, and the Sea People (who are also called the Philistines), who invaded Greece from the Mediterranean Sea. 이제 그리스에는 이민족들이 가득하다. 북쪽 위에서 들어온 도리아인과 지중해에서 그리스로 쳐들어온 (블레셋인이라고도 불리는) 바닷사람들이다.

fancy ⓐ not ordinary, plain or simple

fancier는 fancy의 비교급이다. fancy는 원래 라틴어 phantasia에서 유래한

fantasy의 줄임말로, '보이게 만들기(making visible)'를 의미했다. fancy가 형용
사형으로 쓰이면 '장식이 많은, 화려한, 값비싼, 고급의'라는 뜻이다. 흔히 '팬시'
용품을 산다고 할 때의 그 '팬시(fancy)'의 개념이다.

Their houses became fancier and fancier, with kitchens, rooms for taking baths,
and separate rooms for men and women to entertain their friends. 그들의 주택은
점점 더 화려하고 고급스러워졌다. 부엌과 목욕을 하기 위한 방, 남자와 여자가 따로 친구
들과 어울리는 방이 갖추어졌다.

occasion ⓝ a special or important time or event

occasion에서 접두사 oc-는 '~쪽으로(toward)'이고, 어근에 해당하는 cas-는 '떨
어지다(fall)'를 뜻한다. 세상일은 대부분 나의 의지와 상관없이 정해진다. 종교
적 축일, 명절, 제사, 심지어 내 생일까지도 운명이나 우연, 신의 손에 의해 정
해지는 것이다. 이처럼 occasion은 '특정한 경우, 행사, 일'의 의미이다. on all
occasions는 '모든 행사에서'이다.

As a matter of fact, they soon invented over two hundred dances to use on all
occasions. 사실, 그들은 얼마 지나지 않아 모든 행사에서 사용할 수 있는 200여 가지의
춤을 고안해냈다.

borrow ⓥ to take other people's words or letters and use them in your own language

borrow는 '빌리다'이고, lend는 '빌려주다'이다. 따라서 펜을 빌려 쓰고 싶다면
Can I borrow your pen?이나 Can you lend me your pen?이라고 말해야 한
다. borrow한 '물건'은 주인에게 돌려줘야 하지만 언어나 아이디어와 같은 무
형의 자산을 '차용하다, 도입해서 활용하다'라는 의미로 쓸 때는 돌려줄 필요가
없어서 오히려 지식이 확산되었기 때문에 역사가 발전할 수 있었다.

The alphabet that we use today borrowed many of its letters from the ancient
Greeks. 우리가 오늘날 사용하는 알파벳은 많은 글자를 고대 그리스인에게서 빌려온 것
이다.

alphabet ⓝ the letters of a language in a particular order

본문에 설명되어 있듯이, alphabet은 그리스어 알파벳의 첫 번째 두 글자인 '알
파(alpha)'와 '베타(beta)'가 합쳐진 것이다. 이집트의 문자를 토대로 페니키아가
만든 글자 체계를 그리스에서 차용해 오늘날의 알파벳으로 발전했다고 알려져
있다. 현재 영어의 알파벳에는 21개의 글자(letters)가 있는데, 그 중 5개[a, e, i,

o, u는 모음(vowels)이고, 21개는 자음(consonants)이다.

Our alphabet is named after the Greek letters alpha and beta. 영어의 알파벳은 그리스의 글자 '알파'와 '베타'의 이름에서 온 것이다.

trident ⓝ a weapon made of three sharp points on a long pole

trident에서 dent는 '이, 치아(tooth)'를 나타내며 dentist(치과, 치과 의사)와 어원이 같다. tri-는 '셋, 3(three)'을 의미한다. 즉 trident는 이가 세 개 있는 것인데, 우리말로 '가지가 세 개 있다'는 뜻의 '삼지창(三枝創)'이라고 한다. 그리스 신화에 나오는 바다의 신 '포세이돈(Poseidon)'이 항상 들고 다니는 커다란 포크(fork) 모양의 무기이고, 중국 고전 《서유기》에서 저팔계도 애용한다.

The psi looks a little bit like a trident, a three-pronged weapon carried by the Greek god Poseidon, who lived in the sea. '프사이(psi)'는 바다에 사는 그리스의 신 포세이돈이 들고 다니던 세 개의 창이 달린 무기인 삼지창처럼 생겼다.

owe ⓥ to get something thanks to someone's help

owe는 '~에게 빚을 지고 있다'라는 뜻의 동사이다. 빚을 진 상태를 표현하기 때문에 Don't forget that you owe me 10 dollars(너 나한테 10달러 빚진 거 잊지 마)처럼 거의 항상 현재형 시제를 쓴다. 돈 말고도 다른 신세를 질 경우에도 owe를 쓸 수 있다. owe A to B는 'B에게 A의 신세를 지다, B 덕분에 A를 얻게 되다'라는 뜻이다.

Even though some of the Greek letters are different from ours, we owe a lot of our alphabet to the Greeks. 그리스 알파벳과 영어의 알파벳이 일부 다르기는 하지만, 그리스인 덕분에 영어 알파벳 중 많은 글자를 얻게 되었다.

2 The Stories of Homer

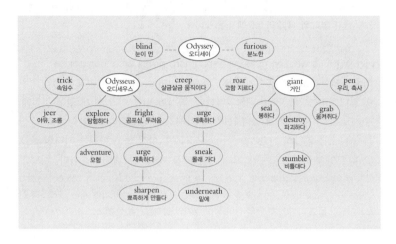

blind @ not able to see

blind는 '눈이 보이지 않는, 앞을 못 보는'을 뜻하는 형용사이다. Homer was
blind(호머는 앞을 보지 못했다)나 He went blind(그는 시력을 잃었다=He lost his
sight)처럼 쓸 수 있다. the blind는 '맹인들'을 뜻한다. 그런데 blind는 다소 직
접적인 표현이기 때문에 보다 완곡하게 visually impaired(시력이 손상된)나
visually handicapped(시각적으로 장애가 있는)로 표현하기도 한다.

Tradition tells us that Homer was blind—so he listened to the stories he heard, and
then wrote them down using the Greek alphabet. 전해 내려온 이야기에 따르면, 호메
로스는 앞을 보지 못해서 들리는 이야기에 귀를 기울여서 그 이야기들을 그리스 알파벳을
이용해 적었다고 한다.

Odyssey ⓝ a long journey or experience during which many things happen

odyssey는 기원전 8세기경 호메로스(Homer)가 쓴 장편 서사시《오디세이
(Odyssey)》의 제목에서 유래했다. 주인공 오디세우스(Odysseus)는 트로이 전쟁
이 끝나고 고향으로 돌아오는 길에 많은 모험을 하며 우여곡절을 겪게 된다. 그
래서 odyssey는 '많은 일을 겪게 되는 긴 여행'을 뜻하는 말로 쓰이게 되었다.
His odyssey to become a politician started in 1990(정치인이 되려는 그의 긴 여
정은 1990년에 시작되었다)처럼 쓸 수 있다.

After he finished the Iliad, he wrote another story, called the Odyssey. 《일리아드》
를 다 쓴 다음에, 그는 《오디세이》라는 제목의 또 다른 이야기를 썼다.

furious ⓐ very angry

furious는 '분노'를 뜻하는 fury의 형용사이다. Dad was furious with me라고 하면 아빠가 보통 화가 난 것이 아니라 엄청나게 화가 난 것을 말한다. 사람에게 분노한 상태를 표현하려면 'furious with 사람'으로, 어떤 행동에 대해 분노한 상태를 표현하려면 'furious at[about] 행동'의 형태로 쓴다.

Poseidon was furious at being left out. 포세이돈은 자기만 빠뜨려진 것에 대해 분노했다.

Q 트로이 전쟁을 실화라고 믿었던 소년이 있었다면서요?

A 《일리아드》,《오디세이》가 서사시로 기록된 것은 실제 전쟁이 일어나고 나서 적어도 400년이 지난 후의 일이었단다. 이미 미케네 문명이 사라지고 3000년이 지나서야 실제 있었던 일로 밝혀졌으니, 그동안 트로이 전쟁을 역사라고 믿는 사람은 거의 없었다고 해.

그러나 어린 시절 선물 받은 책에서 읽은 트로이전쟁 이야기를 그대로 믿은 소년이 바로 '하인리히 슐리만'이야. 그는 어른이 되면 자신의 손으로 트로이를 발견하겠다는 꿈을 꾸게 되었지. 그야말로 소년의 꿈 이야기로 그치지 않고, 그 꿈을 실현하기 위해 다양한 언어를 독학했고, 나중에는 고고학을 배우려고 대학에도 입학했단다. 그렇게 준비를 마치고 일리아드에 등장하는 지역을 찾아 아나톨리아(지금의 터키) 지역으로 갔지. 1870년 그는 히사를리크 언덕을 샅샅이 뒤져 마침내 '트로이'를 찾아냈단다. 슐리만은 이곳이 바로 트로이라고 주장했지만, 지금까지도 고고학자들이 연구를 멈추지 않고 있어.

explore ⓥ to find out about a place by traveling through it

explore는 '밖으로(out)'를 뜻하는 ex-와 '소리 지르다(cry)'라는 뜻의 plore가 합쳐진 것이다. 사냥에서 유래한 말로 추정되는데, 사냥을 할 때 사냥꾼도 소리를 지르고 사냥개도 컹컹 짖는다. 이 사냥감을 '찾기(search)' 위해 큰소리를 내는 것이다. 이 의미에서 확장되어 explore는 '탐험하다, 탐구하다'라는 뜻이 되었다. Internet Explore도 인터넷으로 정보의 바다를 탐험한다는 의미에서 붙여진 이름이다.

And the next morning, when the dawn lit the sky red, they got up to explore. 그리고 다음날 아침, 동이 터서 하늘이 붉게 빛날 때 그들은 탐험을 하기 위해 자리에서 일어났다.

pen ⓝ a small area of land surrounded by a fence, in which farm animals are kept

pen은 '고정시키다, 꼼짝 못하게 하다'라는 뜻을 갖고 있는 pin과 마찬가지로 고대영어의 penn에서 유래했을 것으로 추정한다. '깃털(feather)'을 뜻하는 라틴어에서 유래한 필기구 '펜(pen)'과는 다르다. pen은 '가축이 달아나지 못하게 가두어 두는 곳'을 의미한다. 즉 '우리, 축사'이다.

In front of the cave was a pen, walled with stone and filled with hundreds of sheep and goats. 동굴 앞에는 돌로 담을 쌓고 수백 마리의 양과 염소가 가득한 우리가 있었다.

giant ⓝ a very tall and strong man

지금은 giant가 키가 굉장히 큰 '거인'의 의미이지만, 고대 유럽의 전설 속에서는 괴물(monster)이었다. 덩치가 엄청나게 크고 힘이 있을 뿐만 아니라 인간을 잡아먹는 존재였다. giant의 형용사형으로 '거대한'을 뜻하는 gigantic라는 단어가 있지만, giant도 a giant company(거대 기업)처럼 형용사형으로 자주 쓰인다.

"A giant lives here!" they said. 그들이 말했다. "이곳에 거인이 살아요!"

fright ⓝ a sudden strong feeling of fear

fright는 숨이 턱 막히고 가슴이 덜컥 내려앉을 정도의 '갑작스럽고 심한 공포심'을 뜻한다. 형용사형 frightful은 '무서운, 끔찍한'이고, 동사형 frighten은 '겁먹게[놀라게] 만들다'라는 뜻이다. frightened는 '겁에 질린' 상태를 나타낸다.

He flung them onto the floor of the cave with such noise that Odysseus and his men hid themselves in fright. 거인이 너무도 큰소리를 내며 동굴 바닥에 나무들을 내던졌기 때문에, 오디세우스와 부하들은 겁에 질려 몸을 숨겼다.

creep ⓥ to move slowly and quietly

creep은 원래 몸을 바짝 낮추거나 땅에 대고 움직이는 동작을 뜻한다. 남의 눈에 띄지 않게 움직이는 것으로, 자객이나 도둑이 살금살금 움직이는 모습을 연상하면 된다. 그래서 creep은 '살금살금 움직이다, 몰래 이동하다'라는 뜻이다.

creep-crept-crept

Have you crept into my cave to take my sheep and my cheese? 내 양과 치즈를 훔쳐 가려고 내 동굴로 몰래 들어왔느냐?

destroy ⓥ to break or damage something completely

build와 destroy는 역사의 톱니바퀴 같은 것이다. 지어 놓으면 파괴하고, 파괴하면 그 자리에 또 새로운 것을 지으면서 역사가 흘러왔다고 할 수 있다. destroy는 '반대, 거꾸로(reversal)'를 뜻하는 접두사 de-와 '짓다(build)'를 뜻하는 stroy가 합쳐진 것이다. '짓다'의 반대이므로, '파괴하다, 부수다'라는 의미이다. to destroy the ship(배를 파괴하다)나 Our ship is destroyed(우리 배는 부서졌다)처럼 쓸 수 있다. destroy의 명사형은 destruction(파괴)이다.

But Odysseus was afraid that the Cyclops might want to find the ship and destroy it. 그러나 오디세우스는 키클롭스가 배를 찾아 부수고 싶어 할지 모른다고 걱정했다.

urge ⓥ to try hard to persuade someone to do something

urge는 '압박하다(press), 몰다(drive)'를 뜻하는 라틴어에서 유래했다. 다른 사람에게 어떤 행동을 하도록 '압박하고 몰아붙인다'라는 의미이다. 그래서 urge는 '촉구하다, 재촉하다, 충고하다'라는 뜻이다. urge를 명사형으로 쓰면 어떤 행동을 하게 만드는 '강한 충동, 욕구'라는 뜻이 된다.

"Let's kill him while he sleeps!" Odysseus's men urged him. "잠든 사이에 거인을 죽입시다!" 오디세우스의 부하들은 그에게 재촉했다.

grab ⓥ to take hold of something quickly and roughly

grab은 '쥐다, 붙잡다(hold, seize)'라는 기본적인 의미가 있다. 비슷한 뜻을 갖고 있는 grip, grasp와 어원이 같은 것으로 추정한다. 그런데 grab에는 손으로 거칠게 휙 잡는 느낌이 있기 때문에 폭력성과 강제성이 느껴진다. grab-grabbed-grabbed

When the red dawn came, he woke up, lit his fire, milked the goats, and grabbed two more of Odysseus's men for breakfast. 동이 붉게 트자, 거인은 잠에서 깨어 불을 지피고, 염소의 젖을 짠 후에 아침 식사를 위해 오디세우스 부하들 중 두 명을 움켜잡았다.

sharpen ⓥ to make something sharp

sharpen은 '뾰족한, 날카로운'을 뜻하는 형용사 sharp에 동사형 접미사 -en이 붙은 형태이다. 명사형이나 형용사형 중에는 뒤에 -en 붙어 동사형이 되는 것이 있는데, fright(공포)-frighten(겁주다)도 그 예이다. sharpen은 '뾰족하게 만들다, 날카롭게 하다'라는 뜻이다. '연필을 깎다'가 to sharpen a pencil이고, '연필깎이'가 a pencil sharpener이다.

Let's cut a long piece off the end of this tree, about as long as a man is tall, and sharpen it. 이 나무의 끝을 사람의 키 만한 길이로 자른 다음 끝을 뾰족하게 만들자.

seal ⓥ to close something tightly

seal은 sign(서명)을 뜻하는 라틴어에서 온 것이다. 옛날에는 편지를 보낼 때 봉투 입구에 밀랍을 붓고 그 위에 인장(印章)을 찍어 편지를 봉했는데, 그 인장을 보면 누가 보냈는지 알 수 있었다. 일종의 sign인 것이다. 크리스마스 실 (Christmas Seal)도 처음에는 봉투 입구에 붙여 카드를 봉하는 용도로 썼다. 그래서 지금도 seal은 명사형으로 '인장, 봉인'이고, 동사형으로는 '봉하다, 밀폐하다'이다.

When the monster came back into the cave that evening, he drove his sheep and goats in, and again sealed up the door with the huge stone. 그날 저녁 괴물은 동굴로 돌아와 양과 염소들을 안으로 몰아넣고, 다시 입구를 커다란 바위로 꽉 막아버렸다.

roar ⓥ to make a deep loud noise, like a lion

roar는 사자나 호랑이 같은 야수들이 '으르렁' 울부짖는 소리에서 온 것이다. 소리가 우렁차고 듣는 사람이 위압감을 느낄 정도가 되어야 roar라는 단어를 쓸 수 있다. roar는 '으르렁거리다, 포효하다, 고함치다'의 뜻이다. the roar of the Yellow River(황허 강의 요란한 물소리)나 the roar of the crowd(군중들의 함성)처럼 명사형으로도 쓸 수 있다.

The Cyclops leaped up and roared with pain. 키클롭스는 고통으로 펄쩍 뛰며 고함을 질렀다.

stumble ⓥ to almost fall down while walking

길에서 술에 만취한 사람을 보면, 넘어질 듯 말 듯 S자로 걸어간다. 이렇게 걷는 모습을 '휘청거리다, 비틀대다, 발을 헛딛다'라는 뜻의 동사 stumble로 표현할 수 있다. 그런데 여기에서 s-자를 '똑' 떼어버리면, 어떻게 될까? 넘어진다. 바로 tumble이 '무너지다, 떨어지다'라는 뜻이다.

He stumbled all around his cave, grabbing blindly for Odysseus and his men. 거인은 동굴 여기저기를 비틀비틀 돌아다니면서 앞이 보이지 않는 상태로 오디세우스와 그의 부하들을 붙잡으려고 했다.

sneak ⓥ to go somewhere quietly because you do not want people to see or hear you

sneak는 creep과 의미가 비슷하다. 다만 sneak에는 몸을 낮춘다는 의미가 없는 대신 '몰래, 비밀스럽게'의 의미가 더 강하다는 차이점이 있다. '다른 사람들의 시선을 피해 조용히 몰래 움직이다'라는 뜻이다. '운동화'를 뜻하는 sneakers도 밑창이 고무로 되어 있어 구두에 비해 소리가 작게 나기 때문에 붙여진 이름이다.

But he reached down and patted the back of every animal that went past him, so that neither Odysseus nor his men could sneak out with sheep and goats. 그러나 거인은 아래로 손을 뻗어 자기 앞을 지나가는 모든 가축의 등을 토닥였기 때문에, 오디세우스와 부하들은 양과 염소와 몰래 빠져나갈 수가 없었다.

underneath ⓐ below or under something

underneath는 '아래에(below)'를 뜻하는 neath 앞에 under(밑에, 속에)가 붙은 형태이다. under와 neath 모두 '밑, 아래'라는 의미가 있다. underneath는 '밑에, 아래에'라는 뜻인데, 위에 뭔가 덮여 있거나 싸고 있어야 한다. to hold on underneath(밑에서 붙잡다)처럼 부사형이나 underneath the table(식탁 밑에)처럼 전치사로도 쓰인다.

The Cyclops put his hands right on the sheep's backs—but he couldn't find the men who were holding on underneath. 키클롭스는 양손으로 양의 등을 만져보았지만, 양의 배 밑에 매달려 있는 사내들을 찾아내지 못했다.

trick ⓝ something that you do to deceive someone

trick에는 '속이다(deceive)'라는 뜻이 있다. 그래서 명사형으로 '속임수'를 뜻한다. 만우절에 친구들을 '속이는 장난'도 trick이고, 관객을 감쪽같이 속여 즐겁게 하는 '마술'도 trick으로 표현할 수 있다. 물론 동사형으로 쓰면 '속이다, 속임수를 쓰다'라는 뜻이다.

You should have known better than to fall for my tricks! 얼마나 멍청하면 내 속임수에 넘어갔느냐!

jeer ⓝ laughing in a way that is not nice, or shouting at someone you do not like

jeer의 어원은 정확히 알 수는 없지만 '익살, 농담'의 jest와 '환호성'을 뜻하는 cheer의 철자를 따온 것으로 추측할 수 있다. 왜냐하면 jeer는 듣는 사람이 기분 나쁘게 '큰소리로 조롱하고 야유하다'라는 뜻이기 때문이다. 명사형으로는 '야유, 조롱'을 뜻한다.

The blind Cyclops heard his jeers. 앞이 보이지 않는 키클롭스의 귀에 오디세우스의 야유가 들렸다.

adventure ⑪ an unusual, dangerous or exciting thing that happens to someone

adventure에서 ad-는 '~에게(to), ~쪽으로(toward)'를 뜻하고 vent는 '오다(to come)'를 의미한다. 둘을 합치면 advent가 되는데, 이 자체로 '출현, 도래'를 뜻한다. advent에 명사형 어미 -ure가 붙어서 adventure가 탄생했다. '곧 닥칠 특별한(unusual) 일, 위험한(dangerous) 일, 신나는(exciting) 일'을 겪게 된다는 의미에서 adventure는 '모험'이다.

It took ten long years and many dangerous adventures before Odysseus finally reached his home. 10년이라는 긴 세월과 많은 위험한 모험을 거친 뒤에야 오디세우스는 비로소 고향에 도착했다.

3 The First Olympic Games

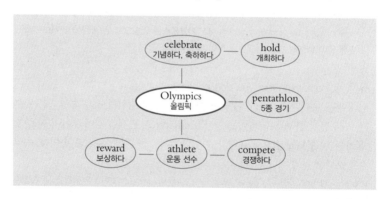

celebrate ⓥ to have a special meal or party because of a particular event

celebrate의 라틴어 어근인 celebr-는 '유명한(famous), 명예로운(honored)'을 의미한다. 그래서 '유명 인사'를 celebrity라고 하고, '유명한 사건이나 명예로운 시간'을 특별하게 기리는 것을 celebrate, 즉 '기념하다, 축하하다'라고 한다. 명사형은 celebration이다.

To celebrate the peace, they decided to have a festival—a big celebration—in honor of the god Zeus, the chief god of the Greeks. 평화를 기념하기 위해 그들은 그리스인의 가장 높은 신인 제우스를 기려 성대한 축제를 열기로 결정했다.

pentathlon ⓝ an athletic event that consists of five different sports

pentathlon에서 pent(e)-는 '다섯, 5(five)'를 뜻한다. 오각형 도형을 pentagon 이라고 하는데, 건물 모양이 오각형이라서 미국 국방부를 '펜타곤(Pentagon)'이라고 부른다. athlon은 '경쟁, 시합(contest)'을 뜻한다. pentathlon은 다섯 종목을 겨루어 전체 순위로 우승을 가리는 한 세트의 시합을 의미하는데, 고대 올림픽의 5종 경기는 원반던지기, 투창, 멀리뛰기, 레슬링, 달리기로 구성되어 있었다.

They even invented a competition called the *pentathlon*, where the athletes had to do five different events. 심지어 그들은 '5종 경기'라고 불리는 시합을 고안해냈는데, 선수들이 각기 다른 다섯 가지 종목을 치러야 하는 시합이었다.

compete ⓥ to take part in a competition or sports event

compete에서 com-은 '함께(together)'이고, pete는 '추구하다(seek), 목표로 하다(aim at)'를 뜻한다. 즉 함께 공동의 목표를 추구하는 것, 같은 목표를 앞에 두고 '서로 경쟁하다'라는 뜻이 compete이다. 명사형 competition은 '경쟁, 시합, 대회'이다.

But only men were allowed to compete in the Greek Olympics. 그러나 그리스 올림픽에는 오직 남자들만 시합에 참여하도록 허용되었다.

hold ⓥ to arrange and make something happen

hold의 기본적인 의미는 '쥐다, 잡다, 들고 있다'이다. 뭔가를 잡고 있으면 행동해야 한다. 야구 배트를 잡고 있으면 휘둘러야 하고, 지휘봉을 쥐고 있으면 지휘를 해야 한다. 그래서 어떤 권한과 책임을 갖고 그에 걸맞은 역할을 한다는 의미로 hold를 쓴다. 이때에는 '개최하다, 주관하다, 열다'라는 뜻이다. We will hold a conference next week(우리는 다음 주에 회의를 개최할 것이다)처럼 쓸 수 있는데, 예문처럼 주어를 '개최되는 행사'로 하고, 수동형(be held)으로 표현하는 것이 일반적이다. hold-held-held

The Olympics were held every four years for almost a thousand years. 올림픽은 거의 천 년 동안 4년마다 한 번씩 열렸다.

athlete ⓝ someone who is good at sports

athlete의 어원은 앞에서 배운 pentathlon의 athlon이다. athlete은 '상을 받기 위해 경쟁하다(to compete for a prize)'라는 뜻에서 유래했다. 물론 참가하는 것만으로도 의미가 있지만, 한 지역과 국가를 대표하는 선수라면 운동 실력이 남달라야 한다. 이처럼 기대할 수 있을 정도로 '운동을 잘하는 사람, 운동선수'가 athlete이다.

People came from all over Greece to compete in the Games and to watch the other athletes. 그리스 전역에서 사람들이 올림픽 경기에 참가하고 다른 선수들을 구경하기 위해 왔다.

reward ⓥ to give something to someone because they have done something good or helpful

reward는 내가 선행을 하거나 누군가에게 도움을 주었을 때 그것에 대한 '보상'을 의미한다. 명사형으로 '보상, 보상금, 답례', 동사로는 '보상하다, 보답하다'를 뜻한다. reward는 경쟁에서 이기거나 성적이 우수해서 받는 '상'인 award와는 성격이 다르다.

And when they went back home, their own cities rewarded them with money and with free food for the rest of their lives. 그리고 우승자들이 고향으로 돌아오면, 그들의 도시에서는 돈과 남은 평생 먹을 공짜 음식을 제공함으로써 그들에게 보상했다.

Chapter 21
The Medes and the Persians

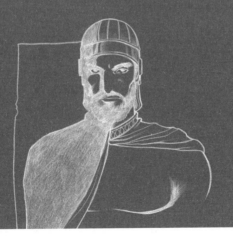

1 A New Empire

지금의 이란(Iran) 사람들이 고대에 건설한 제국을 페르시아라고 하는데, '페르시아(Persia)'라는 명칭은 이란의 남서부 해안에 살던 사람들을 그리스인들이 '파르사'라고 부른 데에서 유래했다. 유목 민족이었던 페르시아인들은 점차 세력을 넓혔고, 키루스 2세가 기원전 550년 메디아를 장악하면서 제국으로 발전하기 시작했다. 페르시아는 바빌로니아를 멸망시키고 메소포타미아 지역을 완전히 통합했으며 소아시아의 그리스 식민 도시와 이집트의 북부 지역, 인도의 인더스 강 유역까지 영토를 넓혀 대제국을 완성했다. 기원전 330년 마케도니아의 알렉산드로스 대왕의 원정대에게 무릎을 꿇음으로써 페르시아 제국 시대는 막을 내린다.

Let's take a minute to review the story of the Assyrians. Earlier, we read about the Assyrian king Shamshi-Adad. He wanted to rule the world. *He conquered the cities all around him and made them obey him. He put his soldiers in the conquered cities, and told them to punish anyone who disobeyed his laws. Soon the Assyrians ruled the whole northern part of Mesopotamia—the land between the Tigris and Euphrates rivers.

*But the Babylonian kingdom ruled the southern part of Mesopotamia, and they were even stronger than the Assyrians. The Babylonian king, Hammurabi, marched his army up and took over Assyria. For a little while, the Assyrians had to obey the Babylonians.

*But the Assyrians didn't like belonging to the Babylonian empire. Eventually, they rebelled and took their kingdom back. Now the Assyrians were in charge, and the Babylonians had to obey them.

*The Assyrians went back to conquering all the cities around them. They fought their way all the way over to Canaan. They captured the Jews who lived there and made them leave their homes.

But the Babylonians made friends with another nation, Media. Together, the Babylonians and the Medes got together and destroyed Assyria. *Now Babylon and Media were in charge, and the Assyrians had to obey. This must have been a very strange time to live! The rulers of the world kept changing—first they were Assyrian, then Babylonian, then Assyrian, then Babylonian again.

*The Babylonians and the Medes must have been pleased with themselves. They had finally gotten rid of Assyria. Now they were the most powerful nations in Mesopotamia! But the Medes and Babylonians weren't in charge for very long. A new nation was becoming stronger and stronger. This new nation was called Persia.

At first, the Persians were just a tribe of shepherds. They lived at the edge of Media, and obeyed the king of the Medes. The Persian shepherds were ruled by a man named Astyges. He wasn't a good man; he liked ruling the Persians, and he would do anything to keep his crown.

One night, Astyges had a dream that scared him. He dreamed that his baby grandson would grow up, take his power away, and become the ruler of the Persians. When he woke up, he was frightened! "If I don't do something about this," he thought, "my grandson will throw me off my throne, and become king in my place!" Astyges sat up all night, thinking about his dream.

In the morning, he called his chief advisor, a man named Harpagus. "I have a job for you," he said.

"I will do anything you tell me to, O King!" said Harpagus.

"Good!" Astyges said. "Take my grandson out to the mountains and kill him. And don't let anyone know what you're doing. Now go!"

Harpagus didn't want to do this terrible thing. But he was afraid to disobey the king. So he took the baby and walked out to the mountains. "I have to obey my king!" he thought to himself. "I have to kill the baby. But I can't make myself do it!"

He looked around and saw a shepherd, grazing his sheep nearby. He called the shepherd over. "Here," he said. "The king wants to get rid of this baby. You do it! If you do, I'll reward you with much wealth. But if you don't, I'll send the king's soldiers to punish you."

The shepherd looked at the baby, and had an idea.

"All right," he said to Harpagus. "I'll get rid of the baby." He took the baby and ran home to his wife, who had no children of her own. "Wife!" he said. "The gods have sent us a son! We can raise him as our own!"

His wife took the baby with tears of joy. And then the shepherd killed a goat, wiped his hands in the blood, and ran back to Harpagus. "Look," he said. "I've done as you told me!" So Harpagus went back to Astyges and told him that the baby was dead. But the shepherd and his wife named the baby Cyrus, and brought him up there on the mountainside.

Cyrus grew up to be tall and strong. He was faster and smarter than any other shepherd's son. And he stood head and shoulders above every other boy his age. One day, the shepherd took him down from the mountainside into town to help with the selling of the sheep. While they were at the marketplace, Astyges, the ruler of the Persians, came by along with Harpagus. As soon as Astyges saw the young boy selling sheep, he knew that this was his grandson.

That evening he sent for Harpagus. "You disobeyed me!" he said to Harpagus. And Harpagus admitted that he had given the baby to a shepherd, rather than killing him. Astyges was so furious that he tried to kill Harpagus and his whole family. But Harpagus fled to the mountains and found Cyrus. "If you want to take the king's power away, and become king of the Persians yourself," he told Cyrus, "I will help you."

Together, Harpagus and Cyrus convinced the Persians to follow Cyrus, rather than Astyges. ˙Cyrus took power away from his grandfather and became the ruler of the Persians, just as Astyges had dreamed, so many years ago. And then he led the Persians in a war against the great empire of Media. ˙After three years of fierce fighting, Cyrus conquered the king of Media as well. ˙Now Cyrus, who had been raised by a shepherd on a mountain, ruled over the combined empires of the Medes and the Persians.

2 Cyrus the Great

키루스 대제는 키루스 2세(Cyrus II)로도 불리고, 《구약 성서》에는 '고레스 왕'으로 기록되어 있는 인물이다. 키루스는 기원전 6세기 초에 메디아의 변방에 위치한, 유목민들의 소왕국 안산에서 태어났다. 기원전 559년에 안산의 왕이 된 이후 세력을 키워 10년 만에 메디아를 멸망시키고, 소아시아를 지배했으며 기원전 538년에는 바빌로니아 제국까지 차지하며 페르시아 제국을 건설했다. 키루스 대제는 정복한 지역에서 토착민의 자치를 허용하고 각 종족의 종교를 인정하는 유화 정책을 폈는데, 바빌론 유수 이후 핍박받던 유대인들도 이때 고향인 가나안으로 돌아가 자신들의 종교를 자유롭게 믿을 수 있게 되었다.

Cyrus was now the king of the Medes and the Persians. ˙He was a great warrior—but he was also known as a good and fair king. Even though he had conquered the Medes, he let the Median people stay in their own homes. He even let Median noblemen have some of the power in his new, combined empire. After all, his empire was so big that he needed help. He couldn't collect all the taxes, judge all the court cases, and settle all the problems himself! So he made both Persians and Medians officials in his kingdom. The Medians felt that they were being treated well—and so they didn't try to rebel against Cyrus's rule.

Now Cyrus decided to make his empire even bigger. He wanted to conquer Asia Minor. Asia Minor was ruled by King Croesus, who was the richest king in the world. He had more gold than anyone else. Cyrus knew that if he could conquer Croesus, he would be rich as well. So he marched his army up to the kingdom of Croesus and conquered it. He captured Croesus and made him stand up on the walls of his city and watch as Persian soldiers looted it. The soldiers went all through the city, carrying away armloads of treasures, gold coins, and

Cyrus the Great

The Persian Empire under Cyrus the Great

jewelry. But Croesus just watched, calmly.

Finally, Cyrus said, "How can you be so calm? They are robbing you of all your gold!"

"No, they aren't," Croesus said. "The city belongs to you now. So they are actually stealing from you." When Cyrus heard this, he stopped the soldiers at once and took all the gold back!

Next, Cyrus turned his army to the east. Cyrus marched the Persian army all the way over to the Indus River. Now he ruled all the land between Asia Minor and India. The Persian Empire was as wide as it was tall.

Cyrus wasn't done conquering yet. There was one big enemy left for him: Babylon. Remember, the Babylonians had been ruling in Mesopotamia for a long time! They were an old kingdom—and a very powerful kingdom. Cyrus wanted all that good, fertile land between the Tigris and the Euphrates rivers. But he knew that the Babylonian army was very strong.

However, Cyrus had one big advantage over Babylon. The Persians liked Cyrus, because he was a good, fair king. But the Babylonians hated their king. He had left the city of Babylon and had gone away to live in a distant desert. In his place, he had given his son Belshazzar control over the city. *Belshazzar spent too much money on feasting and drinking, and not enough on the people of Babylon.

So when Cyrus marched his army to Babylon, he didn't meet much resistance. *The Babylonians were sick and tired of their own king. So they didn't fight very hard when Cyrus's army arrived at the walls. *Some of the Babylonians even opened the gates from the inside and let him in! Babylon fell to the Persians in 539 BC/BCE.

When Cyrus took over Babylon, he also took over Canaan. Canaan (also called Palestine) had been the home of the Jewish people, until Babylon and Assyria conquered it. The Babylonians and Assyrians had made the Jewish people leave their homes. But Cyrus was a merciful king. When he became the king of Babylon, he let the Jews go back to Palestine. And he let them go back to worshipping their own god. This made him even more popular. The Jews were so grateful to Cyrus that they called him, "The Anointed of the Lord."

Now Cyrus was the greatest king in the world.

But there was still one country that didn't obey Cyrus: Greece. And soon the Greeks and the Persians would meet in battle. 📖

Note to Parent: The earliest Persians lived around 700 BC/BCE. Cyrus the Great ruled 559–525 BC/BCE.

The Story of the Words

Chapter 21 The Medes and the Persians

1 A New Empire

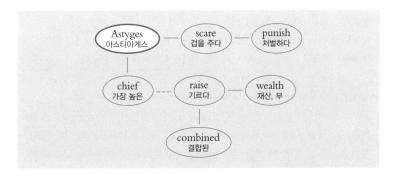

punish ⓥ to make someone suffer because he or she has done something bad or wrong

punish는 '벌주다, 처벌하다'라는 뜻이다. 잘못한 사람을 혼내어 반성하게 하는 방법 중 하나가 '벌'인데, punish는 어떤 방식이든 벌을 주는 행위를 포괄하는 단어이다. 법에 의한 '처벌, 형벌'은 주로 penalty를 쓴다. 명사형은 punishment이다.

He put his soldiers in the conquered cities, and told them to punish anyone who disobeyed his laws. 그는 자신의 병사들을 점령된 도시에 배치하고, 자신의 법을 거역하는 이들은 누구든 처벌하라고 병사들에게 명령했다.

scare ⓥ to make someone feel afraid

scare는 원래 jump(펄쩍 뛰다)를 뜻하는 단어에서 왔다. 운동 삼아 점프하는 것이 아니라, 갑자기 놀라거나 겁을 먹어 뛰는 것이다. '덜컥' 겁을 먹고 '화들짝' 놀라는 모습이다. scare는 '겁을 주다, 무섭게 하다'라는 뜻으로 쓰인다. 앞에서 배운 frighten과 비슷한 단어로, I was scared(나 정말 무서웠어)처럼 수동태로 쓴다. scary는 '무섭게 만드는'의 의미로 '무서운 영화'는 a scary movie라고 한다.

One night, Astyges had a dream that scared him. 어느 날 밤, 아스티아게스는 무서운 꿈을 꿨다.

chief ⓐ highest in position; most important

chief는 head(머리)를 뜻하는 라틴어에서 유래했다. 머리는 가장 높고 중요한 것을 상징한다. 그래서 chief는 명사형으로 '우두머리, 장(長)'이고 형용사형으로는 '최고 지위의, 가장 중요한'을 뜻한다. 회사의 '최고경영자(CEO)'는 Chief Executive Officer이고, 군의 '총사령관'은 commander-in-chief이다. '주방장'을 뜻하는 프랑스어 '셰프(chef)'도 chief와 어원이 같다. chief advisor는 '가장 높은(중요한) 신하(참모)'이다.

In the morning, he called his chief advisor, a man named Harpagus. 아침에 그는 자신의 가장 높은 신하인, '하르파구스'라는 이름의 신하를 불렀다.

wealth ⓝ a large amount of money and other valuable things

wealth의 어근 weal은 '번영, 행복'을 의미한다. 번영과 행복을 이루려면 물질적으로도 풍요로워야 하므로 wealth는 '부(富), 많은 재산, 부유함'이다. 형용사형 wealthy는 '부유한, 재산이 많은(rich)'이고, the wealthy는 the rich와 마찬가지로 '부자들'을 의미한다.

If you do, I will reward you with much wealth. 그렇게 하면, 내가 너에게 그 대가로 많은 재산을 주겠다.

raise ⓥ to take care of; to bring up

raise의 기본 의미는 '들어 올리다'이다. 뭔가를 올리면 높아지고, 커지고, 많아진다. 교실에서 선생님이 Raise your hand라고 하면, 학생들이 손을 높이 든다. We have to raise its price라고 하면 얼마 후 물건 가격이 인상된다. 가축을 raise하면 몸집이 커지고, 살이 찐다. 자식을 raise하면 성장해 어른이 된다. raise를 사람에게 쓰면 성인이 될 때까지 '돌보고 교육시키다(to care for and educate)'라는 의미이다.

We can raise him as our own! 그 아이를 우리 자식으로 삼아 기릅시다!

combined ⓐ joined or united into one

combined는 '결합하다, 섞다'를 뜻하는 동사 combine의 형용사형이다. combine에서 com-은 together(함께)이고, bine은 two(둘)을 뜻한다. 둘이 함께 묶여 '하나'가 되는 것이 combine이다. 그래서 combined는 '결합된, 섞인,

하나가 된'을 뜻한다. combine의 명사형은 combination(결합, 조합)이다. 우리가 주문해서 먹는 '콤비네이션 피자(Combination Pizza)'에도 여러 가지 재료가 다 '섞여' 있다.

Now Cyrus, who had been raised by a shepherd on a mountain, ruled over the combined empires of the Medes and the Persians. 산 위에서 양치기의 손에 길러진 키루스는 이제 메디아와 페르시아가 결합된 제국들을 통치했다.

Q 페르시아가 아니라 '이란'으로 불러야 하나요?

A 1935년 이란 국왕 레자 샤가 세계를 향해 '우리나라를 페르시아가 아니라 이란으로 통일해 불러달라'라고 요구했어. 국왕은 왜 갑작스럽게 이런 요구를 했을까? 실은 갑작스러운 것만은 아니야. 우리가 '페르시아'로 부르는 명칭은 사실은 그리스인이 만든 것이고, 그들 스스로는 '이란'이라고 불렀거든.

그렇다면 그리스인은 왜 그들을 페르시아인이라고 부른 것일까? 자그로스 산맥 아래 '파르시'라는 곳에 도착한 사람들은 중앙아시아에서 인도로 떠난 사람들과 같은 유목민으로, 자신들을 '고귀하다'는 의미로 '아리아'라고 불렀어. 그 아리아인의 나라에서 이란이라는 명칭이 나온 것인데, 그리스 문명의 힘이 세어지다보니 자연스럽게 페르시아로 굳어지게 된 거야.

2 Cyrus the Great

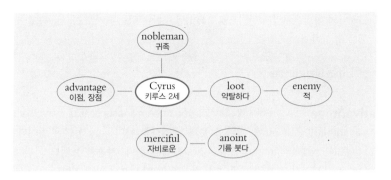

nobleman ⓝ a member of the highest social rank

nobleman에서 noble은 '잘 알려진(well-known)'을 뜻하는 말에서 왔다. '사회적인 신분이 높아서 누구나 다 안다'라는 의미로, 명사형으로 쓰이면 '상류층,

귀족 가문'을 뜻한다. 우리말의 '명문가(名門家)'라는 말도 noble의 의미와 통한다. 높은 사회적 지위에 상응하는 도덕적 의무를 일컫는 '노블레스 오블리주 (noblesse oblige)'의 noblesse도 프랑스어로 '귀족'이고, noble과 어원이 같다. nobleman은 '귀족'이다.

He even let Median noblemen have some of the power in his new, combined empire. 심지어 그는 메디아의 귀족들이 그의 새로운 통합 제국에서 일정 부분 권력을 갖도록 허락했다.

loot ⓥ to steal from shops and houses during a war or disaster

loot는 19세기에 인도어에서 영어로 유입된 단어이다. 남의 재산을 훔치거나 (steal) 강탈하는(rob) 행동을 표현한 것인데, 주로 전쟁이나 폭동이 일어났거나 지진이나 화재 같은 재해가 발생했을 때 상점과 주택에 침입해 '물건을 훔치는 것'을 의미한다. 즉 '약탈하다, 훔치다'이다. looter는 '약탈자'이다.

He captured Croesus and made him stand up on the walls of his city and watch as Persian soldiers looted it. 그는 크로이소스를 잡아서 도시 성벽 위에 세우고, 페르시아 병사들이 그의 도시를 약탈하는 광경을 지켜보게 했다.

enemy ⓝ a person or country that is not friendly to you or wants to harm or fight you

enemy는 not friend를 뜻한다. 즉 친구가 아니라 적대적인 관계를 의미한다. 그래서 전쟁 중인 '적국, 적군'도 enemy이고, 동물 세계의 '천적'도 natural enemy라고 한다. 회사나 학교에서 '적대적인 경쟁 관계에 있는 사람'이나, 페르시아와 바빌론처럼 숙명적으로 '적'이 될 수밖에 없는 관계도 enemy라고 표현할 수 있다.

There was one big enemy left for him: Babylon. 그에게는 거대한 적이 하나 남아 있었다. 바로 바빌론이었다.

advantage ⓝ something that helps you to be more successful than others

advantage는 advant에 '결과'를 뜻하는 명사형 어미 -age가 붙은 말이다. advant는 '앞에(in front), 앞으로(forward)'를 뜻한다. 자동차 브랜드 '아반테 (Avante)'도 '전진, 진보'라는 뜻이다. 경주를 할 때 남보다 한 발이라도 '앞에서' 출발하면 유리하다. 그래서 '앞에 있음'을 의미하는 advantage는 '유리한 점, 이점, 장점'을 뜻한다. '불리한 점, 단점'은 disadvantage이다.

However, Cyrus had one big advantage over Babylon. 그러나 키루스는 바빌론에 비해 큰 장점이 하나 있었다.

merciful ⓐ being kind to people and forgiving them rather than punishing them or being cruel

merciful은 mercy가 '가득한(-ful)' 마음을 의미한다. mercy는 '동정(pity), 감사(thanks)'를 뜻하는 라틴어 merces에서 유래하여 신과 인간의 관계를 담고 있다. 신은 인간을 '불쌍히 여겨' 용서하고, 인간은 그런 신에게 '감사'한다는 의미가 모두 담겼다. 우리말로는 '자비(慈悲)'를 뜻한다. merciful은 형용사형으로 '자비로운, 관대한'을 뜻한다.

But Cyrus was a merciful king. 그러나 키루스는 자비로운 왕이었다.

anoint ⓥ to put oil on a part of someone's body in a religious ceremony

anoint는 '몸에 기름을 바르다'라는 뜻인데, 여기에서 말하는 기름은 요리를 위해 사용하는 참기름, 들기름 같은 것이 아니라 기독교의 종교의식에서 쓰이는 '성유(聖油)'를 말한다. 하느님이 주신 특별한 기름인데, 이 기름은 '이스라엘의 왕'만이 몸에 바를 수 있었다고 한다. 그래서 The Anointed of the Lord는 '하느님이 기름을 부어 이스라엘 민족의 왕으로 선택하신 사람'이라는 의미이다. 거주의 자유와 종교의 자유를 허락한 키루스를 이스라엘인들은 기꺼이 자신들의 왕으로 받아들였던 것이다.

The Jews were so grateful to Cyrus that they called him, "The Anointed of the Lord." 유대인들은 키루스가 너무도 고마워서 '그를 하느님의 기름 부음을 받은 자'라고 불렀다.

진의행(등명중학교 1학년), 진달래(등명중학교 3학년)

Sentence Review 구문은 직접 두 명의 학생이 문장을 선정하고, 저자 지소철이 해설하였다. 구문을 선정한 진의행은 평소 '깊이 읽기 독서'를 즐긴다. 영어 과목은 좋아하지 않았으나 《the Story of the World》 역사 지식을 통해 영어라는 언어와 친해지게 되었다. 진달래는 《the Story of the World》를 시작으로 원서 리딩의 매력에 빠져, 현재 100명의 영향력 있는 인물을 소개하는 《the 100》을 만나고 있다.

The Story of the World

Sentence
Review

20   When the nomads had hunted in one area for a while, all the animals would move away from them.

▶ all the animals(모든 동물들이)가 주어이고, would는 '~하곤 했다'라는 뜻으로 반복되는 상황을 표현하는 조동사이다.

▶ move away from them은 '이동해서(move) 그들로부터(from them) 멀어지다(away)'라는 의미이다.

20   When that happened, the nomads would pack up and follow the game.

▶ game은 '사냥감'이고, follow the game은 '사냥감을 쫓아가다'이다.

20   In warm places, nomads built tents by stretching animal hides over wooden frames.

▶ by는 '수단, 도구, 방법'을 의미하는 전치사이다. 따라서 by stretching animal hides는 '동물의 가죽을 펼침으로써'라고 해석한다.

21   She is sleeping outside, so all she has to do is pick up the piece of animal skin she sleeps on and take it to her mother.

▶ all she has to do는 '그녀가 해야 할 일의 전부'라는 의미로 문장의 주어이다. '그녀가 해야 할 일은 ~뿐이었다'라고 해석한다.

21   She wears the same clothes all the time, so she doesn't have to change out of her pajamas.

▶ out of her pajamas는 '파자마를 벗고'란 뜻이므로 change out of her pajamas는 '파자마를 벗고 다른 옷을 입다'라는 의미이다.

21   In the middle of the nomads' camp, the fire is still burning from the night before.

▶ the night before는 '전날 밤'으로, 불(the fire)이 전날 밤부터 지금까지 계속 타고 있다는 의미이다.

21   Tarak's uncle and some of the other adults have taken turns staying up through the night, watching the fire and keeping it burning.

▶ to take turns -ing는 '교대로 ~을 하다'이다.
▶ to keep A -ing는 'A가 계속 ~하게 유지하다'라는 의미이다.

They heard a wildcat screaming in the night and wanted to keep it away from the camp.

▶ 'to keep A away'는 'A가 계속 멀리 있게 하다. A가 가까이 오지 못하게 하다'라는 표현이다. it이 'a wildcat(사자, 표범 등 고양이과 동물)'을 지칭하므로 keep it away는 '그런 맹수가 가까이 오지 못하게 하다'라는 의미이다.

She and her younger brother get their game bags—small bags made out of skin—and start out to look for food.

▶ start out은 '출발하며 밖으로 나가다'이고, to look for food는 '먹잇감을 찾기 위해'라는 의미이다.

Sure enough, as they walk out of a patch of woods into the sunshine, Tarak sees a lizard dart away into the crack of a log.

▶ sure enough를 문장 앞에 쓰면 그 문장의 내용이 '예상했던 대로' 이루어졌음을 뜻하므로, '아니나 다를까. 예상[기대]했던 대로'라고 해석할 수 있다.

That way, even if it did not rain, they could bring water to their crops.

▶ 문장 앞에 even if가 붙으면 '가정하는 내용이 사실이더라도'라는 의미로 '~할지라도, ~에도 불구하고'라고 해석한다. 따라서 even if it did not rain은 '비가 오지 않더라도'이다.

Then the farmers lowered the bucket into the canal, raised the bucket by pushing down on the weight, and then swung the bucket around to pour the water on the crops.

▶ raised the bucket by pushing down on the weight는 '무거운 것이 달린 쪽으로 밀어서 두레박을 들어 올렸다'라고 이해할 수 있다.

▶ swung the bucket around to pour the water on the crops는 '두레박을 빙글 돌려서 농작물에 물을 쏟아 부었다'라는 의미이다.

They used whatever materials were around them.

▶ whatever는 '어느 것이든, 모든 것을(any or all of the things)'이라는 의미로, whatever materials were around them은 '그들 주위에 있는 재료들은 뭐든지, 그들 주위에 있는 모든 재료들을'이라고 해석한다.

Farmers who lived near the river built houses out of reeds, or out of bricks that were made from mud and left to dry in the sun.

▶ 'out of + 재료[수단]'는 '그 재료[수단]을 이용해'라는 의미로, built houses out of reeds는 '갈대를 이용해 집을 지었다'라는 뜻이 된다.

²⁵ Soon, farmers discovered that it was best to build houses close together so that they could help each other to water and tend their fields.

▶ To build houses close together was best라고 문장을 쓰면 주어가 길다. 그래서 it was best to build houses close together라고 형태를 바꿔 쓴 것이다. '집을 가까이 붙여 짓는 것이 가장 좋았다'라는 의미이다.

²⁶ They just squat on the shore and splash each other.

▶ squat은 '쪼그리고 앉다'라는 뜻의 동사이다. 다리를 굽히고 앉되 엉덩이는 땅에서 뗀 상태가 squat이다.

Chapter 2 Egyptians Lived on the Nile River

³⁶ But the farmers who lived along the banks of the Nile River had a very different kind of river to deal with.

▶ to deal with는 '~을 다루다, 상대하다, 처리하다'를 의미한다. 이 문장에서는 river를 꾸며주는 역할을 하므로 river to deal with는 '다루어야[상대해야] 하는 강'을 뜻한다.

³⁷ If a farmer had a river flood all over his crops today, he'd think it was a disaster.

▶ all over his crops에서 all은 '완전히, 온통'을 뜻하는 부사로, over his crops를 꾸며준다. 따라서 all over his crops는 '그의 농작물 위로 온통[완전히]'를 뜻한다.

³⁷ But the farmers who lived along the Nile liked to see the river flood.

▶ along은 '~을 따라 죽[계속] 이어지는'을 뜻해서, '나일 강의 물줄기를 따라' 산 농부들이라고 해석한다.

Chapter 3 The First Writing

⁵² The pictures stood for certain words.

▶ to stand for A는 'A를 상징[의미]하다'의 표현이다. 따라서 이 문장은 '그 그림들은 특정 단어들을 상징[의미]했다'라고 해석할 수 있다.

⁵⁴ And clay tablets are thick; if you want to store a whole lot of them, you need a lot of space—whole buildings full of rooms for even a

small library.
- ▶ 'hyphen(–)' 다음에 a lot of space를 자세히 설명하는 말이 나와 있는데, whole buildings full of rooms는 '방들로 가득 찬 건물 전체'를 뜻한다.
- ▶ for even a small library는 '작은 도서관 하나를 짓기 위해서도'라는 뜻이다.

And paper took up less room.
- ▶ 'to take up A' 표현은 'A라는 공간이나 시간을 차지하다'이다.
- ▶ less room은 '더 적은 공간'이라는 의미로, 이 문장은 '또한 종이는 공간을 덜 차지했다'라고 해석한다.

 Chapter 4 The Old Kingdom of Egypt

Only priests—men who were in charge of worshipping the gods— were allowed to make mummies.
- ▶ 'in charge of A 표현'은 'A에 대한 권한과 책임이 있는'을 뜻한다. 'A를 담당하는, 주관하는' 으로 해석할 수 있다. 따라서 priests(사제들)를 설명하는 말인 men who were in charge of worshipping the gods는 '신들에 대한 예배를 주관하는 사람들'로 이해하면 된다.

But if his heart is full of sin, it will be heavy—and a monster will eat it!
- ▶ sin은 '신의 뜻을 어긴 죄, 종교의 교리를 어긴 죄'를 뜻하는데, '심각한 범죄, 무거운 죄'를 뜻하는 경우에도 쓸 수 있다. if his heart is full of sin은 '그의 심장이 무거운 죄로 가득 차 있다면'을 뜻한다.

The mummy and all its clothes, furniture, and jewelry were lowered down the shaft into a treasure room.
- ▶ 이 문장에서 lower는 '아래로 천천히 내리다(to move something or someone down slowly)'라는 뜻의 동사이다.
- ▶ shaft는 위아래로 이동할 수 있는 '수직 통로'로, were lowered down the shaft는 '수직 통로 아래로 천천히 내려졌다'로 해석할 수 있다.

They thought that the dead pharaoh would climb up to heaven, using the sides of the pyramids like steps.
- ▶ 동시에 일어나는 동작이나 상황을 '동사의 –ing' 형태로 표현할 수 있다. using the sides of the pyramids like steps는 '피라미드의 측면을 계단처럼 이용하면서'라는 의미이다.

It is called the Great Pyramid, because it is the largest of all the 35 pyramids that the Egyptians built for their pharaohs.

▶ that the Egyptians built for their pharaohs는 앞에 나온 pyramids를 꾸며주면서, 그 피라미드가 어떤 피라미드인지 설명하는 역할을 한다. '이집트인들이 자신들의 파라오를 위해 건설한 피라미드'로 이해하면 된다.

That's as heavy as an elephant!

▶ 'as 형용사 as'는 둘을 비교할 때 쓰는 표현으로 둘이 비슷하다는 의미를 담고 있다. as heavy as는 '~만큼 무거운'을 뜻하므로 이 문장은 '그것은 코끼리만큼 무거웠다'라고 해석한다.

Then they built ramps out of rocks and earth up the sides of the pyramids, and dragged the stone blocks up the ramps with ropes.

▶ 이 문장은 끊어서 순서대로 이해하면 된다. they built ramps는 '그들은 층계를 만들었다'라는 뜻이다. 층계를 무엇으로 만들었냐면 out of rocks and earth, 즉 '돌과 흙으로' 만들었다. up the sides of the pyramids는 층계를 만든 위치가 '피라미드의 측면 위에'라는 의미이다.

But there were also empty chambers and unfinished rooms, and passages that led off into dead ends.

▶ unfinished room은 '완성이 안 된 방'을 말한다. 사방에 벽이 있고 천장까지 갖추어야 완전한 방인데, 그렇지 않은 형태로 남아 있다는 의미이다.

▶ to lead off into는 '도로나 통로가 죽 어떤 곳으로 이어져 있다'라는 뜻이다.

And after the pyramid was finished, workmen sealed off the door to the outside.

▶ 동사 seal은 '밀폐하다, 봉하다'라는 뜻이고, off는 '단절, 폐쇄'를 의미한다. 따라서 workmen sealed off the door to the outside는 '일꾼들이 밖으로 향하는 문을 완전히 밀폐했다'라는 것이다.

The Great Sphinx is as tall as eleven men, standing on each other's shoulders.

▶ 대스핑크의 높이가 '11명만큼 높다(as tall as eleven men)'라고 했는데, 이 말을 설명하기 위해 standing on each other's shoulders를 붙였다. 마치 탑을 쌓듯이, 11명이 어깨 위로 올라가 서면 그 정도의 높이가 된다는 의미이다.

Desert sand keeps burying it and wearing it away.

▶ 동사 wear에는 '닳게 하다, 해어지게 하다'라는 뜻이 있다. 옷을 계속 입으면 닳고 해어지듯이, 뭔가 '점점 닳게 한다'라는 의미이다. to wear away는 '닳아서 없어지게 하다'를 뜻하는 표현이다.

▶ it은 '스핑크스(the sphinx)'이다.

58 By the time archaeologists made their way into the pyramid, Cheops and his gold had disappeared forever.

▶ by the time을 문장 앞에 쓰면, '~할 무렵에, ~할 때가 되면'을 의미한다. 따라서 By the time archaeologists made their way into the pyramid는 '고고학자들이 피라미드로 들어갔을 무렵에는'으로 해석할 수 있다.

Chapter 5 The First Sumerian Dictator

76 Egypt grew richer and stronger, once all the quarrelling Egyptians were united into one.

▶ once는 '한 번, ~하자마자'를 뜻하는 부사로 자주 쓰는데, 문장 앞에 쓰면 '일단 ~하자, ~하자마자'를 뜻한다. 그래서 once all the quarrelling Egyptians were united into one은 '일단 다투던 이집트인들이 전부 하나로 통합되자'로 해석할 수 있다.

76 We call them *city-states* because each city was like a separate country

▶ city-state는 하나의 도시(city)가 곧 하나의 나라(state)인 형태로, '도시 국가'를 의미한다.

Chapter 6 The Jewish People

85 He leaned his arms on the fence surrounding his flocks, and listened to the noise of the sheep and goats.

▶ He leaned his arms on the fence는 '양팔을 펜스 위에 올려놓고 있었다'라는 의미이다.
▶ surrounding his flocks는 the fence를 설명하는 말로, '가축들을 빙 둘러서 가두는'이라는 뜻이다.
▶ flocks는 '가축의 무리[떼]'로, 뒤에 나오는 the sheep and goats를 모두 지칭한다.

9 Down in Egypt, Joseph lived in the house of Potiphar, the captain of the pharaoh's guards.

▶ 지도에서 보면 이집트는 가나안보다 아래쪽에 있다. 그래서 Down in Egypt는 '아래의 이집트에서'를 의미한다.
▶ Potiphar가 어떤 사람인지 설명하는 말이 뒤에 나오는데, 바로 the captain of the Pharaoh's guards는 '파라오의 경비대 대장'이다.

9 He trusted Joseph more and more and gave him more and more responsibility.

▶ He trusted Joseph more and more와 He gave him more and more responsibility가 하나의 문장으로 합쳐진 형태이다. 앞의 문장은 '요셉을 점점 더 많이 신뢰했다'이고, 뒤의 문장은 '요셉에게 점점 더 많은 책임을 주었다'이다.

90 As the dreamer was walking away, Joseph called after him, "Remember me! Tell Pharaoh that I am innocent, so that I can get out of jail!"

▶ 형용사 innocent는 '죄가 없는, 결백한'을 의미한다. 따라서 Tell Pharaoh that I am innocent는 '내가 죄가 없다고 파라오에게 말해달라'며 부탁하는 것이다.

90 "My god gives me the wisdom to understand dreams," Joseph replied.

▶ 파라오의 꿈을 설명하기 전에 자신의 능력이 어디에서 오는지 밝히는 말이다. '내가 믿는 신(my god)'이 '내게 꿈을 이해할 수 있는 지혜를 주신다(gives me the wisdom to understand dreams)'라는 의미이다.

90 He tells me that the seven fat cows stand for seven good years, when the Nile will overflow, the crops will grow, and the Egyptians will have plenty to eat.

▶ A stand for B는 'A가 B를 상징하다[의미하다]'라는 표현이다. 일곱 마리의 살찐 소들은 '7년 동안의 좋았던 시절(seven good years)'을 상징한다.

▶ 뒤에 붙은 when으로 시작하는 문장들은 그 시절을 설명하는 말이다. 7년 동안 풍년이 들어 먹을 것이 많아질 거라는 의미이다.

90 But the seven thin cows stand for seven years of famine. The Nile won't flood, and your crops will die.

▶ 일곱 마리의 마른 소(the seven thin cows)는 7년 동안의 기근(famine)을 상징한다. 그 7년 동안 '나일 강은 범람하지 않을(The Nile won't flood)' 것이어서 '곡식이 죽을(your crops will die)' 것이라는 의미이다.

91 Pharaoh, you should choose a wise man and put him in charge of gathering grain during the seven good years.

▶ to put someone in charge of는 '어떤 사람을 책임과 권한이 있는 위치에 두다'라는 뜻한다. 책임과 권한을 규정하는 말이 of gathering grain으로, '곡식을 모으는' 일이다.

91 Store the grain, so that the Egyptians will have something to eat during the years of famine.

▶ '문장 + so that + 문장'은 '앞의 문장이 원인'이 되어 '뒤의 문장이 결과로' 나타날 때 쓴다. '곡식을 저장하면(Store the grain)' 그 결과로 '이집트인들에게는 기근이 든 해에도 먹을 것이 있을 것이다'라는 의미이다.

The Israelite nation grew larger and larger.

▶ grow는 '성장'이나 '변화'를 표현하는 동사로, 뒤에 형용사가 나온다. grew large라고 하면 '커진다'는 의미인데, 이 문장에서는 large의 비교급 larger가 쓰여서 '점점 더 계속 커졌다' 라는 의미이다.

And as long as Joseph lived, Pharaoh was kind to the Israelites and let them have a part of Egypt for their very own.

▶ as long as는 '~하는 동안에는, ~하는 한'을 의미한다. 그래서 as long as Joseph lived는 '요셉이 살아있는 동안에는'을 뜻한다.

▶ let them have a part of Egypt은 '이집트 땅의 일부를 갖도록 허락했다'라는 의미이고, for their very own은 '그들 자신의 소유로'를 뜻한다.

Chapter 7 Hammurabi and the Babylonians

He convinced the kings of other cities to swear allegiance to him.

▶ convince는 힘들게 노력해서 상대를 '설득하다'라는 뜻이다.

▶ to swear allegiance to him은 '그에게 복종을 맹세하다'이므로, 전체 문장은 '그는 다른 도 시들의 왕들이 그에게 복종을 맹세하도록 강요했다'라고 이해할 수 있다.

He wanted his empire to be governed by just laws.

▶ govern은 규모가 큰 조직을 '운영하다'라는 의미로, '국가를 다스리다, 통치하다'로 쓰였다.

▶ 이 문장에서 his empire(그의 제국)를 다스리는 것은 'just laws(공정한 법)'이다. 따라서 to be governed by just laws는 '공정한 법에 의해 다스려지기를'이라고 해석한다.

He believed that the chief god of Babylon, Marduk, made him king so that he could treat people fairly.

▶ 마르둑(Marduk) 신이 '그를 왕으로 만들었고(made him king)' 그 결과 그가 '백성들을 공정 하게 대할 수 있었다(he could treat people fairly)'라는 의미이다.

He says that his job as king is "to make justice appear in the land, to destroy the evil and the wicked so that the strong might not oppress the weak."

▶ wicked는 '사악한, 못된'을 뜻하는 형용사인데, the wicked로 쓰면 '사악한 사람들'을 뜻한 다.

He had them carved in stone, on a monument that showed him getting the laws from the sun-god.

▶ He carved them in stone이라고 표현하면 '그가 직접 돌에 그것들을 새겼다'라는 의미이지만, 이 문장처럼 He had them carved in stone으로 쓰면 '그가 다른 사람을 시켜서 돌에 그것들을 새기게 했다'라는 의미가 된다.

¹⁰⁶ **If he doesn't have any money to pay with, he will be put to death.**

▶ to put A to death는 'A라는 사람을 처형하다'이다. '처형을 당한다'라고 표현하려면 이 문장처럼 He will be put to death(그는 처형을 당하게 될 것이다)로 써야 한다.

¹⁰⁶ **An eye for an eye, and a tooth for a tooth.**

▶ '눈에는 눈, 이에는 이'라는 뜻의 문장이다. 다른 사람의 눈을 상하게 하면 가해자의 눈을 뽑고, 이를 상하게 하면 이를 뽑아 똑같은 아픔을 겪도록 벌을 줘야 한다는 의미이다.

¹⁰⁶ **If a robber is caught breaking a hole into a house so that he can get in and steal, he will be put to death in front of the hole.**

▶ is caught는 '붙잡히다'라는 뜻이다.

▶ 뒤에 붙은 breaking a hole into a house는 그 사람이 붙잡힐 '당시에 하던 행동'을 표현하는 것이다. '구멍을 뚫어서 집으로 들어가려다가'라는 뜻이다.

¹⁰⁶ **He believed that the gods themselves had given him the Code of Hammurabi.**

▶ themselves는 '그들 자신이, 그들 스스로'라는 뜻의 대명사인데, 여기에서 '그들'은 the gods를 말한다. 함무라비 법전을 '신들이 직접' 그에게 주었다는 의미를 강조해 쓴 것이다.

¹⁰⁷ **From watching the sky, the Babylonians were able to figure out that the earth goes all the way around the sun.**

▶ to figure out은 곰곰이 생각해서 답을 알아내거나 이유를 이해한다는 의미이다.

¹⁰⁷ **So whenever you look at a calendar to see what day of the month it is, or look at a clock to see what time it is, you're using methods that we inherited from the Babylonians.**

▶ what day of the month it is는 '그 달에서 그 날이 며칠인지'라는 의미이다.

▶ to inherit A from B는 'B에게서 A를 물려받다'의 표현인데, methods that we inherited from the Babylonians는 '우리가 바빌로니아인들에게서 물려받은 방법'이다.

Then Shamshi-Adad gathered his army together and set off to conquer the cities of Mesopotamia.

▶ to set off는 '준비를 갖추고(set) 떠나다(off)'라는 의미로, '출발하다, 길을 나서다'이다. 따라서 set off to conquer the cities of Mesopotamia는 '메소포타미아의 도시들을 정복하기 위해 출발했다'라는 의미이다.

Shamshi-Adad would agree to spare their lives—but only if they would do exactly what he said and obey every single one of his decrees.

▶ to spare their lives는 '그들의 목숨을 살려주다'라는 표현이다.

▶ only if는 '~할 경우에만'을 뜻해서, only if로 시작하는 문장은 '목숨을 살려주는 조건'을 표현하고 있다.

But the brothers bickered with each other. They wrote each other nasty letters.

▶ nasty는 '행동이나 말이 무척 기분 나쁘고 불쾌할' 때 쓰는 단어로, nasty letters는 '비꼬는 말이나 욕설 등이 쓰여 있어서 상대를 불쾌하게 만드는 편지'를 의미한다.

But Hammurabi wasn't as cruel as Shamshi-Adad had been.

▶ A is as cruel as B라고 하면 'A가 B만큼 잔인하다'라는 의미가 된다. 따라서 이 문장은 '함무라비는 과거에(had been) 샴시아다드가 그랬던 것만큼 잔인하지는 않았다'라고 해석한다.

The people of Uruk were desperate to get rid of this wicked king.

▶ rid는 '벗어남, 자유'를 의미해서 to get rid of A는 'A라는 존재를 없애서 자유로워지다'이다. 즉 '제거하다'라는 뜻이다.

He dreamed that a huge axe appeared at his door—an axe so big and sharp that he couldn't even lift it.

▶ 'so + 형용사[부사] + that + 문장'의 형태도 앞에서 배운 '문장 + so that + 문장'처럼 '원인과 결과'를 표현한다. an axe so big and sharp(도끼가 너무 크고 예리해서)가 원인이고, that he couldn't even lift it(그것을 들어 올릴 수 없었다)가 결과이다.

But in the forest outside the city's walls, he met the son of a trapper, out checking his father's traps.

▶ out checking은 '덫을 놓는 사냥꾼의 아들(the son of a trapper)'이 있는 위치와 행동을 표현하는 것이다. out은 '밖에 나와 있다'이고, checking his father's traps는 '아버지가 놓은 덫을 (사냥감이 걸렸는지) 살펴보고 있었다'라는 의미이다.

118 He gasped out, "Let us be friends from now on!"

▶ '함께 ~하자'고 제안할 때 흔히 'Let's + 동사'의 표현을 쓰는데, 이때의 Let's가 바로 'Let us'의 줄임말이다. Let us be friends from now on!은 '이제부터는 계속 친구가 되자!'라고 제안하는 것이다.

119 It came charging through Gilgamesh's kingdom, killing hundreds of people.

▶ 동사 charge에는 '돌격하다, 공격하다'라는 뜻이 있다. through는 일직선으로 꿰뚫듯이 '거침없다'는 뉘앙스를 담고 있다. It came charging through Gilgamesh's kingdom은 '신들의 황소가 길가메시의 왕국으로 맹렬히 공격해 들어왔다'라는 의미이다.

119 It was so powerful that whenever it breathed, huge holes and chasms opened up in the earth.

▶ whenever it breathed는 '황소가 숨을 쉴 때마다'라는 의미이다.
▶ chasm은 지진이 나서 땅이 갈라지듯 생긴 '깊은 틈, 구멍'을 뜻한다.

119 Gilgamesh mourned his friend's death.

▶ mourn은 '~에 대해 무척 슬퍼하다'를 의미한다. 슬픔의 정도가 크기 때문에, mourn 다음에는 대개 '사람의 죽음'이나 '비극적인 운명'에 해당하는 표현이 나온다.

120 But his story was told to all the children of Uruk, and has been told to all their children, and to their children's children, until this very day.

▶ until은 '~때까지'를 뜻하므로, until this very day라고 하면 '바로 오늘날까지'라는 의미가 된다. 현재 시점을 강조하기 위해 this와 day 사이에 very를 넣은 것이다.

 Chapter 9 The First Cities of India

129 How long do you think it will take you to walk at the pace of a cow all the way to Assyria?

▶ How long do you think it will take ~는 '그것이 얼마나 오래 걸릴 것이라고 생각하는가?'라는 의미이다.
▶ it은 to walk 이하의 내용을 지칭한다.

▶ at the pace of a cow는 '소의 걸음 속도로'라는 뜻이다.

Cities grew up on rivers because it was easy to ship food, metals, wood, and other goods up and down the water.

▶ to ship ~ the water의 내용을 주어로 대신 표현한 것이 it이다. 내용이 너무 길어서 it으로 바꾼 것이다.

They must have thought that they were in a sea that had no shores and would never end.

▶ 'must have 동사의 완료형'의 형태는 '과거에 분명히 그랬을 것이다'라고 확신을 갖고 추측할 때 쓴다. they must have thought that ~은 '그들은 분명 ~라고 생각했을 것이다'라고 해석한다.

If the people of India had tried to go across the land to Mesopotamia, they would have had to cross a mountain range.

▶ 과거에 '~했다면, …했을 것이다'라고 표현할 때 'If + 주어 + had + 동사의 완료형, 주어 + would + have + 동사의 완료형'의 형태로 쓴다. '인도 사람들이 육로로 메소포타미아에 가고자 했다면, 산맥을 하나 넘어야 했을 것이다'라고 해석한다.

▶ had to는 '~해야만 했다'는 조동사이다.

Each citadel had a stronghold on it—a place to go in case enemies attacked.

▶ stronghold는 '방어가 견고한 곳' 즉, '요새'를 뜻한다. a place to go in case enemies attacked는 stronghold를 설명하는데, '적들이 공격할 경우에 가는 장소'를 뜻한다.

▶ in case는 '~할 경우에, ~할 때를 대비해서'라고 해석한다.

The hunter flung his net over the quail, but they rose up from the ground together, pulled the net out of his hands, and flew away, still side by side.

▶ side by side는 '나란히, 옆에 붙어서 함께'를 뜻하는 말이다. 메추라기들이 '동시에 나란히 모여서' 날아올랐다는 의미이다.

Maybe, if they had united together into one kingdom, the citadel cities would have survived.

▶ 과거를 가정해서 표현하는 문장이다. 사실은 그렇지 않았지만, 만약 그랬다면 어땠을까 가정해보는 것이다. '만약 그들이 하나의 왕국으로 뭉쳤다면(had united together), 그 성채 도시는 망하지 않았을 것이다(would have survived)'라고 해석할 수 있다.

144 But even though they lived far away, the Chinese people chose to live near a river, just like the Egyptians and Babylonians and Assyrians did.

▶ even though나 even if가 문장 앞에 나오면 '비록 ~일지라도, ~이기는 하지만'으로 이해하면 된다. 그래서 even though they lived far away는 '비록 그들은 멀리 떨어져 살았지만'으로 해석한다.

146 Soon Min Lai brought out the empress's favorite meal—turtle meat with garlic and ginger, candied fruit, rice, and a pot of steaming, fragrant tea.

▶ brought은 bring의 과거형이다. bring은 '가져[데려]가다, 가져[데려]오다'라는 뜻이다. the empress's favorite meal은 '제후가 가장 좋아하는 식사'이다. '부엌에서 음식을 만들어 정원으로 '가지고 나왔기' 때문에, brought out으로 표현한 것이다.

147 Only the royal family can know this treasure was yielded by the silkworm cocoons!

▶ 동사 yield는 '생산하다, 산출하다'라는 뜻으로, 비단은 누에고치의 실로 만들기 때문에, this treasure was yield by the silkworm cocoons(이 보물이 누에고치에 의해 생산된다)라고 표현한 것이다.

148 Almost everything that we know about these very ancient Chinese rulers has been passed down in stories and legends, from person to person over thousands of years.

▶ Almost everything부터 Chinese rulers까지가 문장의 주어로, '우리가 바로 이 고대의 중국 통치자들에 대해 알고 있는 거의 모든 것'으로 해석할 수 있다.

148 During the rule of the Shang family, the Chinese began to use bronze.

▶ during은 일정 기간을 의미하는 전치사로, '~하는 동안에'라고 해석한다. 따라서 During the rule of the Shang family는 '상왕조의 통치 기간 동안에'이다.

148 These tools and weapons made of bronze didn't rot away like wooden tools.

▶ rot은 시간이 지나면서 자연스럽게 '썩는' 것을 의미하므로, rot away like wooden tools는 '나무 도구처럼 썩어서 없어졌다'라는 의미이다.

The bronze weapons tell us that the Chinese who lived during the rule of the Shang dynasty knew how to fight with bows and arrows.

▶ 'how to 동사'는 '~하는 법, ~하는 방식'을 뜻하는 표현이다. how to fight with bows and arrows는 '활과 화살로 싸우는 법'을 의미한다.

The farming tools tell us that they grew wheat and mulberries, as well as rice, and that they used plows pulled by horses to farm their fields.

▶ 'tell us that ~'은 '농기구를 통해 ~라는 사실을 알 수 있다'라고 이해해야 한다.

▶ as well as는 '~도 또한, ~뿐만 아니라'로 해석하는데, 의미는 and와 같다.

But he couldn't see out past the stiff paper that covered the windows.

▶ see out은 '밖을 보다'이고, past는 '통과'를 의미한다.

▶ stiff paper는 '빳빳한 종이'이다. 창문이 유리(glass)가 아니라 '문풍지'라서 밖이 보이지 않는다는 의미이다.

Chin got up and tiptoed out of the room, past where his parents, his grandfather, and his little sister lay sleeping on their pallets on the floor.

▶ lay는 '눕다, 누워 있다'란 뜻의 동사 lie의 과거형이다. lay sleeping은 '누워서 잠을 자고 있었다'라는 상태를 나타낸다.

▶ pallet은 천 속에 짚을 넣어서 만든 '돗짚자리'를 뜻한다.

Chin did this every morning; it was his duty, as the oldest son, to make sure that his father had everything that he needed.

▶ to make sure는 모든 것이 잘 갖춰져 있는지, 준비가 잘 되어 있는지 확인한다는 의미이다. '아버지가 필요한 모든 것을 갖고 있는지(that his father had everything that he needed)' 확인하고 챙겨준다는 뜻이다.

Chin waited impatiently by the door.

▶ impatiently는 참기 힘들어서 안달하는 모습을 표현하는 부사형으로, '조바심을 내며, 안절부절 못하는'이라는 뜻이다.

But water still stood ankle-deep all over the rice fields.

▶ stand는 '키나 높이가 ~이다'라는 뜻을 표현할 때 쓸 수 있다. ankle-deep은 '발목이 잠길 만큼 깊은'을 뜻하므로 stood ankle-deep은 물의 깊이가 '발목까지 잠길 정도였다'라는 의미이다.

152 Chin rolled up the legs of his pants and waded out into the water.

▶ wade는 '깊지 않은 물속을 걷다'라는 뜻으로, wade into the water(물속으로 걸어 들어가다)의 자주 쓰인다. out은 '큰 움직임'을 실감나게 표현하기 위해 덧붙인 것이다.

152 Then they started to go numb.

▶ numb은 '감각이 없는'을 뜻하고, go는 '변화'를 의미한다. 따라서 to go numb은 '감각이 없어지다'라는 의미이다.

153 Finally his father called him back to dry land.

▶ call back은 '다시 전화하다, 다시 방문하다'의 의미로도 쓰이지만, 이 문장에서는 '불러서 돌아오게 하다'라는 뜻으로 쓰였다. 따라서 called him back to dry land는 '그(친)를 불러서 마른 땅 쪽으로 돌아오게 했다'는 뜻이 된다.

153 "Let's go back to the house for our midday meal."

▶ midday는 '정오, 한낮'이고, meal은 '한 끼의 식사'를 뜻한다. 즉 midday meal은 '점심(lunch)'이다.

153 But he was proud of the work he had done.

▶ be proud of는 자신과 관련이 있는 사람이나 성과 등에 대해 '자랑스럽게 여기다'라는 뜻이므로, He was proud of the work he had done은 '자신이 한 일에 대해 자랑스러워했다'이다.

153 Chin huddled beside the clay stove, listening to his grandfather tell about the great floods of long ago.

▶ huddle은 추위나 무서움 때문에 몸을 움츠린 모습을 표현한다. Chin huddled beside the clay stove는 '친은 흙난로 옆에서 몸을 움츠리고 있었다'라는 의미이다.

Chapter 11 Ancient Africa

164 We know a great deal about the history of Egypt, because the Egyptians left thousands and thousands of *artifacts* (treasures and everyday objects) behind them.

▶ a great deal은 '많은 양'을 표현하는 말로, We know a great deal about the history of Egypt는 '우리는 이집트의 역사에 대해 많은 것을 알고 있다'라는 의미이다.

165 So we don't know as much about ancient Africa as we do about ancient Egypt.

▶ about ancient Africa와 about ancient Egypt가 'as much as(~만큼 많이)'라는 표현으로
비교되고 있다. we don't know as much about ancient Africa는 '우리는 고대 아프리카에
대해 많이 알지 못한다'이고, as we do about ancient Egypt는 '우리가 고대 이집트에 대해
알고 있는 만큼'을 뜻한다.

365 Sand drifts over the iron-hard ground and piles up in huge drifts
called dunes.
▶ 이 문장에 쓰인 두 개의 동사 중 drift는 '바람에 밀려 움직이다'이고, pile은 '쌓이다'라는 뜻
이다.
▶ and 다음에 나오는 piles up in in huge drifts called dunes는 바람에 이동한 모래가 '사구
(砂丘)라고 부르는 거대한 모래 더미로 쌓인다'라는 의미이다.

368 The yams smelled wonderful, and he couldn't wait to dig in.
▶ to dig in은 '음식을 맘껏 먹다'라는 표현이다.

370 Moral: If you try to be too smart, you might find that someone else
outsmarts you instead.
▶ moral은 '도덕적 교훈'을 뜻한다.
▶ outsmart는 남보다 '더 영리하고 똑똑하다'라는 의미인데, '속임수나 잔꾀를 써서 다른 사람
에게서 이익을 취하다'라는 뜻으로도 쓰인다. someone else outsmarts you instead는 '도
리어 다른 사람이 당신을 속일 수도 있다'라는 의미이다.

Chapter 12 The Middle Kingdom of Egypt

388 They thought that the Hyksos were rude, unclean, and uncivilized.
▶ rude는 말이나 행동이 예의에 벗어날 때 쓴다. '예의 없는, 무례한, 저속한'을 뜻한다.

Chapter 13 The New Kingdom of Egypt

396 Leading the army into wars was what he did best.
▶ leading the army into wars는 '군대를 이끌고 전쟁에 나가는 것'이다.
▶ what he did best는 '그가 가장 잘하는 것'으로 해석한다.

396 Thutmose's first battles were against the Nubians, who were trying
to break away from Egypt.

> ▶ Thutmose's first battles were against the Nubians은 '투트모세의 첫 번째 전투는 누비아인들을 상대로 한 것이었다'이고, 누비안인들을 설명하는 말인 who were trying to break away from Egypt는 '이집트에게서 벗어나고자 하는'을 뜻한다.

197 Next, he took his army and followed the Hyksos all the way up to Canaan.

> ▶ followed the Hyksos to Canaan이라고 하면 '힉소스인들을 가나안까지 쫓아갔다'라는 것인데, all the way up을 더하면 '저 위쪽 멀리'라는 의미이다. 가나안의 위치가 이집트에서 북쪽으로 멀리 떨어져 있기 때문에 쓴 것이다.

197 The Hyksos had come down and taken over Egypt.

> ▶ to take over는 '손에 넣다, 차지하다'이다.
> ▶ The Hyksos had taken over Egypt는 이야기를 하고 있는 과거의 시점보다 더 오래전에 '힉소스인들이 이집트를 차지했었다'라는 것이다.

197 Now he had gone up and taken over the land of the Hyksos.

> ▶ 힉소스 땅이 이집트보다 북쪽에 있기 때문에 had gone up 표현을 쓴 것이다.

197 The victory made him so happy that he wanted to keep on fighting.

> ▶ 'to keep on 동사의 -ing'는 '계속 ~하다'라는 의미의 표현이다. he wanted to keep on fighting은 '그는 계속 싸우고 싶어 했다'라고 해석한다.

198 By the time Thutmose died, Egypt was twice as big as it had been!

> ▶ as big as는 '~만큼 크다'라는 표현으로, 그 앞에 '두 배, 세 배'에 해당하는 수치가 나오면 그만큼 크다는 의미가 된다. twice는 '두 배'이므로, Egypt was twice as big as it had been은 '이집트가 그 전보다 두 배나 커졌다'라는 의미이다.

199 Hatshepsut was so determined to be pharaoh that the Egyptians finally agreed to have her as their ruler.

> ▶ 동사형 determine은 '~을 결정하다'라는 뜻으로, 형용사형 determined는 반드시 하고자 하는 '강한 욕망이나 의지'가 있는 상태를 표현한다. Hatshepsut was so determined to be pharaoh는 '하트셉수트는 파라오가 되고자 하는 의지가 무척 강했다'라고 해석한다.

199 For over twenty years, Hatshepsut ruled Egypt—a queen pretending to be a king.

> ▶ pretend는 '~인 척하다, ~로 가장하다'이다. 따라서 a queen pretending to be a king은 '왕인 척 가장하는 여왕'이다.

There, she bought gold, incense, monkeys, elephants, and other things that the Egyptian people loved.
▶ incense는 불을 붙이면 연기에서 좋은 냄새가 나는 '향'을 말한다.

Amenhotep sacrificed to Amun, gave money to his priests, and held big celebrations to honor this powerful god.
▶ sacrifice는 '제물을 바치다'라는 뜻으로 쓰였다.
▶ hold에는 행사를 '열다, 개최하다'라는 뜻이므로, held big celebrations는 '성대한 기념행사를 열었다'라는 의미이다.

As a matter of fact, he decided that none of Egypt's gods were real.
▶ as a matter of fact는 '사실상, 사실은'으로, 앞에서 한 말에 대해 더 구체적인 말을 덧붙이고자 할 때 쓴다.

The Egyptian people were horrified.
▶ 동사 horrify는 누군가를 '공포에 질리게 하다, 소름끼치게 만들다'이고, 형용사형 horrified는 '공포에 질리고 소름이 끼치는' 상태를 표현한다.

His mind was made up.
▶ to make up one's mind는 '마음을 정하다, 결심하다'라는 표현이다. His mind was made up은 He made up his mind를 수동형으로 쓴 것으로, '그의 마음은 정해졌다'라고 해석한다.

They took him out of all their records.
▶ to take A out of B는 'A를 B에서 빼내다'이다. 그래서 They took him out of all their records는 '이집트인들이 모든 기록에서 그를 빼냈다' 즉, '그의 이름을 지워버렸다'라는 의미가 된다.

They moved out of his new city and let it crumble away into ruins.
▶ 이 문장에서 move는 '이사하다, 이주하다'로, They moved out of his new city는 '이집트인들이 그가 건설한 새로운 도시를 떠나 다른 곳으로 이주했다'라는 의미이다.

King Tut helped to wipe out the worship of Aten.
▶ wipe의 기본적인 의미는 '걸레로 닦다'와 '없애다, 지우다'이다. out은 '완전히'를 뜻하므로, to wipe out the worship of Aten은 걸레로 닦듯이 '아텐 신을 숭배하는 일을 완전히 없애버렸다'라는 의미이다.

He encouraged the people to start worshipping the old gods again.
▶ 'to start 동사의 -ing'는 '~을 시작하다'라는 표현이다. worship은 '숭배하다'라는 의미이므

로, to start worshipping the old gods again은 '다시 과거의 신들을 숭배하기 시작하다'라고 해석한다.

203 Suddenly, a beautiful golden gleam sprang out from the blackness.

▶ spring은 용수철이 튀듯 '갑자기 튀다, 뛰어오르다'라는 뜻이 있는데, 이 문장에서 sprang out은 '빛이 갑자기 반사되었다'라는 의미로 쓴 것이다. a beautiful golden gleam sprang out from the blackness는 '아름다운 황금 빛이 어둠에서 반사되었다'라고 해석한다.

204 The workmen slowly pried the door open.

▶ pry는 '쇠지레'라고 부르는 연장이다. 지레의 원리를 이용해, 강제로 틈을 벌리거나 문을 열 때 쓴다. 그래서 '힘을 주어 지레로 움직이다'라는 뜻의 동사로 쓸 수 있다. pried the door open은 '힘을 주어 쇠지레로 문을 열었다'이다.

204 There was Tutankhamen's mummified body, wrapped in linen and soaked with spices.

▶ mummify는 '미라로 만들다'의 동사로, mummified body는 '미라로 만든 시신'을 뜻한다.

204 The inscription reads, "It is I who hinder the sand from choking the secret chamber. I am for the protection of the deceased."

▶ inscription은 '돌, 금속, 책 표지 등에 적힌[새겨진] 글'이다.

▶ deceased는 '죽어 있는'을 뜻하는데, 앞에 the가 붙어 the deceased하고 하면 '죽은 사람들'이 된다. I am for the protection of the deceased는 '나는 죽은 자들의 보호를 위해 존재한다'라는 의미이다.

 Chapter 14 The Israelites Leave Egypt

214 They packed up their tents, their animals, their families, and all their belongings and traveled down to Egypt.

▶ to pack up은 '짐을 싸다, 빠짐없이 챙기다'라는 표현이다.

▶ belongings는 '소유한 재산, 가지고 있는 물건들'로, 항상 복수형으로 쓴다.

215 What if these people decide to attack us?

▶ 'What if + 문장'은 '~한다면 어쩌겠는가? ~하면 어떻게 하지?'라는 표현이다. What if these people decide to attack us?은 '이 사람들이 우리를 공격하려고 하면 어쩌지?'라고 해석한다.

He started to giggle and coo.

▶ coo도 원래 의성어이다. 비둘기 울음소리인 '구구구'인데, 이 문장에서는 아기가 옹알이하듯 '구구구' 소리를 냈다는 의미이다.

Bring me this woman and she can take care of my baby for me.

▶ to take care of A는 'A를 돌보다, 보살피다'라는 표현이다. she can take care of my baby for me는 '그녀가 나 대신 내 아기를 돌봐줄 수 있다'라는 의미이다.

So Miriam hurried home and got her mother.

▶ hurried home은 '서둘러서 집으로 갔다'이고, got her mother는 '자신의 어머니를 데려왔다'라고 해석했다.

And he saw that his people were being beaten and mistreated.

▶ beat는 '때리다, 구타하다'이고, mistreat는 '학대하다'이다.
▶ his people were being beaten and mistreated은 '자기 민족이 매를 맞으며 학대를 당하고 있었다'라는 의미인데, his people이 '지금' 구타와 학대를 '당하는' 입장이므로 진행형 수동태로 쓴 것이다.

The story of the Exodus shows monotheism winning out over polytheism, because the one god of Israel was able to conquer the many gods of Egypt.

▶ 'to win over A'는 'A에게 승리하다, 이기다'라는 뜻의 표현이고, out은 '결과'를 의미한다. 따라서 monotheism winning out over polytheism은 '다신교를 누르고 승리한 일신교'를 뜻한다.

But now, even a band of slaves without weapons could escape from the clutches of the Egyptian army.

▶ clutch는 뭔가를 '꽉 움켜쥔 동물의 앞발, 사람의 손'을 뜻하는데, '다른 사람을 통제하고 억압하는 힘'의 뜻으로도 쓸 수 있다. the clutches of the Egyptian army는 '이집트 군대의 손아귀'로 해석할 수 있다.

 Chapter 15 The Phoenicians

So she said to the owner of the land, "Will you sell me as much land as I can cover with the skin of a bull?"

▶ 이 문장에서 cover는 '덮다'라는 뜻이다.
▶ as much land as I can cover는 '내가 덮을 수 있을 만큼의 땅'을 뜻한다.

239 Canals brought water into the city, so that all Nineveh's people could drink; and throughout Nineveh, Ashurbanipal had planted gardens of strange and beautiful plants, so that his subjects could wander through green grass and admire the trees and flowers from far away.

▶ wander through green grass는 '푸르른 풀밭을 걸어 다니다'라고 해석한다.

▶ admire the trees and flowers from far away는 '먼 곳에서도 나무들과 꽃들을 보며 감탄하다'라고 이해하면 된다.

240 "But it isn't enough!" Ashurbanipal thought.

▶ enough는 '충분하다'이므로 But it isn't enough!라고 하면 '그것으로는 충분하지 않다, 그것으로는 부족하다'라는 것이다.

240 A voice interrupted him.

▶ interrupt는 '방해하다, 가로막다, 중단시키다'라는 뜻이다. A voice interrupted him은 '목소리가 들려서 그는 생각을 멈추었다'라고 해석할 수 있다.

240 They were always on the lookout for new books for him.

▶ lookout은 명사로 '망보기, 망보는 곳'을 뜻하는데, 'on the lookout for ~'는 마치 망루에 올라가 뭔가를 살펴보듯 '계속 살피다, 주시하다'라는 의미로 쓰였다. 따라서 이 문장은 '그들은 왕을 위해 새로운 책들을 찾으려고 주의를 기울였다'라고 이해할 수 있다.

241 He sent his scribes out into all parts of the vast kingdom of Assyria, ordering them to collect all the tablets they could find and bring them back to Nineveh.

▶ vast는 범위나 크기 또는 양이 '대단히 크거나 많은' 상태를 표현한다. the vast kingdom of Assyria는 '광대한 아시리아 제국'을 뜻한다.

241 These stories had been told to children for centuries—but no one had ever written them down.

▶ no one had ever written them down은 '그 누구도 그것을 적지 않았다'라는 뜻으로, 이야기가 전개되고 있는 과거 시점까지의 일을 표현하기 때문에 had written 형태를 쓴 것이다. 이 문장에서 ever는 '단 한번도'의 의미이다.

241 The court astrologers wrote down the movements of the sun, moon and stars.

▶ astrologer는 '점성술사, 점성가'로, 하늘에 떠 있는 별의 위치와 이동을 통해 미래의 일이나 운명에 대해 점을 치는 사람을 뜻한다.

 Chapter 17 Babylon Takes Over Again!

They broke down the walls and gates, ripped the doors off Ashurbanipal's great library, and smashed hundreds of his precious clay tablets!

▶ broke down the walls and gates는 '성벽과 성문을 부수어 무너뜨렸다'이다.
▶ ripped the doors off Ashurbanipal's great library는 '아슈르바니팔의 위대한 도서관에서 문을 뜯어냈다'라고 해석한다.

Fortunately, some of the books survived so that we can still read them today.

▶ 문장 앞에 fortunately를 쓴 이유는 책들 중 일부가 남아 지금 우리가 그 책들을 읽을 수 있어서 '다행스럽다'라는 의미이다.

The Babylonian Empire wasn't quite as big as the Assyrian Empire, because the Babylonians never took over Egypt.

▶ not quite는 'not completely(완전히 그렇지는 않다)'를 뜻한다. 바빌론 제국은 아시리아 제국만큼 크지는 않았다'라는 의미이다.

Now listen to your doom—you will act like an animal, and eat grass like a cow, until you admit that God is more powerful than you are!

▶ admit은 '사실을 인정하다, 현실을 받아들이다'이므로, until you admit that God is more powerful than you are은 '하느님이 너보다 더 강하다는 사실을 네가 인정할 때까지'라고 해석할 수 있다.

At once Nebuchadnezzar lost his mind.

▶ at once는 '즉시, 곧바로, 당장에'를 뜻한다.
▶ to lose one's mind는 '마음[정신]을 잃다'이나 '미치다, 실성하다'라는 뜻이다.

He drank from the river, slept under bushes, and woke up in the morning wet with dew.

▶ wet with dew는 '아침에 잠을 깬(woke up in the morning)'로 주어 he의 상태를 표현한다. wet 앞에 '상태'를 나타내는 being이 생략된 것으로 이해해서, '이슬에 젖은 상태로, 이슬에 젖은 채로'라고 해석한다.

250 He had a great empire—but what if another country attacked him?

▶ 'What if 의문문'은 일어나지 않은 일을 가정하며 묻는 것으로, '~하면 어쩌지?, ~하면 어떻게 할까?'라는 의미이다. but what if another country attacked him?는 '그런데 만약 다른 나라가 그를 공격하면 어떻게 할까?'로 해석할 수 있다.

252 He ordered his slaves to haul huge slabs of rock in from far away.

▶ huge slabs of rock은 '거대한 돌판'이다.
▶ to haul in은 힘들게 '끌고 오다'이다. 도시나 왕궁 '안으로' 가지고 온다는 의미로 in을 붙인 것이다.

Chapter 18 Life in Early Crete

260 Crete is a long, skinny island in the Mediterranean Sea, a sea that is shaped a little bit like a duck flying.

▶ skinny는 사람이나 동물의 마른 몸을 표현하는 형용사인데, 이 문장에서 skinny island는 크레타 섬의 생김새가 가로로 길쭉하기 때문에 비유적으로 쓴 것이다.

260 The Minoans entertained themselves in an unusual way—by leaping over bulls.

▶ entertained themselves는 '그들 스스로 즐겁게 놀았다'라는 의미이다.
▶ by leaping over bulls는 즐긴 방법을 표현한 것으로, '황소를 뛰어넘으면서'를 뜻한다.

260 Your hands are empty, and all you're wearing is a simple loose garment that allows your arms and legs to move freely.

▶ garment는 '옷, 의복'으로, clothes와 의미가 같다.
▶ loose는 옷을 대충 걸쳐 입었기 때문에 '헐렁한'이라는 의미이다.

261 He snorts and charges straight at you.

▶ charge straight at you는 '너에게 곧장 돌진하다'이다.

261 You turn and see your other teammate vault onto the bull.

▶ '보는(see)' 사람은 You이고, '뛰어넘는(vault)' 사람은 your other teammate이다. 따라서 see your other teammate vault는 '너의 다른 팀 동료가 뛰어넘는 것을 보다'라고 해석한다.

262 So he ordered his craftsmen to build great ships that he could use to wipe out pirates and patrol the Mediterranean Sea.

▶ to wipe out의 의미는 '지워서 없애다'이므로, to wipe out pirates는 '해적들을 소탕하다, 일소하다'를 뜻한다.

No invaders could land on Crete's shores, because the navy kept them away.
▶ keep에는 '현상을 그대로 유지하다'라는 의미가 있다. kept them away는 침략자들 (invaders)이 계속 멀리 떨어져 있게 했다, 즉 '가까이 오지 못하게 막았다'라고 이해할 수 있다.

But this shining palace concealed a dark secret.
▶ conceal은 '감추다, 숨기다'를 뜻한다.
▶ a dark secret는 '어두운 비밀'로 해석할 수 있는데, 여기에서 dark는 '사악한, 추한, 무서운, 슬픈'의 의미가 있다.

Below the foundation of the palace, in a maze so twisty and complicated that no one could find the way in or out, lived a horrible monster—the Minotaur.
▶ 앞에서도 나온 so that 구문이다. twisty and complicated는 '미로(maze)'가 꾸불꾸불하고 (twisty) 복잡한(complicated) 형태라는 의미이다.
▶ 이 문장의 주어는 a horrible monster—the Minotaur이고, 동사는 lived이다.

Every year, Athens had to send seven girls and seven boys to King Minos, or else (he threatened) he would destroy their city.
▶ have to는 must와 같은 '~해야 한다, ~할 수밖에 없다'라는 의미의 조동사이다. 이 표현을 쓴 이유는 or else 다음에 나온다.
▶ or else (he threatened) he would destroy their city는 '그렇지 않으면 그들의 도시를 파괴하겠노라고 (그가 위협했다)'라는 의미이다.

Year after year, the Athenians sent this dreadful tribute to Minos.
▶ tribute는 속국이 종주국에 바치는 '공물, 조공'을 말한다.

But the beach was full of weeping fathers and mothers, and the ship drawn up to the shore had black sails.
▶ the ship drawn up to the shore는 '해안으로 끌어 올린 배'이다.

Let me go to Crete in the place of one of the young men.
▶ 'in the place of A'는 'A의 자리에'인데, 그 자리에 있다는 것은 그 사람을 '대신한다'라는 뜻이다. in the place of one of the young men은 '젊은 남자들 중 한 명을 대신해서'라고 해석한다.

On the shore of Crete, they were greeted by the cruel King Minos himself, with his beautiful daughter Ariadne walking meekly behind him.

▶ meekly는 '점잖게, 조용히, 다소곳하게, 얌전하게'의 부사로, walking meekly behind him 은 '그의 뒤에서 점잖게 걸으며'라고 해석한다.

It stank of some wild animal, and bones littered the floor.

▶ 'A stink of B'는 'A에게서 B의 악취가 나다'이므로, It stank of some wild animal은 '그곳에 서는 어떤 야생동물의 고약한 냄새가 났다'라고 해석한다.

But in their haste, they had forgotten to put a white sail on their ship!

▶ in their haste는 '급히 서두르다가'이다.

Bits of rock called pumice started to spray out of the volcano's funnel.

▶ pumice는 화산의 폭발력 때문에 잘게 부서진 채 분출되는 작은 돌멩이들을 말하는데, '부석(浮石)'이라고 한다.

The volcano exploded, spraying lava and rock all over the island.

▶ spray는 '흩뿌리다, 살포하다'라는 뜻의 동사이다. lava는 땅속에 있던 마그마(magma)가 지표면 밖으로 나온 '용암'을 말한다. 따라서 spraying lava and rock all over the island는 '섬 위의 모든 곳에 용암과 돌을 흩뿌리며'라고 해석한다.

Huge boulders were thrown up from the inside of the volcano and fell like rock bombs on top of the villages of Thera.

▶ boulder는 '크고 둥근 돌'을 말한다. 이 문장은 화산에서 분출된 '거대한 돌들(huge boulders)'이 마치 '돌 폭탄(rock bombs)'처럼 마을로 떨어졌다는 내용이다.

The sea rushed in to fill the hole, and the whole island of Thera sank beneath the sea!

▶ 주어인 the sea는 '바닷물, 파도'로 이해하면 된다. 물은 높은 곳에서 낮은 곳으로 흐르기 때문에 구멍이 생기면 그 구멍 속에 물이 채워지게 된다. The sea rushed in to fill the hole은 '바닷물이 세차게 밀려 들어와 그 구멍을 채웠다'라는 의미이다.

But a tidal wave thrown up by the volcano swept its shores.

▶ a tidal wave는 '해일, 거센 파도'를 말한다. 화산 폭발과 지진으로 인해 발생한 '해일, 쓰나미'이다.

Ash and dust helped bring the first great civilization of Crete to its end.

▶ to bring A to its end는 '끝나게 하다, 종말을 가져오다'라는 뜻으로, bring the first great civilization of Crete to its end는 '크레타의 첫 번째 위대한 문명을 끝나게 하다'라고 해석한다.

Chapter 19 The Early Greeks

The Minoans had been a great nation—but now they were just ragged people trying to find enough food to stay alive.

▶ try는 '노력하다, 애쓰다'라는 의미가 있으므로, trying to find enough food to stay alive는 '계속 생존할 수 있을 만큼의 식량을 찾기 위해 애쓰는'으로 해석할 수 있다.

Greece is the land just north of Crete; it juts out into the Mediterranean Sea like a set of fingers, surrounded by small islands.

▶ jut은 '돌출하다, 튀어나오다'라는 뜻이 있는데, 주로 out을 붙여 쓴다. juts out into the mediterranean Sea는 '지중해 쪽으로 튀어나와 있다'라는 의미이다.

▶ surrounded by small islands는 그리스(Greece)가 '작은 섬들로 둘러싸여 있다'이다.

They learned how to build ships from the Minoans who were left in Crete.

▶ leave는 '떠나다'를 뜻하는데, 수동형 be left는 반대로 '남겨지다'이다. 따라서 the Minoans who were left in Crete는 '크레타 섬에 남겨진 미노아 사람들'을 의미한다.

The Mycenaeans weren't the only people who lived in Greece.

▶ 'not the only ~'는 '유일한 ~은 아닌'이라는 의미이다. 다른 것도 있다는 뜻이므로 이 문장은 '그리스에는 미케네 사람들만 살고 있었던 것은 아니었다'라고 이해하면 된다.

And they hammered out helmets from bronze, and lined them with fur and cloth to protect their heads from enemy swords.

▶ 동사 hammer는 '망치로 치다'라는 뜻으로, hammered out helmets은 '망치로 두드려서 투구를 만들었다'이다.

▶ lined them with fur and cloth는 '그 투구들(them)에 털가죽과 천으로 안감을 대다'라는 의미인데, 여기에서 동사 line은 '안을 덮다'를 뜻한다.

Before this, soldiers had always fought on foot.

▶ Before this는 앞에 나온 내용, 즉, '전투에 말을 이용하기 전까지'를 뜻한다.

▶ on foot은 '걸어서, 서서'이므로, soldiers had always fought on foot은 '병사들이 항상 걸어서[서서] 싸움을 했다'라는 의미이다. 즉 '기마병이 없이 보병들끼리 싸웠다'라는 의미이다.

But the Mycenaeans began to hitch horses to war chariots.

▶ hitch는 밧줄이나 쇠사슬로 '매달다, 연결하다'를 뜻한다. to hitch horses to war chariots는 '말을 전투용 마차에 매달다'라고 해석한다.

It was an insult. You see, the early Greeks thought of themselves as very civilized people.

▶ You see는 앞에 나온 내용의 이유를 설명할 때 '그 이유는, 무슨 말이냐면' 하고 말을 시작할 때 붙이는 표현이다. 왜 Barbarian이란 말이 '모욕적인(insult) 말'인지 설명할 테니 잘 들어보라고 주의를 환기시키는 역할을 한다.

Greek women stayed home most of the day, supervising the household slaves who did most of the housework and cooking.

▶ household slaves는 '집안일을 하는 노예들'이고, supervise는 '감독하다'를 뜻한다. 따라서 supervising the household slaves는 '집안일을 하는 노예들을 감독하면서'라고 해석한다.

And they spent their time wandering around from country to country, attacking the people who lived there and trying to take over.

▶ 'to spend + one's time + 동사의 -ing'는 '~하면서 시간을 보내다'라는 뜻이다.

▶ 동사의 -ing에 해당되는 wandering around from country to country는 '이 나라 저 나라 돌아다니며', attacking the people who lived there는 '그곳에 사는 사람들을 공격하면서', trying to take over는 '정복하려고 애쓰면서'라고 해석한다.

These iron weapons were even stronger than the bronze weapons of the Greeks.

▶ stronger than A는 'A보다 더 강한'을 뜻하는 표현이다. stronger 앞의 even은 '훨씬'을 뜻해서 비교급을 강조할 때 쓰인다. 그래서 even stronger than the bronze weapons of the Greeks는 '그리스인들의 청동 무기보다 훨씬 더 강한'을 의미한다.

These walls were so strong and so big that we can still see them today.

▶ so strong and so big은 '너무 강하고 너무 커서'라는 의미이다. 이 문장은 '이 성벽들은 너무 강하고 너무 컸기 때문에 지금도 우리가 그 성벽들을 볼 수 있다'라고 해석한다.

But no matter how many walls the Mycenaean Greeks built, they couldn't keep the barbarians out.

▶ no matter ~는 '아무리 ~할지라도, ~와는 상관없이'라고 이해하면 된다. no matter how many walls the Mycenaean Greeks built는 '미케네 그리스인들이 아무리 많은 성벽들을 건설해도'로 해석할 수 있다.

 Chapter 20 Greece Gets Civilized Again

Now Greece is full of barbarians—the Dorians from up north, and the Sea People (who are also called the Philistines), who invaded Greece from the Mediterranean Sea.

▶ Now Greece is full of barbarians는 '이제 그리스는 야만인들로 가득 채워졌다'이다.

They're not used to living in cities.

▶ 'be used to 동사의 –ing'는 '~에 익숙하다'를 뜻하는 표현으로, 이 문장은 '그들은 도시에 사는 것에 익숙하지 않았다'라고 해석한다.

Instead of riding out to kill their neighbors, they learned how to enjoy civilized sports like wrestling, chariot racing, and horseback riding.

▶ 말을 타고 자신의 영역 '밖으로 나간다'는 의미로 ride에 out을 붙였다.
▶ Instead of riding out to kill their neighbors는 '인근의 사람들을 죽이려고 말을 타고 나가는 대신에'를 의미한다.

The women no longer went out foraging for food, and they certainly didn't spend their time putting up tents, washing and cooking like barbarian women.

▶ no longer는 '더는 ~않다[아니다]'를 뜻하는 표현이다.
▶ forage는 '분주하게 뭔가를 찾다'라는 의미로, forage for food는 '분주하게 먹을 것을 찾으면서'이다.

Our alphabet is named after the Greek letters alpha and beta.

▶ to name A after B는 'B의 이름을 따서 A의 이름을 짓다'라는 표현이다. 사람들이 알파벳에 이름을 지었기 때문에 be named after로 표현한 것이다. '우리 알파벳은 그리스 글자 알파와 베타를 따서 이름을 지은 것이다'라고 해석한다.

The psi looks a little bit like a trident, a three-pronged weapon carried by the Greek god Poseidon, who lived in the sea.

▶ a trident은 '삼지창'이다. a three-pronged weapon은 '창이 세 개 달린 무기'를 뜻하는데, trident란 단어가 낯설기 때문에 간단히 설명한 것이다.

It is called a theta, and it makes the sound that our letters "th" make when you say them together:

▶ it makes the sound는 '그것이 소리를 낸다'인데, 소리에 대한 설명이 that 이하의 내용이다.

▶ our letters "th" make는 '영어 글자 th가 내는', when you say them together는 '그 글자들 (t와 h)을 동시에 말할 때'라고 이해하면 된다.

Even though some of the Greek letters are different from ours, we owe a lot of our alphabet to the Greeks.

▶ 'even though + 문장'은 '비록 ~이기는 하지만, 비록 ~라고 하더라도'로 해석한다. Even though some of the Greek letters are different from ours는 '비록 그리스 글자들 중 일부 는 우리 글자와 다르지만'이라고 해석한다.

When the Greeks began to learn how to read and write, one of them decided to write down the old Greek stories that had been told out loud around Greek fires for years and years.

▶ to tell A out loud 표현은 'A를 큰소리로 말하다'라는 의미이다. old Greek stories는 아주 오래전부터 과거의 시점까지 사람들에 의해 말해지는 것이므로, '이전부터 큰소리로 말해져 왔다'라는 의미로 had been told out loud라고 썼다.

When Odysseus started to sail back home, he ran into all kinds of trouble!

▶ to run into trouble은 '어려움과 마주치다, 곤경에 처하다'라는 표현이다.

▶ all kinds of는 '갖가지 ~'을 뜻하므로, he ran into all kinds of trouble은 '그는 갖가지 어려 움을 겪게 되었다'로 이해할 수 있다.

Odysseus and his men sailed away from Troy, looking forward to their return home.

▶ sailed away from Troy는 '배를 타고서 트로이(Troy)를 출발해 멀리 항해하다'라는 의미이 다. 즉 '트로이에서 항해를 떠났다'라고 해석한다.

▶ looking forward to their return home은 '귀향[귀국]을 고대하면서'이다.

Poseidon was furious at being left out.

▶ be furious at ~은 '~에 대해 몹시 화가 나다'라는 뜻이다. at 다음에는 분노하게 된 이유가 나오는데, being left out, 즉 '자신이 빠뜨려졌기[제외되었기]' 때문이다.

He sent a strong wind to blow the ships off course, so that Odysseus would have a hard time getting home.

▶ off는 '~에서 벗어난, 멀리 떨어진'을 뜻해서 off course는 '진로[항로]에서 벗어난'이다. to blow the ships off course는 '바람을 불어서 그 배들이 항로를 벗어나게 하다'라는 의미이다.

The walls were lined with racks of cheeses, each cheese bigger than a man's head.

▶ racks of cheeses는 '치즈가 놓인 선반[받침대]들'이다. The walls were lined with racks of cheeses는 '동굴 벽 안쪽으로 치즈 선반들이 줄지어 있었다'라는 의미이다.

▶ each cheese bigger than a man's head는 '치즈가 남자 머리보다 더 컸다'라는 것이다.

And when it was completely dark, they heard footsteps, each one shaking the ground.

▶ each one shaking the ground에서 one은 footstep(발자국, 발소리)이다. 거인이 '한 발자국씩 걸을 때마다 땅이 쿵쿵 흔들렸다'라는 내용이다.

The Cyclops was herding his sheep in front of him.

▶ herd를 동사로 쓰면 '짐승들을 무리 짓게 하다, 한 곳으로 몰다'라는 뜻이다. 따라서 was herding his sheep은 '자신의 양들을 몰고 있었다'이다.

And he carried over his shoulder three or four trees that he had pulled up for firewood.

▶ '운반했다'라는 carried의 목적어는 three or four ~ for firewood이다. 목적어가 길기 때문에 뒤로 보내고, '어깨 위에 얹어'라는 뜻의 over his should를 carried 뒤에 바로 붙인 것이다.

Please, show us some kindness and hospitality—we are hungry and cold!

▶ hospitality는 '친절함, 관대함'을 뜻한다. 주인이 손님을 대하는 넓은 마음이라는 의미에서 '환대, 접대'를 뜻하기도 한다.

So he lied: "We were shipwrecked on your island," he said, "and our ship is destroyed."

▶ be shipwrecked는 항해 중 '배가 부서지다'라는 의미이다.

Instead, he snatched up two of Odysseus's men and ate them on the spot.

▶ '낚아채다'라는 뜻의 동사 snatch에 '위로 들어올렸다'는 up이 더해진 것이다. he snatched up two of Odysseus's men은 '거인이 오디세우스의 부하들 중 두 명을 낚아채서 들어올렸다'라고 해석한다.

296 So Odysseus and his men spent the night huddled at the back of the cave, listening to the Cyclops snore as loud as thunder.

▶ 이 문장에서 huddle은 '여러 사람이 몸을 웅크린 채 모여 있다'라는 의미로 쓴 것이다.

▶ snore는 '코를 골다'이니까 as loud as thunder는 코 고는 소리가 엄청나게 컸기 때문에 '천둥이 치듯 큰소리로'라는 의미이다.

296 But before Odysseus and his men could dash out of the cave, the Cyclops rolled the stone back again, as easy as putting a lid on a jar.

▶ dash는 '급히 달려가다'이고, out of는 '벗어남, 빠져나옴'을 의미해서 dash out of the cave는 '급히 달려 동굴을 빠져나가다'이다.

296 But Odysseus paced up and down the cave and thought, hard.

▶ pace는 '두 방향으로 번갈아 왕복하듯 걷다'라는 의미로, 불안하거나 초조해서 '서성거리다'를 표현한다.

▶ up and down은 높이의 개념이 아니라, '이쪽저쪽'을 나타내 paced up and down the cave는 '동굴 여기저기를 서성거렸다'이다.

297 When the monster came back into the cave that evening, he drove his sheep and goats in, and again sealed up the door with the huge stone.

▶ drove his sheep and goats in은 '자기 양과 염소를 안으로 몰아넣었다'라는 의미이다.

▶ sealed up the door는 '문을 완전히(up) 봉쇄했다(sealed)'이다.

297 And with that he sprawled over and went to sleep, right there on the ground.

▶ with that은 '그 말과 함께'를 뜻한다.

▶ sprawl은 '팔다리를 아무렇게나 뻗고서 눕다'이고, over는 '떨어짐'을 의미한다. 즉 sprawled over는 '쓰러져 대자로 뻗었다'이다.

298 Then he got up, feeling his way around with his hands, and rolled the stone away.

▶ feeling his way around with his hands는 '양손으로 여기저기 더듬어 자기가 가고자 하는 길[방향]을 느끼며'로 해석할 수 있다. 눈을 찔려서 앞이 보이지 않았기 때문에, 손으로 더듬어 촉감으로 길을 찾았다는 것이다.

He told each one of his men to hold on to the stomach fleece of the sheep in the middle of each group, and to let the sheep carry them out past the Cyclops.
▶ the stomach fleece of the sheep은 '양의 복부의 털가죽'이다.

You should have known better than to fall for my tricks!
▶ 'should have + 동사의 완료형'은 과거에 '~했어야 했다'이다.
▶ know better than ~은 '~보다 더 많이[잘] 알다'를 뜻한다. 이 문장은 should have known better than to fall for my tricks은 '멍청하니 내 속임수에 속았지'라고 해석할 수 있다.

In fury, he wrenched a huge boulder off the side of the cliff and threw it towards Odysseus's voice.
▶ in fury는 '몹시 화가 나서'라는 의미이다.
▶ boulder는 '커다란 돌'이고, wrench는 '떼어내다'이므로 wrenched a huge boulder off the side of the cliff는 '절벽 면에서 거대한 돌을 떼어냈다'라는 의미이다.

The winners of the races were given wreaths made out of olive branches to wear on their heads.
▶ made out of olive branches는 '올리브 나뭇가지로 만든'을 뜻한다.

As time went on, more and more Greeks from different Greek cities came to the Olympic Games.
▶ to go on은 '계속 이어지다, 시간이 흐르다'라는 표현이고, 문장을 이끄는 as는 '시간의 흐름, 과정'을 의미한다. 따라서 As time went on은 '시간이 흐르면서, 시간이 지남에 따라'라고 해석할 수 있다.

The winner had to throw a discus (a metal Frisbee) and a javelin (a Greek spear) farther than anyone else.
▶ discus와 javelin 뒤에 붙은 괄호 안의 말이 각 단어의 설명에 해당한다. discus는 '원반'인데, '금속 프리스비(a meal Frisbee)'로 설명했다. javelin은 '그리스의 창(a Greek spear)' '투창'이다.

They thought that the best way to honor the gods was for men to train their bodies to be as graceful and powerful as possible.
▶ the best way to honor the gods는 '신들을 찬미하는 최선의 방법은'이라는 의미이다.
▶ for men to train their bodies는 '남자들이 자신의 신체를 단련시키는 것'이고, to be as graceful and powerful as possible은 '가능한 한 우아하고 강해지는 것'을 의미한다.

301 Poets would recite poems and stories out loud to entertain the crowds.

▶ recite는 '암송하다, 낭독하다'이고, out loud는 '크게 소리 내어'를 뜻한다. 따라서 recite poems and stories out loud는 '시와 이야기들을 큰소리로 암송하다'라는 의미이다.

 Chapter 21 The Medes and the Persians

316 He conquered the cities all around him and made them obey him.

▶ 'to make A 동사'는 'A가 ~하게 만들다'라는 표현이다. made them obey him은 '그 도시들(the cities)이 그에게 복종하게 만들었다'라고 해석한다.

316 But the Assyrians didn't like belonging to the Babylonian empire.

▶ 'belong to A'는 'A의 소유이다, A에 속하다'를 뜻한다. belonging to the Babylonian empire는 '바빌로니아 제국에 속하는 것을'로 해석한다.

316 The Assyrians went back to conquering all the cities around them.

▶ go back to 동사의 ~ing'는 '다시 ~한 상태로 돌아가다'로, 중단했던 일을 '다시 시작하다'라는 뜻이다. 그래서 went back to conquering all the cities around them은 '그들 주변에 있는 모든 도시를 다시 정복하기 시작했다'라고 해석한다.

317 Now Babylon and Media were in charge, and the Assyrians had to obey.

▶ charge는 '권한과 책임'이므로 be in charge는 '통제하는 위치에 있다'라는 의미가 된다.

317 The Babylonians and the Medes must have been pleased with themselves.

▶ 'must have 동사의 완료형'은 과거의 일에 대한 강한 추측을 표현하는 것으로, '분명 ~했을 것이다'라는 의미이다.

▶ be pleased with는 '~에 대해 만족하다, 기쁨을 느끼다'이므로 must have been pleased with themselves는 '분명 스스로에 대해 만족했을 것이다'라고 해석한다.

318 I've done as you told me!

▶ as you told me는 '당신이 내게 말한 대로'라는 의미인데, 이 문장에서 tell은 '명령하다, 시키다'를 뜻한다.

318 But the shepherd and his wife named the baby Cyrus, and brought him up there on the mountainside.

▶ bring up은 '키우다, 성장시키다(raise)'로 brought him up은 '그를 키웠다'이다.

362

▶ there on the mountain은 '산기슭에 있는 그곳에서'라는 의미이다.

Cyrus grew up to be tall and strong.

▶ grew up은 '성장했다, 자라났다'이다. to 이하는 성장한 결과를 표현한 것으로, to be tall and strong은 '키가 크고 힘이 세어졌다'라는 의미이다.

And he stood head and shoulders above every other boy his age.

▶ stood head and shoulders above every other boy his age는 '또래의(his age) 다른 어떤 아이보다도 머리와 어깨가 보일 만큼 키가 월등히 컸다'라고 이해할 수 있고, 비유적으로는 '모든 면에서 우월했다'라는 의미이다.

And Harpagus admitted that he had given the baby to a shepherd, rather than killing him.

▶ admit은 '사실이나 잘못을 인정하다, 받아들이다'를 뜻한다.

▶ rather than killing him은 '그를 죽이지 않고'라는 의미인데, 여기에서 rather than은 instead of(~하는 대신에, ~하지 않고)와 같은 표현이다.

Cyrus took power away from his grandfather and became the ruler of the Persians, just as Astyges had dreamed, so many years ago.

▶ took power away from his grandfather는 '자기 할아버지에게서 힘을 빼앗다'라고 해석한다. power는 '지배력, 권력'을 의미한다.

After three years of fierce fighting, Cyrus conquered the king of Media as well.

▶ as well은 '또한, 역시'를 뜻한다. 다른 왕들도 정복했고, 메디아의 왕도 정복했다는 의미를 담고 있다.

Now Cyrus, who had been raised by a shepherd on a mountain, ruled over the combined empires of the Medes and the Persians.

▶ ruled over는 '전체(over)를 통치했다'라는 의미이다. the combined empires는 메디아와 페르시아를 '합친(combined)' 제국을 뜻한다.

He was a great warrior—but he was also known as a good and fair king.

▶ be known as A는 'A로 알려지다'를 뜻하는 표현으로, but he was also known as a good and fair king는 '그런데 그는 선하고 공정한 왕으로도 알려졌다'라는 의미이다.

So he marched his army up to the kingdom of Croesus and conquered it.

▶ 이 문장에서 march는 '행군[행진]하도록 시키다'이고, up to는 '~끝까지'라는 의미로 '도착' 을 의미한다. 따라서 he marched his army up to the kingdom of Croesus는 '그는 크로이 소스 왕국까지 자기 군대를 행군시켜 갔다'라고 해석할 수 있다.

320   The soldiers went all through the city, carrying away armloads of
treasures, gold coins, and jewelry.

▶ all through는 '사방팔방, 여기저기 빠짐없이'라는 의미이므로 went all through the city는 '도시의 모든 곳으로 갔다'이다.

▶ armload는 양팔을 벌려서 안을 수 있을 만큼의 양, 즉 '한 아름'이다.

322   Belshazzar spent too much money on feasting and drinking, and not
enough on the people of Babylon.

▶ 'to spend A on B'는 'B에 A를 쓰다, B를 위해 A를 쓰다'라는 표현이다.

▶ enough는 'enough money(충분한 돈)'을 뜻하는 것으로 동사는 앞에 나온 spent이다. not enough on the people of Babylon는 '바빌로니아 백성들에게는 돈을 충분히 쓰지 않았다' 라고 해석한다.

322   The Babylonians were sick and tired of their own king.

▶ be sick and tired of ~는 '~이 몹시 싫어지다, ~에 진저리가 나다'라는 표현이다.

322   Some of the Babylonians even opened the gates from the inside and
let him in!

▶ let him in은 '그를 들여보냈다'라는 의미이다. let someone go[come] in의 형태에서 go나 come을 생략해도 의미가 통하기 때문에 그냥 let someone in으로 쓴 것이다.

BC / BCE Date	
7000 BC/BCE	Nomads roam the Fertile Crescent
6800	Stone walls built at Jericho
3500	Climate changes in the Sahara
3000	King Narmer unites Upper and Lower Kingdoms of Egypt
3000-2100	Era of the Old Kingdom of Egypt
3000-1200	Gilgamesh Myth composed
2690	Huang Di rules China
2550	Great Pyramid built (burial place of Cheops)
2334	Sargon becomes king of the city-state of Kish
2200-1450	Peak of Minoan civilization
2040-1720	Middle Kingdom of Egypt
2000-1750	Harappan civilization is at its peak strength
1980-1926	Amenemhet becomes pharaoh of Egypt
1792	Hammurabi inherits the throne of Babylon
1766	T'ang becomes King of China
1766-1122	Shang Dynasty rules
1750	Exodus of Indus Valley
1567	Ahmose expels Hyksos from Egypt
1524	Thutmose I becomes pharaoh
1500	Aryan people enter India
1493-1481	Thutmose I rules Egypt as pharaoh
1473-1458	Hatshepsut rules as pharaoh
1450	Mycenaeans settle in Crete
1357	Tutankhamen born
1352-1336	Amenhotep IV rules Egypt as pharaoh
1339	Tutankhamen dies at age 18
1300-1200	Spread of Assyrian Empire

1200-900	Olmec civilization flourishes
1200-700	Height of Phoenician civilization; Greek "Dark A
mid-800s	Greek city-states begin to arise
814	Carthage is first settled
800	Homer lives during this time
745-727	Reign of Tiglathpileser III
700	Time of the earliest Persians
668-627	Ashurbanipal's reign as king of Assyria
605-561	Nebuchadnezzar rules as king of Babylon
563-483	Siddhartha Gautama (the Buddha) lives
559-525	Cyrus the Great rules over Medes and Persians
551-479	Confucius lives
539	Babylon falls to the Persians
500	War against Persia by Greece begins
500	Aryan civilization in India reaches high point
500	"Period of the Warring States" begins in China
490	First marathon run by Athenian to announce vic over Persia
480	Battle of Salamis
431-404	War between Sparta and Athens (Peloponnesian
338	King Philip of Macedonia conquers Greek city-st
336-323	Alexander the Great rules
321-233	The Mauryan Empire of India
268-233	Asoka rules India; Mauryan empire disintegrates following his death
264-241	First Punic War fought
264-146	Punic Wars
230	Shi Huangdi (Qin Zheng) begins uniting Warring States of China
221	First united Chinese empire, under Shi Huangdi
218	Hannibal's invasion of Italy
218-202	Second Punic War takes place
214	Construction of Great Wall of China begins

212	Qin Zheng orders book burning
200	Nazca civilization flourishes
100	Julius Caesar born
69	Cleopatra born
55-54	Caesar's campaigns in Britain take place
48	Caesar arrives in Egypt
March 15, 44	Caesar is assassinated
43	Octavian becomes a consul in Rome
27	Octavian becomes Caesar Augustus, emperor of the Roman Empire
3 BC/BCE	Probable year of Jesus' birth

AD / CE Dates

14	Caesar Augustus dies
52	Attila the Hun dies
54-68	Nero's reign
61-63	Boadicea revolts against Rome
70	The Temple in Jerusalem is destroyed
284	Diocletian comes to the throne in Rome
286	Diocletian divides the Roman Empire
286-305	Diocletian rules jointly with Maximian
312	The Battle of Milvian Bridge
312-337	The reign of Constantine
395	Stilicho, following Theodosius, becomes regent for the Western Roman Empire
397	Stilicho drives Alaric away
408	Stilicho falls from favor and is executed
410	Visigoths sack Rome
475-476	Romulus Augustus rules

영어로 만나는 역사,
역사로 배우는 영어

우리는 왜 역사를 알아야 하는가? 우리는 왜 영어를 공부해야 하는가? 우리에게 중요한 이 두 가지 질문에 대한 답이 《The Story of the World》 안에 들어 있다.

인간이 만들어온 세상을 이야기하는 것이 역사이다. 변하지 않는 인간의 본성과 그에 따른 행동으로 인해 원인과 결과가 끊임없이 연결되어 지금 우리가 사는 세상이 만들어졌다. '역사란 과거와 현재, 미래의 대화'라는 영국 역사가 토인비(Arnold Toynbee)의 말처럼, 역사를 알아야 과거와 현재를 직시하며 더 나은 미래를 개척할 수 있는 것이다. 그럼에도 우리는 세계사를 힘들게 암기해야만 하는, 굳이 공부하지 않아도 상관없는, 하나의 선택 과목쯤으로 여겨 왔다.

역사에 대한 이런 인식은 《The Story of the World》의 책장을 넘기면서 자연스럽게 바뀌게 된다. 이 책은 제목에서 알 수 있듯이 역사를 이야기 형식으로 풀고 있다. 저자는 부모가 자녀와 함께 읽을 수 있는 역사 이야기, 누구든 신나게 역사 속으로 첫걸음을 내디딜 수 있는 이야기를 쓰고자 했고, 수많은 독자들이 저자의 의도에 고개를 끄덕였다. 이 책 덕분에 많은 독자들이 역사에 관심을 갖게 되었고, 역사에 눈을 뜨게 되었다. 지난 10여 년간 미국은 물론 한국에서도 많은 사랑을 받으며 역사 부문의 베스트셀러로 자리매김한 것은 우연이 아니다.

이제 여러분은 이 책을 원서로 읽고자 한다. 이 시점에서 여러분은 '과연 영어 학습에 도움이 될까? 너무 어렵지 않을까?'라는 의문을 품을 수 있다. 해설서를 쓰면서 먼저 원서를 읽은 독자로서, 나의 대답은 영어 학습에 '대단히 유용한 책'이며 '독해 실력을 확실하게 향상시킬 수 있는 책'이라는 것이다.

우선 중고등학교 과정의 필수 영어 어휘들이 생생한 역사적 상황과 문맥 속에 녹아 있다. 그래서 정확한 의미와 용법을 자연스럽게 익힐 수 있는 것이다. 또한 그 어휘들은 반복되는 역사의 흐름에 따라 빈번하게 등장하기 때문에 머리에 각인되는 효과가 있다. 뿐만 아니라 저자는 미국의 초등학교 저학년부터 성인 독자들까지 모두 쉽게 읽을 수 있게 문장의 난이도를 고려해서 책을 썼다. 영어 수준이 대체로 우리의 중고등학교 수준과 맞다. 독해 실력 향상을 위해 필요한 문법이 총망라되어 있기 때문에 이 책을 일독하면 영어 문장에 대한 자신감이 생길 것이다.

원서를 읽는 과정에서 해설이 힘이 될 것이다. 각 장마다 내용에 맞게 역사적 배경 지식을 덧붙여 원서의 이해를 돕고자 했다. The Story of the Words에서는 영어 학습을 위해 독자들이 반드시 알아야 하는 단어, 내용의 핵심어, 어려운 개념어 등을 선별해 의미를 완전히 이해하고 활용할 수 있도록 했다.

역사와 영어, 이 두 마리 토끼가 이 책 속에서 뛰어다니고 있다. 세계 곳곳을 누비며 시간 여행을 하다가 마지막 책장을 덮을 때, 두 마리 토끼가 여러분의 두 손에 모두 들려 있길 바란다.

지소철

이야기로
이해하는 역사

현재 저는 아이들, 엄마들과 《The Story of the World》를 영어로 읽는 수업을 하고 있어요. 사실 수업이라기보다는 영어를 함께 읽고 역사를 이해하는 나눔의 시간을 갖는 것이지요. 처음에는 영어는 물론 역사에도 관심 없던 아이들이 한 챕터씩 함께 읽어가면서 '피라미드를 직접 보고 싶어요', '스파르타와 아테네 중에 어느 쪽이 더 좋은지' 등 질문을 통해 영어를 읽는 힘과 역사를 보는 힘, 더불어 생각하는 힘이 커가는 것을 보며 보람을 느낍니다.

이 책의 장점을 꼽으라면 크게 세 가지를 말할 수 있어요.

우선 표현력이 뛰어납니다. 기초 단어와 쉽고 간결한 문장으로 역사적 내용을 명쾌하게 설명해내고 있어요. 언어적 측면에서 볼 때 사실 영어는 익히기 쉬운 언어에 속해요. 효과로 보자면 최대한 단순한 문장으로 쓰인 영어책을 많이 읽는 편이 어려운 문장으로 쓰인 책을 힘들게 읽는 편보다 외국어 습득에서는 훨씬 효율적이지요. 꾸준히 읽어가다 보면 읽는 속도도 빨라지고 원서를 읽는다는 부담이 차차 사라지는 것을 아이들을 통해 확인할 수 있었어요.

그 다음은 역사를 바라보는 관점이 어느 한쪽으로 치우침이 없이 균형 잡혀 있다는 것입니다. 고대를 다룬 역사책에서 메소포타미아 문명, 수메르인들의 역할, 아프리카 구전 신화까지 짚어주는 책은 사실상 찾아보기 힘들거든요. 역사란 인류의 발자취이므로 인류가 있던 곳이면 어디에서나 역사가 시작되고 지속되었다고 볼 수 있어요. 동양과 한국의 역사를 좀 더 다뤄주었으면 하는 아쉬움이 남기는 하지만, 나름의 균형 감각을 가지고 써내려간 훌륭한 책이라고 말할 수 있어요.

마지막으로 이야기 중심의 글쓰기입니다. 흔히 역사라고 하면 연대와 사건,

어려운 용어, 왕들의 이름과 각종 지명을 외워야 하는 암기 과목으로 여기지요. 하지만 수잔은 완전히 다른 역사의 세계를 보여줍니다. '아, 역사가 이렇게 재미있구나'라는 생각이 들게 하는 것은 바로 이야기로 풀어썼기 때문이에요. 마치 우리가 그 시대로 날아가 그 시대를 함께 사는 듯한 착각이 들 정도예요. 이야기로 역사를 이해하니 역사 자체에 대한 친근감이 절로 생겨납니다.

훌륭한 한 권의 책은 어떤 선생님보다 배울 점이 많지요. 하지만 문제는 영어로 된 원문을 혼자 힘으로 읽어낼 수 있을까 하는 의문이 들지요. 그래서 이 책이 나오게 되었어요. 영어가 모국어가 아닌 아이들도 단어와 구문을 익히고 나서 원문을 읽을 수 있도록 도와주는 책이에요. 이 책에서 제가 쓴 부분은 Q&A인데요, 실제로 아이들과 함께 공부하며 설명이 부족하거나 놓친 부분들을 선별하여 질문과 대답 형식으로 해설을 달았습니다. 이외에도 더 많은 질문들이 나올 수 있어요. 호기심을 가지고 다른 책을 찾아보기를 권합니다. 공부란 자기가 궁금한 것들을 하나씩 해결하며 지의 세계로 나아가는 과정이거든요.

나아가 아이들뿐만 아니라 어른들도 이 책의 일독을 권합니다. 왜냐하면 영어를 새로 시작하는 어른들에게 영어와 역사를 동시에 공부할 수 있는 거의 유일한 책이거든요. 사실상 어른들과 공부를 해보면 의외로 수준 문제로 적당한 교재를 찾기가 힘든데, 이 책은 우리가 알아야 할 역사 교양을 알려주면서도 영어가 쉬워서 어른들의 지적 호기심을 충분히 만족시킬 수 있어요. 먼저 시작한 사람들이 이웃과 친구에게 권하고 그렇게 입에서 입으로 전해지며 역사 읽기의 재미가 퍼져나가는 상상을 하는 것만으로 마음이 즐겁습니다.

심금숙

지소철

성균관대학교 영어영문학과를 졸업하고 Sungkyunkwan-Georgetown University의 TESOL 과정을 이수하였다. 영어를 보다 재미있게 공부하는 학습법, 영어를 효과적으로 가르치는 교수법 둘 다에 몰두하면서 영어책 저자, 번역가, 도서 기획자로서 영어와 함께하는 삶을 살아왔다. 《플로이드의 오래된 집》《내 인생의 다이아몬드》《해적과 제왕》《제국의 몰락》 등 100여 권의 책을 번역했고 《징글리시가 잉글리시로》《행복한 영어 초등학교》《수능과 직결되는 최정예 영단어 마지노 999》《보카 출생의 비밀》 등 다수의 영어학습서를 저술하였다. 인문서 번역 경험과 영어학습서 집필 노하우를 살려 이 책의 영단어와 구문을 초보자 눈높이에 맞춰 해설하였다. 관심 있는 분야의 원서를 많이 읽는 것, 이것이 그가 제안하는 영어 정복의 지름길이다.

심금숙

대학과 대학원에서 영문학을 전공하였고 《소설 목민심서》를 기점으로 역사책 읽기에 빠져들었다. 책이 좋아 늘 책과 함께 살던 어느 날 급기야 '행복한 왕자'라는 이름의 도서관을 열고 운영한 지 어느덧 18년째다. 책을 권하다 보니 암기식 공부가 아닌 진짜 공부의 즐거움을 찾으러 오는 아이들에게 선생님이 되어 있었고 현재는 영어, 일본어와 역사를 가르치고 있다. 공부가 생활인 삶 속으로 자연스럽게 어른들도 찾아왔고 그들과 인문학 공부를 함께 하며 매일을 바쁘게 보낸다. 인문주의가 삶에 미치는 영향을 아이들과 엄마들을 통해 확인하며 최근에는 그동안 쌓인 내공을 독자들에게 나눠줄 저술에 힘쓰고 있다.

The Story
of the World
세계 역사 이야기 영어 리딩 훈련
고대 1

• 초판 발행 2015년 3월 31일 • 초판 21쇄 발행 2024년 11월 18일
• 지은이 수잔 와이즈 바우어, 지소철, 심금숙
• 펴낸이 이주애, 홍영완 • 편집 김진희, 장정민 • 디자인 오필민디자인 • 마케팅 김진겸
• 펴낸곳 (주)윌북 • 출판등록 제2006-000017호 • 주소 10881 경기도 파주시 광인사길 217
• 전화 031-955-3777 • 팩스 031-955-3778 • 홈페이지 willbookspub.com
• 블로그 blog.naver.com/willbooks • 포스트 post.naver.com/willbooks • 인스타그램 @willbooks_pub
• ISBN 979-11-5581-039-2 (14740)

이 도서의 국립중앙도서관 출판시도서목록(CIP)은 서지정보유통지원시스템 홈페이지(http://seoji.nl.go.kr)와 국가자료공동목록시스템(http://www.nl.go.kr/kolisnet)에서 이용하실 수 있습니다.
책값은 뒤표지에 있습니다. 잘못 만들어진 책은 구입하신 서점에서 바꿔드립니다.